Success in
AS Politics
for Edexcel

Neil McNaughton

Hodder Arnold

www.hoddereducation.co.uk

D0184132

This high quality material is endorsed by Edexcel and has been through a rigorous quality assurance programme to ensure that it is a suitable companion to the specification for both learners and teachers. This does not mean that its contents will be used verbatim when setting examinations nor is it to be read as being the official specification – a copy of which is available at www.edexcel.org.uk

Orders: please contact Bookpoint Ltd, 130 Milton Park, Abingdon, Oxon OX14 4SB. Telephone: (44) 01235 827720. Fax: (44) 01235 400454. Lines are open from 9.00 – 6.00, Monday to Saturday, with a 24 hour message answering service. You can also order through our website www.hoddereducation.co.uk

If you have any comments to make about this, or any of our other titles, please send them to educationenquiries@hodder.co.uk

British Library Cataloguing in Publication Data
A catalogue record for this title is available from the British Library

ISBN-10: 0 340 90576X
ISBN-13: 978 0 340 90576 0

This Edition Published 2006
Impression number 10 9 8 7 6 5 4 3 2 1
Year 2011 2010 2009 2008 2007 2006

Hodder Headline's policy is to use papers that are natural, renewable and recyclable products and made fromwood grown in sustainable forests. The logging and manufacturing processes are expected to conform to the environmental regulations of the country of origin.

Typeset by Dorchester Typesetting Group Ltd
Printed & Bound in Spain for Hodder Arnold, an imprint of Hodder Education, a member of the Hodder Headline Group, 338 Euston Road, London NW1 3BH

iii

Contents

v

Acknowledgements

I should like to acknowledge the help and encouragement of the following:

Matthew Smith and Colin Goodlad at Hodder Arnold

My colleague Jacqueline Heaton

My students at University College School for their criticism and suggestions.

Neil McNaughton, 2006

The authors and publishers should like to thank the following for permission to reproduce illustrative copyright material:

Fiona Hanson/PA/Empics for figure 1.1A; Martial Trezzini/AP/Empics for figure 1.1B; Bettmann/Corbis for figure 1.1C; Alastair Grant/AP/Empics for figure 1.2A; PA/Empics for figure 1.3A; Matt Dunham/AP/Empics for figure 1.3B; Ben Curtis/PA/Empics for figure 1.3C; Jane Mingay/AP/Empics for figure 1.3D; David Cheskin/PA/Empics for figure 1.3E; Martyn Hayhow/AFP/Getty Images for figure 1.3F; Rui Viera/PA/Empics for figure 1.3G; David Jones/PA/Empics for figure 1.4A; Nicolas Khayat/ABACA/Empics for figure 1.4B; Michael Stephens/PA/Empics for figure 1.4C; Joseph Sohm/Visions of America/Corbis for figure 2.1A; PA/Empics for figure 2.2A; PA/Empics for figure 2.2B; PA/Empics for figure 2.2C; PA/Empics for figure 2.2D; Odd Andersen/AFP/Getty Images for figure 2.3B; Michael Stephens/PA/Empics for figure 2.4B; Michael Stephens/PA/Empics for figure 2.4C; David Cairns/Rex Features for figure 3.3A; Barry Batchelor/PA/Empics for figure 3.3B; Toby Melville/PA/Empics for figure 3.3C; Eric Rowley/AP/Empics for figure 3.3E; AP/Empics for figure 3.4B; Franck Prevel/AP/Empics for figure 3.4C; PA/Empics for figure 3.4D; John Stillwell/PA/Empics for figure 3.4E; Sergio Dionisio/AP/WPA Rota/ PA/Empics for figure 3.4F.

The authors and publishers should like to thank the following for permission to reproduce copyright material:

Sage Publications Ltd for tables of 'Membership of all parties' and 'Table of Conservative Party membership' on pages 8 and 60, by Peter Mair and Ingrid van Biezen, 'Party Membership in Twenty European Democracies 1980-2000', *Party Politics* Vol 7 #1 pp 5-21, Sage Publications, 2001; The Electoral Reform Society for tables on pages 33, 261 and 266; Parliamentary material on pages 165-172 is reproduced with the permission of the Controller of HMSO on behalf of Parliament; Phillip Cowley and

Mark Stuart for the tables on page 190, from www.revolts.co.uk; Politics Association Research Centre for the extract on page 325, by Graham Goodlad, 'Devolution in the UK', from *Talking Politics*, vol. 18, no. 1, September 2005.

Introduction

What is politics?

The linguistic origin of the term 'politics' lies in ancient Greek and is derived from the word *polis*. This referred to the city or state – either is appropriate since classical Greece was divided into a number of small city-states, such as Athens and Sparta, each of which was both a city and an independent state. We can hear the legacy of the word *polis* in such terms as 'acro*polis*' (a city or fortress on a hill) and 'metro*polis*' (a capital or important city).

Although *politics* derived from the word *polis*, a general term meaning simply 'of the city' or 'of the state', in practice it came to refer to the activity of managing the affairs of the **state**. This is clearly a very narrow definition of what politics is, but it is one which many conservatives in particular might prefer to use. Politics, therefore, could mean simply the business of managing the state in the best way possible, without any ideological content. It might imply little more than protecting the people from internal or external threat and ensuring their general welfare. But such an incomplete definition would be better described by the word **government**. In today's world, politics suggests *conflict*, that is, conflict between ideas, conflict between sections of the community and conflict between individuals.

Often – perhaps too often – political conflict can break out into violence. This may take the form of general disorder and/or terrorist activity (as in Northern Ireland from 1968 to the mid-1990s, or in the Middle East), revolution (as in Russia in 1917) or civil war (China in the 1930s and 1940s, Sudan and Angola more recently). Such violence can be viewed as a *failure* of politics. If conflict cannot be resolved peacefully within political institutions and processes, groups often resort to violence. In Northern Ireland in the 1990s, for example, successive British governments and leaders sought to persuade political leaders – even those who led extreme groups such as Sinn Fein and the Democratic Unionists – to renounce violence and pursue their goals through conventional, peaceful politics instead.

Professor Bernard Crick, in his celebrated work, *In Defence of Politics* (4th edn, 1992), summed up the meaning and importance of politics thus: **'Politics arises from accepting the fact of the simultaneous existence of different groups, hence different interests and different traditions, within a territorial unit under a common rule.'**

The conflict of ideas

Modern politics would not be politics unless those who take part in it adopt and promote ideas as to how the state should be run and how society should be shaped. The individuals who go to the polling station to cast their votes generally have political ideas in their minds – however mild and

> **State** *The state* is a collective name for the institutions that administer a country. Normally these institutions are non-political and are permanent, such as the civil service, judiciary and law enforcement agencies. *A state*, on the other hand, refers to a country whose government's jurisdiction over a territory is recognised by other states.

> **Government** Can mean the process of organising the state and giving it political direction. It also refers to the institutions that apply political principles to the running of the state.

unformed these may be – when they vote. The ordinary members of political parties presumably join their party in the first place because they have political ideas and hope to further them through their chosen party. Politicians themselves, whether they be local councillors, MPs or ministers, are continuously involved in promoting political ideas. At all levels of politics, therefore, we see and hear the clash of ideas.

On a grand scale, political ideas become *ideologies*. An ideology can be defined as a collection of ideas which propose social change and include some blueprint for a future, idealised society. They are also based upon one or several specific principles, such as equality, common ownership of property or individual liberty. Ideologies are often radical, so those who support them usually flourish on the extremities of moderate western politics. The most influential and successful ideologies have included, for example, socialism, fascism, feminism and radical forms of liberalism and nationalism (for now we will not consider conservatism as an ideology, for reasons that will be explored later). When ideologies come into conflict, politics can become extremely volatile. This occurs because ideologically motivated groups tend to have firmly held views and are especially determined to bring about their political goals. It is for this reason that ideological conflict often breaks out into violence, as described above.

On the whole, however, in the stable, well-established 'democracies' of the world, politics remains a moderate, peaceful activity. Most political activists may wish to create changes in society without proposing any *fundamental* changes. These changes may be based loosely upon ideological thinking, but they may also be viewed as ways of improving the general welfare and security of the people. The table below identifies a number of political ideas which have emerged in the UK in the early years of the twenty-first century, together with their opposing beliefs.

Contemporary political idea	Opposing view
Britain should retain the pound and not join the single European currency for the foreseeable future.	Britain should join the single European currency.
The people of Britain are overtaxed and therefore the general level of taxation should be reduced.	Taxation is at the appropriate level to support a good standard of public services.
We are losing the war on crime and should adopt a harsher attitude towards criminals and criminal behaviour.	The UK needs to concentrate more on the causes of crime and use sentencing to prevent reoffending rather than mere punishment.
Britain must retain the USA as a close ally and so was right to participate in the war in Iraq to depose Saddam Hussein.	The war in Iraq against Saddam was unjustified and Britain should concentrate on its relations with the rest of Europe.

How these conflicting ideas are resolved forms the fabric of politics. At every level of politics – the electorate, the media, party members, MPs, peers, ministers and political advisers – such differences have to be resolved.

The conflict of interests

When we use the term 'interests' we mean sections of the community which have an interest in their own concerns. Various groups may feel they need special protection, that they do not receive their fair share of the national wealth or are not treated fairly by government. The nature of such groups, or interests, varies considerably. They may be occupational groups, such as firefighters, students or nurses; they may be regional, such as those who live in the countryside or inhabitants of regions which are economically depressed; they may be representatives of industries, such as tobacco manufacturers, breweries or horse racing. In essence, an interest, as far as politics is concerned, is any group which seeks to act to achieve some improvements in its own circumstances.

Interests naturally use the political system and the members of the political community to further their own causes. They sometimes attach themselves to a political party. Trade unions, in particular, have always worked closely with the Labour Party (indeed Labour actually emerged from the trade union movement at the start of the twentieth century). More recently, the Countryside Alliance, which defends the interests of members of rural communities, naturally saw the Conservative Party as its most traditional supporter. In more general terms, interests will use a variety of methods to further their aims. This may involve public demonstrations, media campaigns, influence in Parliament, and so on. Their methods will be explored further in Chapter 1.4.

So part of politics is about the clash of such interests. Often their aims conflict with each other and politics is the process of resolving them. Examples of such conflicts are shown below.

Interest group's aims	Opposing interests
Health groups oppose smoking in public places in the interests of reducing smoking-related diseases.	The tobacco industry naturally opposes such restrictions.
All trade unions in the National Health Service campaign for better wages and working conditions.	Taxpayers resist the extra burden on public finances as they naturally hope to pay less tax or prevent the need for tax increases.
Those who live in the countryside campaign for more state aid for rural transport, local services, farming, etc.	Those who live in cities may resist the idea that they should subsidise rural communities.

So some political activity inevitably involves the resolution of such conflicts of interest.

The struggle for power

> **Power** The ability of an individual or an institution to force people to do things, whether they wish to or not. The strongest form of power is force or coercion, while the weakest is influence.

Arguably, the desire for **power** is a natural human characteristic. This is a contentious view, and some ideological groups – anarchists, in particular – may deny it. However, we need not concern ourselves with psychology or philosophy here. What matters to us in our study of political behaviour is that modern society clearly produces many people who do have a drive to achieve and exercise power. Many will say, of course, that their motives for achieving power are altruistic. They have a desire to improve society in some way and must therefore gain power to be able to do so. On the other hand, some may seek power *for its own sake*. Whichever is true – and perhaps both are true – there can be no doubt that politics is about the struggle for power between individuals and groups.

This struggle takes many forms, some of which are shown below:

- Parties compete against each other for power at European, national, regional and local elections.
- Individuals compete at elections to become representatives in local councils, regional assemblies or the Westminster Parliament itself.
- Individual politicians compete to be appointed to senior positions, either in the government or on the opposition front bench.
- At the very highest level of power, there is a struggle to be prime minister within the governing party.

These struggles for political power are what many of us think of when we use the term 'politics'. This is partly because the media tend to concentrate on such issues when reporting on politics, and partly because the struggle for power does, to some extent, reflect the other conflicts we have described. Clearly, which party wins an election will determine to some extent which political ideas become dominant and which interests are more likely to be favoured.

When Margaret Thatcher was elected leader of the Conservative Party in 1975, the policy direction of her party began to change and the nature of British society was ultimately transformed during her premiership in the 1980s. The election of the Labour Party to power in 1997, after 18 years of Conservative government, also began to change the balance of power in Britain. Under Thatcher, for example, financial and business interests certainly found themselves considerably more influential, while trade unions lost much of their political impact. Under Labour, after 1997, Britain became more closely integrated within the European Union and the interests of the poor were more favoured.

So, when individuals seek political power, the effects of the outcome can be far-reaching. At the same time, however, the struggle for power is, to some extent, merely a reflection of a natural desire of some individuals to gain status and influence.

What is government?

Before we attempt definitions of government and the state, it may be useful to consider a number of concepts which are related to such institutions. In particular, it is important to understand the principles which lie behind the activity of governing.

Legitimacy

Here we are asking the question: what gives any government the *right* to rule? This refers both to the *system* of government – for example, monarchy, single-party rule, parliamentary democracy – and the individuals who hold office within the government. It is a difficult question to answer because it has a number of different answers, all of which are plausible.

There are a number of possible ways in which **legitimacy** can be claimed.

Tradition is the first option. This suggests that a system of rule is legitimate if it has existed for a long period of time. Traditionalist conservatives will often support this justification on the grounds that government which evolves *naturally* is most acceptable to its people. The best example of this kind of rule is hereditary monarchy. Of course, it is no longer acceptable in most modern societies for such monarchs to govern (the crown heads of such countries as the UK, Sweden and the Netherlands do not govern as such – they are largely figureheads), but there are societies which accept hereditary rule on traditional grounds. Saudi Arabia and the small emirates around the Arabian Gulf, such as Bahrain and Dubai, are prominent examples.

As long as such states remain stable and there is an absence of significant opposition, it can be argued that hereditary monarchy is a legitimate form of rule.

Force is a more controversial basis for rule. The argument here is that *any* government, no matter how it is constituted, could be seen as legitimate if it is able to maintain peace and security within a country. This is sometimes described as 'might is right'.

Few of us, however, would accept force as a suitable criterion for legitimacy. This is particularly true if the regime in question is seen as unpleasant, through abuses of human rights, discrimination against minorities, and so on. The regime of Saddam Hussein in Iraq, which was removed by force in 2003, was a case in point. Of course, whether the lack of democracy and persecution of ethnic and religious groups in that country was justification for removing the regime is open to question. It is also difficult to establish whether the people of such autocratic regimes do consent to be governed by them, even if their methods do not appeal to us. The fact that a government does not respect human rights does not necessarily make it illegitimate. We may wish to judge the current Chinese regime on this basis.

Consent has now become the most important criterion for legitimacy. The principle itself is simple: if a regime enjoys the broad consent of its

> **Legitimacy** Refers to the degree to which the state or its government can be considered to have the right to exercise power. A state or government can be said to be legitimate if it has a valid claim to rule.

people, it can be considered to be legitimate. Nevertheless, there are some problems in establishing whether sufficient consent exists. The problems include the following:

- People may have consented in the past, but how do we know they still consent? Do we have to see regular referendums to approve the system of government? Even the most open of democracies do not do this.
- What proportion of the people consents? Is a simple majority enough? Should there be a broader consensus of support?
- How do we know whether the people consent? If turnout at elections is low (for example in the UK and the USA), does this signify lack of consent to the *system* of government or does it merely suggest dissatisfaction with the parties and individuals who run the government? Does a lack of open dissent (demonstrations, rioting, and so on) signify consent or merely fear among the people?

In practice, of course, we can use general peace and stability as a sign of consent. In the UK (at least outside Northern Ireland) there is no significant movement to change the system of parliamentary democracy. We can safely conclude, therefore, that the government is legitimate.

Power, authority and sovereignty

Power

In a general sense, power can mean the ability to make other people or groups do what one wants them to do, even if this is against their will. But this is too simple a definition. Clearly we use the term 'power' to signify a whole variety of means by which one individual or institution is able to exert its will over others. In particular, we need to consider different *levels* of power, as set out below.

Coercive power is the strongest form. This can also be described as *force*. Coercion involves the use of physical force, or at least the threat of physical force. In extreme cases, coercion may involve the use of execution, torture, terror and imprisonment of opponents, as has occurred in many totalitarian regimes. Of course, most states do not need to go to such extremes. It is sufficient to reserve the use of force for those who refuse to conform to the laws or who threaten the security of the state itself. In such cases, prison is the most common sanction. Indeed, it has been said that 'all states are founded on force'. What this means is that a state must reserve the right to use force in order to ensure security and peace. The law must be enforced and coercion is a key means of enforcement. But the more stable and united the state, the less coercion that has to be used.

Political power is perhaps how we generally understand the concept. This is the power exercised by members of the political community, including parties, their leaders and other institutions. Political power includes the ability to persuade, but it normally involves the use of rewards and sanctions. Thus prime ministers in the UK have power because of their use of

patronage. Since a prime minister controls the appointment of all ministers and many other senior positions in the apparatus of the state, such as top civil servants and judges, s/he is able to exercise power. This is particularly true when we consider the way in which the party whips in Parliament are able to control MPs. By making it clear that loyalty to the party line may improve an individual's career prospects, power is effectively being exercised.

The strongest form of political power, however, is that which is granted by Parliament – the ultimate source of all political power in the UK. Thus government departments, their ministers, devolved government in Scotland and Wales, local authorities and other public bodies have all been granted powers by Acts of Parliament. The powers of the prime minister, on the other hand, have been largely established by tradition, or *convention*, as such traditions are often known. This means that a prime minister exercises power simply because everybody in the political community accepts that s/he has the traditional right to do so.

In stable democracies, coercion is not needed to reinforce such political powers. Nearly everybody involved in politics, as well as the electorate at large, understands that certain members of the political system should have such power.

Influence is the weakest form of power. We often use the word 'power' when we really mean influence. Thus it is said that the newspapers have power, that public opinion is powerful or that trade unions have power within the Labour Party. In each of these cases, it is really *influence* that is being referred to. In such examples, the press, the people and unions may have some influence over what government and Parliament do, but they cannot enforce their wishes in any way.

Authority

This is a more difficult term than power. Often the terms power and **authority** are used interchangeably, but in politics it is extremely important to distinguish between them. Put simply, authority is the *right* to exercise power; it is not power itself. When we say a teacher exercises authority, for example, what is meant is that s/he has been granted power over the pupils by the head teacher, and, more indirectly, by the parents and the wider community. Thus, the source of the authority allows the teacher to exercise power.

In pure democracies all political authority has its source in the people. The situation in Britain, however, is more complex. While it is true that many of those working within the political system exercise power because they have been directly or indirectly elected by the people, this cannot be said of either the prime minister or the monarch. Their sources of authority have been described as *charismatic* or *traditional*. The ruling party, on the other hand, rules because it has won a general election. This is known as *elective* or *rational* authority. The German sociologist, Max Weber (1864–1920), clarified the nature of political authority by identifying its nature in three ways:

> **Authority** The right to exercise power, rather than the exercise of power itself. Authority is granted to rulers or anyone in power by those over whom power is to be exercised. Without authority, power becomes mere force.

- **Traditional authority**: the right to govern exists because authority has existed over a long period of time. This applies particularly to hereditary monarchies, such as the sheikhdoms of the Middle East. It can be assumed that, if the people have allowed such monarchies to exercise power over a long period of time, they are, by implication, consenting to such rule.
- **Charismatic authority**: the term 'charisma' refers to an individual's ability to inspire, persuade and attract a following, by the force of their personality. Here authority is granted simply by acclaim, because the people wish to be governed by a particular leader. Very often charismatic authority is combined with other forms and so increases the quantity of authority, allowing more power to be exercised. We can say, for example, that President John F. Kennedy in the USA enjoyed charismatic authority to add to his elective authority (US presidents are directly elected, so enjoy direct elective authority). Though we may find it unpalatable, it has to be said that fascist leaders such as Hitler and Mussolini also claimed such authority.
- **Legal-rational authority**: this refers to any rational way of granting authority. In practice, in modern democracies, this is always by election. So it can be best described as 'elective authority'. In current politics, elective authority is undoubtedly the most powerful justification for the exercise of power.

If we now turn to an examination of authority within the political system of the UK, we can discover the source of authority of each of the main institutions, as demonstrated in the table below.

Institution	Main source(s) of authority
Parliament	The authority (which is limited) of the House of Lords is **traditional**. The Commons' main source of authority is by **election** and therefore the people. However, the fact that Parliament *as a whole* is sovereign, has its origins in **tradition**.
The government	Clearly the government's authority is **elective**.
The monarch	Though the power of the monarchy is very limited indeed, the Crown enjoys considerable **traditional** authority.
The prime minister	Much of the PM's authority is **traditional**, but s/he also enjoys indirect **elective** authority in terms of being the leader of the ruling party. Some prime ministers, such as Winston Churchill and Margaret Thatcher, were also said to enjoy **charismatic** authority to reinforce the other two sources.

Before leaving this subject, it is important to note that it can happen that individuals or institutions attempt to exercise more power than their authority warrants. When this occurs we can say they are acting in an *authoritarian* manner. In most cases, however, there will come a time when such authoritarian figures will be brought under control. Certainly some prime ministers have been accused of claiming more power than they have authority to claim. As Margaret Thatcher discovered, when her own party removed her from power in 1990, this is a dangerous practice.

Sovereignty

It is important to avoid a point of potential confusion before examining the meaning of sovereignty. The monarch of the UK is sometimes described as the 'Sovereign', or even the 'Sovereign Lord'. This appears to indicate that the monarch holds supreme power. While this may have been true up to the seventeenth century, it is clearly no longer the case. The reason why this has occurred is that it was certainly true in the past and, being an extremely traditional political system, the term has never fallen into disuse. We must, therefore, ignore this anomaly.

It is useful to divide sovereignty into two main types – legal and political.

Legal sovereignty means the ultimate source of all legal authority. In practice, it amounts to the ultimate source of all laws and all legal power. Although many bodies are granted the authority to exercise power – ministers, local authorities and devolved governments in Scotland and Wales, for example – the ultimate source of that power is Parliament. So we say that Parliament is the legal sovereign. Parliament grants power and sometimes takes it away. Furthermore, all laws in the UK are ultimately determined by Parliament. Parliament either passes laws itself or grants authority for others to make laws. The only exceptions to this lie with the European Union, which has, by various treaties, been granted limited sovereignty in such areas as trade, the environment and consumer protection legislation.

Political sovereignty refers to the location of real political power. Instead of thinking only about where legal power lies in theory, political sovereignty allows us to consider who ultimately makes political decisions *in reality.* Thus, at elections, the people are politically sovereign because they decide who will form the next government. Between elections it is more realistic to think of the prime minister and the government as being politically sovereign. Although Parliament is legally sovereign, we know that government invariably controls it. Though Parliament reserves the right to defy the government, most of the time it is government which rules.

State, government and branches of government

As with many political concepts, the terms 'state' and 'government' can be misunderstood and used as if they had the same meaning. In reality, they are very different and should be employed with great care.

The state

If we refer to '*a* state', rather than '*the* state' we mean different things. *A* state is a country, a territory within which sovereignty can be identified and is widely recognised both within the country and abroad. There is no doubt that France, Italy, the USA and Nigeria are 'states'. Other countries recognise them as states and understand who represents their government. When we say '*the* state', however, we are referring to institutions within the country.

The state normally refers to the *permanent* collection of institutions which administer a territory. Normally we would include the following within the state:

- the armed forces and the security and intelligence establishment;
- law enforcement agencies, including the judges, courts, police and prison service;
- the bureaucracy or civil service – these bodies are politically neutral and may stay in office even when political governments change;
- other institutions which may or may not be part of the permanent apparatus of the state, depending on the arrangements within the country (in the UK, the National Health Service, most educational organisations, the BBC and the Royal Mail are all parts of the state; in the USA, however, health care is largely in the private sector and there is no state-run broadcasting; in France, the railways are part of the state, while in the UK they are not);
- bodies that exist at sub-central level, such as local authorities.

So we can make two assertions about the state: first, it is normally politically neutral, and second, it is permanent.

Government

Here we have to include politics in the definition. The term 'government' (without any article) refers to the act of government. In this context, for example, we might say 'government is a complex operation', or 'political parties aim to achieve government'. But when we say '*the* government', we are referring to specific institutions.

The government is a collection of individuals and bodies which are political in nature and which are not permanent. In the UK, the government consists of the prime minister, Cabinet, junior ministers and political advisers. Should the governing party lose power, all these individuals will cease to be the government and will be replaced by a new team. Normally we expect the government to give political direction to the state. Indeed, the senior members of the state are usually appointed by members of the government.

MPs, peers and Parliament in general do not fit neatly into either the 'state' or the 'government'. Instead they form the legislature, whose role is to provide consent and accountability to government.

Branches of government

It is customary to divide the activity of government into three branches, as follows:

- **Legislature**: in broad terms, this means the lawmaking body. However, this can be misleading, especially in the UK. Parliament, which is Britain's legislature (known as Congress in the USA, the *Chambre des députés* in France and the Bundestag in Germany), does not normally make law. This is the responsibility of the government. Here in Britain, the legislature is primarily concerned with providing formal consent to proposed laws – an activity known as 'promulgation'. Parliament also has limited powers to amend proposals and may, on rare occasions, reject proposed legislation. Legislatures in other countries sometimes *do* develop their own laws, notably the US Congress, but governments are usually more significant than legislatures in this lawmaking role.
- **Executive**: the executive branch has three main roles. The first is to develop new legislation and present it before the legislature for approval (this includes identifying the need for new legislation and drafting the laws themselves). The second is to arrange for the implementation of the laws. Finally, the executive runs the state and so administers the country, making decisions when they are needed and organising state-run services.
- **Judiciary**: this refers to the legal system, and the judges in particular. Most of the judiciary is not concerned with politics, but rather with criminal matters and disputes between individuals and organisations. But at the high levels of the judiciary – in Britain this includes the High Court, Court of Appeal and the senior judges in the House of Lords – some legal cases involve politics. When there are disputes about the meaning of laws, when citizens' rights are in jeopardy or when there are disputes concerning the behaviour of the government or the state, the judiciary has political significance. Nevertheless, as we shall see below, judges are expected to adopt a neutral stance, even though they are concerned with political matters.

Freedom and rights

Freedom and rights are difficult concepts, especially since their precise meaning is disputed by proponents of different political ideologies and traditions. We need not concern ourselves at this stage with such controversy, but we do need to attempt to find neutral meanings.

The clearest conception of freedom is perhaps **civil liberties**, also described as **civil rights**. These are rights and freedoms which exist for citizens in their relationship to the state and its laws. Some civil rights are 'positive' in nature, that is, they are affirmations of what we are permitted to do by the state. Indeed, such rights will also be enforced by the state, especially the judiciary. These include the following:

- the right to vote;
- the right to form a political party or any other kind of political group;
- the right to form associations, such as trade unions, pressure groups, religious groups (freedom of association and freedom of worship);
- the right to express opinions, provided they will not result in breaches of the law (freedom of the press and freedom of speech);
- the right to move freely around the country, to leave and return to the country (freedom of movement).

The other kind of civil rights or liberties refer to restrictions on the state. That is, the citizen is protected and so enjoys greater freedom. These include:

- the right not to be imprisoned without trial;
- the right to a fair trial with legal representation;
- the right to privacy and not to have one's home violated by agents of the state.

Most of these rights and freedoms exist to a large extent in modern, democratic societies. There may be exceptions in some countries, and some rights may be suspended in times of national emergency, such as war or terrorist attack. But, on the whole, democratic states respect our basic rights and freedoms.

If we consider a wider aspect of rights – for example, in the economic and social spheres – there is less clarity and more conflict. These refer to our rights and freedoms with regard to employment, business activity, trade union activity, welfare benefits and the like. In general terms, those who hold liberal or socialist views tend to favour the wide application of such rights and freedoms, while conservatives tend to be less enthusiastic and even oppose some of them. Typical examples of such rights include:

- the right to form or join trade unions;
- the right of trade unions to take industrial action in the case of industrial disputes;
- the rights of women and minority groups to equal treatment in employment and in the application of welfare benefits;
- the rights of workers to reasonable and safe working conditions;
- the right to be free from unfair dismissal;
- the right to a decent standard of education and health care (this is a contentious example and in some countries it is not guaranteed);
- the right to a decent pension in old age;
- the right to engage in business enterprise without state interference;
- the right to purchase property.

After centuries of political battles, most of these rights and freedoms have been won for the citizens of most western democracies. Nevertheless, they remain the subject of political conflict from time to time. Governments which have become anxious to improve law and order provi-

sion and to combat international terrorism, for example, have argued that some individual liberties have to be sacrificed. Should the state be allowed to imprison suspected terrorists without trial in the interests of protecting society, for example? Freedom from imprisonment without a fair trial is, after all, an ancient right and many have died to protect it.

There remain many countries, too, where human rights and freedoms are not respected. Liberals have therefore turned their attention to campaigning on behalf of the citizens of such countries. But here there remains a difficult dilemma. To what extent should 'liberal' societies tolerate other cultures which do not appear to respect the rights which we hold dear? Do we have a right to intervene? To a large extent this issue remains unresolved.

Tolerance (toleration)

The concept of tolerance did not enter the political arena in Britain in any significant way until the late sixteenth and early seventeenth centuries. But it was not in the arena of worldly politics that tolerance was to become a major philosophical and ethical issue. It was religious tolerance, or rather the lack of it, which came to be challenged by the newly emerging liberal philosophy of the seventeenth century. The English philosopher, John Locke (1632–1704), argued strongly that the pursuit of religions other than orthodox Anglican Christianity should be tolerated. Nobody, he asserted, has a monopoly on the truth and so there can be no justification for stifling alternative thought and beliefs.

Thus began a long struggle for the tolerance of religious thought. It was not until the creation of the American Constitution in the 1780s and the emancipation of Catholics in England in the nineteenth century that significant political progress was to be seen. Thereafter attention shifted to the more general field of political tolerance. For liberals, any mode of thought and behaviour should be tolerated, as long as its exercise does no harm to others. Conservatives have tended to resist this principle, mainly on the grounds that social order and unity are crucial and are best preserved if excessive variety of belief and thought is discouraged.

Ultimately, the liberal argument has prevailed and minorities, especially religions, have achieved widespread legal protection for their activities. Furthermore, the conservative movement has now also accepted tolerance as a necessary feature of modern democracy. So there is now no significant political disagreement about toleration. Rather it is the issue of the *limits* to toleration which still provoke argument. What forms of behaviour *cannot* be tolerated, even in a free society? Some examples of these difficulties are suggested below:

- Should a political party, such as the British National Party, which campaigns on barely concealed racist policies, be allowed to campaign openly?
- Should the publication of material which may be offensive to some, though not all people, such as pornography, be freely allowed?

- To what extent should legitimate political demonstrations be allowed to disrupt people's everyday lives by blocking thoroughfares and causing transport closures?
- In the early years of the twenty-first century, the issue of hunting with dogs flared up as a highly contentious issue. The question was asked: should a centuries-old pastime – especially fox hunting – be tolerated, even though a majority of the elected House of Commons and the community believe it to be cruel to wild animals?
- Should religious leaders be permitted to make statements that criticise the British 'way of life' and culture, thereby perhaps promoting terrorism?

So tolerance and, more particularly, its limits are likely to remain the subject of political conflict for the foreseeable future.

Law and order

In 1790 the great conservative thinker, Edmund Burke (1729–97), asserted that 'Good order is the foundation of all good things'. He was referring especially to the effects of the French Revolution, which had occurred a year earlier. Without order, society will fall apart, just as it had in France, he observed. With order, however, individuals can flourish in an atmosphere of security and stability.

Burke's views formed the foundation of conservatism's stress on the need for stability. Indeed, this is perhaps the most enduring value of the political movement that we call conservatism. Conservatives have always claimed that their guarantee to lay great stress on order stands in contrast to other political ideologies, notably liberalism and socialism, which, they claim, threaten stability.

There is a constant tension in all democratic societies between the basic human need for law and order and the claims of tolerance, freedom and the rights of the individual. For example, to what extent should the law enforcement agencies bend over backwards to protect the rights of suspects in criminal cases, and to what extent should they merely concentrate on securing convictions? Similarly, what rights should householders have to protect their property even if this may result in serious injury, or even death, to intruders?

Law and order became a major party political issue in the UK during the 1980s, when it became apparent that the sharp increase in crime experienced at that time was not going to diminish. But it is not simply a case of which party has the best law and order policies. There is a fundamental question about how far a free society is willing to threaten the individual rights of its citizens to preserve public order and private security. In other words, it is likely to remain an eternal theme.

Equality

This is one of the most difficult words in the vocabulary of political concepts. It has meant very different things to a variety of political movements.

It is therefore essential to avoid the temptation of believing that it has any fixed meaning. Nevertheless, it is possible to identify two variations on the theme of equality which have been accepted within mainstream politics. These are the concepts of equal rights and equality of opportunity.

Equal rights

It is now established in western democracies that all citizens are entitled to equal rights. The women's movement of the twentieth century led the way, of course, especially with its demands for voting rights and, later, full political rights for women on an equal basis with men. This has been extended more recently to full legal, political, economic and social rights for such groups as homosexuals, the disabled and ethnic minorities. This stems from the notion that all citizens are entitled to the same treatment and that the law should underpin such rights. This does not mean that prejudice and inequality have been eliminated, but the political principle is now well established that the law has a role in attempting to eliminate unequal treatment.

Equality of opportunity

However much we may believe that individuals are naturally unequal in terms of their character, abilities and potential, it is now widely accepted that all citizens should start life with the same opportunities. This means that society should find ways to reduce the advantages and disadvantages which different people have at the time of their birth. A number of practical issues and measures are involved in this process:

- No section of society, such as a hereditary aristocracy, should be born with privileges which are not enjoyed by all.
- No section of the community, such as women, the disabled, followers of a particular religion, homosexuals or members of ethnic minorities, should be excluded from access to opportunities and choices which the rest of society enjoys.
- The fact that some individuals are born into disadvantaged family situations, especially of poverty and other kinds of deprivation, should not prevent them from achieving their full potential in life. This is mainly achieved through widening and equalising educational opportunity.
- Where a group suffers routine discrimination, that discrimination should be combated and, if possible, eliminated. Failing that, some argue (though many disagree) that positive discrimination should be used, giving these groups an artificial advantage to balance the disadvantage caused by prejudice.

Justice

Of all the political concepts we are considering, justice is perhaps the most difficult and contentious. It is, of course, a term most of us use frequently in

everyday conversation, and we tend to use it to mean 'fairness'. But it can also be used to denote the successful outcome of criminal or civil trials. We often speak of 'bringing wrongdoers to justice' or 'seeing justice done'. Sometimes the phrase 'natural justice' can be heard, referring to some abstract concept of what would generally be considered 'fair', although different people would undoubtedly disagree about what 'natural justice' actually is.

So we are presented with a widely used term, clearly significant in the world of politics, but one which has no clear or agreed meaning. Hence the problems. To tackle these, it is advisable to break the term 'justice' into a number of distinct usages. We may then examine each of them in turn.

Natural justice

For some, this may imply that nature is a force which has some control over the affairs of mankind; that we could, theoretically, discover some laws of nature which would constitute justice. All we have to do is to undertake a rational study of the world and we could discover what natural justice is. The problem, of course, is that a socialist, communist, liberal, feminist or conservative will undoubtedly discover different conceptions of natural justice. A communist will declare that complete economic and social equality constitutes natural justice, while a liberal or a conservative will claim that inequality is natural. A feminist will be adamant that equality between the sexes is naturally just, while a conservative might counter this by pointing to important biological (and therefore natural) differences between men and women.

Of course, for many, the term 'nature' implies 'God'. In this sense, justice becomes a gift granted to us by our creator. Indeed, in societies where religion has become fundamental and all-pervading (for example, some Islamic states), natural or God-given justice can be discovered by careful reference to scriptures and to the teaching of prophets. Jewish people, in particular, refer to the Old Testament of their bible to find important examples of how God has influenced kings and prophets to administer real justice. They refer, for example, to the 'wisdom of Solomon' (who enjoyed a reputation as the wisest of all the kings of Israel) as an important model for how apparently insoluble disputes may be resolved on the basis of natural justice.

Even in the highest levels of the British legal system, judges may find themselves with no known guide as to how to adjudicate in a dispute, no precedents from other countries or from their own past. In such cases they may rule on the basis of natural justice. Here the judges mean what 'normal, everyday folk' would consider to be a just outcome, rather than some philosophical notion of the truth. So, in the end, natural justice must remain a highly subjective concept.

Legal justice and the rule of law

With legal justice we can stand on firmer ground. In western democratic society the principles of legal justice are well established. Important

documents, such as the American Constitution (1787) and the work of the English nineteenth-century constitutionalist, A.V. Dicey (1835–1922), have established certain key elements which are now widely accepted and enforced.

The main principle is that all (adult) citizens of the state are treated equally under the law. This means that the law will be enforced against all on an equal basis and that nobody can be considered 'above the law'. This includes members of the government and those who must enforce those laws. Dicey called these concepts the 'rule of law' and this is an important aspect of legal justice.

It also means that government itself must abide by the laws; it is, in effect, limited by law. Normally it is a country's constitution which sets out the legal limits of government's power. Should a government exceed its legal powers, we would say it is acting *arbitrarily* and *unconstitutionally*; there will be safeguards to ensure that this cannot happen – in truly democratic societies, that is. There is a problem with this principle in the UK. This is because there is no such document as the 'British Constitution'. Therefore, as long as Parliament gives its approval, government can do whatever it likes. There is no constitutional law to constrain it. Fortunately for the principles of the rule of law and legal justice, Parliament has always been robust in preventing governments from overstepping their powers.

Finally, legal justice also implies that every citizen has an equal right to a fair trial if accused of an offence. It must also mean that the judges who try them must be independent of the government. This is, in fact, probably the most common understanding of what justice means. On the whole, it has nothing to do with politics as such, but is simply a long-established right. But it can have political significance in some circumstances. If governments were permitted to imprison individuals without trial, there is a danger they would use that power to silence their opponents and critics. In the past, absolute monarchs and totalitarian regimes have done this. British monarchs were prone to lock people in the Tower of London if they were a threat, while some modern regimes keep thousands of political prisoners in their jails, offering none of them a trial.

Social justice

Different conceptions of social justice lie at the heart of a number of political ideologies. As such it has become a highly contentious term, not least because each ideology which claims it as its own believes that it has a monopoly on what constitutes social justice. In short, therefore, some ideologies claim they are superior because they, and they alone, know what this kind of justice is; furthermore, justice is often placed on a pedestal (frequently alongside freedom) above all other human aspirations.

Ideas of social justice refer to the way in which goods are distributed within a society. By 'goods' we mean anything that people find desirable. Of course, income and wealth, and what they can buy, fit into this category. But goods can also mean power, status, privileges, social honour and even freedom itself. Some ideologies believe, as we shall see below, that all these goods should be distributed equally throughout the population. Others, however, assert that there is a natural inequality within mankind, so it must also be natural to expect that goods will be distributed very unevenly, with some enjoying large quantities and others being relatively poor.

The clearest approach to this subject is to examine the basic beliefs of some of these ideologies so that we can understand the various usages of the term.

Communism

Karl Marx and Vladimir Lenin, the two main architects of twentieth-century communism, both subscribed to the slogan, **'from each according to his ability, to each according to his need'**. For them, the ultimate destination of human society would be reached when this principle was established. It is an expression of total equality. No one should have significantly more than any other. There was to be equality of wealth as well as social and economic power. This is the only kind of social justice which they would accept. Taking this principle one step further, communists see private property as the root of most inequality. The best way to deal with this, they assert, is to abolish private property altogether.

Fundamentalist socialism

Slightly less radical than communism, fundamentalist socialists also propose economic equality. However, they accept that society requires some incentives to ensure that there will be some who are willing to undertake long periods of education and training, and who are prepared to take on stressful and difficult employment. In other words, some jobs should enjoy higher rewards than others. This changes the Marxist slogan shown above to one which is slightly different: **'from each according to his ability, to each according to his contribution'**. Here there is room for some inequality, since each person's contribution is likely to have a different value to society.

But these two ideas do have one common aspect, that is, they both reject the idea that rewards should be distributed on a 'random' basis. The operation of completely free markets, with no state interference, they argue, is an irrational and unjust way of organising society. Instead they propose a rational way of distributing rewards on the basis of merit rather than market power. Thus the fact that premier league footballers may earn more in a week that many of their supporters earn in a year is seen as fundamentally unjust by communists and socialists. This is not a comment on the quality and worth of professional footballers, of course (though fans of some unsuccessful teams may argue that it is!), but simply an argument against the completely free market in footballers' wages which creates the apparent 'injustice'.

In practice, this effectively implies that socialists are prepared to tolerate some inequality of wealth and income, but would propose that differences should be rather modest. They would also insist that every individual has equal opportunity to aspire to the higher rewards which are on offer.

Liberals

Since liberals place freedom above social justice in their hierarchy of principles, it is clear that, for them, a just society must be one where individuals enjoy extensive liberty. This also means that we must be 'free to be unequal'. Where free markets are allowed to operate, therefore, there will be freedom to move about within the market to seek the highest rewards. For liberals, a society which seeks to *impose* greater equality cannot be just because it will not be free.

Liberals are aware that the 'struggle' to achieve higher rewards, greater wealth, status and power is not a just one if some are born with advantages over others (in the form of wealthy parents, privileged background, and so on). They argue, therefore, that a free and unequal society can only be just if there is equality of opportunity for all. In other words, unjust privileges and social disadvantages should be counteracted by the full availability of good education for all and guarantees of equal treatment to all groups in society.

Libertarians

Also known as extreme neo-liberals, or even anarcho-capitalists, this group has extremely radical ideas about social justice. They propose a society in which all markets – for goods, labour and money – should be completely free, with no state interference whatsoever. They insist that the outcomes of such a free market are always just (provided that individuals act lawfully, that is). They say that, as long as we are all free and have equal chances, we receive rewards that are due to us according to our own efforts. Furthermore, they would reinforce this principle by eliminating all forms of state subsidy to individuals (i.e. no welfare benefits). In this way, everyone is treated equally. They argue, therefore, that freedom and social justice can coexist without contradiction.

An overview of government and politics in the UK

Before we examine the various parts of the political system of the UK, together with the issues associated with them, it will be useful to consider a general overview of how the whole system works.

We can usefully adopt two approaches. One may be described as *linear*, while the other is *pluralist*. We should examine each in turn.

The linear analysis

This views the political system as a production process. First, there are inputs (the raw material of politics). A process then takes place involving various institutions and individuals. This processing converts the inputs into decisions. Finally, the outcomes of the political process emerge in the form of action.

The inputs

- **Demands** made by different groups in society. These will usually entail the need for action to promote their interests or to protect them from some perceived threat. For example, farmers will campaign for subsidies and price support systems through the Common Agricultural Policy of the European Union; nurses will look for a better deal from the NHS funding pool; home owners will demand tougher action by the law enforcement system against burglaries. Such demands may be made by pressure groups, media campaigns or from within political parties themselves.

- **Responses** will be required to various problems which may arise. Most commonly, economic action is needed to deal with inflation, unemployment, lack of economic growth or any other such difficulties. If crime begins to rise alarmingly, a response is needed again. Similarly, a rise in homelessness needs a response from the appropriate public bodies. All governments know they will be forced, from time to time, to make decisions to deal with unexpected issues.

- **Ideological** initiatives can promote political action. That is to say, politicians and the parties they represent develop strong political beliefs which they wish to promote when they achieve power. Ideological beliefs concern the more long-term development and character of the country and its society. Conservatives, for example, typically oppose high levels of taxation. When in power, therefore, they will usually attempt to reduce the tax burden. On the other side of the same coin, Labour normally seeks to reduce poverty levels. This may entail higher taxes for the majority, in order to pay for measures to help the poor minority. Liberal Democrats prefer to promote personal liberty. They oppose such perceived threats to freedom as the introduction of identity cards or the reduction in the rights of those accused of criminal offences.

- **Crises** obviously create a need for rapid decision making. After the attack on the World Trade Center in New York, for example, and the atrocities in London that began in the summer of 2005, a whole raft of anti-terrorism measures were suddenly needed. The alarming rise of poverty in Africa has also led to the British government considering international debt cancellation.

- **Paternalism** also plays a part in policy making. This occurs when politicians themselves believe they understand what is best for the country at any particular time. Indeed, the term 'paternalism' suggests that the decision makers claim a superior understanding of issues compared with that of the public at large. The management of the economy, education and health policy and defence matters are typical examples of such common political behaviour.

The political process

These inputs then have to be processed within the political system. In other words, they are subjected to a *political process*. This involves a variety of individuals and bodies. The main examples are discussed next.

Parties, though of decreasing importance in modern politics, do attempt to have influence over the outcomes. From ordinary members, right up to party leaders, the inputs will be considered and sifted within the parties. Of course, it is here that ideological demands most commonly appear, as many party members are highly politically aware and motivated.

Political leaders (broadly, the so-called front benches of the major parties) are those who, ultimately, will have to make decisions and be held accountable for those decisions. It is therefore to be expected that they play a major part in processing inputs. The leaders in government are clearly more influential, but opposition party leaders must always prepare alternatives in the event that they may take power in the future.

Civil servants and political advisers have a dual role. Clearly, they advise political leaders, as we would expect, but it must be emphasised that they are also sometimes called on to make decisions themselves. They are less accountable than elected leaders, but remain highly influential.

Quangos (quasi-autonomous national government organisations) **and other committees** play a similar role to that of civil servants. They consider policy options and advise ministers on possible political action.

Parliament also has two main roles. One is to take part in the consideration of political demands. However, on the whole, it does not take the initiative in such matters. When issues are debated, it is normally under the tight control of political leaders. The House of Lords has become more independent than the Commons, but its power remains limited. The other role is to formalise decisions which have been made elsewhere. When Parliament passes a new Act, or amends or repeals an old one, it is granting formal consent on behalf of the people.

The Cabinet – about 20–25 senior government ministers appointed by the prime minister – now performs the main task of granting the official stamp of government approval on any political decision. The Cabinet cannot make laws, but once it has formally approved a proposal, it is normally the case that the proposal will lead to action. Occasionally the Cabinet does process decisions itself, but its role in this respect has been much eroded in recent decades.

The prime minister is, as one might expect, at the apex of the process. Though s/he has to take account of all the other parts of the political system and can be overruled by Parliament or Cabinet, it is clear that key decisions are often made in 10 Downing Street. Usually, prime ministers gather round them a small 'inner cabinet' of trusted allies to advise them. These, too, are a vital part of the political system.

The outputs

This is somewhat clearer. The outcomes of the political process fall into four main categories.

Legislation obviously refers to new laws which may emerge from Parliament. However, under this heading we should add the possible repeal of old laws and the amendment of existing ones.

Ministerial decisions can often be made without recourse to Parliament.

Ministers are granted wide powers to make such decisions as when to go to war (in the hands of the prime minister him/herself), how government expenditure should be distributed, what adjustments need to be made to economic policy (the Chancellor of the Exchequer's responsibility) or what kind of weapons the armed forces should purchase.

Broad policy may not involve *specific* decisions, but does concern the general direction of the government's plans and priorities. In other words, such policy will be converted into action in the future. Typical examples are long-term policies on the economy, foreign affairs, defence, education or transport.

Judicial review is the final stage of the process. It occurs when laws and decisions by government are challenged by citizens or groups of citizens. This may be because laws are unclear, or because there is a suspicion that a public body has exceeded its legal powers. In general, such reviews are a tidying-up process, ensuring that there is clarity in the laws and that they are being applied properly. If serious shortcomings are revealed by the judges in the senior courts during these reviews, it is for government and Parliament to consider whether new or revised legislation is needed.

1. The linear analysis

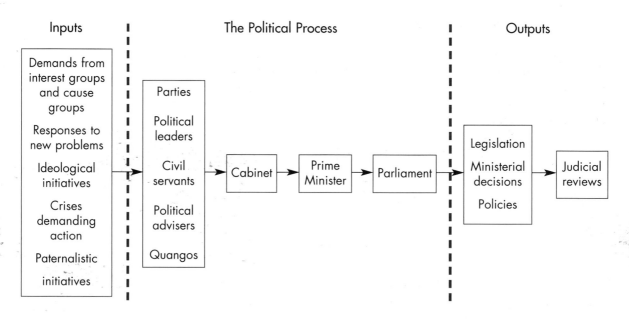

FIG 1

The pluralist analysis

This is a more complex and less formal version of the political system. It places a relatively small number of political actors at the centre of the process. These include the prime minister, Cabinet members, some senior political advisers and a number of other influential members of the governing party.

This group is surrounded by a wide variety of organisations which seek to influence them. They will have varying levels of influence, depending on circumstances. The role of the central group of key decision makers is to mediate between competing demands and beliefs, to develop a coherent political programme and to drive their decisions through to decisive action. As we would expect, since the central group comprises party politicians, they will also take into account public opinion and the effects their decisions will have on their party's re-election prospects.

The groups which clamour to gain the ear of the decision makers include the following, most of which we can also see in the linear analysis:

- the wider membership of political parties;
- pressure groups;
- Parliament (MPs and peers);
- senior civil servants;
- the media;
- public opinion;
- overseas influences, including the European Union.

The pluralist analysis suggests that the process is highly informal and does not necessarily follow any set pattern. By contrast, the linear picture presents a view of the process which is both formal and predictable. However, for the purposes of the student who is new to political study, either analysis can be adopted.

2. The pluralist analysis

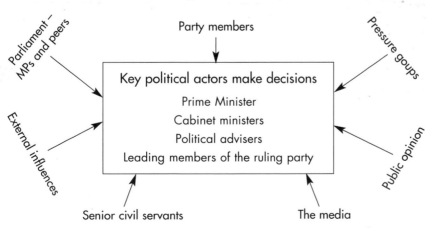

FIG 2

KEY CONCEPTS

State	*The state* is a collective name for the institutions that administer a country. Normally these institutions are non-political and are permanent, such as the civil service, judiciary and law enforcement agencies. *A state*, on the other hand, refers to a country whose government's jurisdiction over a territory is recognised by other states.
Government	Can mean the process of organising the state and giving it political direction. It also refers to the institutions that apply political principles to the running of the state.
Power	The ability of an individual or an institution to force people to do things, whether they wish to or not. The strongest form of power is force or coercion, while the weakest is influence.
Legitimacy	Refers to the degree to which the state or its government can be considered to have the right to exercise power. A state or government can be said to be legitimate if it has a valid claim to rule.
Authority	The right to exercise power, rather than the exercise of power itself. Authority is granted to rulers or anyone in power by those over whom power is to be exercised. Without authority, power becomes mere force.

The concepts of legitimacy (page xi), power (pages xii–xiii), authority (pages xiii–xv), state and government (pages xv–xvii), tolerance (pages xix–xx) and equality (pages xx–xxi) are particularly relevant to Unit 1. The concepts of sovereignty (page xv), freedom and rights (pages xvii–xix), law and order (page xx) and justice (pages xxi–xxv) are particularly relevant to Unit 2.

1

People and Politics

1.1
Democracy, representation and participation

A definition of democracy

We could spend a great deal of time attempting to develop a watertight definition of **democracy**, but this would not be of great use for a study of this kind. Instead it is better to define the term in a more straightforward manner. The best approach is to adapt the nineteenth-century American president, Abraham Lincoln's description of democracy and examine its meaning. This has three parts:

1. **Government by the people**. This is a state of affairs where the people themselves make the important decisions which affect them. In effect, we could describe this as *direct democracy*, an arrangement that would entail constant use of referendums or direct consultation processes. Government by the people could also describe a circumstance where the government is intensely sensitive to public opinion. In practice, this would be virtually direct democracy. All democratic governments consult the people, so this is a useful part of our definition.
2. **Government for the people**. This phrase suggests that whoever governs us does so in the broad interests of the people. In other words, they are not governing in their *own* interests; nor do they concern themselves only with *one section* of the community. They should take into account, therefore, the interests and needs of all sections of society, as far as possible. Since pure direct democracy all the time is not feasible, it is inevitable that government for the people will be carried out by representatives. Thus we speak of *representative democracy* as the most common form. As long as our representatives – MPs, ministers, and so on – are accountable to the people, we usually entrust government to them.
3. **Government with the people**. Here we are straying furthest from Lincoln's definition. We now expect that most of the citizens are able to participate in political activity. This does not merely include standing for elected office or voting in elections, but also means being active in parties or pressure groups, being aware and letting our political views be known. Many people in modern democracies remain politically inactive, but the majority are active, and everyone certainly has the *opportunity* to participate, even if they do not take up that opportunity. We can describe this aspect as *participatory democracy*. It is often claimed that, if citizens cease to be active in politics, democracy will wither and die.

> **Democracy** A very general description of various political systems which are organised on the basis that government should serve the interests of the people. In liberal democracies it is also expected that citizens should influence decisions, or make decisions themselves. It is also expected that government should be accountable, in various ways, to the people.

The importance of democracy

Although there was a brief episode in the history of ancient Greece when democracy of different kinds flourished in the various city-states of that age, it had a relatively short life as a political system. Even the most direct forms of democracy, where all free citizens gathered regularly to make important decisions, excluded slaves, women and the uneducated. It was, in essence, reserved for the prominent citizens who enjoyed most of the wealth of the city. They were the only people who were considered to be sufficiently informed to vote. Democracy was short-lived in Greece, and once it had disappeared, it did not reappear in any recognisable form until the eighteenth century.

Two and a half thousand years later, democracy has established itself as the political system preferred by all economically advanced nations. In the meantime, most peoples had been governed by hereditary monarchs, auto-cratic rulers or had effectively not been properly governed at all. It is worth examining why democracy was resurrected after so many centuries in the wilderness. What is it about modern society that seems to make democracy so important? We can identify a number of theories to try to answer this question.

Democracy establishes and protects freedom. Towards the end of the eighteenth century a number of new philosophical and political move-ments developed. They were largely based on the principle that mankind should be free, both as individuals and collectively, as nations. The new democratic spirit was carried forward, in particular, by the French and the Americans. The French Revolution of 1789 was a bold attempt to free the people from the autocratic rule of the monarchy. For the revolutionaries, the monarchy ruled in the interests only of itself and the aristocracy; it was time the political system took into account the demands of the middle and working classes. If such people were to be truly free, they should also have a place in the new political system.

Similarly, the Americans, during their revolution against British rule, fought to establish freedom for all individuals from the oppressive rule of George III. The constitution which they wrote and approved in 1787 enshrined freedom of the individual in a form of government which could certainly be described as a representative democracy. By ensuring that all citizens could participate and be represented, they believed their newly found freedom would be safe.

Today democracy continues to ensure that no government can threaten freedom unless it is with the expressed consent of the people. To illustrate this, when the Soviet Union collapsed in 1990 and its satellite states declared their freedom, most of the new governments adopted democratic systems. This process guaranteed that such domination as had occurred during the cold war could never reassert itself. The most dramatic demonstration of the power of the new democratic spirit took place in Ukraine in 2003–04. When it was rumoured that apparently democratic elections had been fixed, and that Russia was behind the plot, the people simply took to the streets and stayed there until new, clean elections were held and their chosen government was installed. In this way Ukrainians believed their liberty was assured and traditional Russian domination could finally be broken.

Democracy protects minorities. If a democracy is to be effective and enduring, the system must take into account the interests and demands of minority groups. Democracy ensures that all groups have access to the political process. It also guarantees that minorities have a free voice and are free from discrimination. Indeed, democracy is sometimes described as a political system where minorities rule. Of course, popular democracy can become little more than government by the majority, and early forms of democracy looked like this. But in the nineteenth century John Stuart Mill (1806–1873), the liberal philosopher, described such a circumstance as no more than the *tyranny of the majority*. It is democracy of a sort, but unless the rights and interests of minorities are protected, it does not conform to the modern meaning of the term.

Democracy controls government power. It is a well-established belief that power tends to corrupt those who wield it. If those who govern us are left to their own devices, there is a danger that they will simply claim increasing amounts of power and begin to abuse their position. Therefore democracy is vital in preventing this. By making governments accountable to the people, by ensuring that they must submit themselves regularly to re-election and by guaranteeing that they are controlled by elected representatives, the people can feel safe from the corruption of power.

The alternative to democracy is a form of politics were decisions are made without reference to the people, where governments are not accountable to the people and where there are no guarantees that individuals and minorities will be protected.

Democracy encourages popular participation. As it is commonly believed that tyranny can be prevented by ensuring that the people are able to participate freely in politics, democracy is critical in ensuring the prevention of such tyranny.

In a free democracy the people have the opportunity to become informed and be directly involved in influencing decision making. A docile and uninformed population is vulnerable to autocratic government. Democracy can prevent such a situation arising, helping to ensure that citizens remain fully involved.

Is democracy always appropriate?

So far we have been uncritical of democracy, suggesting that it is a universally 'good thing' to which all societies should aspire. But there may be circumstances when democracy might not be the most appropriate political system.

We are assuming that the principles that all individuals should be free, that there should be freedom of thought and expression and that all minorities should be respected are shared by all. Certainly it is true that they are firmly established in the USA, in much of Europe and in many

other economically developed countries. But there are cultures and societies which do not share these and other democratic principles. In societies that are governed by a strict religious code, for example, there is much less room for alternative belief systems to flourish. There are cultures where the people do not expect or desire personal liberty. In some Islamic states, for instance, most aspects of life are governed by the teachings of the prophet Muhammad, as expressed in the Koran. Muslims in such states expect to be guided in their actions by such teachings. Since Islamic governments view it as their duty to oversee the moral and social principles of the Koran, there can be no reason for them to be democratic in the sense we have described. People do not lament their lack of personal freedom, as they wish to be guided towards the most righteous way of life.

There may also be circumstances in the history of a people when decisive government action is needed. Democracy may well slow down and hinder the decision-making process at a time when speed and purpose are most important. Indeed, even established democracies, such as those in the UK and the USA, have suspended aspects of their democracy when faced with a major war. In the longer term, some poorer countries may feel that the need for economic development takes precedence over democratic principles. Thus a number of African states, such as Tanzania and Zambia, introduced one-party systems in order to try to solve their chronic problems in a more effective way.

Having said this, many democrats still insist that democratic principles cannot be sacrificed in the name of religion, emergency circumstances or the need for economic development. When it was suggested to Nelson Mandela that democracy and black majority rule in South Africa could lead to the economic decline of his country, he insisted that the people would prefer to be free than to be well fed.

Citizenship and participation

Citizenship

Citizenship This term refers to the idea that members of the political community have certain rights with respect to political institutions. It also implies that an individual has the right to live within a particular state and thus enjoy all its rights and benefits. Citizenship also implies a certain level of obligation, mainly to obey the law, to give military service in some circumstances, to pay taxes and, arguably, to vote and to engage in some kinds of service to the community.

It is well understood that a citizen is one who enjoys all the rights and privileges which a country can bestow. Since the time of the French Revolution, when the modern concept of **citizenship** was established, the principle of equal rights has always been emphasised. Under absolute monarchies the people were merely seen as *subjects*. In other words, they were expected to obey, perform their duties and not to question the legitimacy of government.

Once people became citizens of democratic states, however, they had rights and were encouraged to call government to account and exercise their own liberty. But in order to prevent all coherent government being swept away by 'people power', it remains necessary to impose duties upon the citizens. What has happened, therefore, is that the citizens of democracies have both rights and duties (or obligations), and that these are balanced against each other. The table below shows the main examples of the citizen's rights and obligations.

Rights	Obligations
■ To be a resident in the state. ■ To vote in free elections. ■ To stand for public office. ■ To be treated equally under the law. ■ To a fair trial if accused of a crime. ■ To enjoy the modern concept of civil liberties such as freedom of expression, association, movement, religion and thought.	■ To obey the laws. ■ To accept the legitimacy of the properly constituted government. ■ To pay taxes. ■ Possibly to join the armed forces if there is a need for conscription (compulsory draft).

Participation

When Tony Blair and his allies developed the New Labour movement in the 1990s, however, he introduced the concept of *active citizenship* as a new kind of obligation which was to be undertaken and which would serve as a price to be paid for a wide range of guaranteed rights. Thus Britain signed up to the European Convention on Human Rights (by passing the Human Rights Act), adopted the European Union Social Chapter, guaranteeing a range of employment rights, and introduced the Freedom of Information Act, which gave citizens the right to see official documents. But Blair and his supporters were also anxious that citizens should demonstrate a greater commitment to protecting democracy and community life.

Active citizenship had two purposes. First, it was to balance the extension of individual rights which was being undertaken. Second, it was seen as a vital way of preserving and extending a 'community spirit', which, it was felt, had been threatened by excessive levels of individualism and the pursuit of self-interest. The active citizen is expected to become involved in such activities as:

- Making themselves aware of political issues and voting in elections.
- Becoming actively involved in the promotion of issues in which they are interested. This may be at local or national level and could involve membership of pressure groups.
- Becoming involved in community action of some kind. Examples include voluntary work among the disadvantaged in the community, helping in environmental projects, neighbourhood watch schemes to deter crime and becoming closely involved with one's children's schooling.
- Joining and being active in a political party (this might apply to the most active of citizens).

Of course, it was impossible to consider legislation to guarantee such active citizenship. The main way of promoting it, therefore, has been through education. A subject entitled 'citizenship' has become part of the compulsory national curriculum, so all school pupils will be taught the principles of what it is to be an active and effective citizen.

Participation
Opportunities for, and tendencies of, the people to become involved in the political process. At a minimum level this will involve voting, but may also involve active work in political parties or pressure groups. At the highest level it implies standing for public office.

Despite these initiatives, falling levels of political **participation** have become a major concern for policy makers. The main evidence of lower levels of active participation include the following:

1. **Turnout** at elections has been declining. The table below, showing general election participation, demonstrates this decline, which has clearly accelerated in recent years.

Election year	Turnout
1979	79.0%
1983	72.7%
1987	75.3%
1992	77.7%
1997	71.4%
2001	59.4%
2005	61.3%

Turnout in local and regional elections has also remained worryingly low.

2. **Party membership** has been declining. The figures for the UK shown below demonstrate this trend.

Year	Membership of all parties	Membership as % of total electorate
1980	1,693,156	4.12
1989	1,136,723	2.63
1998	840,000	1.92

Source: P. Mair and I. van Biezen, 'Party Membership in Europe', in Party Politics, vol. 7, no. 1, 2001.

Even more dramatic has been the collapse of membership in the British Conservative Party, where, traditionally, participation has been very high. Estimated figures are as follows.

Year	Conservative Party membership
1980	1.20 million
1988	0.75 million
1998	0.35 million
2005	0.24 million

Source: P. Mair and I. van Biezen, 'Party Membership in Europe', in Party Politics, vol. 7, no. 1, 2001.

FIG 1.1A The anti-war demonstrations in 2003 challenged government authority

3. A third indication of falling levels of participation has been indicated by a great deal of research material which suggests that, in general, people identify much less closely with political parties than they used to. This is a process known as **partisan dealignment**. So, not only are considerably fewer people joining political parties, but fewer people are taking any close interest in party politics.

The news for our participatory democracy is not all bad, however. It may be true that much of the electorate has turned away from traditional party involvement, and even from voting, but it seems that pressure group activity has never been higher. Furthermore, rather than relying on parties to represent their concerns, many people are taking direct action themselves. In 1990 hundreds of thousands took to the streets of London to protest against the imposition of the unpopular local poll tax. Their action succeeded in getting the legislation repealed within two years. Similarly, the Countryside Alliance managed to muster up to 300,000 supporters in 2003–04 to demonstrate against the proposed ban on hunting with dogs and the general neglect of rural issues. They may not have prevented the ban on hunting, but they did push rural issues to the top of the political agenda. Also in 2003 over a million protesters made their opposition to the Iraq war of that year clearly known.

Membership numbers of some of Britain's leading pressure groups are shown in the following table. It is interesting to compare them with party membership statistics, shown above.

Pressure group	Main concerns	Membership
Countryside Alliance	The interests of those who live in the countryside	100,000
Royal Society for the Protection of Birds (RSPB)	Protection of bird species and their natural habitats, plus other environmental issues	1,000,000
Friends of the Earth	Various environmental issues	200,000
Liberty	Human rights issues	5000

Source: Membership figures are estimates published by the organisations themselves

Thus many millions of citizens are engaged in fundraising, campaigning and undertaking research for thousands of pressure groups, all of which are participating fully in the democratic process.

Direct democracy

Earlier we referred to the dawn of democracy in ancient Greece. Some of the states at that time instituted direct democracy (albeit for a relatively short time). In other words, the free people themselves made key decisions, literally by gathering together, listening to speeches made by their leading citizens and then being invited to vote. The majority verdict was accepted.

Clearly this kind of activity is not feasible today. Many more important decisions have to be made, and the population is now so much larger than in classical times, when the voting strength may have been below 10,000. But direct democracy can still be exercised and it appears to be on the rise again.

To some degree direct democracy involves any form of direct consultation which government makes with the people. The Labour Party, for example, retains a large 'focus group' of ordinary citizens which it consults regularly on various issues. This group is not making any decisions, of course, but it certainly has a direct influence on how the Labour leadership behaves. Similarly, many local authorities regularly consult members of their community, principally on how expenditure is allocated between various services. On an even smaller level, some small parishes in rural areas hold public meetings to discuss and decide upon minor local issues, such as the provision of street lights, parking restrictions and planning concerns. So, to an increasing extent, Britain is becoming a **consultative** democracy – a limited kind of direct system. But the true meaning of direct democracy suggests that the citizens themselves make critical decisions. The device by which this is done is the **referendum**.

Referendum
A popular vote where the people are asked to determine an important political or constitutional issue directly.

The use of referendums

We need first to define the term 'referendum'.

- It is an occasion when citizens (either all of them or those in a certain region) are asked to determine a question of public importance.
- In some countries the result of a referendum is binding on the government, in others it is not. In the UK, for instance, a referendum result is not binding on Parliament because Parliament remains sovereign. But it has to be stressed that it is virtually unthinkable that the UK Parliament would defy the expressed result of a referendum.
- Referendums always have either a 'yes' or a 'no' answer. Otherwise the result would be indecisive.
- Normally only one question is posed, though in 1997 a referendum to decide whether Scotland should have devolved government did have two questions: first, whether the Scots wanted their own parliament, and second, whether such a parliament should have tax-varying powers. The questions were linked since, if the Scots had rejected devolution (in the event they did not), the second question would have been irrelevant.
- It is Parliament and government that determine whether a referendum is to be held and what the question may be. When a referendum is called for by the people themselves it is known as an **initiative**. In some states of the USA, for example, there is provision for such initiatives. A minimum number of genuine signatures is required to create an initiative, after which the question is put on a ballot paper. Initiatives have been held in California, for example, on such issues as levels of taxation and education provision.

We can now review the use of referendums in the UK. The table that follows shows the nature and outcome of all major referendums used in UK history.

A referendum was held in Northern Ireland in 1973 to decide whether the province should remain in the UK or be united with the Republic of Ireland. Most of the Catholic community boycotted the referendum so its result became irrelevant.

Although the 1979 referendum of devolution in Scotland produced a yes vote, there was a requirement that at least 40 per cent of the total Scottish electorate (not just those who voted) had to approve. This figure was not achieved so the proposal was effectively rejected.

Apart from these referendums, it is proposed that two future polls will be held. One will be on whether Britain should agree to a new European Union Constitution (though the draft constitution was rejected in French and Dutch referendums and so remains in doubt). The other will be on whether Britain should adopt the single European currency (the euro).

Year	Location	Question	Yes	No	Turnout
1975	UK	Do you think that the UK should stay in the European Community?	67.2%	32.8%	64.5%
1979	Scotland	Do you want the provisions of the Scotland Act to be put into effect?	51.6%	48.4%	63.8%
1979	Wales	Do you want the provisions of the Wales Act to be put into effect?	20.3%	79.7%	58.8%
1997	Scotland	Do you agree that there should be a Scottish Parliament?	74.3%	25.7%	60.4%
1997	Scotland	Do you agree that the Scottish Parliament should have tax-varying powers?	63.5%	36.5%	60.4%
1997	Wales	Do you agree that there should be a Welsh assembly?	50.3%	49.7%	50.1%
1998	London	Are you in favour of the government's proposals for a Greater London Authority made up of an elected mayor and a separately elected assembly?	72.0%	28.0%	34.1%
1998	Northern Ireland	Do you support the agreement reached at the multi-party talks on Northern Ireland and set out in Command Paper 3883?	71.7%	28.9%	81.0%
2004	North-east England	Should there be an elected assembly for the North-east region?	22.1%	77.9%	47.7%
2002–04	Various (31) localities	Should a community introduce an elected mayor?	11 votes	20 votes	Between 10% and 64%

Why were these referendums held?

All the referendums shown above had one factor in common. That was that they were all concerned with important constitutional changes; in other words, they were about proposed changes to the system of government. In the past, constitutional changes have not been subject to popular approval, but the electorate is now considered to be better informed and so insists on being consulted. A further reason for submitting constitutional changes to a referendum is that it has the effect of entrenching the changes. This means that future governments and parliaments will not be able to reverse the changes unless they again consult the people; they will thus become permanent.

It is also possible to identify other individual reasons why it was deemed necessary to secure the consent of the people. These are outlined below.

The 1975 vote on European Community membership. The Labour Government of the day was itself split on whether Britain should remain a member. Prime Minister Harold Wilson therefore ordered the referendum to settle the issue and to avoid the collapse of his government. During the campaign ministers were free to oppose the official line, that Britain should remain a member. The decisive yes vote ensured the government's survival.

The 1979 votes on Scottish and Welsh devolution. These both failed, partly because the Labour Government of the day was less than enthusiastic itself. It was forced to put the issue to the vote by the Liberal Party. Lacking a parliamentary majority, the government relied on the support of a small group of Liberal MPs to survive. The Liberals pushed the devolution issue, but were obviously thwarted by the failure to achieve sufficiently large majorities.

The 1998 vote to approve of an elected London mayor. This was going to change the governance of London so the consent of Londoners was vital. It also implied some increase in taxation, again making consent essential.

The 1998 referendum in Northern Ireland on the Good Friday Agreement. This was a critical vote. After 30 years of inter-community conflict, the agreement held the promise of permanent peace. It was necessary to secure not just a yes vote, but a decisive one to ensure that all sections of Northern Ireland were in favour. The yes vote of over 70 per cent was considered good enough.

The 2004 referendum in the North-east. This was really a test run for future referendums in other English regions, such as the North-west. The decisive rejection of the proposal led to the government abandoning the policy of setting up more assemblies in the English regions. At least the government could take comfort in the fact that the no vote stopped them introducing a policy which would have proved highly unpopular.

Various referendums in localities. The idea that local communities might have powerful elected mayors had already been established for London. This was extended to various parts of the country. Between 2001 and 2004, 31 votes were held, of which only 11 were positive. It was considered unacceptable that elected mayors should be imposed upon communities from the London government. In other words, the *local* system of government should be determined by *local* decisions.

Assessment of referendum use

It has become clear that referendums are here to stay for the foreseeable future. This is not to say, however, that they are necessarily the best way of resolving issues. The next two sections present a balanced view of the use of referendums.

The benefits of referendum use

- It is, of course, the most direct form of democracy. The people's views on a particular question are clearly indicated; there is no confusion which may be caused if politicians simply *claim* to be representing public opinion. In other words, a referendum helps to make decisions *legitimate* and confirms the principle of *government by consent.*

- If the people have demonstrated their expressed consent, they are more likely to accept the decision. This was especially important in Northern Ireland, where the Good Friday Agreement of 1998 could only have a chance of success if it received widespread and *clear* support from most of the community. The yes vote of over 70 per cent was therefore crucial. (The Agreement ran into difficulties later, but the peace did last, even if the political settlement faltered.)

- Referendums may prevent governments from making unpopular decisions when a no vote is delivered. This occurred in 2004 when regional government was rejected by the people of North-east England.

- There are occasions when the government and the parties in general are likely to fail to resolve an issue effectively. In 1975, the Labour Government, as well as the Conservative Opposition, were divided on whether Britain should remain in the European Community. The decisive yes vote resolved this key issue. It may well be that a similar deadlock in the party system would occur over whether Britain should adopt the single European currency – the euro. A referendum would again solve the problem.

- A referendum effectively entrenches constitutional changes. It protects them from attacks by future governments whose policies may be only short-term. In order to reverse a referendum decision, it is widely accepted that a fresh referendum would have to be held. This principle prevents the possibility that a future government would simply dismantle constitutional reforms already made. For example, as the Scots voted for their own parliament in 1997, it would be extremely disruptive if a future Conservative government simply decided to abolish that parliament. Only the Scots will be able to undo what they did in 1997.

The problems of referendum use

- In ancient Greece the philosopher Plato argued against direct democracy of this kind by suggesting that the people will not respect the decisions which they make themselves. At first sight this seems to make no sense, but further consideration reveals that perhaps Plato had a point. Many people prefer to be led, especially if they can believe that their elected representatives have better judgement than themselves. Plato also pointed out that if people make their own laws, they will get used to the idea of simply repealing the same laws when they do not suit them any more. The result would be lack of continuity at best, chaos at worst. In a modern context, Plato's objections can be translated to mean that the excessive use of referendums will lead to a loss of respect for our elected representatives and institutions. Of course, it is certainly true that there has been a general loss of confidence in politicians and parties in the modern period, but their replacement by regular referendums might cause the political system to collapse altogether. There are few, if any, political commentators who believe that the people can replace the political system entirely.

- Many issues may be simply too complex for the majority of the people to understand and make a judgement on. We may be better educated than ever, but some political questions remain difficult and technical. It may well be, for example, that the issue of whether Britain should sign up to the European Constitution is beyond the understanding of many. The danger of such situations is that the debate will be presented as a few simple, emotional arguments and the true, detailed nature of the issues will be neglected. There are many who feel particularly uneasy about the way in which tabloid newspapers tend to reduce such issues to oversimplified symbols. In referendum campaigns the tabloids (and therefore their owners and editors) may well have a disproportionate influence over the result. Perhaps, many would argue, such matters should be left to our elected representatives under the guidance of experts, rather than to the mood swings of newspaper proprietors and their readership.

- Referendum campaigns are expensive operations. There is, therefore, a danger that one side will prevail simply because it has more resources. Although many legal limitations are placed on campaign expenditure, it seems inevitable that money will play a decisive role. It was often suggested, for example, that the yes campaign in the 1975 European Community referendum spent vastly more money than the opposing side. Most businesses were in favour of membership and they clearly used their wealth to good effect. Furthermore, if the government itself supports one side of the argument, it should give that side a distinct advantage. But we need to be cautious here. Government support for one side may prove to be a double-edged sword, as we shall see in the next point.

- There is a danger that people will use a referendum as an opportunity to express their dissatisfaction with the government of the day and ignore the issue in question altogether! The decisive no vote to devolution for the North-east of England in 2004 may well have been the result of such an effect, especially as the minister who was promoting such devolution – John Prescott – was personally unpopular. It would indeed be irrational if Britain adopted the euro or rejected it simply on the basis of whether the government of the day was popular or unpopular. In parts of Europe where referendums are used more often than in the UK there is evidence that this is a common occurrence.

- Finally, we may turn to perhaps the most serious objection of all. This can be described as the danger of the *tyranny of the majority*. Referendums are, effectively, government by majority. The minority which loses is not taken account of in any way. Elected representatives are able to weigh up the interests of the majority against those of minorities. We expect modern democratic governments to protect minorities. Referendums leave them defenceless. This danger was recognised by liberal philosophers such as John Stuart Mill as long ago as the mid-nineteenth century, when popular democracy was emerging. Most issues, it can be argued, can be resolved without a simple yes or no response. Our representatives are in a position to modify decisions to take account of minorities; referendum verdicts cannot do this. If we imagine future referendums on such issues as the level of taxation, euthanasia or abortion,

it can be seen how a blunt yes or no may not be the best resolution. Having said that, however, there are many issues which *do* only have two possible outcomes (such as the European single currency question). In these cases we may have less fear of the referendum as a political device.

A summary of the arguments for and against the use of referendums follows below.

For	Against
■ They are the most direct form of democracy. ■ People may be more likely to respect and conform to decisions they have made themselves. ■ They represent true government by consent. ■ They may prevent governments making unpopular decisions. ■ They may resolve issues that cause special problems for government and parties. ■ They entrench constitutional change.	■ They may undermine respect for representative institutions. ■ Some issues may be too complex for people to understand. ■ They may produce an emotional rather than a rational response. ■ Wealthy groups or the tabloid press may influence the result unjustifiably. ■ People may use referendums as a verdict on the general popularity of the government rather than on the issue in question. ■ They may represent the 'tyranny of the majority'. Minorities may suffer.

FIG 1.1B Referendums have become a more common way of gaining consent for governmental changes

Representative democracy

The democratic spirit began to spread across Europe and North America from the seventeenth to the nineteenth centuries. But it was not direct democracy that was being proposed. States were larger and more complex than those that had flourished in classical Greece. The idea that the people should assemble at regular intervals was simply not practical. Perhaps, more importantly, however, political philosophers opposed direct democracy on several grounds:

- Most people remained illiterate and ill-educated. Expecting them to reach important political decisions was, therefore, unrealistic.
- There was a widespread fear that minority groups would suffer discrimination at the hands of the majority. The interests of landowners, merchants, manufacturers and other entrepreneurs might be swamped by the numerical superiority of the ordinary people. In particular, the property-owning minority might suffer at the hands of the non-property-owning majority.
- In the larger, more complex states of the modern world, it was impractical to expect the people to assemble regularly to exercise their democratic rights.

So a modified form of democracy was seen as desirable. This became *representative* democracy. The mass of the people was to be represented by a minority of office holders. If we concentrate on the British experience of the growth of such democracy, we can identify a number of key developments:

- **1649–53**: Following the execution of King Charles I, a number of attempts were made to govern by means of Parliament. However, the system by which MPs were called to Parliament was not democratic and the new representative institution lacked legitimacy. By 1653 parliamentary government had collapsed and was replaced by the autocratic rule of Oliver Cromwell.
- **1688**: In the Glorious (and largely peaceful) Revolution, King James I was replaced by the joint monarchy of William III and his wife, Mary. At the same time, the Bill of Rights was agreed between the new monarchy and Parliament. This effectively transferred sovereignty to Parliament (it declared that all laws required the sanction of Parliament). However, both the Commons and the Lords continued to lack democratic legitimacy.
- **1689**: The great English philosopher, John Locke, published *Two Treatises of Government*. This highly influential work set out the principles of representative democracy operating within a limited monarchy.
- **1832**: The Great Reform Act introduced a fairer, regular system for the election of MPs. It also widened the franchise to include all of the property-owning middle classes (still a small proportion of the total

FIG 1.1C Robert Peel, often seen as the founder of the Conservative Party

population). This had the effect of making the House of Commons legitimate and can be treated as the dawn of **parliamentary democracy** as we understand it today.

- **1830s–1900**: The party system developed over this period. The Conservative Party evolved under Robert Peel (1788–1850) in the 1830s, the Liberals under William Gladstone (1809–98) in the 1870s and Labour was founded in 1900. Increasingly, voting was based on the party affiliation of a candidate rather than his personal philosophy and qualities. Thus **party representation** evolved.
- **1884**: The Third Reform Act granted voting rights to most of the male population. The House of Commons could claim even more legitimacy and thus gained superiority over the unelected House of Lords.
- **1928**: In this year the principle of universal adult suffrage was finally established. Virtually all adults, men and women, over the age of 21, were granted the franchise. Britain could now be said to be a true **liberal democracy**.
- **1945**: The first true election manifesto appeared, published by the Labour Party, which was duly elected with a clear programme of reform, approved by the electorate. The existence of a detailed manifesto, setting out the party's policies, implied that the new government had a mandate to carry out the policies contained in the manifesto. This introduced the representative concept of **mandate and manifesto**. Since 1945 manifestos have become gradually more detailed and the mandate of the electorate has become clearer.

Representation
The *political* idea is that people elect or appoint representatives to make decisions on their behalf, rather than making those decisions themselves. On a *social* level, it implies that political institutions should have a membership that is broadly a social cross-section of society in general.

Alongside these specific developments, the nature of **representation**, as it is generally understood, was also evolving. It passed through three main stages.

Burkean representation was expounded by the Whig MP and writer, Edmund Burke (who ultimately came to be seen as a conservative), at the end of the eighteenth century. Burke argued that an elected representative should be expected to use his judgement in the best interests of his constituents. He should not be expected merely to follow the instructions of those who have elected him.

Parliamentary representation combines Burke's idea that representatives should be independent-minded with the development of united political parties in the nineteenth century. Here representatives were expected to strike a balance between their own judgement, the stated policies of their party and the interests of their parliamentary constituents. The middle part of the nineteenth century has often been described as the '*golden age* of the British MP'; this was because representatives in that

period retained their independence within the party structure. In so doing they were able to retain real influence over government policy.

Of course, there are still occasions when the party whips are called off and MPs are allowed to vote free of their discipline (so-called 'free votes'). When such situations occur, MPs may revert to the Burkean principle – that they should use their own judgement – or will consult their constituents on the issue and follow their wishes. Parliamentary votes on hunting with dogs, abortion laws and public smoking bans are modern examples of such circumstances.

Party delegation evolved during the twentieth century. The parties became increasingly disciplined and monolithic. MPs were subjected to ever greater control by their party leadership. Parliamentary whips became the agents of this discipline, so the age of the independent MP had more or less ended. With a few exceptions, MPs toe the party line. In other words, MPs have become largely delegates of their party. Such discipline can be justified on the grounds that the voters typically base their decision on the merits of each party's election manifesto, not on the personal qualities of the candidates. The MP who is elected, therefore, has a moral duty to support the party's manifesto commitments as that is what their constituents voted for. MPs who wish to defy their party's line on an issue are certainly expected to consult their local party members and, ideally, their constituents before doing so.

Representation in the UK

We may now review the state of representation in the UK today. In doing so, it is important to appreciate that there is now widespread disillusionment with representative institutions. As we have seen above, party membership has declined dramatically, turnout at elections has fallen markedly and a decreasing number of citizens claim to have any close identification with a political party. Nevertheless, there is a wide variety of ways in which people continue to feel represented.

- Each MP represents a constituency. This is also true of Members of the Scottish Parliament, the Welsh Assembly and every local councillor. As such they are expected to represent the interests of the constituency as a whole and their constituents as individuals. Occasionally this may conflict with their party's policy, but there are many occasions when such representatives are able to protect their constituencies and take up their grievances with members of the government and other public bodies. It is a key part of the democratic system that each individual feels that there is an elected representative who will listen to their problems and injustices and, if appropriate, try to resolve them.
- Both Houses of Parliament are, to some extent, expected to act as a representative cross-section of society as a whole. When debates and committee hearings take place in either House, MPs and peers do express what they believe to be the views and interests of various sections of the community. Unfortunately, neither House of Parliament can claim to be

truly socially representative of the nation as a whole. The table below indicates the social profile of Commons and Lords just before the 2005 general election.

Social group	% in the House of Commons	% in the House of Lords	% in the whole population
Women	19.6	18.3	50.5
Ethnic minorities	1.4	1.5	8

We can clearly see that Parliament as a whole is far from socially representative. Women and ethnic minorities especially are under-represented. Nevertheless, it is true that various sections of the community are represented in Parliament, especially in the House of Lords. Peers come from a wide variety of backgrounds and thus represent all the main professions – law, medicine, teaching, and so on – trade unions, pressure groups, industries and leisure groups. Within the constrictions of party discipline, the interests of these and other groups are represented, to a limited extent.

- All mainstream parties in the UK claim that they represent the whole nation. The days when the Conservative Party represented the middle class and Labour represented the working class are now gone. So we enjoy party representation. As we have seen, this is exercised through the principle of mandate and manifesto. Each party manifesto claims to represent the national interest.
- As faith in political parties has declined, people in Britain increasingly feel represented by pressure groups of various kinds. It is not felt that parties can represent all the interests of all the people at the same time. Pressure groups, on the other hand, represent us very precisely and accurately. By pursuing the interests of a particular section of society or by promoting a particular cause, pressure groups are seen as more effective vehicles for the demands and views of the electorate today.
- Finally, it can be argued that the media, especially newspapers, represent the general public. Certainly newspaper editors claim they are representing the typical views of their readership. What is more, political leaders pay more attention to the press than was the case in the past. Whether or not newspapers have influence, it is widely believed that they do, so the views they express are important.

Direct and representative democracy compared

Representative democracy has a number of distinct advantages over the direct form. Among these are:

- Elected representatives may be expected to use superior knowledge, judgement and experience to consider issues more deeply and so avoid over-emotional, hasty conclusions.

- Representatives, especially political parties, are in a position to mediate between the conflicting demands of different groups in society. For example, what are the merits of high petrol taxes to deter its use, reduce emissions and so improve the environment, against those groups who wish to see fuel prices as low as possible? Should we allow into the country large numbers of immigrants as a source of cheap labour, or should we restrict immigration in case the country becomes dangerously overpopulated with low-income families? These are difficult, controversial issues, which require lengthy, sober reflection.

- In a similar way, representatives are in a position to protect minorities against the 'tyranny of the majority', as described above. For example, elected representatives may be able to protect the interests of cyclists against the majority who drive cars. Similarly, the cause of tobacco smokers conflicts with the wishes of the majority of non-smokers, who want to see the practice restricted. If either issue were resolved by direct democracy, the majority would always prevail.

- The demands of different sections of the community are often incoherent and do not collectively add up to a logical political programme. It is therefore crucial that representative institutions – parties, Parliament and government in particular – 'aggregate' or collate the many demands placed on the political system and convert them into practical, coordinated programmes of action.

Despite these clear advantages of representative institutions, direct democracy has a great deal to commend it. This has become especially true since the 1990s, when there has been considerable disillusionment with representative bodies, especially the party leaderships. People are probably better educated, and certainly better informed than they have ever been, so they are well placed to make decisions for themselves. It can be observed that an increasing proportion of key political issues are now being resolved either by pressure group activity or by the use of referendums.

We can now summarise the main advantages of each of the two main types of democracy:

Comparison of Direct and Representative Democracy

Relative Advantages of Direct Democracy
- It is the purest form of democracy.
- Avoids distortion of the views of the electorate by the time they are communicated to representatives.
- Avoids issues of distorted decision making by representatives to serve their own electoral prospects.

Relative Advantages of Representative Democracy
- Elected representatives may use superior knowledge and judgement. This avoids hasty and emotional decisions made directly by the people.
- Representatives and parties are able to mediate between the interests of different sections of society. Direct democracy means the will of the majority always prevails, making minorities very vulnerable.

Continued on next page

Comparison of Direct and Representative Democracy

Relative Advantages of Direct Democracy
- People are becoming increasingly well informed and educated and so can make their own judgements.
- When there is disillusionment with representative institutions, people prefer to make decisions for themselves.
- Decision made directly by the people may now carry more authority.

Relative Advantages of Representative Democracy
- Issues which involve such conflicting interests require complex solutions. Direct democracy tends to reduce all questions to over-simplified answers.
- Demands made directly by the people are often incoherent and illogical. Representative democracy can make better sense of these demands and convert them into practical programmes.

KEY CONCEPTS

Democracy A very general description of various political systems which are organised on the basis that government should serve the interests of the people. In liberal democracies it is also expected that citizens should influence decisions, or make decisions themselves. It is also expected that government should be accountable, in various ways, to the people.

Citizenship This term refers to the idea that members of the political community have certain rights with respect to political institutions. It also implies that an individual has the right to live within a particular state and thus enjoy all its rights and benefits. Citizenship also implies a certain level of obligation, mainly to obey the law, to give military service in some circumstances, to pay taxes and, arguably, to vote and to engage in some kinds of service to the community.

Participation Opportunities for, and tendencies of, the people to become involved in the political process. At a minimum level this will involve voting, but may also involve active work in political parties or pressure groups. At the highest level it implies standing for public office.

Referendum A popular vote where the people are asked to determine an important political or constitutional issue directly.

Representation The *political* idea is that people elect or appoint representatives to make decisions on their behalf, rather than making those decisions themselves. On a *social* level, it implies that political institutions should have a membership that is broadly a social cross-section of society in general.

Revision topics and examination questions

Revision topics

- What is meant by democracy
- How citizens can participate in politics in the UK
- Nature of direct democracy
- Why referendums have been held
- Arguments for and against referendums
- Nature of representative democracy
- Direct and representative democracy compared
- How citizens are represented in the UK

Short answers (approx. 50–100 words)

- What is meant by the term 'direct democracy'?
- What is a referendum?
- What is meant by the term 'representative democracy'?
- Outline any THREE ways in which UK citizens can participate in politics.

Medium answers (approx. 250 words)

- Distinguish between direct and representative democracy.
- Under what circumstances have referendums been used in the UK?
- How are citizens represented in the UK political system?
- What is meant by the term 'political participation'?
- Distinguish between a referendum and an election.

Long answers (approx. 500 words)

- What are the main arguments in favour of the use of referendums?
- What are the arguments against the use of referendums?
- Compare the relative merits of direct and representative democracy.
- In what senses can the UK be described as a democracy?
- How representative is the UK political system?

Resources and Web Guide

Books

A good general discussion on issues surrounding democracy can be found in:
A. Heywood, *Politics*, Palgrave Macmillan, 2002.
Another general discussion of democracy in Britain is:
S. Weir and D. Beetham, *Political Power and Democratic Control in Britain*, Routledge, 1999.
General contemporary issues in UK democracy can be found in:
S. Weir *et al.*, *Democracy Under Blair*, Politico's, 2002.

Useful websites

For information about referendums look at the website of the UK Electoral Commission:
www.electoralcommission.gov.uk

1.2
Elections and electoral systems

The purposes of elections

At first sight, the reasons why we hold elections, especially general elections, may seem obvious. We use them to elect a government, of course. But closer inspection reveals that when we vote in a general election we are actually performing a number of different functions, different but connected, that is.

■ We are electing a Member of Parliament to represent the constituency as a whole and us as individuals if we feel we have a grievance against the state.

■ We are delivering a verdict on the performance of the government in power. If we are broadly satisfied we will vote for its party's candidate; if not, we will vote for another party's candidate, or perhaps abstain by not voting at all. This occurred most notably in 1997 when the electorate decided it wished to express dissatisfaction with past Conservative administrations.

■ Since we understand that the collective result of all the voting will decide who governs us for the next few years, we are also deciding between several alternative political programmes. We know what these programmes are likely to be, either by reading the party manifestos if we are especially interested or, more likely, by following what the media have to say about the different policies. Some, who take relatively little interest in politics, may only have the vaguest ideas of what each party stands for and what each intends to do if it is elected to government.

■ Even if we have little idea of competing party policies, we almost certainly know about the party leaders, that is, the prospective prime ministers and their front bench teams who would become ministers. So we are choosing between different teams of political leaders.

■ Finally, we are effectively granting a **mandate** to the new government. In other words, we are granting authority to whichever party wins the election. This applies both to the party we have voted for and those we have rejected. By voting, by taking an active and voluntary part in the electoral process, we grant our mandate to whichever party wins.

The **electoral mandate** means two things: first, that the winning party has authority to put into effect the commitments in its election **manifesto** (this can be referred to as the doctrine of **mandate and manifesto**); second, that it grants authority to the new government to do whatever it feels necessary to promote the security and welfare of the country. This therefore covers unforeseen events, such as a military crisis, economic problems,

> **Electoral mandate**
> Refers to the authority to govern granted to the winning party at an election by the voters. The mandate suggests that the government may implement the measures in its election manifesto. It also implies that the government has authority to use its judgement in dealing with unforeseen circumstances (the 'doctor's mandate').

> **Manifesto** A statement produced by a political party at election times, stating what policies it intends to implement if it gains power.

unexpected public demands or any other crisis or emergency. This can be described as the **doctor's mandate** (which those facing an operation must sign to cover anything the surgeon may find when s/he opens us up).

This is not a blank cheque, of course. Parliament is there to ensure that the government sticks to its manifesto commitments (unless it has good reason to stray from them) and that it does not abuse its doctor's mandate.

So an election is an event with several different functions. It can be added, indeed, that the election campaign also provides an opportunity for the major political issues and philosophies of the day to be subjected to public scrutiny. It has, in a sense, an educative function, informing the public of what alternative programmes of action are available.

Elections to the Scottish Parliament and to the Welsh and Northern Ireland Assemblies serve a very similar function to UK-wide general elections, though the issues are on a regional basis. The Northern Ireland Assembly elections have one further function. The overwhelming issue in the province, one that overshadows all other political conflicts, is the question of the status of Northern Ireland in relation to the UK. Thus the election result there tells us much about the strength of feeling on that fundamental issue. If Sinn Fein does well, it indicates growing support for independence from the UK. If the radical loyalists, the Democratic Unionists, gain support, it demonstrates resistance to the demands of the nationalist community. Northern Ireland, in other words, is a separate political system, and elections there have their own special meaning.

Finally, turning to local elections, the functions are more limited. The local community is not really electing a 'government' as such. Rather, it is electing a number of councillors to represent them and showing a rather generalised party preference, which is often based more on national than local issues. So local elections tend to be something of an opinion poll on the performance of *national* government, illogical though that may seem. To some extent, local parties can determine their own fortunes based on the quality of the services they provide when in power, but voting usually follows national trends.

The British electoral system in general elections

How the system works

Electoral system
A system that converts votes in an election into seats. It may also refer to the process of electing a single leader, such as a president or a mayor.

The main British **electoral system** is properly titled **simple majorities in single-member constituencies**, but this is not how it is generally known. The common description is **first-past-the-post**, usually abbreviated to **FPTP** (we will use the expression FPTP from here onwards).

The features of FPTP are as follows:

- Each constituency returns one Member of Parliament.
- Each party may only nominate one candidate in each constituency.
- Voters have only one vote each. They choose their preferred candidate by means of the proverbial cross on the ballot paper.

Whichever candidate wins the largest number of votes is declared elected. This is known as gaining a **simple majority** or **plurality**. It is not necessary for a candidate to achieve over 50 per cent of the votes.

To demonstrate how this plurality or simple majority system works, below are the results from the 2005 election, in the constituency of Finchley and Golders Green (London):

Candidate	Party	Votes	% of votes
Rudi Vis	Labour	17,487	40.5
Karl Mennear	Conservative	16,746	38.8
Sue Garden	Liberal Democrat	7282	16.9
Noel Lynch	Green Party	1136	2.6
Jeremy Jacobs	UKIP	453	1.0
George Weiss	Rainbow Ticket	110	0.3

Thus Rudi Vis was elected with barely 40 per cent of the votes cast, but he did beat all the other candidates.

There are 646 seats in a British general election (this is the 2005 figure – from time to time the number of seats has varied slightly). Of these only 190 (29 per cent) of the elected MPs achieved over 50 per cent (i.e. an **absolute majority**) of the votes in their constituency. The rest gained only a plurality – less than 50 per cent.

The effects of FPTP

The most striking feature of FPTP is that it discriminates in favour of some parties and against others. It certainly does not award seats in proportion to the total votes cast. If we study the results of recent general elections we can see how FPTP has such effects. The table below looks at results between 1979 and 2005, showing the advantage given to the winning party and the disadvantages to the third party. The third party was the Liberals in 1979, a union between Liberals and Social Democrats (known as the Alliance) in 1983 and 1987, and the Liberal Democrats since then.

Year	Winning party	% of vote	No. of seats	% of seats	Third party	% of vote	No. of seats	% of seats
1979	Cons.	43.9	339	53.4	Liberal	13.8	11	1.7
1983	Cons.	42.4	397	61.1	Alliance	25.4	23	3.5
1987	Cons.	42.3	376	57.8	Alliance	22.6	22	3.4
1992	Cons.	41.9	336	51.6	Lib. Dem.	17.8	20	3.1
1997	Lab.	43.3	418	63.4	Lib. Dem.	16.7	46	7.0
2001	Lab.	40.7	412	62.5	Lib. Dem.	18.3	52	7.9
2005	Lab.	35.2	356	55.1	Lib. Dem.	22.0	62	9.6

It can be seen that the winning party always won a considerably higher proportion of seats than votes. This was seen at its most stark in 1997, when Labour won 43.3 per cent of the vote, but converted this to a landslide 63.4 per cent of the available seats. The opposite effect has occurred for the third party. Most dramatically, the Liberal/Social Democrat Alliance won an impressive 25.4 per cent of the vote in 1983, but this yielded a meagre 23 seats, that is 3.5 per cent of the total. Indeed the 1983 election was extraordinary in that Labour, the second party, won only 27.6 per cent of the vote, barely 2 per cent more than the Alliance, yet still obtained 209 seats – 186 more!

FPTP has also produced several anomalies in modern history:

- Back in 1951 the Labour Party actually won more total votes than the Conservatives, but the Conservatives won 26 more seats than Labour and formed the next government. Not surprisingly, this brought strong demands within the Labour Party for electoral reform.
- In February 1974 the Conservatives beat Labour by over 200,000 total votes, but ended with four fewer seats.
- In 2005, if we look at England alone, the Conservatives won 0.3 per cent more of the votes, but were awarded 92 fewer seats than Labour.
- Meanwhile in Wales, also in 2005, Labour won 42.7 per cent of the total vote there and 29 seats. Three other parties – Conservatives, Liberal Democrats and Plaid Cymru – put together won 52.4 per cent of the vote, but only ten seats in total.

So we can say with great certainty that the FPTP electoral system converts votes into parliamentary seats in a totally disproportionate way. Why is this so? The best clue lies in the results of the Finchley and Golders Green constituency shown above. Rudi Vis scraped home by a few hundred votes, but he won the seat. This kind of result was replicated up and down the country. Conservatives commonly came second in constituencies, but they did not win enough to make a serious challenge. Labour won a comfortable majority mainly because it was able to concentrate its support in a large enough number of constituencies. The Conservatives' 32.4 per cent of the popular vote was simply spread too thinly. The same was true of the Liberal Democrats.

The Liberal Democrat performance in 1992 and 1997 is also instructive. The Liberal Democrat vote actually fell between 1992 and 1997 (from 6 million to 5.2 million), but the number of seats won went up from 20 to 46. What happened was that the Liberal Democrats managed to concentrate their support in a number of 'target' seats by putting more electoral effort into them than into seats they knew they could not win. In other words, they were able to convert their votes into seats *more efficiently*.

One other statistic can help us to illustrate the disproportionality of FPTP. If we divide the number of votes won by each of the three main parties by the number of seats obtained, we have a statistic that demonstrates the *average number of votes* needed to elect an MP for each party in 2005.

Party	Total votes	Total seats	Average votes per seat
Labour	9,566,618	356	26,872
Conservative	8,785,941	198	44,373
Liberal Democrat	5,985,414	62	96,538

What this means, effectively, is that a vote for Labour is worth more than a vote for the Conservatives and considerably more than a vote for the Liberal Democrats. Thus it could be said that votes in UK general elections are not of equal value.

Turning to the effect on the formation of governments, FPTP has one overwhelming result. That is that a single party virtually always wins an overall majority in the House of Commons. This is because the system always seems to discriminate in favour of the leading party. The table below shows the overall majority won by the winning party in recent times.

Year	Winning party	Overall Commons majority
1979	Conservative	43
1983	Conservative	144
1987	Conservative	102
1992	Conservative	21
1997	Labour	179
2001	Labour	167
2005	Labour	65

This means that it has not been necessary to form coalition governments and that single-party administrations have enjoyed a clear electoral mandate.

It is also interesting to compare the *actual* results of the 2005 general election with the results as they *would have been* if the seats had been awarded strictly in line with the proportion of total votes cast for each party. This is shown in the table on the next page (excluding Northern Ireland, with six seats unallocated).

With strictly proportional results, shown in the right-hand column, we can see that the business of forming a decisive government would be extremely difficult. But, of course, each of the parties would be *proportionally* represented in Parliament.

Party	Actual seats won	Seats in proportion to votes
Labour	356	227
Conservative	198	209
Liberal Democrat	62	142
Scots Nats	6	10
Plaid Cymru	3	5
Respect	1	2
UKIP	0	14
Green	0	6
Others	2	13

We can now summarise the main effects of the FPTP system:

1. There is a strong, unique relationship between a single MP and every constituency.
2. The majority of MPs are elected without securing an overall majority of the votes in their constituency. In other words, more constituents usually vote *against* their MP than *for* him/her.
3. The system favours the leading party, almost guaranteeing that a single party will win an overall majority in the House of Commons and so be able to form a government with a clear mandate.
4. The system favours those parties that are able to concentrate their votes in specific constituencies.
5. It makes it extremely difficult for a third party to break into the domination of the two main parties.
6. Votes are not, in effect, of equal value. Votes are more valuable in 'marginal' constituencies where the result is in doubt. Votes for the second and third parties are of less value than votes for the winning party.
7. Votes for very small parties that have no hope of winning any constituencies are virtually completely wasted. Voters who are considering voting for a losing party increasingly tend to vote for their second, not their first choice of party. This is known as *tactical* voting.
8. The House of Commons does not reflect accurately the political balance of the whole electorate.

A discussion of the advantages and disadvantages of FPTP can be found in Unit 3.

The 2005 general election: a general assessment

Introduction

In strict political terms, the 2005 general election changed very little. Labour remained in power, of course, and the Conservatives remained frustrated in Opposition. The Labour majority was slashed, but the remaining majority of 66 is still comfortable and is unlikely to create too many problems for the new government (however, the government still suffered an early defeat on the detention of terrorist suspects in the autumn of 2005). The turnout remained stubbornly low, so any hopes of a recovery in political participation were dashed. The Liberal Democrats did not make a further breakthrough and are still very much the third party. But when we examine the results below the surface, can we detect any significant developments in British politics?

Labour

This was a bad election for the Labour Party. Its majority was cut to 66 seats and this means its leadership is more vulnerable to relatively small revolts among its own backbenchers. But, perhaps more significantly, its share of the vote was severely reduced, from 40.68 per cent in 2001 to 35.1 per cent in 2005. This fall represented a total loss of more than 1 million votes, from 10.72 million to 9.56 million. Nearly 1 million votes were lost to Labour in English constituencies alone. The party lost 85 seats.

There is, of course, a different angle to be taken on Labour's performance. First, they did not lose. Despite the highly unpopular decision to support the US invasion of Iraq – perhaps *the* most unpopular foreign policy decision since the Second World War – Labour hung on to power. Victory was also secured against the background of a modest recovery in the Conservative Party's reputation and a sharp decline in Tony Blair's popularity. Second, three outright victories in succession was a record for Labour and they are almost certain to retain power for 12 or 13 uninterrupted years – a totally unprecedented situation. This has led to some triumphant members of the party suggesting that Labour had become 'the natural party of government' – a claim that had hitherto been the property of the Tories.

Conservatives

It was also a very bad result for the Tories. True, their representation had risen from 165 to 198 seats and Labour's lead was severely reduced, but all other indications were dire. The Conservative share of the vote rose from 31.7 per cent to 32.3 per cent – an increase of just 0.6 per cent! The party gained a total of 430,000 votes – from 8.36 million in 2001 to 8.79 million. Although the party gained 30 more seats in England, the number of votes won there rose by barely 30,000.

This lack of success occurred in a context, as we have seen above, of government disarray. At the beginning of the campaign a genuine recovery seemed in sight for the Tories, but these hopes withered on the vine as such issues as immigration, law and order and public service reform all failed to strike a chord with the electorate.

Liberal Democrats

There was no new surge for the Liberal Democrats. They gained ten seats (an increase from 52 to 62), but this was a disappointment. More encouraging were the raw voting figures. The party gained over 1 million votes – from 4.81 million in 2001 to 5.98 million in 2005. Their share of the vote rose from 18.3 per cent to 22 per cent.

What the Liberal Democrats had failed to do was to convert the increase in their voting strength into seats as successfully as they had done in 1997 and 2001. The party's problem was that it was uncertain whether to try to win over disillusioned Labour voters or disappointed Conservatives. In 1997 and 2001 they had targeted Conservative supporters with considerable success. In 2005 the tactics were less successful. It was also disappointing in that the Liberal Democrats seemed to hold two trump cards in their pack of policies. The party had opposed both the war in Iraq and the introduction of university top-up fees, two of the government's most dangerously unpopular issues. It may have been that the party's commitment to raising the top rate of tax from 40 to 50 per cent for the very well-off had led voters to believe that the Liberal Democrats were a 'high tax' party.

Others

It was not a good election for nationalist parties. The Scottish Nationalists gained only one seat and Plaid Cymru lost one seat in Wales, even though Labour support declined there. The UK Independence Party also failed to make its hoped-for breakthrough, gaining an increase of just over 1 per cent in its vote from 2001. Led by notorious left-winger, George Galloway, the new Respect Party won one seat in London, but this was largely due to the special circumstances which saw a large Muslim anti-Iraq war vote bring Galloway home. Elsewhere the anti-war party made little impact.

It was in Northern Ireland where the most dramatic change took place. The formerly dominant Ulster Unionist Party lost all but one of its seats. The party leader, David Trimble, lost his own seat and resigned shortly after the election. By contrast, the more extreme Loyalist Democratic Unionist Party, led by hardliner Ian Paisley, won nine seats, up from five in 2001. This may not seem significant, but in the parochial politics of Northern Ireland it represented a seismic shift. It meant that the whole peace process was placed in danger, as Paisley's party was unwilling to do business with Sinn Fein (which gained one seat). Perhaps, of course, it was the success of the Democratic Unionists that led the IRA to declare a total end to hostilities later in the summer of 2005. It may indeed be the case that, in years to come, the most significant feature of the 2005 election was, in fact, the effect it had on events in Northern Ireland.

The results of the 2005 general election can be seen in the next table.

Turnout

In 2001 the low turnout had been blamed largely on the fact that the result was a foregone conclusion. This could not be offered as an explanation for

Party	Seats won	% of seats won	Gain or loss over 2001	% of vote	Gain or loss over 2001	No. of votes won (millions)
Labour	355	54.9	-57	35.2	-5.5	9.55
Conservative	198	30.7	+32	32.4	+0.5	8.79
Lib. Dem.	62	9.7	+10	22.0	+1.8	5.98
Respect	1	0.2	n/a	0.4	n/a	0.11
Others	2	0.3	+1	5.8	+1.2	1.08
Scots Nats	6	0.9	+1	1.4	-0.4	0.41
Plaid Cymru	3	0.5	-1	0.6	+0.1	0.17
Democratic Unionist	9	1.4	+4	0.8	-0.1	0.24
Sinn Fein	5	0.8	+1	0.6	+0.1	0.17
SDLP	3	0.5	0	0.4	-0.6	0.13
Ulster Unionist	1	0.2	-5	0.4	-0.4	0.13
Speaker*	1	0.2	0	n/a	n/a	n/a

*Elected unopposed

Source: Electoral Reform Society

the failure of turnout to recover in 2005. A Labour victory seemed likely, but there remained the possibility of a hung Parliament and a late surge by either the Liberal Democrats or the Conservatives. Furthermore, many of the younger electorate seemed to have been 'politicised' by the Iraq war and the issue of university top-up fees. But these factors had little or no effect. The proportion of the electorate who voted rose only from 59.4 per cent in 2001 to 61.3 per cent. The experiment of encouraging more people to exercise postal votes worked in the sense that a large proportion of voting took place in this way, but the postal voters did not seem to be new voters.

Placing the turnout figures into context, it is a striking fact that turnout in the UK in 2005 was the lowest of all the most recent general elections held by the 15 members of the European Union before the 2004 enlargement. A selection of general election turnout figures is shown below as an illustration.

Country	Election year	Turnout %	% of votes won by the government
Denmark	2005	84.5	39.5
Germany	2002	79.1	47.1
Netherlands	2003	79.9	50.6
Italy	2001	77.2	42.6
Finland	2003	66.6	52.2
France	2002	64.4	38.5
Ireland	2002	63.0	45.5
UK	2005	61.3	35.2

FIG 1.2A Voting turnout tumbled in 2001 and 2005

If we take out short-term factors, the possibility must now be faced that disillusionment with conventional party politics has become both deep and long term.

The electoral system

The verdict of the Electoral Reform Society on the 2005 general election was summed up by the following statement: 'Labour's control of the 2005 parliament is somewhat less lopsided than its dominance in the parliaments of 1997 and 2001. But parliament is still a grossly distorted version of what Britain's voters chose in 2005' (Electoral Reform Society, *Report on the General Election*, 2005).

This represents, perhaps, a surprisingly gentle criticism of the effects of the electoral system in 2005. The most striking fact seems to be that a government has been elected, with a comfortable Commons majority, on a mere 35.2 per cent of the national vote. This is the lowest percentage for a winning party since the extension of the franchise in 1918. Furthermore, if we factor in the turnout of 61.3 per cent, we discover that only 21.5 per cent of the *total* electorate (i.e. including both those who voted and those who did not) voted for the Labour Party. In other words, nearly four out of every five adult citizens did not support the winning party! The result is perhaps even more shocking for the Conservatives. They achieved the support of just under 20 per cent of the total electorate. The once great Tory party – the so-called 'natural party of government' – can barely persuade one in five adults to support it.

By calculating the average number of votes required to elect each MP from the three main parties, as discussed above, the inequities of FPTP make it possible to say that a Liberal Democrat vote was worth considerably less than a Labour vote in the general election of 2005. But the most damaging indictment of the effects of FPTP occurred in England. Separating England from the rest of the UK, the results are shown below.

Party	% of vote	Seats won
Labour	35.4	286
Conservative	35.7	195
Liberal Democrat	22.9	47

If England were a separate, sovereign state, Labour would enjoy a majority of 44 seats, despite the fact that the Conservatives obtained more votes! One has to believe that such a result would signal the demise of an electoral system that could produce a government without elective legitimacy.

But in case we think that England was the only example of gross distortion, a glance at Northern Ireland is worthwhile. There the Democratic Unionist Party (DUP) won 33.7 per cent of the total vote, but obtained half the 18 seats on offer. By contrast, the two nationalist parties, the SDLP and Sinn Fein, together won more votes (41.8 per cent) than the DUP, but were awarded one less seat.

In Scotland, meanwhile, FPTP was seen at its most favourable to Labour. The party won 39.5 per cent of the votes, but this was converted into 41 of the 59 (nearly 70 per cent) seats available. Only the Liberal Democrats appeared to beat the system in Scotland, converting 22.6 per cent of the vote into 18 per cent of the seats.

So the legitimacy of the Labour Government can certainly be challenged on the basis of these statistics. On the other hand, it can also be said that the FPTP system has done its work most effectively. It delivered a working government majority, despite the fact that the electorate split their votes relatively liberally between three parties.

Conclusions

It is now a real issue as to whether the Conservatives should consider electoral reform as a policy. Almost certainly there needs to be one more election defeat for the Tories for them to abandon a system which they have always supported on the grounds that it delivers strong government. Perversely, perhaps, there may also be further calls for reform from within the Labour Party itself. Members are likely to become increasingly uneasy about their lack of legitimacy.

Apart from the influence on the issue of reform, the **party system** itself looks remarkably similar to how it was before 2005. The description 'two-and-a-half-party system' remains appropriate, but the legitimacy of this system must now be called into question seriously.

Party system The typical structure of parties within a political system. It describes the normal number of parties that compete effectively. Thus we may speak of two-, three- or multi-party systems. It also refers to the typical party make-up of governments – for example, single-party government, coalitions, and so on.

Electoral systems explained

Majority systems

This term describes an electoral system which is designed to try to ensure that the person or party elected enjoys a broad majority of support from the electorate. Of course, if there are only two candidates or parties to choose from, the winner must, by definition, receive a majority of support (except in the highly unlikely event of a tie). However, few elections have only two candidates. Majority systems, therefore, normally have two parts. The first part is designed to reduce the contest down to only two candidates. The second part is a 'run-off' between the two survivors. As we have said above, in a two-horse race, one must achieve an absolute majority.

Of course, we need to be careful here. Majority systems where there are more than two candidates do not usually produce a winner who enjoys over 50 per cent of the *first-choice* support of the electorate. Sometimes they will, but if not, we can only say that the majority support includes the first and second choices of the majority. This is a broad majority of support, rather than a specific absolute majority.

The only major political example of a majority system operating in Britain is that which elects the London mayor. It is known as the **supplementary vote**. A similar system is used to elect the French president every seven years. The figures below demonstrate the way the most recent elections in London and France worked.

London mayoral election, 2004

Each voter has two votes, a first and second choice. Had one candidate secured over 50 per cent of the first choices s/he would have been elected. Failing that, the top two candidates go to a second round. The second-preference votes on all the losing candidates' ballots are added to the top two candidates' totals. One of them must then have a majority over the other.

The figures for 2004 are shown below.

Candidate	First-choice votes	Total with second preferences
Livingstone	685,541	828,380
Norris	542,423	667,178
Hughes	284,645	
Maloney	115,665	
German	61,731	
Leppert	58,405	
Johnson	57,331	
Gidoomal	41,696	
Reid	9451	
Nagalingam	6692	

So, Ken Livingstone was elected with a final majority of 55 per cent over Steve Norris's 45 per cent. On the first ballot Livingstone was very far from securing an absolute majority, but he picked up a total of 142,839 second preferences, while Norris won 124,755 second preferences.

French presidential election, 2002

In France the voters show their second preferences on a separate date, not on the same ballot paper. On the first Sunday ballot, all the candidates stand. A week later a second vote is held (unless one of the candidates secures over 50 per cent of the first vote, in which case they are elected). In the second ballot, only the top two candidates from the first ballot stand.

The results for first ballot in 2002 follow below.

Candidate	Votes (millions)	%
Chirac	5.7	19.9
Le Pen	4.8	16.9
Jospin	4.6	16.2
Bayrou	1.9	6.8
Laguiller	1.6	5.7
Chevenement	1.5	5.3
Mamere	1.5	5.3
9 other candidates	16.8	24.0

This was a remarkable result, with no candidate securing a significant proportion of the total vote. Under a plurality system, Jacques Chirac would have won with the support of a mere 20 per cent of the voters. The second ballot was a very different story. The voters abandoned the extreme right-wing candidate, Jean-Marie Le Pen, in their millions. Indeed, his share of the second-ballot vote was scarcely more than his total on the first ballot. Here was the outcome.

Candidate	Votes (millions)	%
Chirac	25.5	82.2
Le Pen	5.5	17.8

Chirac was not a particularly popular candidate, but over 80 per cent of the electorate preferred him to Le Pen.

Alternative vote

The most common type of majority system is known as the **alternative vote** system, known normally as **AV**. Here voters are given two votes, a first and second choice. If, when the first-choice votes are counted, one of the candidates achieves 50 per cent or more – an absolute majority – s/he is elected automatically. If none of the candidates achieves this, however, the second-choice votes have to be taken into account. The top two candidates retain their first-choice votes. The other (losing) candidates are eliminated, but not before the second choices on their ballot papers are added to the first-choice votes already won by the two leaders. The final totals for the two leading candidates now must produce an outright winner.

A slightly more complex version of the alternative vote is used to elect Members of the Australian House of Representatives. In their system, voters may place *all* candidates in order of preference. If no candidate achieves an overall majority on first preferences, the bottom candidate drops out. His/her second preferences are then added to the others. If a candidate now has an overall majority, s/he is elected. If not, the candidate now at the bottom drops out and his/her second preferences are added to the surviving candidates. The process continues until one candidate has an overall majority.

As an example, the results from 2001 for the candidates of one constituency (Melbourne Ports) are shown below.

Counting round	G. Chipp	J. Beck	M. Danby	J. Kavanagh	J. McLorinan
1	7328	305	31,110	8912	31,384
2	7428	Eliminated	31,170	9004	31,437
3	Eliminated		33,192	13,456	32,391
4			44,018	Eliminated	35,021
			Elected		

We can see that Danby was elected even though he did not win more first-preference votes than his main rival, McLorinan. Under FPTP, McLorinan would have won because the second, third and fourth preferences of those who voted for losing candidates would not have been taken into account.

Plurality systems

The term 'plurality' refers to a candidate who wins more votes than any of their opponents, but who does not necessarily achieve an overall majority of more than 50 per cent. It is essentially the way in which the current British electoral system for the Westminster Parliament works, as shown above. Today, plurality systems are relatively uncommon. The UK and the USA are the most prominent examples of its use. In the USA both the Senate and the House of Representatives use a plurality system.

Plurality, or FPTP, is not particularly controversial in the USA. This is because, in nearly all Senate and House of Representative contests, there are only two serious candidates. There are no significant third or fourth

parties, as in the UK, so, effectively, every election is contested between just two serious candidates – the Democrat and the Republican. This means that the winner virtually always has an absolute majority – more than 50 per cent – and not just a plurality. It is in the UK, where Liberal Democrats, nationalists and others win significant numbers of votes, that the plurality system throws up many winners who have failed to gain an absolute majority of support in their constituencies. A full explanation of the UK system is shown on pages 26–30.

Proportional representation

It must be emphasised at the outset that **proportional representation** (we will refer to this as PR from now on) is *not* an electoral system. PR is a description of a number of different electoral systems and the effect that they have.

Proportional representation defined

PR is a description of any electoral system which tends to produce institutions which are representative of the people who have elected them. The term *representative* normally refers to the balance of party representation in the institution. However, it can also refer to the *social* make-up of the body – are women, ethnic minorities, social classes and age groups, for example, appropriately represented? If a system is exactly proportional, parties will be represented in accordance with the proportion of the total votes that they win. Under pure PR, if a party wins 40 per cent of the vote, it receives 40 per cent of the seats available, and so on. Such a system operates today in Israel. Similarly, a system which returned 50 per cent of women Members would be representative. Nevertheless, it is unlikely that *any* electoral system can be exactly proportional in its result. Therefore we describe any system as PR if it *tends* to produce results which reflect *reasonably* accurately the social and political divisions within the electorate as a whole.

A variety of different kinds of PR systems are examined below.

Single transferable vote (STV)

This is possibly the most complex electoral system, but is favoured by many for both its fairness and the amount of choice it gives to voters. It dates from the 1850s, so it has stood the test of time. It is used in local and assembly elections in Northern Ireland. It is also the system operating in the Republic of Ireland and will be used for local govenment in Scotland from 2007.

STV works in the following way:

- Constituencies return more than one Member each. In Northern Ireland, the normal number is six.
- In order to be elected, a candidate must achieve a 'quota'. The quota is calculated by taking the total votes cast and dividing it by the number of

> **Proportional representation**
> Describes any electoral system that converts votes into seats in a broadly proportional way.

seats plus one (i.e. if there are six seats, the number is seven; the whole result, plus one, is the quota).

■ Voters may vote for all the candidates in their own order of preference. They do not have to vote for all candidates, but only the number they wish to select.

■ Voters may vote for candidates from different parties and may show a preference between candidates of the same party.

■ Candidates who achieve the quota on their first preference are elected. When that happens, their second and subsequent preferences are redistributed among the other candidates.

■ When more candidates achieve the quota by adding redistributed votes to their first preferences, their spare votes are also redistributed. This continues until no more candidates can achieve the quota. At this point the votes of the candidates at the bottom of the poll begin to have their subsequent preferences redistributed.

■ When the required number of candidates has achieved the quota, the counting can end.

STV was chosen for Northern Ireland partly because it was the system used over the border in the Republic of Ireland, so it was reasonably familiar, but largely because it fitted the special needs of a community which suffered from a number of serious problems.

Essentially, the new electoral system of Northern Ireland, adopted in 1998 under the terms of the Good Friday Agreement, was chosen to achieve a number of objectives. First, it had to reflect the different sections of a very divided society. Second, it was used to prevent the Unionist parties winning an overall majority, which they would have done under FPTP. This was essential as one of the main problems in the history of the province was the so-called abuse of power by the Unionist, Protestant majority. Third, there was a very strong civil rights movement in Northern Ireland. These campaigners insisted on an electoral system which maximised voter choice. STV was able to achieve all three aims.

List systems

A list system is one where there are no individual candidates. Instead, the voters are offered a choice of political parties. Each party produces a list of candidates. This list is shown on the ballot paper. The voter chooses one of the lists and casts their vote for it. The seats are awarded in proportion to the votes cast for each party. This is the most proportional of all systems and this is its greatest attraction.

There are three main variations. First, there is the **national list system**, as used in Israel. Each party list covers representation for the whole country. Second, there are **regional list** systems, the most common form in Europe. The country votes in regions, rather than nationally. Regional systems are either **closed** or **open**. With a closed system it is the party leaderships who decide in what order their candidates are elected. In an open system the voters may determine both how many seats each party wins and the order

in which candidates are elected. The UK operates a closed regional list system to elect Members of the European Parliament.

List systems normally include a **threshold** system. The threshold is a minimum proportion of the total votes which a party must receive to win any seats at all. In other words, if a party fails to achieve the threshold figure, it is eliminated and its seats distributed among the other parties. The purpose of the threshold is to keep out very small, extremist parties. In Germany, for example, where the similar AMS system was adopted after the Second World War, a high minimum threshold of 5 per cent was adopted to prevent Nazis or communists gaining representation.

How the regional list system works

- The country is divided into regions.
- In each region the parties produce lists of candidates.
- The voters are invited to vote for one of the lists.
- Seats are awarded to each party in exact proportion to the votes cast.
- If a party wins, say, 40 per cent of the total votes, the top 40 per cent of its candidates on the list are elected.
- In some cases, including the UK elections to the European Parliament, a small adjustment is made, depending on the performance of parties at the previous election.
- If it is a **closed** system, voters have no influence over which individuals are elected from the list. The order of the list is determined by the party leaderships.
- If it is an **open** system, voters can, if they wish, show a preference for certain candidates on a party list. This will influence which individuals are elected from the lists.
- There is normally a threshold of between 1 and 5 per cent, or a minimum proportion of the votes, which a party must win to gain *any* seats.

Additional Member systems (AMS)

AMS systems are known as **hybrids** or **mixed**. They are a combination of FPTP with a regional list system. A proportion (which varies from country to country) of the seats is awarded through FPTP. The rest are awarded on a regional list system. This means that every voter has two votes. One is for a constituency candidate in the normal way. The other is from a choice of party lists.

So, some of the elected representatives have a constituency to look after, while others do not. They have been elected from the lists and are free of constituency responsibilities. No real distinction is made between them, though the senior party members tend to be elected from lists rather than in constituencies.

AMS is something of a compromise. It is designed to make a system *partly* proportional, but also preserves the idea of parliamentary constituencies with an MP to represent them. It helps smaller parties, but also favours the larger ones. It achieves two objectives at the same time, preserving the idea of constituencies and a constituency representative, but producing a much more proportional result than FPTP.

How AMS works in Scotland and Wales

- Two-thirds of the seats are elected using FPTP, as for UK general elections.
- The other third of the seats is elected on the basis of closed regional list voting (see above to show how the regional list system works).
- There is an important variation in the regional list part of the vote.
- The variable top-up system adjusts the proportions of votes cast on the list system.
- This is a complex calculation, but, in essence, what happens is that the seats awarded from the list system are adjusted to give a more proportional result.
- Parties which do less well in the constituencies (typically Conservatives or Greens) have their proportion of list votes adjusted upwards. Those who do proportionally well under FPTP (typically Labour) have their list votes adjusted downwards.
- The overall effect of variable top-up is to make the total result close to proportional of the total votes cast in both systems.

AV+ system

We can now begin to see how many different systems can be devised for the conversion of votes into parliamentary seats. The descriptions above, indeed, show only the main variations. In practice, there are even more variations on these themes.

One such possible variation is known as AV+, a system which is not currently used, but which was recommended for general elections for the UK by a Commission led by Lord Jenkins in 1998. The Jenkins Commission recommended that general elections should be held under this system. It is essentially the AMS system, as adopted in Scotland and Wales, except that the constituency MPs would be elected using the alternative vote (AV). This would retain constituency MPs, but would give the smaller parties, notably the Liberal Democrats, a much fairer degree of representation. The proposals for electoral reform were ultimately dropped by the Labour Government after 1997, but the Jenkins proposal remains on the table if reform is considered again.

The issue of whether Britain should reform its system for general elections is further considered in Unit 3 of this book.

A summary of electoral systems

System	Examples of use	Main features	Main effects
First-past-the-post	UK general elections; US Congress.	Plurality in single-member constituencies.	Strong constituency–MP link, strong, single-party government.
Single transferable vote	Northern Ireland Assembly; Republic of Ireland.	Multi-member constituencies with wide voter choice.	Highly proportional result; many parties gain representation.
Closed regional list	European Parliament elections.	Voters select a party, not an individual.	Highly proportional result; no constituencies.
Open regional list	Various in Europe.	As for closed regional list, except that voters influence which individuals are elected.	As for closed regional list.
Additional member systems	Germany, Greater London Assembly, Scottish Parliament, Welsh Assembly.	A hybrid system of FPTP and regional list with a variable top-up system.	More proportional than FPTP, but constituencies are preserved; small parties do well.
Alternative vote	Australian House of Representatives.	Voters show two preferences; guarantees an overall majority for the winner.	Helps small parties, but not very small parties.
AV+	Not used, only proposed.	As for AMS, except that constituency MPs would be elected by the AV system.	Would be very beneficial to small parties, especially Liberal Democrats.
Supplementary vote	London mayor.	Used to elect individuals; voters show two preferences.	Guarantees that the winner enjoys an absolute majority.
Second-ballot majority system	French president.	Voters vote twice on successive weeks; only top two candidates run off in second ballot.	Guarantees that the winner enjoys an absolute majority.

Effects of and comparisons between different electoral systems

STV in Northern Ireland

Shown below are the results of the election to the Northern Ireland Assembly in 2003.

Party	Type	Seats won	% of votes	% of seats
Democratic Unionist (DUP)	Strong Loyalist	30	25.6	27.8
Ulster Unionist (UUP)	Moderate Loyalist	27	22.7	25.0
Alliance Party	Neutral	6	3.7	5.6
SDLP	Moderate nationalist	18	17.0	16.7
Sinn Fein	Strong nationalist	24	23.5	22.2
Others	Various	3	7.5	2.8

The figures below are an extract from the 2003 results of one constituency, **Belfast North**.

Number of seats available	Number of voters	Electoral quota
6	41,125	5876

The electoral quota was calculated by dividing 41,125 by 7 = 5875. One is added to complete the calculation at 5876.

If we look at the results for individual candidates, certain conclusions can be drawn.

Candidate	Party	1st preferences	%	Final result
Dodds	DUP	7476	18	Elected
Maginnes	SDLP	6196	15	Elected
Kelly	Sinn Fein	5610	14	Elected
Hutchinson	Other	3751	9	Elected
McIlkenny	Sinn Fein	3165	8	Not elected
Agnew	Other	2976	7	Elected
Morgan	SDLP	2465	6	Not elected
Cobain	UUP	2415	6	Elected
Browne	UUP	2064	5	Not elected
Smyth	DUP	1288	3	Not elected
Roberts	Alliance	1267	3	Not elected
White	Other	911	2	Not elected
Cooper	Other	748	2	Not elected
Emerson	Other	257	1	Not elected
McAughtrey	Other	255	1	Not elected
Doran	Other	155	0	Not elected
Blair	Other	76	0	Not elected
Quinn	Other	50	0	Not elected

The following features are important:

- There is a large variety of candidates with a number of independents.
- The large parties do not put up more candidates than they expect to be elected.
- The six elected were not the same six who came top of the first-preference votes.
- Two candidates from small parties, Hutchinson and Agnew, were elected. This could not have happened under FPTP. They picked up enough lower-preference votes from other candidates to achieve the quota.
- The candidates at the bottom end of the poll were significant in that some of the lower preferences on their ballots were added to the more popular candidates. In other words, those who supported such candidates as Blair or Quinn, did have an influence on the overall result through their second, third and subsequent preferences.
- The constituency is clearly very mixed as there was significant support for nationalists and Loyalists of various kinds. Candidates from six different parties were elected, which is representative of the fragmented social and political nature of Belfast North. If the election were by FPTP, the DUP might have won outright, with all the other groups excluded.

We can draw a number of conclusions from this. STV is clearly a very representative system, an example of a highly proportional representation system. The voters have been given a very wide choice and their second and subsequent choices are taken into account, not just their first choice.

The overall result was fairly even between the four main parties – DUP, UUP, SDLP and Sinn Fein. This was important for the province as the different political groupings needed to have decent representation. It was expected that they would share power.

Of course, such a system would have produced a very indecisive result in a more 'conventional' system. If we require strong, single-party government, STV will not produce it, as these results indicate. If STV were used throughout the UK in general elections we could expect that the three main parties would dominate and that smaller parties such as the Greens or UKIP would also gain a few seats. This would be good for representation, but bad for those who want to see strong government.

It is also clear that STV is a very complicated system. Some voters may be confused by the sight of a very large ballot paper with many names on it. They may also not understand the result. But the Irish on both sides of the border where STV is used seem reasonably happy with their electoral system, however well or badly they understand it. It is a slow system to count and final results can take several days to be calculated. However, such a delay seems a small price to pay for fair representation.

Additional member system in Scotland and Wales

The results of the elections to the Scottish Parliament in 2003 are shown below. The country is divided into eight regions. The figures show how the constituency results were divided between the parties and then how many seats were awarded under the differential top-up system.

	Constituency seats won	Top-up seats
Central Scotland		
Labour	9	0
Scottish Nationalist	3	3
Conservative	1	1
Liberal Democrat	1	1
Scottish Socialist	1	1
Other	2	1
Glasgow		
Labour	10	0
Scottish Nationalist	2	2
Conservative	1	1
Liberal Democrat	1	1
Green	1	1
Scottish Socialist	2	2

	Constituency seats won	Top-up seats
Highlands and Islands		
Labour	3	2
Scottish Nationalist	4	2
Conservative	2	2
Liberal Democrat	5	0
Green	1	1
Lothians		
Labour	6	0
Scottish Nationalist	2	2
Conservative	2	1
Liberal Democrat	2	0
Scottish Socialist	1	1
Green	2	2
Other	1	1
Aggregate of four remaining regions		
Labour	22	2
Scottish Nationalist	16	9
Conservative	12	10
Liberal Democrat	8	2
Scottish Socialist	2	2
Green	3	3
Other	1	0
NATIONAL TOTALS		
Labour	46	4
Scottish Nationalist	9	18
Conservative	3	15
Liberal Democrat	13	4
Scottish Socialist	0	6
Green	0	7
Other	2	2

	Total seats won	% of regional list votes
Labour	50	29.1
Scottish Nationalist	27	20.9
Conservative	18	15.3
Liberal Democrat	17	12.1
Scottish Socialist	6	
Green	7	
Others	4	

We can see that Labour won the constituency contest comfortably, winning an overall majority of 19 over all other parties. However, once the top-up, regional list seats were added in, Labour was in a minority and thus forced to enter a coalition with the Liberal Democrats. The smaller parties, notably the Greens and Scottish Socialists, were squeezed out of the constituency contests (the Greens, in fact, put up no constituency candidates), but gained decent representation of seven and six respectively, reflecting electoral support for them more accurately.

The 2003 Welsh Assembly election demonstrated similar trends. The results shown below are presented in less detail, but indicate clearly how AMS operates.

Party	Constituencies won and (% of vote)	Top-up seats awarded and (% of vote)	Total
Labour	30 (40.0)	0 (36.6)	30
Conservative	1 (19.9)	10 (19.2)	11
Liberal Democrat	3 (14.1)	3 (12.7)	6
Plaid Cymru	5 (21.2)	7 (19.7)	12
UKIP	0 (2.3)	0 (3.5)	0
Others	1 (2.4)	0 (8.4)	1

The result in Wales is particularly startling. Labour won the battle in the constituencies very comfortably, annihilating the other parties. Yet the party won only 40 per cent of the constituency votes. Support for the other three main parties had the effect of splitting the non-Labour vote so much that most constituencies fell to Labour. Thus the FPTP system worked dramatically in their favour. The differential top-up, however, brought the results back closer to a proportional result. The overall outcome was a dead heat between Labour and all the other parties added together.

One other interesting feature of the Welsh election was the fact that a fair number of voters clearly 'split the ticket', that is, voted for different parties in the constituency from the regional list. Labour lost over 3 per cent of its support in the regional ballot, while others – mainly Greens – added 6 per cent to their support on the regional vote. Clearly some voters recognised that a vote for a small party in the constituency poll was wasted, but this was not the case in the regional list vote, where every vote counts.

The regional list system in the UK

Used to elect Members of the European Parliament, the regional list system has had the effect of awarding seats broadly in proportion to the votes cast and gives the smaller parties a greater chance of gaining some representation. This can be seen in the results of the 2004 UK elections to the European Parliament.

Party	% votes	Seats won	% of total seats
Conservative	26.7	27	36
Labour	22.6	19	25
UKIP	16.2	12	16
Liberal Democrat	14.9	12	16
Green	6.2	2	3
BNP	4.9	0	–
Respect	1.5	0	–
SNP	1.4*	2*	3
Plaid Cymru	1.0*	1*	1
Others	4.6	0	–

*The Scottish Nationalists (SNP) and Plaid Cymru were awarded seats on a small proportion of the vote as they only put up candidates in Scotland and Wales respectively.

Plurality System
An electoral system where the winning candidate does not require an overall majority but merely needs to win more votes than any other candidate.

Majority System
A description of an electoral system where the winning candidate is required to win an overall majority, i.e. more than 50% of the votes cast.

So we can see how much more proportional this system is (even with the adjustments made). Interestingly, the UK Independence Party (UKIP) was able to win seats to an assembly of which they do not approve. But this was justified by the fact that 16 per cent of the electorate wished to express their disapproval of the European Union and their view was given representation. The Greens also won some seats, but Respect, a socialist party, did not. This was the first time they had entered a list, so they received no adjustment in their favour. Next time they may well win some seats, having gained a foothold. Above all, it can be seen that the regional list system breaks the two-party domination of Labour and the Conservatives.

Manifestos and mandates

Before leaving the subject of elections, we need to consider one of the principles of election politics in the UK. This is the doctrine of manifesto and mandate. One of the purposes of an election in the UK is to give the governing party a mandate to govern, that is, to give it elective authority. But the mandate does not give the government carte blanche. The authority granted to the government at elections is based very much on the manifesto of the party. This represents the policies of which the electorate has approved.

The mandate is subject to certain conditions. The first is that the government should only go beyond its manifesto commitments, or amend them significantly, if it can carry Parliament with it. Indeed, the House of Lords, which is more independent than the Commons, sometimes sees its role as that of guardian of the mandate. They tend to obstruct proposals for which they feel the government has no mandate. The second condition is that the government will be judged by the electorate on its performance against its previous manifesto proposals at the next general election. The third condition is that we expect the government to use its judgement when unforeseen circumstances arise. Again, it is for Parliament to judge the performance of the government in this respect.

Elections, therefore, provide a triple opportunity for the electorate. First, they can judge between the competing manifestos of the parties. Second, they can deliver their verdict on how well – or how badly – they feel the outgoing government has delivered its mandate. Third, they can give a fresh mandate to the existing governing party, or give a mandate to a different party.

KEY CONCEPTS

Electoral mandate

Refers to the authority to govern granted to the winning party at an election by the voters. The mandate suggests that the government may implement the measures in its election manifesto. It also implies that the government has authority to use its judgement in dealing with unforeseen circumstances (the 'doctor's mandate').

Manifesto

A statement produced by a political party at election times, stating what policies it intends to implement if it gains power.

Electoral system

A system that converts votes in an election into seats. It may also refer to the process of electing a single leader, such as a president or a mayor.

Party system

The typical structure of parties within a political system. It describes the normal number of parties that compete effectively. Thus we may speak of two-, three- or multi-party systems. It also refers to the typical party make-up of governments – for example, single-party government, coalitions, and so on.

Proportional representation

Describes any electoral system that converts votes into seats in a broadly proportional way.

Revision topics and examination questions

Revision topics
- The functions of elections
- Meaning of the term 'proportional representation'
- How FPTP works
- How STV, AMS and regional list systems work
- The effects of FPTP
- The effects of the use of other electoral systems in the UK
- The nature of mandate and manifesto

Short answers
- Outline the FPTP electoral system.
- What is meant by 'proportional representation'?
- What is meant by the term 'electoral mandate'?
- Outline the main functions of elections.

Medium answers
- What are the main effects of the use of FPTP in UK general elections?
- Describe the operation of any TWO electoral systems used in the UK.
- Describe the operation of STV and AMS in the UK.
- What is the significance of the doctrine of mandate and manifesto?

Long answers
- Describe the effects of the use of proportional electoral systems in the UK.
- Distinguish between the effects of FPTP and other electoral systems used in the UK.
- To what extent do elections in the UK produce representative government?

Resources and Web Guide

Books

The key description of a UK general election can be found in:
D. Butler and D. Kavanagh, *The British General Election of 2005*, Macmillan, 2005.
For information on electoral systems in general, look at:
D. Farrell, *Comparing Electoral Systems*, Prentice-Hall, 1997.

Useful websites

The Electoral Reform Society discusses the British electoral system plus alternative electoral systems and the arguments for reform:
www.electoral-reform.org.uk (accessed 11 November 2005)
The UK Electoral Commission contains a large amount of information about British elections and referendums:
www.electoralcommission.gov.uk (accessed 11 November 2005)

1.3
Political parties and the party system

Features of political parties

Before describing the nature of political parties, it is worth establishing a working definition:

A political party is an organisation that develops a set of political goals and policies, which it seeks to convert into political action by obtaining government office, or a share in government, or by influencing the government of the day. It pursues its goals by mobilising public opinion in its favour, selecting candidates for office, competing at elections and identifying suitable political leaders.

If we now look at each of the elements in our definition we can also develop a useful set of features, to which most parties conform.

■ Political parties have to be organised. They need to do this in order to carry out their many functions. A vague and disorganised group of people will find it difficult to create a coherent political programme and will be unable to fight elections successfully. Organisations will tend to be relatively formal, especially among well-established parties. An exception is the British Green Party, which prefers to remain a loose, informal organisation, but even so it has developed a mechanism for producing election manifestos and selecting candidates. New parties, such as the UK Independence Party (UKIP) find organisation difficult at first and this can prevent them making inroads into support for the other parties. Unlike the situation in the USA, where small parties can suddenly make an impact, as did Ross Perot's Reform Party in the 1990s, new British parties find it difficult to become established quickly. The problem is partly financial. Wealthy individuals like Perot are able to provide the funding for a new party in the USA. Such benefactors are rare in the UK. Even when a rich individual appears, success is elusive. A large organisation of activists is needed to mobilise public opinion and to fight elections on the ground. Multimillionaire James Goldsmith's anti-EU party, the Referendum Party, started in 1997 with £20 million of funding, failed largely because it was unable to attract enough ordinary members. Indeed, British politics is a graveyard of failed parties, mainly because of an inability to create a sufficiently effective organisation quickly enough.

■ Parties must develop policies and programmes to present to the electorate in order to secure the election of its candidates. Behind such policies usually lies some kind of ideology. This may be relatively weak, as has been the case with the Conservatives and the Labour Party since the 1990s, but it remains important for a party to have some sort of 'ideological identity' with which people can identify. This may be little more than, say, '*releasing individuals from the excessive burdens of government*' (a contemporary Conservative slogan), or '*governing on behalf of the many rather than the few*' (Labour). Labour before the mid-1990s, of course, considered itself to be democratic socialist, a far clearer ideological identity. The Liberal Democrats claim to base themselves on the primacy of individual freedom and social justice. There are ideological parties in UK politics, such as the Greens and the ultra-left Respect Party, but these have failed to make a significant electoral impact.

■ Large parties have the securing of government office as their primary goal. It is indeed arguable that a party which does seek to become the government – or at least to share government – is not a party at all, but rather a pressure group. The reason is clear. There is little point in developing a political programme unless there is a prospect of putting it into practice. Of course, smaller parties like the Liberal Democrats have to be realistic. They are unlikely to win enough seats in the Commons to be able to form a majority administration, so their immediate goal has to be to share power with one of the larger parties. From this starting point they may hope to govern alone in the future. The hopes of even smaller parties remain very much further away. Their immediate objective may be simply to gain supporters and perhaps win a few seats in Parliament. But even these political minnows may harbour dreams of forming governments in the distant future. All parties must start somewhere.

■ If parties are to make progress they must gain public support for their policies. This means they must have strategies for winning such support. They must devote much of their work to presenting their policies, educating the public and engaging in persuasion. This must be carried out on two main levels. One is in the media. Successful parties must attract the attention of TV, radio and the press if they are to have any hope of reaching the mass of the people. The other involves more work. This is the slow, gradual building up of support in neighbourhoods, persuading people to attend meetings, to read the party's literature and perhaps even to become active members.

■ When a party is in a position to fight elections it must select suitable candidates. Procedures must be put in place for selecting the best – always assuming, that is, that there is competition for such positions. This is normally a local function in the UK, as elections are essentially local in nature. Councillors and MPs are expected to represent a locality, so it is logical that they should be selected at a local level.

■ The Green Party in the UK has always been reluctant to recognise leaders. It is an intensely democratic party which is highly suspicious of the exercise of political power. But it is an exception. Parties ultimately rely upon successful leadership. Leaders give the party direction and are essential for the mobilisation of public support.

We can now see what features most, if not all political parties display. There are exceptions – loose political groups which call themselves parties (even some anarchists have described themselves as parties) – but a modern party is clearly recognisable.

Functions of parties

Having identified the main features of political parties and distinguished them from other organisations, we can summarise the functions of a modern **political party**.

Perhaps the most recognisable function of a political party is the **development of policies and political programmes**. This is a role which becomes especially important when a party is in opposition and is seeking to replace the government of the day. Opposition parties are, therefore, in a fundamentally different position to the party in power. When a ruling party controls the government, its leadership *is* the government; there is virtually no distinction between the two. Therefore the policy-making function of the ruling party is the same as the policy-making function of the government. It involves not only political leaders, but also civil servants, advisory units and committees and private advisers. Of course, the rest of the party – backbench MPs and peers, local activists and ordinary members – have some say through policy conferences and committees, but their role remains very much in the background. Ministers and their advisers make most policy in the ruling party.

In opposition, the leadership of a party is not in such a pre-eminent policy-making position. True, the leadership group will have most influence – the leader especially – but it is in opposition that the general membership of the party can have most input into policy making. 'Policy' relates to the political objectives of the party: how to run the economy, public services, defence and foreign policy, law and order, social affairs, and so on. A political programme is more specific: it describes what priorities the party should have and corresponds generally to what can be achieved in a five-year term of office, or even longer if the party is confident of a sustained period in government.

The policy-formulating function is also sometimes known as *aggregation*. This involves identifying the wide range of demands which are made on the political system, by the mass of individuals in society as well as many different groups, and then converting these into programmes of action that are consistent and compatible.

Parties claim to have a **representative function**. As we have seen above, parties have their origins in the representation of social classes. This is a weaker function in contemporary politics because all the main parties argue that they represent the *national* interest and not just the interests of specific classes or groups. So when we suggest that parties have a representative function, we mean today that they seek to ensure that all groups in society have their interests and demands at least considered by government.

Parties spend a great deal of their time and effort **selecting candidates for office** at all levels. They need to find prospective local councillors, elected mayors in those localities where such a position exists (notably London), members of the devolved assemblies and the Scottish Parliament, candidates for the European Parliament and, most prominently of

Political party
An association of people who have similar political philosophies and beliefs. Normally a party will seek power and develop an organisation whose purpose is to fight elections.

all, for the Westminster Parliament. This is mostly done at local and regional level, through party committees staffed by activists, but the party leaderships do have some say in which candidates should be chosen. But it is in this role that constituency parties have the greatest part to play.

Parties need leaders and, in the case of the main parties, this means potential government ministers. They therefore have procedures for **identifying political leaders**. It is in this area that the established party leaders play a key role. For the ruling party, the prime minister completely controls the appointment of ministers. In opposition parties the leader will choose a smaller group of frontbench spokespersons who form the leadership. But despite the dominance of party leaders in this field, potential leaders cut their teeth to some extent in internal party organisations and committees. The formal organisations of parties give opportunities for members to become 'trained' as leaders.

At **election time** parties play a critical role. Apart from supplying approved candidates, the party organisations form part of the process of publicising election issues, persuading people to vote and informing them about the candidates. Without the huge efforts of thousands of party activists at election time, the already modest turnout at the polls would be even lower.

It is not only at election time that parties have an **educative function**. They are also continuously involved in the process of informing the people about the political issues of the day, explaining the main areas of conflict and putting forward their own solutions to the problems which they have identified. Part of this process is also educating the public about how the political system itself operates.

The senior members of the party in Parliament, especially the 'business managers' – the whips and other parliamentary managers – **play a vital role in the workings of Parliament**. The party leaderships, in consultation with each other, determine the proceedings of Parliament, organise debates, manage the legislative process and ensure that MPs and peers themselves are well informed about proceedings.

Finally, parties also have a 'hidden' function, but a vital one nonetheless. This can be described as **the mobilisation and reinforcement of consent**. All the main parties support the political system of the UK – that is, parliamentary democracy. By operating and supporting this system, parties are part of the process which ensures that the general population consents to the system. If parties were to challenge the nature of the political system in any fundamental way, this would create political conflict within society at large. Parties which challenge the basis of the political system – those of the far left and right wings of politics – are generally seen as extremists and only marginal elements in the system.

We can now summarise the various features and functions of political parties in the UK.

Features	Functions
■ Some kind of organisation. ■ Developing political policies and programmes. ■ Seeking government office. ■ Putting up candidates for election. ■ Campaigning to achieve public support. ■ Training and recruiting leaders.	■ Developing policies and programmes (including aggregation). ■ Selecting candidates for office. ■ Representation. ■ Selecting political leaders. ■ Helping to run elections. ■ Political education among the people. ■ Organisation of parliamentary procedure. ■ Mobilising popular consent for the political system.

The nature of party government

It is normal to describe the British political system as 'parliamentary government', and this is largely accurate. However, a viable alternative would be to call it 'party government'. This suggests that parties are a vital element in the way in which the system operates, and this is certainly true.

First, we rely upon parties to determine who shall form the government. The prime minister is, virtually automatically, the leader of the largest party in Parliament. This, in turn, relies upon the fact that parties have a clear system for determining who their legitimate leader is. Thereafter we expect that the prime minister will form a government from the leading ranks of the ruling party. Here, again, it is party activity that determines who the candidates are to be in that leading group. Normally, British governments are drawn from a single, relatively unified party. This gives the activity of governing great stability and a strong sense of purpose, which is sometimes lacking in systems where parties are relatively weak (such as the USA) or where coalition governments are common (Ireland, Holland, Italy).

Second, parties are an essential element in the conversion of the many demands which are placed on the political system, and the variations in political belief, into workable programmes for action. Without this *aggregating* function, decision makers in government would be faced with a bewildering range of uncoordinated demands and public goals.

Third, elections in the UK depend heavily upon parties for their coherence and organisation. Parties organise the creation of policies and election manifestos, select most of the candidates (at least most of those who have a realistic chance of winning), inform the electorate about the key issues and even play a large part in the administration of elections, not least by trying to ensure that as many people as possible turn out to vote.

Fourth, Parliament itself is largely run by the parties. They determine the business of both Houses, organise the activities of MPs and peers, also keeping them informed, as well as controlling debates so that they remain relevant and effective.

Finally, we can say that the nature of the participation of the people is very much reinforced and shaped by the activities of parties. It is parties that identify key issues and conflicts and educate the public about the work of government, both by explaining it (the governing party) and criticising it (opposition parties). Parties recruit activists who can encourage participation, who raise funds for political activity and who act as a channel of communication and representation between the general public and political leaders.

So without a strong party system, political processes in the UK would be disorganised and incoherent. The public would be ill-informed and it is difficult to imagine how elections could work without them. But they are not merely a practical necessity. The whole *character* of British politics is determined by the activities of parties. In other words, we tend to think of politics in terms of the conflict between the parties, rather than just the clash of ideas and interests.

Parties and democracy

Positive features

So far we have painted a relatively positive picture of the role of political parties in the UK. It is suggested that they play a vital role in the political system and that without them there would be political chaos. But we should now undertake a more critical analysis of their role in a modern democracy.

Parties certainly do serve the interests of democracy, in the broadest sense of the word. They do this in a number of ways:

- If the main feature of any democracy is that the people should have a role to play in the development of policy, the making of decisions and the implementation of those policies, then parties carry out an important part in the process. As channels for popular demands and interests they can inform the political system and its institutions of popular sentiment.
- It is important that all sections of society receive representation in the political system. Parties help to achieve this. As we have seen above, most parties today do not represent any particular section of society (such as a social class or a region), but they do seek to ensure that the whole society is taken into consideration when policy is being made.
- They have a key role to play in informing and educating the public about political issues which will affect their lives and determine the future shape of society.
- A feature of any healthy democracy is high levels of participation by the public. Since as long ago as the 1830s, when the French philosopher, Alexis de Tocqueville, was writing in praise of North American society, theorists have insisted that it is not just necessary that the people be well informed, but also that they should take an active role in politics. This is essential, it is argued, in order to keep government under popular

control. Parties, therefore, enable people to remain active for such purposes. A passive population is in danger of subjecting itself to tyranny. Participation can take place at several levels, from mere support and voting, to local activism, local and regional office-holding, right up to national-level political activity. Parties provide opportunities for participation at all these levels.

Negative features

There are two aspects to this issue. First, the reality that parties are simply becoming *less important* in the British political system. Their democratic role is, therefore, simply weakening. Second, there are features of modern parties which may have the effect of *inhibiting* democracy, rather than enhancing it.

The declining role of parties can be charted by considering falling membership levels. The table below demonstrates the dramatic decline.

Year	Membership of all parties	Cons.	Lab.	Lib. Dem.
1980	1.69 million	1.20 million	0.35 million	0.15 million
1989	1.14 million	0.75 million	0.29 million	0.08 million
1998	0.84 million	0.35 million	0.39 million	0.10 million

Source: P. Mair and I. van Biezen, 'Party Membership 1980–2000', in Party Politics, vol. 7, no. 1, 2001.

Accurate figures are difficult to verify since 2000, but there is little doubt that membership of at least the two main parties has declined further. This means that the role of parties in encouraging participation is clearly failing. Similarly, turnout at elections, especially general elections, has also been falling. The following table shows general election turnout (as a proportion of the total electorate actually voting) is shown below.

Year	Turnout (%)
1970	72.0
1974 (Feb.)	78.8
1974 (Oct.)	72.8
1979	76.0
1983	72.7
1987	75.3
1992	77.7
1997	71.5
2001	59.4
2005	61.3

On a more general level, it is also true that modern parties in the UK play a relatively limited role in policy making. Policy now tends to remain largely in the hands of a leadership elite. It would be wrong to say that ordinary party members have no influence over policy, but it is certainly the case that such influence has declined. Mass membership participation in the policy process has been replaced largely by external think tanks, private advisers and professional researchers. Furthermore, the balance of power in the main parties has shifted markedly to the leaders, rather than the wider party organisation.

This is not a uniform process. The Liberal Democrats continue to consult regularly with their ordinary membership; and the Conservative Party, traditionally leadership-oriented, has realised that the constituency members do need to be involved to some extent if they are not to become totally alienated from the process. But the parties have all understood that, if they are to succeed in elections, there is more mileage in consulting the *general public* directly, rather than merely their own membership.

Parties, in the sense of mass political movements, are simply less significant than they used to be. As we shall see in the next chapter, pressure groups have replaced them as the main way in which most people become active in politics.

We can now examine the senses in which parties inhibit democracy in the UK.

- As we have suggested above, parties are now less *internally* democratic than they used to be. In other words, they are less efficient in translating the views of their own members into policies and action. They are perhaps more reflective of the opinions of experts and influential groups in society than of political activists. Of course, if parties are successfully reflecting wider *public opinion* through such research processes, we need not be concerned that they are becoming less democratic. Perhaps, indeed, quite the opposite.
- There is now a high degree of ideological rigidity within parties. There is a growing recognition that, if parties are to do well in elections, they need to present a united front to the electorate. Divided parties do not win elections, so the accepted wisdom goes. Vociferous dissidents, such as the left wing of the Labour Party and ultra-right-wingers among Conservatives, are viewed as dangerous elements that need to be suppressed as much as possible. The result has been a stifling of internal political debate within parties. This is seen most dramatically in Parliament when critical votes are imminent.
- The doctrine of the electoral mandate can been seen as fundamentally flawed. This principle – that the ruling party has a mandate to carry out *all* the proposals in its last election manifesto – can become undemocratic. There are two causes for concern. One is that ruling parties in the UK are always elected on a minority of the popular vote. Indeed, the Labour Government which was elected in 2005 received only 35.2 per cent of the total votes in the general election. Despite this, the government claims to have a popular mandate for its whole political

programme. The second is that it cannot reasonably be claimed that the electorate supports *every* element in the party manifesto just because that party won the election. But when the whips are persuading governing party MPs to support their own leadership in a critical vote, they often do so on the grounds that the government has a *popular mandate* and this should not be defied.

■ If we concentrate on the parliamentary process, we can find further suggestions that parties stifle democracy. Tight party discipline and the activities of the party whips, who persuade, cajole and threaten MPs into supporting the leadership when a contentious piece of legislation is being debated, have the effect of inhibiting the democratic process on the floor of the House of Commons. Indeed, it has been argued that, because party discipline is weaker in the House of Lords, it is the more democratic of the two chambers, even though it is not elected!

Political Parties – Positive and Negative features

Positive features

■ The means by which popular opinion can be translated into viable political programmes.
■ Represent all sections of society.
■ Inform and educate the public about political issues.
■ Provide opportunities for the public to participate in politics.
■ Help to run and administer elections.
■ Manage parliamentary business.
■ Recruit and train political activists and leaders.

Negative features

■ May not be internally democratic. May be dominated by leaders who may not reflect wider opinion.
■ Tend to discourage open discussion of policies, preferring to impose rigid discipline on their members.
■ The doctrine of the mandate is flawed in that it distorts public opinion, claiming authority which cannot always be justified.
■ Tight party control over parliament prevents sufficient debate of issues and legislation.

On a more general level, there has certainly been a growth in the importance of *direct* rather than *representative* democracy in the UK (and, indeed, in other modern democracies). Parties have, for over two centuries, been the main instruments of representative democracy. But if representative democracy is in decline, it is logical to assume that parties will follow. The introduction of referendums, focus group research and direct action by mass membership pressure groups (often known as 'New Social Movements') is now seen as central to the democratic process. Parties have become increasingly marginalised and specialised. Their role has become less concentrated on democratic representation, and more concerned with ensuring that the party wins elections and retains its position in power.

Having examined the role and importance of parties in the UK in general terms, we can consider the specific beliefs and policies of current parties. In the case of the three main parties, we will consider first the fundamental, traditional beliefs which have underpinned their development, followed by a consideration of current specific policies.

Conservative ideas

The task of determining the basic conservative philosophy is complicated by the fact that, since the 1970s, a second, distinctive tradition has emerged. These two very different philosophies are normally described as **traditional conservatism** – the pre-1970s type – and **New Right conservatism** – which came to prominence under the Conservative Party leadership of Margaret Thatcher. We must look at these in turn.

Traditional conservatism

Originating in the late part of the eighteenth century, traditional **conservatism** emerged as a reaction against the newly emerging liberal ideas which were the inspiration behind the revolutions in North America (1776) and France (1789). Conservative thinkers, such as Edmund Burke, became alarmed at the rise of ideas such as freedom of the individual, tolerance of different political and religious beliefs, representative government and a laissez-faire attitude towards economic activity (that is, the state avoiding significant interference in the way in which wealth is distributed in society). Conservatives believed that such a free society, with so little control by government, would lead to major social disorder.

Thereafter conservatives have consistently opposed the rise of any new ideology, so, later in the nineteenth century, the rise of socialism was opposed. This anti-socialist position remained in place until the 1970s, when it reached its height under Margaret Thatcher.

But conservatism is not merely a reaction to any dominant ideology. It is not simply a political philosophy opposed to change. There are some enduring principles, which are described below.

Human nature

Perhaps the most fundamental conservative value is its belief about basic human nature. In short, this is more pessimistic than the attitude of most other ideologies, notably **liberalism** and **socialism**. The following examples of these beliefs are typical:

■ The deepest conservatives take the Roman Catholic view that man is born with original sin. Therefore, s/he is, and must remain, severely flawed in character. However much s/he tries, s/he will be unable to achieve perfection. Ideologies such as socialism and anarchism have argued that mankind can be moulded by a just society into more perfect creatures. Not so, say such conservatives, thus rendering these ideologies impractical and merely utopian. Mankind is driven not by reason, but by basic appetites: these include the desire for physical prosperity, property and power, and the avoidance of deprivation. This implies that people generally cannot be trusted with government as they will simply use it for their own ends rather than for the welfare of the whole community.

Conservatism
A state of mind and a political movement that is naturally averse to excessive change and reform. It is sceptical about strongly held political views, prefers the known to the unknown and generally supports the retention of traditional institutions and values.

Liberalism A state of political mind or political movement that places freedom, rights and tolerance high on its scale of values.

Socialism A state of mind and political movement that places such values as equality of opportunity, social justice and collectivism high on its scale of values. It is either opposed to free market capitalism or proposes measures to moderate the effects of capitalism.

■ It is a conservative tradition to see people as, on the whole, untrustworthy, self-seeking and generally feckless. This adds up to the clear conclusion that mankind is sorely in need of firm government. This should not be government by dictatorial figures – they may rise to power too easily as people are often led by populist figures. Rather they need to be governed by benevolent rulers, who should be firm, but who have the general interests of the populace at heart. As Edmund Burke, the father of English conservatism, observed in the eighteenth century, the relationship between government and the people should be similar to that between a parent and a child. This view is often referred to as *conservative paternalism.*

■ It is normal for human beings to think of themselves first; the interests of the rest of society tend to be a secondary consideration. This implies that the state needs to intervene if the pursuit of self-interest is not to take over completely. It also led to the conservative stress on social unity rather than social conflict.

There are two further practical implications of the conservative view of human nature. The field of law and order is an obvious example. The causes of crime and disorder, they believe, lie with the individual. Indeed some have argued that it is the product of mankind's inherent sinfulness. This directly opposes the more liberal view that criminal behaviour is the result of economic and social deprivation. The application of these beliefs therefore involves exemplary punishment rather than social remedies.

A second, very different application of this conservative philosophy concerns the nature of government. If there is an excess of popular democracy, the country is likely to be poorly governed. As long ago as the 1870s, the great Tory prime minister, Benjamin Disraeli (1804–1881), had advocated that conservatives accept the need for universal suffrage, but this did not imply that the people could be completely trusted with government. The conservative view of representation is that governments should not slavishly follow the fluctuating desires and demands of the people, but should use their wise judgement to serve the best interests of the whole community. In a modern context this is reflected in the conservative suspicion of the referendum as a governing mechanism (though the British Conservative Party has supported the use of referendums in some circumstances, such as possible approval for a European Union Constitution in 2005 – a typical example of Conservative pragmatism).

Order

In the most basic terms, it could be said that liberals see mankind's most fundamental need, after food, clothing and shelter, as individual freedom. Socialists and anarchists, on the other hand, stress man's social nature and his preference for the collective rather than the individual pursuit of goals. The conservative view is clear and stands in opposition to these beliefs. It affirms that mankind's most basic need is for order and security.

We can trace this key aspect of conservative philosophy to two English

thinkers, Hobbes and Burke. Thomas Hobbes (1588–1679), writing shortly after the end of the English Civil War in 1651, examined mankind's basic predicament. On the one hand, we have a desire to be free and to exercise all our rights. On the other hand, we are intensely competitive and self-seeking. This would, if allowed to flourish, lead to an intolerable situation. Life, he famously argued, would become 'nasty, brutish and short'. In practice, everyone would consider themselves to be in competition with every other person and therefore live in fear of the results of that restless society. Hobbes believed that, faced with such a dilemma, mankind would choose to sacrifice much of its freedom and rights in favour of a secure existence. The only way to assure this was to allow an absolute ruler to govern and so protect us from each other.

Ever since Hobbes, conservatives have preferred strong government and have tended to favour the needs of the community for security above the rights of individuals. We see this philosophy most clearly in the conservative attitude to law and order and reluctance to champion the cause of civil liberties.

Edmund Burke's great work, *Reflections on the Revolution in France,* was written in 1790, one year after the French had dismissed their monarchy and at a time when there was growing hysteria in England in case revolution crossed the Channel. Starting as a vehement criticism of the actions of the revolutionaries, the book turned into a general manual of conservatism. Above all, Burke's *Reflections* is a plea for the preservation of order and gradual reform, rather than the disorder which results from revolutionary change. The French Revolution thus sacrificed order and security for the sake of the imposition of abstract theories which were premature, unnecessary and not generally supported by the majority of the people. Since Burke, conservatives have always erred on the side of caution and preserving order above promoting dubious new ideas – until Margaret Thatcher, that is.

A clear contemporary example of how the conservative preference for social order over individual rights and freedoms has occurred is the struggle against terrorism. The typical conservative view is that individual rights and freedoms must be sacrificed for the sake of public security in the face of such a desperate challenge.

Tradition and preservation

The conservative preference for the preservation of tradition is related closely to their desire for public order. When we refer to tradition in this context we mean both traditional *institutions,* such as monarchy, established Church and political constitutions, and *values,* such as the preservation of marriage, the importance of the nuclear family, religion and established morality. Here, again, it is an attitude which traces itself back to Burke.

The greatest crime of the French revolutionaries, said Burke, was to abandon traditional forms of authority which, according to him anyway, had stood the test of time. This is summarised in his ringing criticism: 'No

generation should ever be so rash as to consider itself superior to its predecessors.'

The very fact that values and institutions have survived, argue conservatives in general, is a testament to their quality. Furthermore, they carry the 'accumulated wisdom of the past' and should therefore be respected. In a similar way, traditions bring to an existing society some of the best aspects of past societies. How people thought and behaved in the past can inform current generations. Thus the nineteenth-century poet and philosopher, G.K. Chesterton, called tradition the 'democracy of the dead', allowing the wisdom of previous generations to be involved in the activities of current society.

Burke also praised traditions for their ability to provide continuity between the past and the present, claiming that they give a sense of security and help to prevent violent transformations in society. He referred to 'a partnership between those who are living, those who are dead and those who are to be born'.

A typical example concerns monarchy. Elected governments, political ideologies and social change may come and go, but if monarchy endures in its traditional form the people will retain a sense of security and continuity amid the turmoil. Conservatives take a similar view of traditional morality, based around the family. This helps each new generation to hold on to a lasting set of values in an ever-changing world, giving them a sense of security which they can pass on to the next generation.

Allied to their theories of tradition, conservatives also believe that, where institutions and values have proved to be helpful in promoting order and stability in the past, they should be preserved. It is irresponsible, they argue, to reject them for the sake of ideological principles or new theories. But this is not a recipe for 'no change'. Rather, it is a tendency to conserve what is seen to be good and reform what is proving to be undesirable.

Modern British conservatism has largely ignored the importance of tradition, especially since the 1980s. It has embraced new social theories, such as opposition to the dependency culture, privatisation and economic monetarism, and has attacked some traditional institutions, such as the civil service, the Church of England, the legal establishment and the long-standing practices of the financial centre in London. However, we can still see strong support for traditional institutions and values in North American and French conservatism, which have proved resistant to 'excessive' social reform.

The organic society and 'one-nation Toryism'

Dating back to the leadership of Disraeli in the 1860s and 1870s, conservatives in the UK have stressed the need to unite the nation and to prevent social conflict. To this end they have stressed the *organic* nature of society. This suggests that the people are part of one single body – the nation – and that they are all interdependent. Even though we may be divided into different social classes, these classes should work together to maintain the welfare of the nation, rather than engage in conflict with each other.

Organic society theory also denies the notion that we are merely individuals pursuing our own interests without any regard for the well-being of society as a whole.

This does not add up to a socialist vision of society. Conservatives accept that individuals should be able to pursue their own goals and that we are all fundamentally unequal. In the organic society, however, individuals should be expected to accept that they do have responsibilities to society as a whole. It is, furthermore, the role of the state to ensure the unity of society by caring for the welfare of *all* the people, not just particular social classes. The danger of social conflict, Disraeli had argued, is that the nation will become divided. By maintaining the welfare of all, he added, Britain can remain *one nation*, rather than *two nations* – the wealthy and the deprived. For that reason, Disraeli's brand of conservatism is still known as one-nation Toryism to this day. As we shall see below, it was this organic vision of society which was most fiercely attacked in the 1980s when Margaret Thatcher transformed the Conservative Party.

FIG 1.3A Margaret Thatcher dominated conservatism in the 1980s

Pragmatism

It would be entirely wrong to suggest that conservatism is a doctrine of no change, or that it treats its own principles as eternal and fixed. Conservatives are, above all, pragmatists. Michael Oakeshott (1901–1990), a leading conservative philosopher of modern times, particularly advocated this kind of political action. He asserted that politics should be 'a conversation, not an argument'. What he meant was that political action should never be the result of conflict over political dogma and theory. Instead it should be the result of a more gentle relationship between government and the governed. The good conservative politician should engage in a relationship with the people which would allow him/her to reach decisions based on the 'intimations and traditions' of the community.

Pragmatism implies a flexible approach to politics, incorporating an understanding of what is best for people, what is acceptable to them and what will preserve a stable society. It is also a rejection of the politics of strongly held ideology, a dogmatic approach to decision making. Perhaps the most striking example of this approach occurred in the 1950s. A series of moderate Conservative governments in the UK were faced with dealing with a number of radical reforms which had been undertaken by the Labour Governments of 1945–51. Should the Conservatives cancel the widespread nationalisation of major industries, dismantle the newly created welfare state and remove freshly granted powers from local government? In principle the party was opposed to the reforms, but had to recognise that they were both popular and seemingly successful. Therefore they reached a pragmatic decision to retain Labour's radical initiatives.

Individualism

This is perhaps the most difficult of conservative principles to pin down. It has also lost much of its distinctiveness as it is a value which is now shared by liberals, by most European democratic parties, both Republicans and Democrats in the USA and by the British Labour Party. There is also a problem in distinguishing individualism from individual liberty. Though they are linked ideas, they are not necessarily the same concept, and represent very distinctive political traditions.

Conservative individualism has two main elements. First, it suggests that each individual and household should be presented with the widest possible range of choices and opportunities. The state should restrict such choices as little as possible, providing a link with liberal freedom, but it is distinguished from it in that the state can also *enhance and facilitate* choice and opportunity. In other words, the state can play a positive rather than a negative role. Second, individualism implies a sense of *privacy*. There are many areas where interference by the state may be seen as legitimate – for example, in the fields of law and order, national defence and management of the currency – but there is also an extensive private sphere. For conservatives, private life is not the concern of the state. Such matters as operating private businesses, religious belief, enjoyment of property and family expenditure decisions are not normally to be interfered with by government. So it is part of the *essence* of conservatism that a strong barrier should be preserved between what may be described as the *public* sphere, and *private* or *individual* spheres.

There is one further important implication of the conservative support for individualism. For them, individualism can best flourish in a stable social, moral and economic environment. The continuity provided by morality, law and order and tradition provides the necessary scenery in which individuals can play their roles securely. Indeed, in many circumstances, the excessive exercise of individual liberties, as advocated by pure liberals, threatens individualism. A society that allows too much personal freedom may threaten its own security and stability. Given the choice between a free society and a collectively secure society in which individuals can flourish, conservatives normally favour the latter.

Property

For much of the nineteenth century, conservatives (then usually referred to as *Tories*) feared the rise of the property-owning middle classes. This was mainly because they believed that they would sweep away traditional authority by using their vast economic wealth to wield political power. It was the Whig Party which was seen as the promoter of capitalist property.

After Disraeli in the 1860s and 1870s, however, the British Tories (then turning themselves into the Conservative Party), accepted that they too must incorporate the interests of property owners.

In the modern context, conservatives have always attempted to defend the interests of home owners and the owners of businesses. For them, the right to own and enjoy one's own property in security is a fundamental aspect of a civilised existence. Furthermore, property owners are seen to have a greater vested interest in order and so will ensure that there is stability in society.

Opposition to ideology

We have seen above that conservatism has changed its character according to the dominant ideology which it may be resisting at any time. However, the movement's opposition to ideologies in general runs more deeply than merely a suspicion of radical change. There are a number of different aspects to this belief.

First, conservatives fear that an excessive attachment to a political ideology can lead to tyranny. They point to the experience of fascism and communism to prove their theory. In both these cases there was a slavish attachment to a ruling ideology. Second, they do not believe that society should be driven towards any particular goals. Instead, society should be allowed to develop naturally. Nobody has the right to declare what the nature of a future society should be, conservatives argue. Thus socialists, in particular, are wrong to attempt to create an 'idealised' form of society. Third, conservatives note that ideologies make false assumptions about human nature. Thus socialists believe that mankind is naturally sociable and seeks equality; liberals believe that man seeks freedom and is able to use such freedom well. Holding a much more pessimistic view of man's nature, conservatives reject such ideological notions.

Empiricism

Most conservatives consider themselves to be 'empiricists'. Empiricism involves judging current actions against our experience of the past. Respect for tradition, pragmatism and suspicion of the new and the untried are all aspects of this empirical approach. The wise politician, it is suggested, builds on the wisdom of the past and is informed by that past. This is a preference for the known (what has gone before) over the unknown (what may be in the future). This view follows Chesterton's concept of the 'democracy of the dead' and respects Burke's plea not to believe that the current generation is wiser than those who have gone before. Critics see this as permanently looking backwards, but conservatives respond by pointing out how much of a positive nature has been achieved in the past, from which we can still learn.

Before moving on to the New Right variety of conservative thought, we can summarise the traditional view by quoting the words of Benjamin Disraeli in a speech of 1872: 'the Tory Party has three great objects…to maintain the institutions of the country…to uphold the Empire of

England…and to elevate the condition of the people'.

There is no longer an Empire, of course, but if we substitute 'British values' for 'Empire', Disraeli's words remain relevant to traditional conservatism.

New Right Conservatism

The British Conservative Party was dominated by traditional conservatism until the latter part of the 1970s. But, at that time, politicians of all opinions were faced by an apparent crisis in British society. The economy had descended into a major slump, with high unemployment, inflation and lack of growth, all at the same time. Public sector (state) debt was reaching new heights, placing enormous burdens on taxpayers to pay the interest on that debt. There was a great deal of persistent industrial unrest. Crime levels were also increasing. The Labour Party's response to this crisis was to propose more radical socialist plans, with greater intervention by the state to solve the problems. In the Conservative Party, by contrast, a radically new set of beliefs was taking hold, largely imported from the USA. This became known as the 'New Right', and it became the basis of the policies of the new Conservative leader, Margaret Thatcher, and her close advisers, notably Keith Joseph. Her policies stood in complete contrast to those of the Labour Party. When the Conservatives won the election of 1979, a period of remarkable social and economic reform was ushered in. This process was to last until well into the 1990s and beyond.

The main beliefs of New Right Conservatism (sometimes also described as 'Thatcherism') are described below.

Deregulation

While socialists were arguing that the answer to Britain's problems in the early 1980s was *more* intervention by the state, the New Right was suggesting that the source of the problems was *too much* intervention by the state, especially in industry, welfare policy and the management of the economy. They therefore proposed that, as far as was practical, the state should 'disengage' from those parts of society which promoted wealth.

The key policy flowing from the idea of deregulation was the privatisation of major industries which were formerly under state control and public ownership. Thus such industries as telecommunications, gas, electricity generation and supply, coal, steel and even, as late as 1996, the railways, were all sold off to private shareholders. In addition, most of these former nationalised industries had been monopolies. Competition was either forbidden or discouraged. They were therefore forced to allow competition, both from home and abroad. Thus they would be forced to become more efficient and to provide a better service.

At the same time, other industries which were already in the private sector, such as banking, building societies and stockbroking, were forced to allow more competition. The domination of large companies (notably the big banks) was thus broken, to the benefit of consumers. In this way, the

whole of the financial sector was deregulated, allowing for the much freer flow of money in the economy, creating more rapid growth.

Disengagement

Since the Second World War, governments in the UK had commonly intervened when a major industry found itself in financial difficulties. In the interests of protecting traditional industries, and employment levels in particular, the state would find ways of providing artificial support. Similarly, when the economy began to fail, governments would tend to raise public expenditure on various projects and on welfare benefits such as pensions, in order to promote more economic activity and bring the economy out of its slump. Such measures had certainly prevented the return of mass unemployment and a major economic depression, as had occurred in the 1930s, but the New Right challenged such policies on the grounds that they were merely *short-term* remedies that inflicted *long-term* damage on the economy. In other words, they were treating the symptoms of economic decline, but not the causes.

Two main policies were thus introduced, together known as *disengagement*. First, the New Right declared that the state would no longer intervene to save declining industries or firms. If they were failing, the argument went, it was because they were not efficient enough to compete. By not intervening, therefore, they would either disappear altogether, allowing resources to move to other, growing industries, or they would be *forced* to make themselves more efficient. In this way, the structure of British industry would be reformed, with a concentration on modern, efficient industries and the decline of traditional, failing industries which could never compete in world markets.

Second, there was to be less intervention in the economy. The argument of the New Right was that the practice of raising public expenditure in order to raise economic activity was both an excessive burden upon taxpayers and an artificial way of promoting economic activity which could not be sustained in the long term. In other words, constantly 'bailing out the economy' masked the real problems. These were mainly, the New Right insisted, lack of efficiency and competitiveness. Exposing the economy to competition from abroad, without giving it any aid, would be the perfect discipline, forcing it to make itself more efficient. This resulted in high levels of unemployment in the short term, but, the New Right pointed out, it would have the desired effect in the long run.

Trade union reform

Followers of the New Right saw trade unions as the main culprits in sustaining industrial inefficiency and in the maintenance of excessive inflation. They were using their power, it was argued, to maintain inefficient working practices, prevent technological innovation (because of the threat to jobs and traditional skills) and force companies to employ more labour than they really needed. In this way, inefficiency was retained and caused excessive price levels because production costs were relatively high.

Trade unions were also the cause of excessively high wages, it was said, leading to alarming price increases and making British industry uncompetitive in world markets. In the past, governments had intervened directly to try to control wages and prices (so-called prices and incomes policy, used in the 1960s and 1970s). The New Right was ideologically opposed to such intervention and so attacked the problem from a different angle.

The first measure was to reform trade unions in such a way as to reduce their power. This was achieved by making it more difficult for strikes to be called in support of wage claims (secret ballots in favour were introduced by law), and making them effectively unlawful if they had a political aim. The unions were also forced to make themselves internally democratic. But, above all, the traditional legal immunity of trade unions was removed. This had prevented unions from being sued by businesses who had lost trade and profit as a result of a trade union's actions. The effect of this was to make striking a dangerous practice. A union whose actions caused problems for businesses not directly involved in the strike ran the risk of sustaining orders to pay out heavy financial damages and so face ruin. The result of these reforms was significant reductions in industrial unrest and the destruction of trade union power ever since.

Low taxation

By the early 1980s, levels of income taxes and taxes on business had reached a high level. The justification for this had been that the state was using funds raised through such taxes to create a fair society, to support failing industries and to maintain a high quality of public services. The New Right thinkers, on the other hand, insisted that high levels of such direct taxation were a disincentive to enterprise and to hard work. Conversely, reducing taxes on incomes and on business would be an incentive to more entrepreneurial activity, research and development and general investment in economic growth.

To this end the Thatcher Government rapidly reduced levels of income tax, especially on higher-income earners. The top rate of income tax on the very wealthy was reduced from 83 per cent to 60 per cent. By the end of the 1980s the highest rate of tax had been reduced to 40 per cent. At the same time, a range of other taxes, including corporation tax on company profits, was reduced. Of course, there was a price to pay, and some indirect taxes, especially VAT, were raised to compensate. In the long run, however, it was argued that low taxes would be an incentive to wealth creation. The greater wealth would reduce the need for government spending on welfare, while, at the same time, the 'tax base' would increase, meaning that as people's prosperity rose they would automatically pay more in tax (even though rates were lower).

Dependency culture

The New Right inspiration for a general attack on the use of welfare benefits had its origins in the nineteenth century, when a strong political

movement, led by the ultra-liberal philosopher, Herbert Spencer (1820–1903), had led to opposition to government intervention to alleviate the conditions of the poor. For Spencer, the poor deserved to be where they were because they lacked a work ethic or a sense of enterprise. Therefore the state was not justified in helping them; they should be responsible for their own welfare.

The New Right of the late twentieth century was less dogmatic than Spencer had been, but they shared the same general attitude. Its followers argued that levels of state welfare benefits were too high. They had created a *dependency culture* where many members of society had grown used to depending on state welfare benefits and had no incentive to improve their own economic circumstances. Successive generations in some families simply learned to depend on the state in the same way as their parents had done.

During the 1980s and 1990s the levels of state benefits were gradually eroded. Nobody was expected to fall into total poverty (as Spencer had accepted), but lower benefits were certainly seen as an incentive for the unemployed to seek work, for the low-paid to seek improvements in their skills and earning power, and for everybody to make better private pension provision for themselves. Those who chose to remain dependent on state benefits found their standard of living falling significantly.

We can now offer a summary of the distinctions between traditional conservative ideals and the New Right philosophy.

Traditional conservatism	The New Right
■ A pessimistic view of human nature. ■ Order. ■ Respect for traditional institutions and values. ■ The organic society and the need to preserve 'one nation'. ■ A pragmatic approach to political action. ■ Stress on individualism. ■ Need to defend the interests of private property. ■ Opposition to ideologies and dogmatic political principles. ■ Empiricism – a stress on the importance of following the lessons of past experience.	■ Deregulation – the privatisation of industry and the introduction of more competition. ■ Disengagement – reluctance to interfere in the economy or to support failing industry (also known as laissez-faire policy). ■ Opposition to trade union power. ■ Low levels of personal and business taxation as an incentive to wealth creation. ■ Opposition to the dependency culture created by high levels of welfare benefits.

It would be a mistake to assume that these two traditions were in complete opposition to each other. There are elements of traditional conservatism which have been retained by the New Right. Thus they accept the need for good order and for the state to take a strong position on law and order. Both wings of the conservative movement are strongly nationalist and support the retention of traditional British values.

The aspects of New Right philosophy which conform to traditional conservatism have come to be known as *neoconservatism*. The neoconservatives, perhaps, take an even more authoritarian position on the role of the state in social and moral issues than their traditionalist colleagues. The economic and social New Right ideas shown above have also been described as *neo-liberalism*, because they aim to extend personal freedom and are suspicious of the role of the state. Thus the New Right is sometimes described as a combination of neo-liberalism and neoconservatism.

The policies of the Conservative Party today

The Conservative Party entered a difficult period of its history after 1992, an experience which seems likely to persist until the general election of 2009 or 2010. There are a number of reasons why policy making within the Conservative Party has become confused.

Three traumatic election defeats, in 1997, 2001 and 2005 have been a unique experience for the party. Before this period they had considered themselves to be the 'natural party of government', a party to which the British people have regularly turned for periods of stability. As a result of

FIG 1.3B David Cameron, who became Conservative leader in 2005

these shocks there has been considerable turmoil within the party. After John Major resigned the party leadership in 1997, there have been four more leaders, a rate of turnover that illustrates the problems in the party.

The division within the party over the appropriate attitude to the European Union for a conservative to take persists. This conflict has been so damaging and overwhelming that the normal task of adopting a winning set of policies has been suspended.

Many of the recently successful policies of the Conservative Party, especially of the New Right, have been adopted by the Labour Party since the mid-1990s. This has left the party with a dilemma – whether to accept the situation and campaign on the basis that they are more competent than the Labour Party, or whether to adopt a different set of policies to attract the electorate.

Perhaps the most important reason is that there are still two distinctive wings of the party, broadly represented by the traditions described above. The New Right section is certainly stronger, but the rest of the party retains a desire to return to a less dogmatic position and to maintain the one nation philosophy that seeks to prevent social conflict and to unite the country. The two sides remain incompatible.

Despite this internal division, there are a number of policies that remain distinctly conservative and that most members of the party can agree upon.

Less government

The party believes that Britain is over-governed. This includes the over-regulation of business and commerce, excessive interference in people's lives and an overprotective attitude towards the vulnerable in society. The European Union is seen as one of the main culprits in this area.

Reduced taxation

Similarly, they continue to argue for the reduction of taxation in general, income and company taxation in particular. Like the New Right, all conservatives see taxation as a disincentive to enterprise and to individualism. It is viewed, by and large, as a necessary evil which should be minimised. The Conservative Party promotes itself as 'business-friendly'. Low business taxes form a key part of this attitude.

Law and order

Conservatives remain concerned that there are excessive levels of crime and disorder. While they clearly wish to see the main thrust of anti-crime policy in terms of a more authoritarian approach to sentencing and policing (with many more police employed), they also see the causes of crime in terms of the breakdown in family life and too many modern, 'liberal' methods in education.

Choice in public services

Conservatives share with the other main parties a desire to retain high quality public services, especially health and education. However, they argue that individuals do not have enough choice in their experience of the use of these services. They wish to see services arranged so that the public may have a variety of provision available to them, the means to search out the best services available and even some financial assistance if they choose to use private sector health or education. This is sometimes known as a 'voucher' or 'passport' system of public services.

Euroscepticism

Most Conservatives (though not all members of the party) are suspicious of the power and activities of the European Union. Only a minority proposes that Britain should withdraw completely, but most agree that there are too many European regulations and that members do not retain enough of their own independence within the Union. It remains official policy that Britain should not join the European single currency.

There remain fundamental policy issues which the Conservative Party has to reconcile. There are many who would like to see the UK distance itself significantly from the European Union. Others are comfortable with a close relationship and there is a minority that would like to see Britain adopt the single European currency. Some, on the right wing of the party, wish to see very extensive reductions in taxation, with cuts in state welfare provision to pay for them. The more radical members of the New Right even propose that several elements of the welfare state should be replaced by a voluntary system in which people will be free to opt in or out of public sector services and adjust their tax liability accordingly.

There are also disputes over immigration and multiculturalism. Some conservatives would like to see a hard line taken to reduce or almost eliminate immigration. For them, Britain should remain a country dominated by a single 'British' culture. Their opponents view Britain as a multicultural society which can tolerate different cultural traditions and lifestyle choices. The latter, known as 'modernisers', argue that there should be equal opportunities for all, a policy which was formerly the preserve of liberals and social democrats.

As the first decade of the twenty-first century progresses, however, the Conservative Party remains in a state which, at worst, might be described as 'turmoil', and, at best, can be seen as 'transitional'. It remains to be seen whether its leader, David Cameron, can facilitate a smooth change into modernity.

Socialism and Labour in the UK

Supporters of the British Labour Party have, in the past, often been described as 'socialists'. But in most cases this is misleading. For most of its

life – dating back to the end of the eighteenth century – socialism has been a more radical ideology than the one followed by Labour in Britain in the twentieth century. British 'socialism' has certainly been traditionally more moderate than those forms which have flourished in the rest of Europe and elsewhere.

The most radical form of socialism has been Marxism (which can also be described as communism). In fact, Marxism has had relatively little influence on British Labour. Above all, Marxists are revolutionary, desiring the complete destruction of capitalism and the political system that has supported it. Labour has never been revolutionary, but has always argued that its brand of socialism can be achieved through peaceful, parliamentary means. Of almost equal importance is the fact that Labour has always accepted that a limited, regulated form of capitalism is acceptable and desirable. Marxists and other radical socialists have always insisted that capitalism must be completely destroyed and replaced by forms of common ownership (i.e. by all) of all the means of production, distribution and finance.

Some non-Marxist forms of socialism have been almost as radical as communism. Particularly in the nineteenth century, a number of European socialist movements were either revolutionary or radical or both. Such a form of socialism never caught hold in Britain. The one attempt to create such a movement – the Social Democratic Foundation in 1884 – soon withered away. Parliamentary candidates representing radical socialist parties have been remarkably unsuccessful. Only the Independent Labour Party (ILP), a radical offshoot of the main Labour Party, has ever won significant representation. The Scottish Socialist Party did win six seats in the Scottish parliamentary election of 2003, and George Galloway's socialist-inspired Respect Party won a Westminster seat in 2005, but these have been isolated successes. So British socialism, as represented by the Labour Party, has been remarkably moderate.

The socialist ideas described below can be viewed both in terms of *fundamental* principles, and in terms of the way they have been adapted by British Labour.

Core values of British socialism and 'Old Labour'

Class

All but the more moderate socialists have seen social class as a crucial aspect of society. It has been assumed by socialists that most people define their position in society, to some extent, in terms of their social class. This implies that they develop a sense of common interests and common purpose with other members of their class. Marx described this effect as 'class consciousness', but most socialists use the more moderate expression 'common class interest'. Thus, for example, the middle classes feel they have a strong common need to protect private property interests, to promote and protect business, and to keep taxes as low as is reasonably possible. The working classes, on the other hand, are more concerned with welfare issues, sympathetic industrial relations, fair wages, good working conditions and policies which promote greater equality. These two sets of interests conflict with each other. Low taxation and high welfare expenditure together are not feasible. The business classes normally oppose higher wages as they conflict with the need to make profits and generate funds for further investment.

British Labour certainly adopted such a 'class position' at least until the 1980s. However, two reservations must be included here. First, Labour has always been forced to consider in its policies the interests of all classes in British society, not just those of the working class. The reason has, to a large extent, been the fact that the party has always needed to attract electoral support. For most of the twentieth century, about one-third of the British working class habitually voted Conservative. Electoral arithmetic determined, therefore, that Labour could not win by winning the votes of the other two-thirds of the working class alone. Therefore Labour has always pursued the support of a wider constituency than that of the working class. Yes, it was a working-class party, but its policies always reflected wider interests.

Second, the size and unity of the British working class declined steadily in the second half of the twentieth century. This meant that the electoral calculations for Labour were becoming worse. The party therefore gradually shed its class-based image and steadily moved towards a more moderate position. In the mid-1980s, especially at the 1983 election, Labour did move back, temporarily, towards its former position by supporting pro-working-class policies, such as the restoration of trade union power, nationalisation of large industries and greater redistribution of income, but these policies proved so unpopular that the party was finally forced to abandon its position as a working-class party.

Equality

Although equality is seen as the central principle of socialism, it is not a simple issue and has created conflict both between socialists and others and *within* the socialist movement itself.

It is worth beginning with the aspects of equality upon which all, or the vast majority of socialists can agree. First, there is a belief that we are all born with equal rights. Socialists share this belief with liberals. It suggests that we are created equal in terms of our right to both justice and access to power. Second, all socialists reject the idea that society has any kind of natural order. Instead, every individual has the potential to take up any position in society to which they may aspire. Third, equality of opportunity is a key principle. However unequal people may prove to be, all are entitled to the same life chances.

None of this is particularly contentious, which is why there is unity over these principles among socialists. When we look more deeply, however, fragmentation appears within the movement. The most controversial issue is the extent to which *equality of outcome* should be pursued. This principle is relatively simple – that the resources of a society should be distributed equally throughout the community. Whatever the contribution made by individuals, they are entitled to equal rewards. Clearly this has a number of

problems. It eliminates the conventional incentives upon which a modern economy is said to rely. It also does not acknowledge the variety of contributions which each person makes. It can be seen, indeed, as fundamentally *unjust*, even though many socialists see it as the ultimate expression of social justice.

British Labour has always supported the cause of equal rights – for women, for ethnic minorities and for those who are economically deprived. But it has never proposed that the state should sponsor absolute economic equality among the population. It *has*, however, always proposed that some of the inequalities between the richer and poorer elements in society should be reduced. This can be achieved through the tax system and by the redistribution of income through welfare benefits. Radical elements in the party have proposed large redistributions of wealth and income, but most members have supported relatively mild redistribution policies.

Equality of welfare provision has, however, been pursued rigorously by the Labour Party. The welfare state, created in the 1940s, adopted the principle that every adult should contribute to the country's welfare provisions – health care, education, pensions, subsidised housing, a variety of benefits to combat poverty and unemployment, and so on. At the same time, everybody has been *equally* entitled to the benefits of the welfare state.

Social justice

So, the desire for economic and social equality has not been stressed particularly within the Labour Party. Instead, British socialists have tended to discuss *social justice*. This concept accepts that full-scale equality is neither practical nor desirable. However, it does include a sense that some inequalities in society are excessive.

The socialist idea of social justice argues that there are some who are deprived through no fault of their own (the 'deserving poor'), and that some have become wealthy through windfalls rather than their own efforts (for example, inherited wealth, or fortunes made through mere speculation). Where these occur, a socialist would argue, there is a very strong case for redistributing income from the rich to the poor. On the other hand, those who achieve personal prosperity through enterprise, special talent or wealth creation may deserve to retain their fortune. Similarly, there are those who are deprived because they make no effort to improve their situation. For them, only a minimum level of state benefit is appropriate.

Social justice also means that all are entitled to equality of opportunity. The state is justified in intervening both to eliminate artificial privilege and to create greater opportunities for those who are born with a lack of opportunity.

Equality of opportunity

British socialists in the Labour Party, as we have seen, have never pursued absolute economic equality. They have accepted that unequal rewards in a capitalist-based society are inevitable and, indeed, desirable, because they provide incentives to enterprise, wealth creation and hard work. But they have also recognised that inequality can be unjust. In particular, therefore, they have been anxious to ensure that all in our society are provided with equal opportunities. The provision of a good standard of free education for all has always been the principal means of achieving such equality of opportunity. But there are three other aspects to this question.

First, socialists tend to emphasise the belief that people who live in deprived circumstances do not have equal opportunities. This is not merely a question of education. Socialists believe that there is generalised discrimination against those who come from poorer backgrounds. If living standards can be raised for all, there will also be more opportunities for all.

Second, socialists believe that there are social forces in society which operate against the interests of some sections of society. In the fields of higher education, the professions, government itself and business in general, there remains a certain degree of class-based bias which discriminates in subtle ways against those who come from more humble backgrounds. Equality of opportunity therefore demands that such institutions must make themselves more open to a wider social spectrum of society. Members of the middle classes still seem to have advantages in a number of walks of life, especially university education. The answer that socialists have offered is to break into this cycle of discrimination, either by positive discrimination or by introducing laws and codes of practice which outlaw social discrimination.

Third, the modern Labour Party, along with liberals, has sought to open up more opportunities for a wider section of the community to become involved in business and so secure for themselves a greater share of society's wealth. In other words, one of the ways in which the prosperity of the poorer sections of society can be improved is by allowing them to take part in capitalist enterprises themselves.

Collectivism

The term 'collectivism' refers to two main ideas: first, that people usually prefer to achieve goals collectively rather than independently; second, and more fundamentally, that action taken by people in organised groups is likely to be more effective than merely the sum of many individual actions. These ideas stem from a socialist view of human nature that man is a social animal who will prefer to live in social groups than alone.

Of course, the degree to which society should be organised on the basis of collectivism has varied with different branches of socialism. Marxists and other state socialists have proposed that the centralised state should be the vehicle for collective action in the form of organising all or most production and distribution. Socialists who accept some degree of free market capitalism have promoted collectivism alongside individualism.

Socialist collectivism, of the kind described above, became very much the norm for socialists throughout Europe after the Second World War. Indeed, the collectivist arrangements which they introduced came to be accepted by non-socialist governments, albeit reluctantly. Three main

examples of collectivism, as practised by the British Labour Party, are shown below:

1. In the 1940s several large British industries were nationalised. These included the railways, coal, steel, electricity, gas and telecommunications. Nationalisation was a collectivist enterprise which had two main purposes. The first was to prevent the industrial muscle of such private industries from exploiting its workers. The second was to ensure that these industries were run in the interests of the whole community, rather than merely for the benefit of their owners. By bringing them under public ownership and state control, the interests of the workers and the whole community could be safeguarded.

2. Labour has always supported trade union power. Having accepted that capitalism will be allowed to flourish, British socialists have agreed that there is an unbalanced relationship between workers and employers. The more radical of the socialists have argued that workers are effectively exploited by capitalist employers. In order to redress this balance to some extent, therefore, Labour has sought to ensure that workers have strong *collective* representation through unions.

3. The welfare state in all its forms is a collective enterprise, organised by the state. Rather than allowing or forcing people to make their own individual provision for such services as health, education, pensions, housing and insurance against unemployment or poverty, the welfare state does this on their behalf. The welfare state collects funds through taxation and National Insurance contributions and distributes the benefits according to need. Indeed, the welfare state is perhaps the most enduring symbol of Labour's attachment to collectivism.

Common ownership

A feature of socialism which is closely related to collectivism is common ownership of the means of production and distribution. Indeed, common ownership is a key form of collectivism. It is perhaps the oldest socialist idea as it pre-dates the onset of capitalism.

Some socialists have claimed that common ownership of property is a Christian principle, pointing to the fact that Christ insisted that his followers pool their resources and share them out equally. There have also been many movements – mostly among the poor peasantry – throughout history which have demanded the seizure of land and its transfer to a communal system of production. In England the Levellers (or Diggers) purchased tracts of land in the South of England and began to farm collectively with the equal distribution of its output. But it was the development of capitalism which brought about a more complex set of ideas about the evils of private property and the virtues of common ownership.

As with most socialist principles, however, there is a great deal of variation in thought in this area. But before looking at common ownership itself, it is useful to look at the variety of reasons why socialists have objected to private property. These have included the following:

- The earth is given to mankind in general. No individual has a right to claim that any part of it belongs to him/her.
- Claiming private property deprives someone else of its use.
- Property gives rise to inequality, especially between those who have and those who lack property.
- Ownership of property, particularly land and capital goods, gives rise to exploitation by property owners of those without property.

By contrast, common ownership can give rise to a number of good outcomes, including:

- The possibility of imposing economic equality, as described above.
- Since many socialists see collectivism as natural, it creates, or re-creates a natural state of society.
- It is possible to direct commonly owned property to serve the interests of the whole community, not just that of fortunate owners of property.

The value of common ownership has, along with the evolution of the principles of equality, social justice and collectivism among socialists, certainly declined in the modern age. The failure of the socialist 'experiments' which were introduced in the USSR, China, Cuba and much of Eastern Europe during the twentieth century served to destroy faith in the idea of common ownership by the state (on behalf of the people). Socialists have therefore tended to modify their attitude to common ownership, seeing it as a complement to private property rather than a replacement for it.

The Labour Party appeared to have adopted the principle of common ownership when it wrote its first constitution in 1918. Clause 4 of that constitution contained a commitment to

> secure for the workers by hand or brain the full fruits of their industry and the most equitable distribution thereof that may be possible upon the basis of common ownership of the means of production, distribution and exchange and the best obtainable system of popular administration and control of each industry or service.

This appeared to be a clear call to nationalise all major industries. In fact, Labour never approached the full implications of the original Clause 4. The nearest they came was the nationalisation of several major industries. Most production, distribution and exchange remained in the private sector.

In recent times, Labour has retained some elements of common ownership, organised by the state – the welfare state institutions in particular – but the party has also encouraged free enterprise where this is seen as the best method of wealth creation and distribution. As the twentieth century progressed, however, Labour gradually lost its commitment to common ownership through the state (central and local government), accepting that, in modern society, most individuals prefer to own and control their own private property.

Policies of the Labour Party – 'New Labour'

The Labour Party experienced a huge trauma in the 1980s. It found itself completely divided over how to deal with the challenge of Thatcherism and the New Right. Some of the party believed it should move to a more moderate, centre position in politics. This group lost the internal argument and many of them therefore left the party, forming the Social Democrat Party (SDP) in 1981. Electoral support for Labour fell to a meagre 27.6 per cent of the popular vote in 1983 (only 2 per cent ahead of the SDP–Liberal Alliance which was formed for that election). This figure recovered only slightly, to 30.8 per cent, in 1987. Labour had been taken over by a large left-wing faction, led by Michael Foot and Tony Benn, that believed that the correct response to Thatcherism was more, not less, socialism. Unfortunately for them, the electorate did not agree.

The leftward-leaning Labour Party of the mid-1980s was routed at the polls by the Conservatives. There were some at the time who believed that the party was doomed for ever, but forces were gathering which were to transform Labour fortunes in the 1990s. Led by Neil Kinnock, who was the party leader through the defeats in 1987 and 1992, a new group of reformers began to emerge. They understood that there had now been a massive change in the nature of British society. Traditional socialist policies were no longer appropriate, they argued. In short, the party needed to find a new direction without abandoning its traditional values. A cohort led by John Smith (party leader from 1992–1994) and including such figures as Tony Blair, Gordon Brown, Bryan Gould, Peter Mandelson and Robin Cook, set about creating what has come to be known as the *Third Way*. So great was the proposed change that the party itself came to be known as *New Labour*. It is the policies of the Third Way and of New Labour which have dominated party policy since then.

The expression 'Third Way' refers to the idea that New Labour policies were to be distinct from one way, which was traditional socialism, as described above, and another way, which was Thatcherism and the New Right. Labour should not pursue traditional socialism, because it made the party unelectable. Thatcherism was unacceptable because it flew in the face of the values of the Labour Party. The principles of the Third Way are shown in the table on the next page, contrasted with the two alternatives.

FIG 1.3C Robin Cook, Labour cabinet minister who resigned over the Iraq war in 2003

Policy area	New Right policy	Socialist policy	Third Way policy
Attitude to capitalism	Capitalism should be given a free rein, with as little state interference as possible.	Large-scale industry should be brought under state control. Capitalism should be controlled by the state.	Capitalism should be allowed to flourish, but the state should enforce competition and fair trade.
Industrial relations	Trade union power should be minimised.	Trade unions should be powerful to protect the interests of workers.	A limited role for trade unions, but individual workers' rights to be protected by law.
Welfare state and its services	Welfare benefits create a dependency culture and are a disincentive to work and enterprise. Individuals should be able to choose freely between public and private sector. Maximum choice of services for families.	Welfare benefits are a vital way of compensating for disadvantage and in redistributing income from rich to poor. The welfare state is to be protected. All welfare services should fall under the control of the state.	Welfare benefits should be used as an incentive to work and to take responsibility for one's own prosperity. Their role is not to redistribute income. High quality public services are to be preserved. Private sector is to be involved if this improves quality and efficiency.
Economic management	State interference in the economy should be minimised. Above all, public sector debt is to be avoided and inflation kept under control.	State should interfere extensively in the economy to keep unemployment low. Public sector borrowing is acceptable when needed to stimulate the economy.	Similar to the New Right, but public sector borrowing is acceptable if used for investment in public services.
Law and order	An authoritarian position, with punishment to be the main deterrent to crime.	Concentration on the causes of crime, especially economic causes.	'Tough on crime, tough on the causes of crime' (Tony Blair, 1994). A combination of authoritarian attitudes and tackling social causes of crime.

Policy area	New Right policy	Socialist policy	Third Way policy
European Union	Highly suspicious, keeping Britain away from close integration. Opposed to single European currency.	Anti-European on the whole. Britain probably to relinquish membership. Britain to be free to protect domestic industries from foreign competition.	Britain to remain at the centre of the EU, but retaining its independence. Cautious support for the single currency.
Foreign policy	Britain to defend its vital national interests.	As far as possible, Britain to distance itself from international affairs, only becoming involved when there is no alternative.	Britain to take a leading role in world affairs. 'Ethical foreign policy' designed to help poor countries and to defend human rights.
The constitution	Opposed to reform of the constitution on the whole.	Radical proposals to democratise institutions, destroy inherited privilege and promote equal rights.	Less radical reform, concentrating on decentralisation of government, mild Lords reform, Human Rights Act.

For most of its period in office after 1997, Labour has followed the principles of the Third Way. Many have argued that it has gradually shifted towards a more 'New Right position', that is, even further away from its core socialist values, and this is certainly true in some areas of policy. On the other hand, Labour supporters can claim, with some justification, that a number of key values have been preserved and even extended.

A generalised term for Labour's social and economic policies is **communitarianism**. This could be described as a synthesis between the creation of a society where individualism can flourish successfully, but where individuals also retain a sense of social responsibility towards the community as a whole. A healthy and prosperous economy, argue New Labour thinkers, does require a great deal of freedom for individuals to undertake their own enterprises and to fend for themselves in the labour market. But, they add, there is a danger that the old socialist benefits of collectivism will be lost, that the uncontrolled pursuit of self-interest (an idea in neo-liberal thinking that they criticise) threatens the unity of society.

In place of socialist collectivist ideals or the authoritarian, traditional approach of conservatism, New Labour has argued that individual citizens themselves should take responsibility for ensuring the cohesion of society. To this end they should be politically active, should engage in voluntary initiatives to protect and develop their local communities (for example, in

FIG 1.3D Tony Blair, the driving force behind New Labour

the fields of law and order and the environment) and should support voluntary organisations which seek to help the disadvantaged. This adds up to a kind of voluntary, locally based socialism. The role of the state in communitarianism is different to its role in a socialist-based society. Rather than undertaking the function of maintaining social unity, protecting communities and caring for the disadvantaged *itself*, the state should facilitate individuals and private or voluntary sector organisations that wish to undertake this role. Underpinning such a society, however, education has to play a key role. For that reason, education as a whole was to be strengthened in order to help individuals to make the most of opportunities available to them, and it was also to undertake the task of promoting the kind of responsible citizenship that communitarianism demands. Hence Tony Blair's famous declaration in 1996 that his government's priorities would be 'education, education, education'.

We can now look at Labour policies after their 2005 election victory in a little more detail.

Anti-poverty

New Labour has largely abandoned the traditional socialist aim of redistributing income to create more economic equality. Instead, the party has adopted an attack on poverty, especially child poverty. This is a priority largely sponsored by Gordon Brown, one of the more socialist-leaning members of New Labour's leading cohort.

While it is accepted that economic inequality is inevitable, Labour also seeks to ensure that everybody who is either willing to work, is unable to work though no fault of their own, or accepts very poorly paid employment, should enjoy a decent standard of living. Families with children, especially, have been targeted. This has meant rises in some welfare payments, such as child benefit, and a system of tax credits which subsidises the income of deserving poorer families, lone parents, the disabled and pensioners. Part of the anti-poverty programme also involves a policy known as *selective universality*. This means that benefits are being targeted at specific groups in society who are poor through no fault of their own. The real value of benefits which are available to *all*, such as old-age pensioners, have been eroded, but large subsidies are available to those in need.

Economic policy

Here, New Labour has largely followed New Right principles, with additional methods introduced to control the public finances. Thus direct taxes have been kept at a much lower level than has been normal under Labour; there is a resistance to heavy government borrowing (though this began to creep up from 2003 onwards); inflation has been controlled by the independent intervention of the Bank of England Monetary Policy Committee (using interest rates as the control mechanism); and Gordon Brown's '*Golden Rule*' was designed to prevent excessive government borrowing unless it is to be used for investment in public services.

Labour governments' economic management and the policies of Chancellor Gordon Brown have been acknowledged, even by Conservatives, as the most successful aspect of their administration. From the mid-1990s (suggesting that the improvement actually began under the Conservative Government of

FIG 1.3E Gordon Brown, Tony Blair's great political rival

1992–97), for at least ten years, the British economy achieved steady growth, low inflation, interest rates and unemployment, and no significant slumps. This was something that had not been achieved through most of the twentieth century. However, from 2004 onwards it was becoming clear that the maintenance of this healthy position was coming under some strain, partly because a lack of investment was causing a serious decline in British manufacturing industry and a loss of international competitiveness.

Welfare services

Labour inherited public services – health, education, policing and public transport, in particular – that were seriously run down by long-term lack of investment and low levels of efficiency. Labour has adopted a two-pronged attack on these problems. One has been to divert large increases in public expenditure (financed partly by the rewards of economic growth, partly from higher taxation) to these services. The other has been to attempt to drive up standards. Rising standards have been pursued through the use of performance target setting, incentives for success and sanctions for failure.

Education

As we saw above, education forms the central theme in Labour's social policy. Improvements in education have been seen as critical in its policies towards poverty reduction, equality of opportunity, law and order (especially youth offending), communitarianism and long-term economic prosperity. The most controversial aspect of education policy has been in the field of higher education. Labour governments have adopted a target of creating places in higher education for 50 per cent of each generation of school leavers. While this target itself has been criticised as being unnecessary and ignoring the need for skilled manual labour, it is the funding issue that has caused most problems. The decision to pay for the greater provision of higher education places by levying extra fees (so-called top-up fees) on students, thus forcing them to take on high levels of debt and possibly therefore deterring students from less well-off families, is controversial. Socialist-minded left-wingers in the Labour Party see such fees as a denial of the principles of the welfare state. Liberals have criticised such funding policy on the grounds that it is unjust and will cause hardship for poorer individuals and families.

Law and order

Labour's intentions towards law and order issues were based on Tony Blair's assertion in 1994 (when he was shadow Home Secretary) that the party would follow a policy of 'tough on crime, tough on the causes of crime'. Although at the beginning, in the late 1990s, the government attempted to develop 'joined-up' policies to combat crime (through education, poverty reduction, community work, etc.), especially youth offending, policy has evolved in a different direction. The party leadership has gradually adopted a more authoritarian position on crime. This has led to increasingly harsh measures against young offenders – tagging, curfews and the well-known antisocial behaviour orders (ASBOs), as well as persuasion of the judiciary to give out more severe sentences. Not surprisingly, after the 9/11 attack on New York and the 7/7 attacks in London, the police and security services have been given additional powers to deal with actual and suspected terrorists.

In the early years of the twenty-first century, policy has concentrated on increasing police numbers, setting performance targets for forces and the recruitment of ever more community officers to assist the police and to create a clear, visible policing presence on the streets. The community approach to crime prevention continues, but it is a long-term policy. In the short term, Labour shares with Conservatives an authoritarian approach to crime. Successive Home Secretaries – Jack Straw, David Blunkett and Charles Clarke – have moved towards 'tough on crime' positions as opposed to 'tough on the causes of crime'.

Welfare benefits

A number of key groups in society have been targeted in Labour's anti-poverty programme. These are poor pensioners (those who rely totally on a state pension), the deserving disabled, lone families and members of families who are working, or seeking work, for low wages. Indeed, targeting welfare is a fundamental social policy. The main device for raising the living standards of these groups is a variety of tax credits, whereby such individuals and families receive additions to their incomes through the tax system.

This policy has three main objectives. First, it targets benefits more specifically on the most needy. Second, it is a system designed to create *incentives* for those who can, to find work and to make it worth their while to take up low-paid employment where there are labour shortages. Third, it is designed to take people out of poverty *permanently* by persuading them to join the workforce and so have no need to rely on the state. As an adjunct to this policy, people are also encouraged to make their own private pension provision (the government offers a subsidised scheme) so that they will not need support in old age.

Constitutional reform

When Labour swept to power in 1997 it did so with a policy of major constitutional reform. This included devolution, the passage of the Human Rights and Freedom of Information Acts and reform of the House of Lords, and it even opened up the possibility of electoral reform. After a brief spurt of reforming zeal, Labour's enthusiasm for constitutional reform has waned. Policies include the completion of Lords reform (left in the hands of the House of Commons) and a greater degree of independence for the judiciary. But constitutional reform has ceased to be a central element in New Labour policy.

Europe

Since 1997 Labour's support for closer European integration has declined. All three Labour administrations have refused to hold a referendum on joining the single European currency on the grounds that conditions were not favourable. In fact, Labour's enthusiasm for the single currency has certainly declined since 1997.

While the party remains pro-European, and supported the proposed European Constitution up to 2005, it is committed to reform of the European Union, with the intention of making it more democratic, more sensitive to the national interests of its members, more financially responsible and less bureaucratic. The leadership also campaigns for the reform or even abolition of the Common Agricultural Policy (CAP).

Tony Blair did attempt to push forward an agenda for a Europe of independent nation states, governed by a clear constitution and with a wide range of shared aims, during 2005. However, the EU failed to ratify a proposed new constitution, thwarting Blair's vision for the foreseeable future. In the same year British attempts to reform the Common Agricultural Policy, in particular, and the EU's financial arrangements, in general, also largely failed. By the end of 2005 New Labour's enthusiasm for the European project had been very much reduced.

Defence and foreign policy

New Labour has been considerably more international in its outlook than past Labour (or even Conservative) administrations. This has largely been caused by the personal objectives of Tony Blair and the commitment of Gordon Brown to the reduction of world poverty. So, under Labour, Britain takes a leading role in such international issues as debt reduction, foreign aid, climate change and the introduction of free world trade.

In other fields Labour follows a foreign policy which is tied very firmly to that of the USA. Thus there remains strong support for US Middle East policy, notably in Iraq, and for its anti-terrorism policies. Labour governments have been very ready to intervene in international conflicts, notably in Kosovo, Sierra Leone, Afghanistan and Iraq. The general thrust of policy, therefore, has been to be active in the pursuit of what the government perceives to be British national interest. Furthermore, British and US interests are seen as largely synonymous.

Conclusion

In its first years, New Labour was very much a reforming and modernising party, but not a radical one. It did not make any significant departures from Conservative policies which had preceded it, but it did seek to improve the way in which policy was implemented, and it has also attempted to make government action more sensitive to the needs of the disadvantaged in society. Its principal reforms, therefore, have been to public services and to the welfare system. As time has passed, the party has turned increasingly to consolidation rather than reform. Policy tends to concentrate now on improving the delivery of the policies it has already implemented.

Liberalism in the UK

Liberalism is perhaps the oldest of Britain's political traditions, dating back to the late seventeenth century. Arguably, the writings of the English philosopher, John Locke, were the earliest examples of liberal thought. Locke believed that all of us are born with natural rights that could justify a much wider range of freedoms than had existed up to his time. Furthermore, he argued that people should only accept government if it was the result of their clear consent and that different modes of thought and religious belief should be tolerated in a modern society. Locke's idea of government (basically a limited form of monarchy) was that it should be limited by representative institutions and that it should respect individual rights. British government after 1700 was largely based on Locke's philosophy. He also had a major influence on the French and American revolutionaries a century later.

Liberal thought in Britain developed a great deal further with the writings of John Stuart Mill. Mill became the key historical figure in the development of English liberalism. He argued that all citizens have an absolute

right to exercise their freedom, provided they did not interfere with the freedom of others. He shared Locke's support for tolerance and representative government, but added that it was essential that the role of government should be extremely limited. It should certainly protect citizens' rights, but should not attempt to interfere with the social and economic life of the country. So it was that Mill established three of the main pillars of liberalism – individual liberty, tolerance and limited government.

Liberalism was attacked in Britain in the later nineteenth century by both conservatives, who were suspicious of the exercise of too much liberty, and by socialists, who argued that too much economic liberty resulted in inequality and the exploitation of the working class by free market capitalism. Liberals had to respond and did so towards the end of the nineteenth and into the early part of the twentieth century. They introduced two new aspects to their philosophy. One was the principle of equality of opportunity (which they shared with socialists) and the other was the introduction of state-sponsored welfare. Indeed it was a liberal – William Beveridge (1879–1963) – who instigated the introduction of the welfare state in Britain in the 1940s.

It has to be emphasised that, by the middle of the twentieth century, the core values of liberalism, which are described below, had been adopted by all moderate politicians in Britain, whether they were members of the Labour, Conservative or Liberal parties. In other words, liberal principles formed the basis of a political consensus in modern Britain.

We can now summarise the main principles of liberalism in the twentieth century and beyond.

Core liberal values

Freedom and rights

As in Mill's day, all liberals are supporters of individual liberty. This does not mean that society should be left to its own devices. Freedom should only be exercised, say liberals, if it does not threaten the peace and freedom of others. Certainly the power of the state should not be used to curtail freedom unless there is an overwhelming reason to do so.

A related theme is the liberal defence of human rights. The traditional rights of members of British society include freedom of expression, thought, worship, movement and association. It is the role of the law and the state in general to defend these rights. The main practical application of this support for rights concerns the position of minorities. In democratic society minority groups are vulnerable to the will of the majority. Liberals have traditionally defended the rights of such minorities. The interests of the gay community, ethnic groups, the disabled and women (who are not, of course, a minority, but have been treated as one) have all been championed by liberalism.

Tolerance

Tolerance is a principle that is closely allied to that of freedom. Liberals insist that all forms of expression, belief, thought and lifestyle should be tolerated in a free society. There is a proviso to this. Where the words or deeds of an individual or a group are harmful to the rights and freedom of others, the state is justified in suppressing them.

In the modern multicultural society of Britain, the liberal support for tolerance has become a key social issue. It has also come under great pressure with the terrorist activities of Irish Republicans and Islamic extremists, suggesting that tolerance might be overplayed. But the liberal principle is clear – that it is for individuals to decide what they believe and what lifestyle they adopt, as long as their activities do not affect others adversely.

Equality of opportunity

As we have seen, socialists and many conservatives share this essentially liberal principle. It contains two main aspects. One is that inherited and undeserved privilege should not be allowed to give an individual or a group an artificial advantage in life. This has meant that liberals have always argued that political power should rest only in the hands of elected representatives and should never be exercised by those who enjoy inherited social privilege. It also implies that people in general should advance in life purely on merit rather than on the basis of social position.

The second is that, no matter what our circumstances of birth, we are all entitled to the same life chances. Liberals therefore champion the cause both of those who are born into deprived circumstances and of various minorities who have traditionally been disadvantaged. As we have seen above, education is seen as the key to this principle.

Social justice

For most of the nineteenth century, many liberals saw justice in terms of individual merit. In a free society, they argued, people were responsible for their own prosperity. If they worked hard and showed enterprise they would do well; if they were not prepared to use their initiative they would remain poor. This was seen as a just outcome. But, as it became apparent that many were deprived through no fault of their own, liberalism began to adopt a new conception of social justice.

It remains true that a liberal will argue that a free economy is bound to result in inequality of economic outcome. But they now insist that the most dramatic examples of inequality – especially when wealth is seen as the result of market forces rather than deserving effort and enterprise – should be reduced by the state. So liberals have become committed to the reduction of excessive inequality, protection for deprived groups in society and the principle that taxation must always be based on the ability to pay. In other words, they see it as 'just' that the wealthy should be subject to considerably higher tax rates than those who live on more modest means. In this sense, liberalism has a great deal in common with socialism.

Welfare

Associated with the liberal/socialist position on social justice is support for state-organised welfare. Indeed, it was governments formed by the Liberal Party, under Herbert Asquith and David Lloyd George in the early decades of the twentieth century, that introduced the first forms of state-run pensions, housing, health and unemployment insurance schemes. As we have seen above, another liberal, Beveridge, extended these services into the full-scale welfare state we know today.

Liberals support welfare partly because it constitutes social justice, partly because they recognise that the whole community has a responsibility to help those in need and partly because they believe that everybody is entitled to a reasonable standard of living and prospects of future well-being. In addition, as Beveridge pointed out, the most serious threats to individual freedom were not just government power, but also poverty, unemployment, poor health and lack of education.

Constitutionalism and democracy

Liberals are instinctively suspicious of the power of government. They see the power of the state as perhaps the main threat to liberty. At the same time, it is a guarantee of freedom that government should be under the democratic control of the people. This has given rise to two practical applications of liberal political thought. One is that governments should be controlled by law. In effect, this means a constitution which sets out the powers of the different branches of government and which asserts the limits of governmental power. Constitutions also describe and protect the rights of citizens (civil liberties) against government and between themselves.

The second application requires that government must be highly democratic. This means it must accurately represent the demands and interests of the people, must be fully accountable to the people and must allow full participation by all citizens on an equal basis. This does not necessarily mean that governments need be 'slaves' to the will of the people (that would be 'direct democracy', which carries dangers of its own), but it certainly implies that government should be open and responsive and that its institutions should fall under the general control of the people.

The policies of the Liberal Democrats

The Liberal Democrat Party was formed in 1988, the result of an amalgamation of the

FIG 1.3F Charles Kennedy led a revival in Liberal Democrat fortunes in 2001

original Liberal Party (which dated back to the nineteenth century) and the very young Social Democrat Party, which had broken away from the Labour Party in 1981. Its policies have always been, therefore, something of a synthesis of core liberal values (as shown above) and social democracy, a very moderate form of socialism.

At the time of the 2005 general election, the main Liberal Democrat policies were as follows.

Fair taxation

Two main policies are prominent in this category. First, Liberal Democrats wish to replace council tax by a system of local income tax. As council tax is based on property rather than income, it contains certain anomalies whereby relatively poor families are forced to pay relatively high local taxes, while the better-off pay proportionally less. A local income tax would be based purely on ability to pay. Second, there was a proposal for a higher rate of income tax – at 50 per cent – to be paid on incomes above £100,000 per annum (a proposal which was dropped after its failure to make an impact in the 2005 general election). The additional revenue from the higher tax rate would be used to eliminate top-up fees for higher education and to provide free residential care for poor pensioners. A longer-term objective of the party is to take many more of the poorest families out of taxation altogether.

Economic management

Liberal Democrats have few arguments with the way in which Labour governments have run the economy since 1997. There is a general tendency in the party to believe that more intervention is necessary to ensure greater industrial democracy – more power for employers in principle – and to protect some industries which are in decline. But, on the whole, Liberal Democrats are included in part of a widespread consensus on an economic policy which sees the state taking a minimum role in management of the economy, leaving control largely to the Bank of England and to a responsible attitude to the public finances by the Treasury.

The welfare state

The Liberal Democrat Party is now, perhaps, the main defender of the principles of the welfare state in Britain. It argues that services should be an extremely high priority in public spending decisions. It also insists that quality should be guaranteed for all. Liberal Democrats oppose the Conservative view, that there should be more choice for users of public services, on the grounds that the same high quality services should be available for all, with choice, therefore, unnecessary. They also oppose the Labour policy of driving up standards through the use of performance targets, incentives and sanctions. Instead they would simply ensure that the welfare state has the necessary resources and allow its natural tendency to want to deliver first-class services to flourish.

Law and order and rights

For most Liberal Democrats the most effective way of dealing with criminal behaviour is to concentrate on tackling the *causes* of crime rather than on punishment and sanctions in general. Education is seen to be on the front line of law and order policy, as is the role of other state agencies in supporting families. The excessive use of prison sentences, and the lengthening of sentences in general is opposed. Liberal Democrats support instead the wider use of 'community-based' and innovative methods of attempting to deal with criminal behaviour.

As we have seen, liberals are firm defenders of the rights of citizens. They see modern law and order policies as a profound threat to civil liberties. The Liberal Democrat Party, therefore, has argued consistently that human rights must not be sacrificed merely in the interests of a firmer position on law and order. This policy has been thrown into greater focus with the increasing pressure on government to take ever more authoritarian powers to deal with the threat of terrorism.

Thus, although the Human Rights Act went a long way to satisfying Liberal Democrats in their pursuit of the defence of human rights, the party still insists that the Act is too weak as it is not binding on Parliament. It proposes an *entrenched* Bill of Rights that cannot be overturned by Parliament.

Constitutional reform

The programme of reform undertaken by Labour Governments after 1997 was supported by Liberal Democrats. However, they criticised Labour on the grounds that the reforms did not go far enough.

As we have seen, they wished to see a stronger Human Rights Act. They also believe that devolution has not gone far enough. More power should have been devolved to Scotland, Northern Ireland and Wales, say Liberal Democrats, including full legislative and taxation powers. Liberal Democrats support decentralised government on the grounds that it will be more democratic. Therefore they support the general weakening of central government and the strengthening of regional and local government institutions.

But the key Liberal Democrat proposal for reform concerns the electoral system. They see FPTP (the current system) as fundamentally unjust, distorting political representation and granting excessive power to the executive over Parliament. It has to be said, of course, that electoral reform is most supported by Liberal Democrats because they have the most to gain from it. But this also indicates that they are the greatest sufferers in a system that discriminates against smaller parties. Elections at all levels of government, therefore, should be conducted under some form of proportional representation, they argue. This would include elections to a reformed House of Lords. Liberal Democrats will not compromise on the second chamber. It must, they argue, be fully elected in the future.

European Union

Liberal Democrats are the most enthusiastic of all the three main parties about the European project. While they agree that its institutions must be made more democratic, they are content to see a good deal of power being transferred to the EU. This is not, however, because they wish to see power centralised in Brussels. On the contrary, Liberal Democrats support a 'Europe of the Regions', where most power will be exercised by regional and local government. This will bring government closer to the people and thereby make it more democratic.

Foreign policy

The Labour policy, supported by most Conservatives, of seeing British national interests as largely identical to those of the USA, is opposed by Liberal Democrats. In fact, the party is instinctively suspicious of any attempts by Britain to intervene directly in the affairs of other countries. It is committed to promoting human rights throughout the world, but believes that this should be achieved through diplomatic and economic means, not by military intervention.

The environment

The Liberal Democrat Party emphasises the need for environmental protection more than the other main parties. They argue that government should be more committed to such issues, both domestically and on the international stage. They therefore support the causes of public transport, recycling programmes and controls on carbon emissions. While they support the Green movement's exhortation to 'act locally', they also wish to see the state take a leading role on environmental issues.

Other parties in the UK

Scottish National Party (SNP)

Not surprisingly, the main policy of the SNP is the achievement of complete independence for Scotland. They believe that the Scots have a historical right to complete self-determination. They also believe that Scotland has enough of its own resources – human and physical – to be viable as an autonomous economic unit. It is their aspiration to become the largest group in the Scottish Parliament and then call for a referendum on Scottish independence.

In the meantime, the policies of the SNP are similar to those of the Liberal Democrats. They support local democracy, the defence of human rights (a long Scottish tradition) and the importance of education. One area of special emphasis, however, concerns the development of Scottish industry. Scottish Nationalists recognise that, if a small country is to survive in a highly competitive world trade environment, its industry must be efficient and capable of producing high value output. They stress the need for low business taxes and investment incentives. For similar reasons, the SNP is pro-European. They understand that the regional and industrial development policies of the EU are of special benefit to small countries like Scotland. 'An independent Scotland in a strong European Union' is a typical SNP slogan.

At the 2005 general election the SNP won 17.7 per cent of the Scottish vote, converting to six parliamentary seats. In the 2003 election to the Scottish Parliament they won 27 (out of 129) seats. This represents a small decline in their electoral fortunes since 2001.

Plaid Cymru (PC – the Welsh Nationalists)

Plaid Cymru does not demand full independence for Wales. However, most of its members do want to see the Welsh Assembly turned into a Parliament, with a wide range of legislative powers. This will give greater autonomy for Wales, but not sovereignty. They are also committed to the development of a completely bilingual Wales, aspiring to the wider dissemination of Welsh speaking and encouraging the maintenance of a distinctive Welsh culture.

The general policies of the party are socialist-leaning on the whole, proposing some redistribution of income from rich to poor and stronger employment rights. The party is also very supportive of environmental protection policies, especially concerning the preservation of the countryside and agriculture.

Plaid Cymru won 12.6 per cent of the Welsh vote in the 2005 general election, but only three seats in Parliament. In the 2003 Welsh Assembly election they won only 12 (out of 60) seats.

UK Independence Party (UKIP)

UKIP is, in some senses, a breakaway movement from the Conservative Party. Many of its members are former Conservatives. Their overwhelmingly dominant policy is that Britain should withdraw from the European Union altogether. The party has also developed a stronger anti-immigration policy than that of the Conservative Party. In other words, it is largely a *nationalist* party. The other policies of the party are close to Conservative proposals, mostly at the more authoritarian right-wing tendency of modern conservatism.

UKIP won 2.2 per cent of the popular vote in the 2005 general election, but no seats. However, they held ten seats in the European Parliament after the 2004 elections to that assembly.

FIG 1.3G Robert Kilroy Silk, whose new party, Veritas, collapsed after failing in the 2005 election

The Green Party

Clearly the main thrust of Green Party policy concerns environmental issues. These also include such concerns as biodiversity and animal rights. But the party has adopted a full range of policies across the spectrum of government responsibilities. Most of these are similar to Liberal Democrat policy, with an even greater emphasis on tolerance and human rights.

The Greens won no seats at the 2005 general election, with a 1 per cent share of the vote. However, they won two seats in the 2004 election to the European Parliament.

Other parties

There are many other parties on the British electoral scene, but virtually none of them make any significant impact. The ultra-right British National Party (BNP) has won a few local council seats in urban districts with racial problems, and the Respect Party, formed by left-winger George Galloway, did win a parliamentary seat in London's East End on an anti-Iraq war platform, but both failed badly elsewhere. Indeed, even if proportional representation were introduced, it is difficult to believe that any other parties would win seats in Parliament.

Consensus and adversary politics

There are two models of party politics that are often seen as competing with each other as the most appropriate way of conducting the processes of government. These are 'consensus' and 'adversary' models. They can be described in the following way.

Consensus politics refers to a process whereby decision makers seek to find a wide level of general agreement within the political community before attempting to bring forward proposals. This may be a formal process, whereby representatives of all parties are consulted before decisions are reached, or it may be informal, with government only adopting policies that they are confident will enjoy cross-party support.

In recent times there has been a high degree of *formal* consensus on such issues as Northern Ireland policy and anti-terrorism measures. There has also been a good deal of *informal* consensus over the management of the economy.

Consensus politics also refers to periods when it is noticeable that there is little difference between the policies of the parties on a wide range of public policy. It was said that for much of the 1950s and 1960s Britain enjoyed *consensus politics* only because the parties were largely agreed on policies towards the economy, law and order, defence and social policy

Consensus politics
A circumstance where two or more major political parties broadly agree on most basic policies. In other words, a period when there are few or no major political conflicts. It may also refer to a single issue where different parties agree to support the same policies.

generally. Indeed, this consensus remained largely intact until the 1980s. Some commentators have spoken since the 1990s of a *post-Thatcher consensus*. This consensus includes agreement on the need to allow free market capitalism to flourish, to maintain responsible financial policies (especially in keeping inflation under control) and to promote the development of private enterprise. Only the more radical members of the Labour and Liberal Democrat parties question these consensual values.

On the whole, British politicians are uncomfortable with such a form of politics. They much prefer that proposals are subject to critical examination in a process known as adversarial politics.

Adversarial politics is the more common characterisation of what happens in Britain. Indeed it is sometimes claimed that Britain's is the most adversarial system in the democratic world. The 1980s were perhaps the most significant period of such adversarial politics in modern times.

The main quality of adversarial politics is that all government policies are subjected to hostile critical examination by opposition parties. This, it is often claimed, improves the quality of decision making (it is sometimes likened to a classical Greek method of philosophical inquiry, known as dialectics, wherein every proposition is confronted by its own opposite proposition in the search for truth). In practice, adversary politics demands that opposition politicians oppose virtually every government proposal. This takes place in Parliament during debates and also in the media. By being forced to face adversary politics, it is assumed that the government is forced to justify its policies. It also means that decision makers have to consider what opposition they will face and ensure that their proposals are robust enough to withstand such attacks.

Even in this hostile environment some consensus politics can take place. As we have seen above, some recent policy areas have been the subject of cross-party agreement, notably over Northern Ireland. For the most part, however, opposition politicians prefer to be free to be as critical as they wish.

We can now review the main policy areas following the 2005 general election, dividing them between those that enjoy largely consensus support and those that remain hotly contested.

> **Adversarial politics** The opposite of consensus. This is a circumstance where political parties are engaged in considerable conflict over political issues. It can also mean a process where opposition parties adopt adversarial attitudes simply in order to force a government to justify its policies.

Consensus issues	Contested issues
■ Responsible management of the economy. ■ Keeping personal taxation relatively low by European standards. ■ The maintenance of largely free markets, with relatively little state interference. ■ Policy in Northern Ireland. ■ The maintenance of good quality public services within the basic principles of the welfare state. ■ Support for the system of parliamentary democracy.	■ The degree to which the private sector should be involved in the provision of welfare state services. ■ The degree to which law and order policy should concentrate on punishment as opposed to dealing with the social causes of crime. ■ Britain's relationship to the European Union and whether Britain should adopt the single European currency. ■ The degree to which Britain should be open to immigrants and asylum seekers. ■ How much Britain should support US foreign policy.

KEY CONCEPTS

Political party
An association of people who have similar political philosophies and beliefs. Normally a party will seek power and develop an organisation whose purpose is to fight elections.

Conservatism
A state of mind and a political movement that is naturally averse to excessive change and reform. It is sceptical about strongly held political views, prefers the known to the unknown and generally supports the retention of traditional institutions and values.

Liberalism
A state of political mind or political movement that places freedom, rights and tolerance high on its scale of values.

Socialism
A state of mind and political movement that places such values as equality of opportunity, social justice and collectivism high on its scale of values. It is either opposed to free market capitalism or proposes measures to moderate the effects of capitalism.

Consensus politics
A circumstance where two or more major political parties broadly agree on most basic policies. In other words, a period when there are few or no major political conflicts. It may also refer to a single issue where different parties agree to support the same policies.

Adversarial politics
The opposite of consensus. This is a circumstance where political parties are engaged in considerable conflict over political issues. It can also mean a process where opposition parties adopt adversarial attitudes simply in order to force a government to justify its policies.

Revision topics and examination questions

Revision topics

- Definition of a party
- Features of parties
- Functions of parties
- Democratic role of parties
- Undemocratic features of parties
- Role of parties in political participation
- Nature of party government
- Nature of two-party system
- Nature of conservatism
- Nature of British socialism
- Nature of liberalism
- Policies of all three parties
- Difference between consensus and adversary politics
- Main policies on which parties agree
- Main policies on which parties disagree

Short answers

- What is a political party?
- Outline THREE features of a political party.
- Outline THREE functions of a political party.
- What is meant by the term 'party government'?

Medium answers

- How do parties encourage political participation?
- In what senses is politics in the UK a two-party system?
- Outline the main policies on which the main UK parties agree.
- Outline the main political issues on which the main UK parties disagree.
- Distinguish between consensus and adversary politics.

Long answers

- In what ways do parties enhance democracy?
- How, and to what extent, can parties be said to be undemocratic in the UK?
- How far has the current Conservative Party retained basic conservative principles?
- To what extent is Labour still a socialist party?
- How liberal are the beliefs of UK political parties?

Resources and Web Guide

Books

For general discussions of political ideologies and their relation to current parties:
A. Heywood, *Political Ideologies*, Palgrave, 2003.
N. McNaughton, *Political Ideologies*, Philip Allan, 2005.
And for discussion of modern parties in general:
P. Webb, *The Modern British Party System*, Sage, 2000.
R. Garner and R. Kelly, *British Political Parties Today*, MUP, 1998.
Two excellent books on conservatism are:
T. Honderich, *Conservatism*, Pluto Press, 2005.
R. Scruton, *The Meaning of Conservatism*, Macmillan, 2001.
On liberalism, look at:
J. Gray, *Liberalism*, OUP, 1995.
C. Cook, *A Short History of the Liberal Party 1900–2001*, Macmillan, 2002.
For Labour, see:
P. Riddell, *The Blair Government*, Politico's, 2002.
A. Seldon (ed.), *The Blair Effect*, Little Brown, 2001.

Useful websites

Websites of parties include the following:
www.labour.org.uk (accessed 11 November 2005)
www.conservatives.com (accessed 11 November 2005)
www.libdems.org.uk (accessed 11 November 2005)
www.greenparty.org.uk (accessed 11 November 2005)
www.ukip.org (accessed 11 November 2005)
www.plaidcymru.org (accessed 11 November 2005)
www.snp.org.uk (accessed 11 November 2005)

1.4
Pressure groups and pluralism

The nature and functions of pressure groups

The most informative beginning to this section would be to consult two leading authorities on pressure groups, which offer useful definitions.

> [A **pressure group** is] an organisation which seeks to influence the details of a comparatively small range of public policies and which is not a faction of a recognised political party. (Robert Baggott)
>
> [A pressure group is] an organisation which seeks as one of its functions to influence the formulation and implementation of public policy, public policy representing a set of authoritative decisions taken by the executive, the legislature and the judiciary, and by local government and the European Union. (Wyn Grant)
>
> *Both quoted in R. Baggott,* Pressure Groups: A Question of Interest, *1994.*

> **Pressure group**
> An association that may be formal or informal, whose purpose is to further the interests of a specific section of society or to promote a particular cause.

We now need to examine these definitions in a little more detail.

1. The most important feature is that pressure groups are trying to *influence* decisions. They do not expect to make the decisions themselves.
2. As Grant points out, they may seek to influence not just the decisions themselves, but also the details of those decisions and even their implementation. A good example of this occurred in the period 2003–04. Parliament was debating the issue of hunting with dogs, especially fox hunting. At first, the pro-hunt lobby – mainly the *Countryside Alliance* pressure group – opposed any kind of ban. When this was clearly going to fail, they sought to influence the *details* of the legislation. Perhaps hunting could be allowed, for example, if it was to be strictly regulated to prevent cruelty. When that failed and the full ban was enacted, they turned their attention to ways in which they could thwart the police's attempts to enforce the ban. So the Alliance had operated at every stage of the decision-making process, including implementation.
3. Baggott's quote suggests that pressure groups operate in a relatively *narrow* range of issues. This may be a single issue, such as *Fathers4Justice*, which emerged in 2003 and campaigned for better child custody rights for divorced and separated fathers. Their issue affected only a few thousand people and applied to very specific purposes. It may also be a whole cluster of related issues – for example, the environment, where *Greenpeace* and *Friends of the Earth* operate.
4. Grant points out that pressure groups operate at different *levels* of government. They must first identify where key decisions are made and

then apply their pressure in that location. This may be at the level of central ministers and civil servants, the Westminster Parliament, the Welsh, Scottish or Northern Ireland governments or local government. Issues which are resolved at the European Union level, such as agriculture, fisheries and trade, force pressure groups to work with the relevant institutions in Brussels, Strasbourg and the other centres of power. Grant also mentions the judiciary. Why would pressure groups be interested in legal cases? The answer is that there are some issues which may have to be resolved in the courts because the law is not clear or because there may be disputes about the meaning of law. In such cases, pressure groups may promote legal cases themselves, or may seek to give evidence in court in support of their position.

The Countryside Alliance can be used as an example again. Having lost the battle in Parliament, the Alliance turned to the courts. First, they tried to claim that the government had misused parliamentary procedures so the law was invalid. When this failed, they returned to the High Court to protest that the anti-hunting ban conflicted with the European Convention on Human Rights. Again they failed, but the process indicates how widely some groups seek to cast their net of influence. Trade unions and consumer groups also use the courts when they feel their members' rights may not have been enforced satisfactorily.

FIG 1.4A The Countryside Alliance has been one of the most successful of the new social movements

It must also be pointed out that many government policies take several years to develop. During that time they may be considered by a variety of committees, commissions and agencies. As they begin to take shape, ministers and civil servants become involved. Once the details are published, MPs, peers and the media will seek to add their contributions to the debate, and, of course, public opinion has to be considered. All this happens before any legislation appears at Westminster. Pressure groups need to be aware of these processes and become involved at every stage if they are to be successful.

Our description of what pressure groups seek to do, however, remains a little narrow, perhaps. They also have a number of general functions which go well beyond simply influencing government decisions.

We have discussed the nature of representative democracy above. Most of that discussion revolved around political parties, but it is important to remember that pressure groups also have a representative function. Those that have a formal membership, such as the Automobile Association (AA) or any trade union, clearly wish to further their interests. But some pressure groups claim that they represent the best interests of the whole community – for example, environmentalists, the anti-smoking lobby and Transport 2000 (which campaigns for a better public transport system).

Like parties, pressure groups also have a function of educating the public. They inform us about issues, offering both specific facts and competing points of view which can help us to form our own opinions. Before the Countryside Alliance emerged in the late 1990s, few sections of the population were aware of the problems of those who live in rural areas. Similarly, *Liberty* and *Charter 88*, groups which promote individual human rights, have alerted us to various examples of shortcomings in the British experience of rights. The passage of the Human Rights Act in 1998 was a crowning achievement for them.

The relationship between pressure groups and parties is explored in some depth below, but it should be pointed out at this stage that there has been some transfer of functions from parties to pressure groups. Members of the public who are not directly involved in politics may wish, nevertheless, to have more influence than merely by voting. Party membership may also demand an excessive degree of involvement. Pressure groups, on the other hand, can provide opportunities for a less intensive form of political activity. Furthermore, such groups deal specifically with narrower issues. Parties require support across the whole spectrum of public policy. Most people do not think about politics in that way. They think more of individual issues and how they feel about them. So pressure groups today offer a more relevant and acceptable form of political participation than parties are able to.

The functions of pressure groups

We can now usefully summarise the various functions which pressure groups perform:

■ They play a key part in the governing process. Their involvement at all stages of the policy- and decision-making process helps to inform government itself and ensures that the interests and views of sections of the public are taken into account. In this sense they can improve the quality of policy making.

- They have a representative function. Either they represent specific sections of the public or claim to represent the best interests of the whole community.
- Pressure groups help to educate and inform the public about politically important issues (they also try to educate and inform governing institutions).
- They provide a less intensive, but more relevant opportunity for political participation than political parties.
- One further general function can be added. We may call this 'tension release'. There are times when significant sections of society feel very strongly about a particular issue. If we are to remain a peaceful society, it is vital that there is an outlet for such feelings which does not necessarily result in violence. People need, from time to time, the opportunity to give full expression to their feelings, sometimes their outrage. Issues such as opposition to the 2003 Iraq war, to university tuition fees, to the proposed ban on hunting with dogs, all create extremely strong feelings. Relevant pressure groups were able to channel the emotions that were generated by these issues into limited forms of political action (some violence did occur, but it was limited and remained controlled).

The distinctions between pressure groups and parties

Clearly there are a number of areas where the roles of parties and pressure groups overlap. Both types of organisation attempt to influence the policy-making process. In different ways they are also both representative bodies, claiming to be channels of communication between sections of the community and those who govern us. They also try to mould and to mobilise public opinion in order to promote the issues which concern them.

But there are also critical differences. The most important of these is that parties are seeking to achieve power, either as the governing party or as part of a governing coalition. Pressure groups do not seek governmental power. If they do, they must turn themselves into political parties. This begs the question: how does being a party rather than a pressure group affect the way in which members behave? There are two main answers to this question. First, a party must address the full range of political issues. If it were to become part of government it would have to address all government responsibilities. Second, parties must accept responsibility for all the policies they propose. Governments must be accountable for what they do. Pressure groups do not face this problem. They will never be in power and will never have to account for their actions and beliefs. This truth affects their attitudes fundamentally. Two examples can illustrate this.

The environmental action group, Greenpeace, has waged a long campaign against trials of genetically modified (GM) food crops. They believe that such developments are dangerous and environmentally unsound. But there are also great potential benefits in GM foods, including long-term solutions to poverty in some developing countries. Greenpeace can safely oppose GM crops without having to be accountable for the fact that their opposition might condemn millions of people to starvation. Governments cannot abdicate such responsibility. They have to weigh up the benefits of GM foods against the possible problems. Similarly, *Action on Smoking and Health* (ASH) campaigns against tobacco use. But if ASH is successful and smoking is severely reduced, how will we replace the lost taxation from tobacco duties? ASH does not have this problem; government does.

Some confusion may arise from the fact that some pressure groups offer candidates for election to Parliament, to the Scottish Parliament and other devolved assemblies or to local councils. They do this in order to create publicity for themselves. But does this make them into political parties? The answer must be no, because they are not seeking power; they merely want representation and publicity. There is, it has to be noted, a history of pressure groups turning themselves into parties in this way.

Most significantly, at the start of the twentieth century, the trade union movement began to put up candidates for election. At first they were simply drawing attention to the fact that the working class was underrepresented and had a wide range of grievances. But the trade unions had considerable success in having its candidates elected, so much so that they decided in 1906 to become a political party. Thus was created the Labour Party. Similarly, but with less impact, the British ecology movement fought a number of elections in the 1980s and eventually decided to become a party – the Greens. More recently, the single-issue United Kingdom Independence Party (UKIP) was a pressure group in the 1990s, campaigning to bring the UK out of the European Union, but by 2005 it was a fully fledged party, with policies on all issues.

We can now summarise the main distinctions between parties and pressure groups, together with the features which serve to blur the differences.

Parties	Pressure groups	Blurring
Seek governmental power.	Do not seek power.	Both may put up candidates for election. In addition, some pressure groups may be converting themselves into parties.
Adopt policies across full range of government responsibility.	Usually have narrow range of issues.	Some pressure groups, such as trade unions or business groups, may develop a wide range of policies.
Have to be accountable for their policies.	Do not have to be accountable.	
Must behave in a responsible way.	Some pressure groups may act illegally or promote civil disobedience.	Some pressure groups work so closely with parties and government it is difficult to distinguish between their roles.

Classification of pressure groups

It is important to establish a classification of pressure groups because it can help to explain their behaviour. It is normal to divide them into two types: sectional (or interest) groups and cause, issue or promotional groups.

Sectional or interest groups are those which represent a specific section of society. They are self-interested and thus concerned only with promoting the best interests of their members.

The best examples are trade unions, but there are many groups which represent other economic sections, such as the *Institute of Directors* (employers in general), the *National Farmers' Union* (NFU) or the *Engineering Employers' Federation.* Medical groups are also prominent. They represent members who are suffering from specific diseases or conditions. The *Multiple Sclerosis Society* or the *Heart Foundation* are important examples. There are also sectional groups which represent various sports organisations, pensioners, children, students, industries and the like. Wherever there is an identifiable social section or organisation, it is most likely that it will be represented by a pressure group.

Cause, issue or promotional groups do not have a specific section of the community to represent. They claim to be serving the interests of the whole community. They have one issue, or a cluster of issues, which they are seeking to promote. They often do not have a specific membership, or at most a small group of activists. They are altruistic in that they consider that they serve us all, not their own members.

The most obvious examples are environmental groups such as *Greenpeace* or *Friends of the Earth.* Many other organisations which flourish in Britain are concerned with both specific environmental issues as well as quality of life in general. The *Royal Society for the Protection of Birds* (RSPB) or the *National Trust* are typical. Some campaign for changes in the political system itself, such as the *Electoral Reform Society* and *Liberty.* These groups may also be temporary in nature, as the issue with which they are concerned may be short-lived. The *Anti-Poll Tax Federation* was an example of this in 1989–90. Campaigning against the unpopular local poll tax, they succeeded in persuading the government to relent and abolish the tax. Naturally, the group immediately ceased to exist. It may be that *Fathers4Justice* (described below) will experience the same fate.

Dual-function groups may be both sectional and cause-based, so we should not be too inflexible in our classification. The Countryside Alliance, for example, represents people who live in rural areas, but also campaigns for a better quality of life in the countryside, which can benefit us all. Similarly, Transport 2000 believes that better public transport is an issue which affects us all, but they also represent existing users of such transport. It is, therefore, both cause and sectional in nature.

There are also other types of dual-function pressure groups. These are groups that perform a specific service, or set of services, for their members, as well as campaigning within the political system on their behalf. Trade unions are an obvious example, as is the *AA* or the *RAC.* Many charities,

---

Sectional group
A pressure group that represents a specific section of society, such as a trade union or an employers' association. Also known as an *interest group.*

Promotional group A pressure group that seeks to promote a cause rather than the interests of its own members. Also known as a *cause group* or an *issue group.*

such as *Cancer Research* or the *National Society for the Prevention of Cruelty to Children* (NSPCC), are also pressure groups. They are seeking funds and/or legislation from government to help those whom they serve. But they also offer a wide range of other care services and expend much effort in raising finance from the general public.

It should not be forgotten that there are also many thousands of local pressure groups operating within communities. Often they are environmental in nature, being concerned with local areas of natural beauty, parks and problems arising from industry or agriculture. Local action groups are also often concerned with temporary issues, such as the building of bypasses, threatened closure of hospitals and schools, erection of wind turbines, various planning issues and the like. Whenever a major change is proposed for a locality, you can be almost sure that groups will spring up either to oppose, amend or support the initiative. Indeed, it is in this domain that the majority of political activity probably takes place. It is much more likely that citizens will become motivated to act locally than to become involved in national politics.

Finally, there are some examples of organisations where it is not clear whether they are pressure groups at all. For example, are terrorist groups, such as the IRA, pressure groups? What about so-called think tanks – agencies which obtain funds from a variety of sources to carry out research into policy issues and report their findings to governing bodies? The Adam Smith Institute, which researches issues concerning free markets, is an example of such a think tank. Arguably they are pressure groups, but for our purposes they will not be considered as such.

Insiders and outsiders

Professor Wyn Grant (with whose definition of pressure groups this chapter opens) introduced another classification of pressure groups. This divided them into *insiders* and *outsiders*.

Insiders

An insider pressure group is one that has succeeded in becoming a part of the decision-making process itself. They are 'inside' the process, not outside, hoping to influence. Naturally we would expect that insiders have something of an advantage. They take part in the development of policy and so can hope to mould it to their own benefit. They may also be able to prevent unfavourable legislation at an early stage. Their activities can be understood better by identifying the ways in which they are considered to be insiders:

■ They may be consulted regularly by government bodies. This is because they can provide useful information and may also be able to express the views of their members. If policies are to secure support, it is important for government to understand the attitudes of those who will be affected by their implementation. The *Confederation of British Industry* (CBI) is a typical example of such an insider. The CBI regularly produces reports on how businesses are operating and what are their attitudes towards such issues as business taxation, employment regulations, trade and economic policy in general. They also inform government about how business is performing with regard to such issues as investment, sales expectations, exports and production costs.

- Some pressure groups have permanent seats on government policy committees and agencies. These groups therefore find themselves at the centre of the decision-making process. The National Farmers' Union is a typical example. It is advantageous to government that all agricultural policy should be considered by representatives of the farming community at an early stage, as they will have to conform to these policies.

- There are groups which have actually been set up by government itself, and may be funded from taxpayers' money. Naturally these are insiders of a special kind. They are almost *part* of government, not just **insider groups**. The *Commission for Racial Equality* (CRE), for example, was set up specifically to advise government on matters of racial discrimination and equality. The *Equal Opportunities Commission* (equality of rights and opportunities for women) and the *National Consumer Council* (a fair deal for consumers) are similar examples of such *ultra-insider* groups.

- Select committees in both the House of Commons and the Lords investigate the work of government departments and produce reports of policy proposals. They have the power to call witnesses in the course of their proceedings. Insider pressure groups are often called to their meetings and so have a direct input into the process of making government fully accountable.

It should also be noted that some groups need to achieve insider status at local, regional and European level.

European insider groups, typically trade unions and business employers' organisations, have been able to attach themselves to the various sections of the European Commission, which develops policy for the European Union. They also operate extensively with the European Parliament, which is having an increasing impact on policy. Representation is notoriously weak in the European Union, as Members of the Parliament (MEPs) have huge constituencies and relatively modest influence, as individuals or even as political groupings. Pressure groups – some of them joined up into European-wide organisations – therefore have a special role to play in the flow of information and influence.

We can also see a similar phenomenon in the governments of Scotland, Northern Ireland and Wales, which have similar institutions to those to be found at central level. In local government there are some insiders which operate with council committees, but more often they work with the permanent council officials who run local services.

Although insider status may appear to be an enormous advantage for those groups that enjoy it, there is a price to be paid. Insiders must, by implication, act in a responsible way. Government institutions cannot be seen to be closely associated with groups who are prepared to operate

---

Insider groups
Pressure groups that operate inside the political system through contacts with ministers, MPs, peers and official committees. They are regularly consulted by government.

outside the parliamentary system and even engage in illegal activities. Insiders, therefore, are constrained in the kind of methods they use. There is also a danger that they will lose their independence. If they begin to work too closely with government they may begin to find that their position is compromised, in other words, they will begin to adopt the same policies as their political contacts. If this occurs, their membership may well feel that they are ceasing to be genuinely representative. Organisations such as environmental groups and trade unions, in particular, must guard against this danger. For these reasons some groups prefer to remain as outsiders.

Outsiders

There may be two reasons why a pressure group is not an insider. One is that it prefers to remain outside the governing process in order to preserve its independence and freedom of action. This is certainly true of Greenpeace, for instance. As an organisation they undertake acts of civil disobedience, such as destroying GM crops or disrupting international conferences. If they enjoyed insider status they would not have the option of doing this. They certainly feel they can make more impact by remaining as outsiders.

> **Outsider groups**
> Unlike insider groups, outsiders have no special links with government, but seek to influence decision makers by mobilising public opinion.

The other reason is that they would like to be insiders but simply have not been invited into the governing process. These have been described as **aspiring insiders**. No doubt the Countryside Alliance would like to find itself in the position of an insider. However, it is relatively young as an organisation and, throughout its existence, has been faced with an unsympathetic Labour Government. Certainly the most important factor in outsider status is conflict between the aims of government and the aims of the group. Trade unions, for example, having enjoyed a special status within the Labour Party since 1900, found themselves total outsiders after Margaret Thatcher came to power in 1979. She was opposed to trade union power in general and therefore had no intention of consulting with them regularly. Even after Labour took power in 1997, unions were unable to regain fully their insider status. Having attracted the support of business, Labour under Tony Blair decided to retain business pressure groups as insiders. This left unions still out in the cold.

The 1980s saw the rise of a new kind of political action group that did not fit into any of the existing pressure group classifications. These have been described as **new social movements**, or NSMs.

An NSM is a broadly based, fairly informal movement that emerges, sometimes very rapidly, around a particular issue. They are characterised by the organisation of mass demonstrations and media campaigns that are designed to create maximum publicity and put political pressure upon decision makers. They have become possible largely because of the development of telecommunications, such as the internet and mobile phone texting. Opinion can spread like a forest fire by means of such communication.

Perhaps the first modern example (mass movements in a very general sense are nothing new) of a new social movement was the Anti-Poll Tax

FIG 1.4B Live 8 enjoyed limited success

Federation of the late 1980s. This arose out of widespread discontent about the replacement of domestic property rates, with a flat-rate tax per head (poll tax) to finance local government services. This movement organised demonstrations, some of which led to considerable violence and damaged property, as well as a 'tax strike'. The tax strike involved hundreds of thousands of people who simply refused to pay the tax. It was highly successful and the poll tax was abolished in 1991.

In 2000 sharp rises in fuel prices led to the formation of the *People's Fuel Lobby*, an alliance of farmers, motorists, road hauliers and other interested parties. This group blockaded fuel depots and blocked main roads to publicise the issue. Though the government criticised their tactics, it did lead to a cancellation that year of a tax increase on petrol. In the same period the Countryside Alliance was developing, campaigning on a variety of rural issues, including the proposed ban on hunting with dogs. In the event, the Alliance formed itself into a permanent pressure group and now seeks insider status.

More recent examples have been the *Anti-Iraq War Coalition* of 2002–04 and *Make Poverty History* (backed by Bob Geldof's *Live Aid* and *Live 8* movement) in the early years of the twenty-first century, which campaigned for more aid for poor countries. In a looser sense, there is a recognised movement of anarchists, radical environmentalists and anti-globalisation campaigners which regularly appears at international conferences, such as those of the G8 or the World Trade Organisation.

The main common characteristics of new social movements are as follows:

- They appear on the political scene very rapidly.
- They are mass movements, with many thousands of instant followers.
- They are concerned with a narrow range of issues or one single issue.
- They are often temporary, especially when they achieve some success.
- Their methods are striking and flamboyant, sometimes including acts of civil disobedience.
- They have loose, informal organisations.
- Their followers tend to have an intense attachment to the issue(s) in question.

As we shall see below, insiders and outsiders tend to adopt very different methods. At this stage, however, we can say that an outsider group will always try to mobilise widespread public support as a means of influencing government. Insiders, by contrast, may welcome such support, but prefer to work directly with decision makers and opinion formers.

We can now formalise our classification of pressure groups.

Type	Examples	Insider or outsider
Cause (promotional or issue)	Action on Smoking and Health (ASH)	Insider
	Greenpeace	Outsider
	Shelter (homelessness)	Insider
	Animal Liberation Front	Outsider
Sectional	British Medical Association	Insider
	Fuel Forum (against high fuel prices for road users)	Outsider
	Confederation of British Industry (CBI)	Insider
	Institute of Directors	Outsider
Mixed (both cause and sectional)	Countryside Alliance	Outsider
	Equal Opportunities Commission	Insider
New social movements	Anti-Poll Tax Federation	Outsider
	People's Fuel Lobby	Outsider
	Make Poverty History	Outsider

Pluralism, civil society and group politics

Now that we have established the nature and main functions of pressure groups, it is important to consider how they fit into modern political society. It is common to refer to the political culture in the UK as being one of **pluralism** in nature. This means that we expect a wide range of groups, interests, beliefs and ideologies to flourish together, all competing for attention and influence. The UK is fundamentally a free society, tolerant of

> **Pluralism** A description of a political system where a wide range of beliefs, ideologies and ideas is tolerated and allowed to flourish. It also implies a society where many different groups are active and are free to operate.

different cultures, ideas and demands. As long as a group does not break the law, threaten the security of the state or incite others to commit crime or adopt racist ideas, it will be tolerated and protected from discrimination. Thus pressure groups are able to operate in an extremely free and tolerant environment. In short, they are a key element in a pluralist society.

Britain also enjoys an extremely free and active civil society. The term *civil society* refers to the many types of groups that flourish and to which people owe some kind of allegiance or sense of attachment. Civil society includes individual families, but also larger sections of the community, such as religions, political parties, the media, the arts, sports organisations, associations, schools, universities, and so on. A key part of civil society is taken up by pressure groups.

Until the 1970s, politics in the UK was largely based upon social class and the two-party system. Most political issues were seen in terms of party conflict. They were also usually based upon class conflict. Political conflict was a reflection of class conflict. On the whole, policies supported by Conservatives were seen as middle class-based (whether or not they were actually aimed at middle-class interests). Conversely, Labour was considered to be the party of the working class. The political attitudes of the electorate tended to revolve around these certainties. But in the 1970s two processes began to take shape.

First, the class divisions in the UK were breaking down. Fewer and fewer people could be identified as members of one particular class. Much of the working class was becoming affluent, thus adopting formerly 'middle-class' lifestyles and attitudes. The middle class was dividing itself up into subgroups – those who worked in the private sector and those who were part of the public sector, for example. There were increasing differences between those who were 'professionals' – doctors, teachers, lawyers, and so on – and those who were employed in managerial positions. There was also a growing distinction between the self-employed and the employed. As such groups no longer identified with one great common class, they began to concern themselves with the narrower interests of their own smaller section of society. Thus so-called 'group politics' was coming into being.

Second, there was a process called 'partisan dealignment' taking place. This was a process whereby people identified less and less closely with the aims of political parties. Group politics, as described above, was taking hold. Parties were unable to represent satisfactorily the smaller sections of society that were now making political demands. They seek to develop policies that attract broad, not specialised support. The gap had to be filled and the growth in the number, membership and influence of pressure groups has gone a long way to filling that gap.

Pressure groups and democracy

Here we ask, what is a healthy modern democracy, and what part do pressure groups play in such a democracy? As a supplementary issue, we can also ask whether there are any ways in which pressure groups may be seen to be *undemocratic*.

A generalised view of democracy suggests that it should enjoy the following features:

- It is a society where knowledge flows freely and people have wide access to sources of information independent of government. In other words, there is a well-informed citizenry.
- People will feel they are effectively represented in government circles. Furthermore, institutions should be politically and socially representative.
- Government itself is fully accountable to the people and to the people's representatives.
- There are free and extensive opportunities for people to participate actively in political processes. Participation can range from deep and intensive to shallow and sporadic, depending on a citizen's preferences.
- The rights and interests of individuals and groups are taken into account in decision-making processes.
- The full range of constitutional, democratic principles are in place, notably free and fair elections and the rule of law, including equal rights, an independent judiciary and defences against arbitrary government.

We can now ask what part pressure groups play in sustaining the features described above.

Democratic features of pressure groups

Education

It is clear that pressure groups offer a considerable amount of information to the people. They are, by definition, independent of government (if they were not, we could not describe them as pressure groups), so we are receiving important messages from which we can make sound judgements. Of course, we cannot always rely upon the information being totally accurate, but if we combine all the various sources of information available to us, we are able to form some kind of reasonable judgement. So pressure groups certainly help to inform and educate us.

Representation

Whether we take an active part or not, pressure groups represent our interests to those who govern. In virtually all our activities there is probably a group which is seeking to secure favourable legislation or decisions and to avoid unfavourable ones. As motorists, hospital patients, students, sportspeople, environmentalists, cyclists, walkers, birdwatchers, holidaymakers, workers, and so on, we can be sure there is a group which is fighting our corner. In some cases we may be active members and so know exactly what issues are being addressed. In other cases we are not active, but are nevertheless being passively represented. Even the smallest minorities are likely

to enjoy such benefits. So pressure groups have important representative functions to perform.

Participation

A passive citizenry is often seen as a danger to democracy. When people do not involve themselves in political activity there is a strong probability that government will become dictatorial, safe in the knowledge that its power is unlikely to be challenged. Political activism is therefore important both to prevent excessive accumulation of power and to ensure that government remains accountable to the people. With declining levels of popular involvement in political parties, pressure groups have provided a vital opportunity for political participation.

Minority interests

But perhaps the most important democratic function of pressure groups is to ensure that all of us, in small or large groups, are taken account of, protected and awarded equal status. If this does not occur there is a danger that democracy simply becomes rule by the majority. The nineteenth-century liberal philosopher, John Stuart Mill, referred to the dangers of the *tyranny of the majority* in this context. Majority rule, he argued, is not true democracy. Seeking majority support, political parties will inevitably have to ignore the interests of many minorities. It is therefore necessary for pressure groups to ensure that party rule is not converted into tyranny.

The picture is not completely rosy, however, where pressure groups are concerned. There are a number of senses in which they may not fulfil democratic principles.

Some undemocratic features

Disproportionate influence

The question of whether some pressure groups do not conform to demo-cratic principles revolves around the nature of influence. If all groups enjoyed the amount of influence which their size and importance warranted, the outcome might be considered democratic. But this perfect state of affairs does not exist. Some groups wield more power than their relative importance might suggest.

Some sectional groups, for example, hold a particularly strategic posi-tion in society. That is, we rely on them a great deal and therefore have to take their demands into account. The farming community, for instance, accounts for a tiny proportion of the total population, but farmers are responsible for much of our food supply and create much of the country-side which many of us enjoy. Similarly, emergency and medical workers may have more power than groups which are employed in the private sector.

Finance

Related to their position in society is the issue of wealth. Clearly some groups have access to considerably more funds than others. All those sectional interests that represent employers and business in general inevitably have more finance available to them than charities, which have to rely on handouts from the public or scarce lottery funding. In particular, wealthy groups, including individual companies, have adopted the practice of giving donations to political parties. Clearly they are hoping for a sympathetic attitude if their chosen party wins power. Most notoriously, Bernie Ecclestone, who controls Formula One racing, gave £1 million to Labour before the 2001 general election. He was hoping to hold off a proposed ban on tobacco sponsorship of sport, a ban which would have hit motor racing especially hard. In the event, this caused such a scandal that the money had to be returned by Labour. But the Ecclestone case was only one of many which did not result in such an outcome.

Size

So finance undoubtedly can distort the democratic process. So too can sheer weight of numbers. When the Countryside Alliance put an estimated 300,000 on the streets in 2003 to protest about the ban on hunting with dogs and other rural issues, the government was panicked into action on a number of fronts, including an attempt to water down the hunting bill in Parliament. But the huge numbers on the demonstration certainly did not reflect public opinion on the main issue of fox hunting. This was firmly in favour of a full ban. Similarly, the million-strong march against the 2003 Iraq war was extremely impressive, but, in truth, the country was divided quite evenly on the issue.

Other factors

We can add several other factors that might lead some groups to enjoy a disproportionate amount of power. Insider status, as we have seen, gives some an advantage over others. There may also be sudden waves of public emotion that can thrust an issue into the limelight, possibly without full justification. The Snowdrop Campaign, for example, worked successfully for a ban on the keeping of handguns after public outrage following a school massacre at Dunblane in 1996. The result was rushed, unsatisfactory legislation that appears to have done little to reduce gun crime. Finally, there may simply be periods when a particular group enjoys the support of the government of the day. This has been true of ASH (Action on Smoking and Health) after 1997. But who can say that their successes do not infringe the rights of smokers to pursue their own pastime without persecution?

Finally, we must accept that some pressure group leaders may not truly represent the views of their members. This used to be a charge levelled at trade union leaders (less so since democratic reforms were introduced to unions in the 1980s), and it remains a danger. Party politicians are made accountable for their actions through the electoral process and through representative institutions. This may not be the case with pressure group leaders. Though such a problem may not be widespread, it is certainly true that democratic controls over pressure groups are weaker than those affecting parties and politicians.

Pressure Groups and Democracy

Democratic Features

- Educating and informing the public about important political issues.
- A channel of representation between the people and the government, keeping government in touch with public opinion.
- Provide opportunities for political participation.
- Protect the interests of minority groups and opinions.
- Act as a safeguard against the power of the state.

Undemocratic Features

- Some groups wield more influence that their place in society warrants.
- Some groups have influence simply because they have large financial resources available to them. This may be to the detriment of poorer groups who may also have a strong case.
- Insiders have influence at the expense of outsiders.
- Some groups' leaderships may not represent accurately the views of their members, i.e. they are undemocratic internally.
- Pressure groups cannot be made democratically accountable for what they do and propose.

Methods of pressure groups

Insiders

Lobbying

The way in which insider pressure groups operate has been described above. Much of what they do is hidden behind closed doors and receives little publicity. Britain, though, is a consultative democracy and so we should expect discussions with pressure groups to be going on all the time. For insiders this is a constant process. Committees and commissions, including group representatives, meet to develop policy; ministers consult with interested groups to ensure consent to their policies; MPs and peers use pressure groups as a source of information or to help in their task of scrutinising legislation and investigating the work of government departments.

Parliamentary methods

Although Parliament has been increasingly marginalised in modern times, pressure groups recognise that Westminster remains fertile ground for

their causes. Some groups, indeed, pay retaining fees to MPs in return for which they will raise relevant issues as much as possible in the House (it should be pointed out that it is unlawful to attempt to persuade an MP actually to vote in a certain way or to ask a parliamentary question in return for money). All the large pressure groups have a number of MPs who are committed to representing them in Parliament, either for financial return or simply because the MP is a sympathiser. Of course, the party whips usually have the final say, but where MPs have the opportunity to act independently, they often engage in group politics rather than party politics.

The House of Lords has become more significant since it was reformed, and there has certainly been a corresponding growth in interest from pressure groups. The Lords is mainly an amending chamber and it is in this field that interested pressure groups seek to gain some leverage. On issues such as university tuition fees, deregulation of casino gambling, the protection of human rights and the extension of pub licensing hours, the Lords has been successful in securing amendments in recent times. In such examples, campaigning peers have been backed by the relevant pressure groups. Peers are more independent of party control than are MPs in the Commons, so pressure groups are more likely to find a sympathetic ear there than in the Commons.

Outsiders

Direct action

At the other end of the spectrum to such private consultations lies direct action. This occurs when pressure groups seek to obtain the maximum possible amount of publicity for their cause. The mass demonstration is the most common example. In recent years there have been impressive demonstrations of mass support over such issues as the 2003 Iraq war, the grievances of the Countryside Alliance and opposition to university tuition fees. There was even a large gathering of old-age pensioners at Westminster to put pressure on government for higher pensions and other benefits.

Direct action can also involve 'stunts' and provocative action to draw attention to an issue. Most famously, members of Fathers4Justice have often dressed up as 'superheroes' and placed themselves in positions, such as Buckingham Palace, where they will attract media attention. In 2004 members of the Countryside Alliance invaded the floor of the House of Commons while Tony Blair was speaking. Feminists and anti-war groups have also staged demonstrations in the House where they know the TV cameras will pick them up.

Lawbreaking and civil disobedience have also been used in extreme circumstances. The anti-fuel tax lobby group, for example, has blockaded fuel depots in order to publicise their case for lower petrol taxes. Similarly Greenpeace destroys GM crops and the *Animal Liberation Front* lives up to its name by freeing animals from experimentation laboratories or by threatening laboratory workers.

There is no doubt that such direct forms of action have been increasing

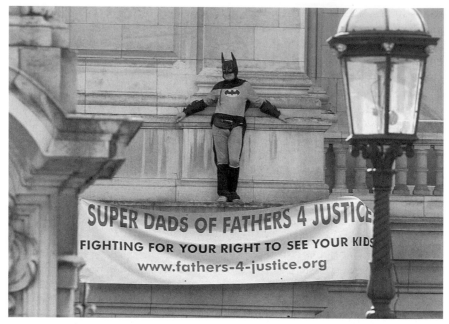

FIG 1.4C Fathers 4 Justice successfully gained media and public attention

in recent years. The reason is, quite simply, that it often works. Governments are forced to respond to powerful demonstrations of feeling, especially when the media take up the same cause. Furthermore, technological advances such as the internet and mobile phones have made such direct action more feasible. Campaigns can be mounted at short notice and large numbers of people can be mobilised simply because communications systems have improved so much.

Mobilising public opinion

As public attachment to political parties has weakened in modern times, so governments have become increasingly sensitive to the shifting sands of public opinion. If a party wishes to retain or regain power it can no longer rely upon a large and permanent bedrock of support. Instead it must try to ensure that it promotes issues which will win it votes at elections. This reality gives pressure groups a great deal of political leverage. If they can demonstrate to political leaders that the issue or issues they support command widespread interest among the people, and so deliver many votes, those leaders are forced to listen.

In the 2005 election campaign, for instance, there is no doubt that the old-age pensioner vote was a critical factor. The elderly vote in much larger numbers than the young. For this reason politicians are forced to woo the so-called 'grey vote'. The two main pressure groups that represent the elderly – *Help the Aged* and *Age Concern* – knew that they were in a position to influence policy in the run-up to the election. Thus they pushed hard on

issues such as the size of the pension, rebates on council tax for the elderly and law and order measures (older people display a greater fear of crime than the rest of the population). By demonstrating that this particular group of voters was interested in these demands, they were able to force concessions from aspiring party leaders.

Similarly, some smaller groups have attempted to publicise their concerns forcefully enough to bring public opinion round to their cause. The Countryside Alliance has pursued this objective (over rural issues), as have Fathers4Justice (over child custodial rights for separated and divorced fathers) and Greenpeace (anti-GM foods).

The media play a key role in such mobilisation of opinion. Thus many groups employ professional public relations operators, whose role it is to ensure good press or TV coverage for a particular campaign. Sometimes, too, the press take it upon themselves to mount their own campaigns. In 2005, for example, the *Independent* newspaper instituted a major campaign to reform the electoral system (much to the delight of the Electoral Reform Society, the main pressure group in this area). The *Daily Mail*, too, usually supports those groups which are pressing for a tougher government line on law and order issues.

Why some groups are more successful than others

It is worth asking first: what do we mean by 'success'? Clearly a pressure group can be considered successful if it achieves the passage of particular legislation for which it has been campaigning. This has certainly been the case for ASH, which successfully campaigned for a ban on tobacco advertising and on smoking in public places. But groups sometimes seek to *prevent* unfriendly legislation. Business groups such as the Institute of Directors, for example, helped to persuade the British government to negotiate an opt-out from the European Union Working Time Directive, which limited the working week to 48 hours. Similarly, amendments to legislation may be sought. Pressure group activity (mainly religious groups) certainly resulted in changes to the Gambling Act of 2005, which partially deregulated gambling activity in the UK. In a wide range of technical and specialised areas of policy too, pressure groups, large and small, are constantly successful in moulding proposed legislation for their own benefit.

However, pressure group success should not be measured merely in terms of legislation. In some cases, such groups simply wish to raise the profile of an issue, to place it on the political agenda where it has been ignored in the past. In recent years, for example, such issues as rural problems, child abuse, mental health, infertility treatment, euthanasia and abortion have all risen up the political agenda as a result of pressure group activity.

So success can come in a number of ways. But why are some groups more successful than others?

Philosophy

Where a group's beliefs and aspirations are close to those of the government of the day, success is very likely. Business groups have certainly done well under the Conservatives in the past, and since 1997 have also been achieving success under New Labour. Trade unions used to be highly favoured by Labour, but have now lost their strategic position. On the other hand, the anti-poverty policies pursued by Gordon Brown under Labour have put pensioner and lone parent groups in a good position. Since 1997, Labour has also placed great emphasis on improving the quality of public services, so that teacher and medical associations have been influential. By contrast, rights campaigners, such as Liberty and Charter 88, have discovered resistance to their demands from recent governments, which have sought to introduce a more authoritarian stance on law and order and asylum seeking.

Finance

Being wealthy is no guarantee of a group's success, as the tobacco lobby has discovered over smoking curbs, but it can yield positive results. The Electoral Commission, in its report on the 2005 general election, noted that some £20 million had been donated to political parties towards their election expenses. Clearly the groups that spent this money felt that it could lead to favourable outcomes. Donations to political parties do not represent the only use of money, however. Those groups that have considerable funds can mount expensive campaigns to press their cause. Many industries, such as farming, oil, tobacco, supermarkets and banks, spend large sums on lobbying behind the scenes and on public campaigning. This is not to say, however, that wealthy groups will be successful automatically. Large trade unions, for example, have considerable funds available for political purposes, but, with an unsympathetic government, even this can be futile.

Size

We have seen above how large some groups have become. The Royal Society for the Protection of Birds (1 million members), Friends of the Earth (200,000) and the Countryside Alliance (100,000) all claim influence through the weight of public opinion. If we consider the two major motoring organisations – the AA and RAC – as pressure groups, we can see how much leverage they have, since both have several million members. The private motoring lobby has a considerable advantage as so many of us are motorists.

Size often translates itself into finance and also voting power. The recent success of groups which represent the elderly – Age Concern and Help the Aged – can largely be put down to the fact that this age group votes in much larger numbers than the rest of the population. Turnout among pensioners is usually 70–80 per cent, compared with less than 40 per cent among the under-thirties.

Of course, there is no guarantee that a large pressure group will be successful. As we have seen, trade unions have fallen out of favour with governments from both parties, so even the biggest unions, such as *UNISON* (1.2 million members working in the public services) and *AMACUS* (1.1 million general workers), do not 'punch their weight' in political circles as they used to do before the 1980s.

Organisation

The ability of a group to organise successful demonstrations, to raise its public profile and to persuade its members to take visible action, can replace both size and finance as factors in success. The Countryside Alliance, Fathers4Justice and Live Aid are all examples of movements that have been successful because they have been well led and have captured the imagination of the public and the media. Images of these and other similar groups appear regularly on our TV screens. Careful planning and organisation are behind their successes.

Opposition groups

It is often the case that groups are faced by adversaries who are arguing the opposite case. When this happens, pressure group activity becomes battle of wills and the result is uncertain. (Where a group is lucky enough to have no serious opposition, such as old-age pensioners, poor families and financial establishments, there is a greater chance of success.) The table below shows some examples of how such groups line up against each other.

Group	Opposition
Action on Smoking and Health	Tobacco industry
Private motoring lobby	Environmentalists and public transport campaigners
Trade unions	Employers' groups
Farming industry	Free trade campaigners
Countryside Alliance	Anti-hunting lobby
Animal rights groups	Pharmaceutical industry

These groups which face powerful opposition have to hope they can capture the attention of government and attract the support of public opinion. But they do have special problems that are not faced by other groups.

Insider status

There is no certainty that insider groups will be more successful than outsiders, and it would be a mistake to assume that insiders are always treated favourably. However, there is no doubt that those groups that have

regular contact with government and Parliament do enjoy some advantage. They are regularly consulted and governments rely upon them for both information and support.

Celebrity involvement

Most groups attempt to gain endorsements from well-known celebrities. One well-placed individual, one useful photo opportunity, can replace huge amounts of finance and public support in terms of influence. Indeed, in 2004–05 celebrity chef Jamie Oliver single-handedly won a commitment from government to provide more funding for school meals. Elton John has campaigned for many years on behalf of AIDS charities, and Bob Geldof has become a legendary leader of various campaigns on behalf of the world's poor and disadvantaged. What lies behind the success of those groups with celebrity support is the fact that such success can be achieved by any movement which is able to capture the public imagination.

The changing nature and activities of pressure groups

There is no doubt that pressure groups have a considerably significant place in British society in general and the political system in particular. Furthermore, it is clear that the importance of their role has been increasing and is likely to continue to do so. We can identify a number of reasons why this is so.

Participation

We have seen that the importance of parties has been declining. Party memberships have fallen dramatically (as have voting turnouts), and the ordinary members of parties now have relatively little influence over the policy-making process. But membership of pressure groups has been growing – so too have their activities. Social and political research indicates strongly that political participation and a general interest in politics is not declining as statistics might suggest. Rather the nature of interest and participation is changing. The large numbers of non-voters and apparently disillusioned non-participants (concentrated among the young) have shifted their political awareness away from party politics in favour of specific political issues. Clearly pressure groups provide a more appropriate vehicle for such interest than do parties.

Access points

Pressure groups now have many more 'access points' to the decision-making institutions than has been true in the past. It used to be the case that pressure groups concentrated the vast majority of their efforts on government ministers, civil servants and their advisers, or on Parliament. But decision making in Britain today has become spread over a much wider range of institutions. This process has four facets: the importance of the European Union; devolution of power to national regions; the growth of policy-making bodies outside the traditional party system; and the increasing importance of the courts as a result of the passage of the Human Rights Act.

The European Union

The clearest example has been the growing jurisdiction of the European Union. Those decisions that are made in the Union have forced pressure groups to adopt two new methods. First, they have switched many of their activities to the European Commission, the Committee of the Regions, the Social and Economic Committee and various other Union institutions whose task it is to develop policy. At the same time, the European Parliament is becoming more influential. Therefore, lobby groups have sent increasing numbers of representatives to the Parliament and its committees. In 2005 there were more than 4200 accredited (that is, permitted to operate freely) lobbyists attached to the European Parliament.

Of course, pressure groups continue to lobby national ministers, who make the final decisions, but there is ample opportunity for groups to put pressure on permanent institutions that have consciously opened their doors to representatives of interest groups. It is often argued that the European Union is an undemocratic body and, in the traditional sense of 'parliamentary democracy', that is probably so. But it is also noteworthy that the European Union accepts that the representation of interests is vital if they are to recommend policy which will enjoy popular consent.

Second, groups have understood that they must unite with their European counterparts if they are to exert effective pressure. So we have seen the development of an increasing number of 'federated' groups in Europe. All major trade unions, producer groups and environmental campaign organisations, for example, have developed their own European-wide institutions. The brief list of examples of European pressure and interest groups shown below gives a flavour of the range of issues being treated in this way:

- European Automobile Manufacturers Association
- Friends of the Earth Europe
- Association of Electricity Producers
- European Fair Trade Association
- European Mine, Chemical and Energy Workers Federation
- European Small Business Alliance
- Association of Commercial Television in Europe
- European Association for the Defence of Human Rights

Devolution

A considerable amount of power has been devolved to Scottish and Welsh government (and to Northern Ireland, when devolved government is operating there). The main policy areas which have been devolved are: health, education, transport, planning, industrial development, agriculture and local government services. Pressure groups that are involved in these policy areas have naturally been forced to move some of their operations to Edinburgh, Cardiff and Belfast. Of course, the main thrust of their activities remains in London or Brussels, but there has been a considerable shift in their operations.

Extra-party institutions

As we have seen, the early consideration of policy has shifted away from party institutions. Instead, there is now a wide range of external think tanks, policy units, private advisers and working parties, which have the task of feeding policy options into the government machinery. Pressure groups have a vital interest in becoming involved in the *early stages* of policy consideration. The main way in which they can achieve this is by employing *professional* lobbyists, who can find their way through the maze of policy-making institutions which now flourish at the centre of British politics. Professional lobbyists undertake the critical task of identifying the key decision makers, securing contact with them and ensuring that the information that a pressure group wishes to disseminate finds the appropriate targets.

The Human Rights Act

This Act was passed in 1998 and brought the European Convention on Human Rights into British law in 2000. Its effect was to reinforce and introduce a wide range of rights, many of which were designed to protect minority interests. Since many pressure and interest groups represent such minorities, the Act provided many new opportunities for them to assert their interests. By applying to the courts, a minority group may be able to seek a judgement that protects them from oppressive legislation. The human rights campaign group, Liberty, for example, has been especially active in this judicial field since the passage of the Act.

Direct action

It used to be the case that *insider* pressure groups were seen to have a distinct advantage in gaining the attention of policy and decision makers over **outsider groups**. This was because they had direct access, were generally felt to be more responsible in their demands and had developed long-term links with government and Parliament. This picture has been changing, however. Many groups now feel that they can exert more pressure on government by mobilising public opinion than by pursuing direct links with decision makers. Certainly there is a good deal of evidence to suggest that modern governments are responsive to mass political movements – nearly always outsiders – provided they can demonstrate widespread support. The Countryside Alliance has certainly found this, as have old-age pensioner groups, development aid campaigners and environmentalists. Direct action, when properly organised and well supported, is growing in importance.

Summary

Many millions of British citizens consider themselves to be detached from the political process. There has been growing disillusionment with traditional party politics; fewer people than ever bother to vote in elections; and party membership has been falling steadily. But there is a different perspective that we can adopt. In terms of pressure group activity, especially since the emergence of new social movements, it could be claimed that political activity and participation have never been higher.

Though a decreasing number of people identify closely with any political party or ideology, a growing number are willing to take positive action in pursuit of a cause about which they feel passionate. Furthermore, as representative institutions – especially parties and Parliament – have become increasingly marginalised and impotent, there has been a renewed interest in the influence of direct action. As long as we enjoy an independent civil society, and as long as politicians remain sensitive to public opinion, pressure groups will remain a key feature of British democracy.

KEY CONCEPTS

Pressure group	An association that may be formal or informal, whose purpose is to further the interests of a specific section of society or to promote a particular cause.
Sectional group	A pressure group that represents a specific section of society, such as a trade union or an employers' association. Also known as an *interest group*.
Promotional group	A pressure group that seeks to promote a cause rather than the interests of its own members. Also known as a *cause group* or an *issue group*.
Insider groups	Pressure groups that operate inside the political system through contacts with ministers, MPs, peers and official committees. They are regularly consulted by government.
Outsider groups	Unlike insider groups, outsiders have no special links with government, but seek to influence decision makers by mobilising public opinion.
Pluralism	A description of a political system where a wide range of beliefs, ideologies and ideas is tolerated and allowed to flourish. It also implies a society where many different groups are active and are free to operate.

Revision topics and examination questions

Revision topics

- Classification of groups
- Functions of pressure groups
- Methods of groups
- Changing role of pressure groups
- Nature of direct action
- Factors in success or failure of groups
- Distinctions between parties and pressure groups
- Democratic role of pressure groups
- Undemocratic features of pressure groups

Short answers

- What is a pressure group?
- Describe briefly any TWO types of pressure group.
- Outline THREE functions of pressure groups.
- Distinguish between a pressure group and a party.
- Distinguish between a sectional and a promotional (cause) pressure group.
- Distinguish between an insider and an outsider pressure group.

Medium answers

- Why is it sometimes difficult to distinguish pressure groups from parties?
- Describe the main methods used by modern pressure groups.
- What is meant by the term 'direct action'?
- How do pressure groups encourage political participation?

Long answers

- In what ways do pressure groups enhance democracy?
- In what senses can pressure groups be considered undemocratic?
- Why are some pressure groups more successful than others?
- How has the role of pressure groups changed in recent years?
- How and why have the methods of pressure groups changed in recent years?

Resources and Web Guide

Books

Two books stand out as classic works:
W. Grant, *Pressure Groups and British Politics*, Palgrave, 2000.
R. Baggot, *Pressure Groups Today*, MUP, 1995.

Useful websites

A sample of prominent pressure groups is:
www.ash.org.uk (Action on Smoking and Health) (accessed 11 November 2005)
www.cbi.org.uk (Confederation of British Industry) (accessed 11 November 2005)
www.rspb.org.uk (Royal Society for the Protection of Birds) (accessed 11 November 2005)
www.greenpeace.org (Greenpeace) (accessed 11 November 2005)

2

Governing the UK

2.1
The UK constitution

The functions of a constitution

Virtually every country in the world operates its political system within the constraints of a **constitution**. In most cases the constitution of the state is a written document which has been agreed on some occasion. Such constitutions are usually described as *codified*. There are a few countries, however, including the UK, that operate without such a specifically written constitution. Even so, these countries have a general 'sense' that a set of constitutional rules exists. So constitutions, whether codified or not, are a vital aspect of most stable political systems. All constitutions, no matter where they exist, perform the same set of functions. These are as follows:

> **Constitution** A set of principles, which may be written or unwritten, that set out the distribution of power within a political system, relationships between political institutions, the limits of government jurisdiction, the rights of citizens and the method of amending the constitution itself.

1. They determine how political power should be distributed within the state. This includes **federal** settlements, where power is divided between the central government and regional institutions, as in the USA, or **unitary** states, where ultimate power lies firmly in one place, as with the UK's parliamentary system. Similarly, constitutions determine the balance of power between government and parliament, between president and prime minister and between two chambers in systems that are **bicameral** (two houses of parliament).
2. Linked to this first function, constitutions also establish the political processes which make the system work. This includes the relationships between institutions and the rules which govern how they operate.
3. A constitution normally states what the limits of governmental power should be. In other words, what is the **competence** of government. The British constitution is unusual in this sense as it places no limits at all on the competence of Parliament. Being sovereign, Parliament is able to do what it likes. Of course, we would not expect it to act in a dictatorial way, but it has the legal power to do what it wishes. By contrast, North American government is very circumscribed by that country's constitution.
4. Just as constitutions limit governmental power, so too they assert the rights of the citizens against the state. Most countries which at least claim to be democratic have some kind of bill of rights – a statement that prevents the government from trampling on the civil liberties of its citizens.
5. Constitutions set out the rules by which nationality is established, in other words, who is entitled to be a citizen and how outsiders may become citizens. This also implies that a constitution defines the territory that makes up the state.
6. Finally, we must remember that constitutions have to be amended from time to time. It is essential, therefore, that a constitution contains within itself the rules for its own amendment. The UK is, once again, unusual

in this respect as its constitution changes in two ways. One is through a simple parliamentary statute, the other is the slow evolution of unwritten rules, known as **conventions**. Normally states have special arrangements for amending their constitution. In France and Ireland, for example, a referendum is needed to approve a change. In the USA it is necessary to secure a two-thirds majority of both Houses of Congress and the approval of three-quarters of the 50 states which make up the Union. Britain has no such methods of amendment; its constitution has largely evolved naturally over the course of history.

So we have established six main functions of a constitution. Issues which concern any of these matters are therefore described as *constitutional* in nature.

Codification and entrenchment

Two aspects of constitutionalism need further explanation. They are codification and entrenchment.

A **codified** constitution is one that is written in an organised way in a single document. The advantage of this arrangement is that the constitution is clear and every citizen is able to access it. Similarly, when there is a dispute concerning constitutional arrangements, having a codified document is a considerable advantage.

Codification of a constitution normally occurs at some critical moment in a country's history. This may be the aftermath of a revolution, civil war or *coup d'état*; it may come about following the actual creation of a new state or the re-formation of troubled country. The following examples demonstrate how constitutions can come about.

Country	Year of current constitution	Circumstances
USA	1787	The creation of a new political union after independence of 13 former British colonies.
Ireland	1937	Renounced the British Crown and became a Republic.
France	1958	After a *coup d'état* and a new president – Charles de Gaulle – taking over.
Nigeria	1999	Changed from military rule to democracy.
China	1949	Upon the victory of communist forces after a civil war.
Norway	1814	On the country's freedom from Danish rule.
Malaysia	1957	On independence from Britain.

A codified constitution has one additional benefit. As a single document it can provide the people of a state with something with which they can identify. Americans, for example, virtually worship their historic constitution, treating it with great reverence and pledging allegiance to it regularly. When each new president takes office, it is part of his oath of allegiance that he agrees to 'protect and defend' the constitution.

The British constitution is unusual in that it is not codified. Many even argue, therefore, that it does not actually exist at all. Parts of it are written, but there is certainly no single document and there are important parts of it which are not written at all. Israel, New Zealand and Canada also lack codified constitutions, but in all three cases there are 'Basic Laws' which describe constitutional principles and are differentiated from other laws. By contrast, the UK makes no distinction between constitutional and other laws.

Entrenchment is a rather more important matter. This is the device which protects a constitution from short-term amendment. It is important because constitutional change makes a fundamental and important difference to the political system of a country. The constitution is too important to be placed in the hands of a *temporary* government. A country must be sure that any proposed constitutional change meets two tests: one is that there is widespread popular support for it; the other is that it is in the long-term interests of the country.

An example of this principle concerns the guarantees of human rights that exist in most states. It may be in the interests of a particular government to set aside some of these rights by amending that part of the constitution which deals with civil rights. But this would clearly damage the long-term interests of the people. Similarly, a dictatorial government might seek to grant itself additional powers to protect its own position. If this occurred, democracy in general would be under threat.

To ensure that the two tests are met, therefore, special arrangements need to be established. Thus a referendum, for example, guarantees popular support for change, while special parliamentary procedures can ensure that constitutional amendment is in the long-term interests of the state.

But the situation in the UK is unusual. It is not possible to entrench constitutional principles. This is because Parliament is sovereign. The sovereignty of Parliament asserts that each individual parliament cannot be bound by its predecessors, nor can it bind its successors. This means, in effect, that every new parliament is able to amend the constitution as it wishes. All Parliament has to do is to pass a new parliamentary statute, using the same procedure as for any other statute. It can be done in as little as two days. Furthermore, the government in power is normally able to dominate Parliament, using its majority in the House of Commons and the mandate of the people which is granted at elections. So a dominant government can effectively control the constitution.

An example of executive power was demonstrated when the UK Parliament passed the Human Rights Act in 1998. This incorporated the European Convention on Human Rights into British law. It became binding on all political bodies other than Parliament itself. No special procedures were needed. A fundamental change to the British constitution was made through a simple Act of Parliament. It occurred in this way because the British constitution is not entrenched.

Having said that, it is now becoming common practice in the UK to hold a referendum when constitutional change is proposed. This was done for devolution of power to Scotland and Wales in 1997, the introduction of elected mayors in London and a number of other locations, and to approve the Good Friday Agreement in Northern Ireland in 1998. Referendums have also been proposed to approve the adoption of the single European currency and the new European Union constitution. The effect of such referendums is to entrench constitutional developments. It is inconceivable that the changes would be reversed without another referendum to approve such a reversal.

Unitary and federal constitutions

There are two fundamental types of constitution in the world of politics. These are unitary and federal.

A **unitary** constitution is one where sovereignty – ultimate political power – resides in one location. This is at the centre. It is possible that some power may be distributed to regions and local government, but this is not the same as sovereignty. In a unitary constitution the central sovereign power can overrule all other bodies and has the right to restore all political power to itself. Thus, although Britain has devolved much power to Wales, Scotland and Northern Ireland, the Westminster Parliament remains firmly sovereign.

In a **federal** constitution sovereignty is divided between central bodies and regional institutions. Such constitutions normally arise when a number of sovereign states come together and agree to surrender some of their sovereignty – but not all of it – to a central authority. The political reason for such an arrangement is usually that a country contains strong regional differences and identities. These can be protected by ensuring that regions retain some of their own sovereignty.

The USA is possibly the best-known federal constitution, negotiated and written in 1787 and ratified by the 13 states (there are now 50) in the three years that followed. To illustrate the principle, some of the main sovereign powers as they are divided in the USA are shown below.

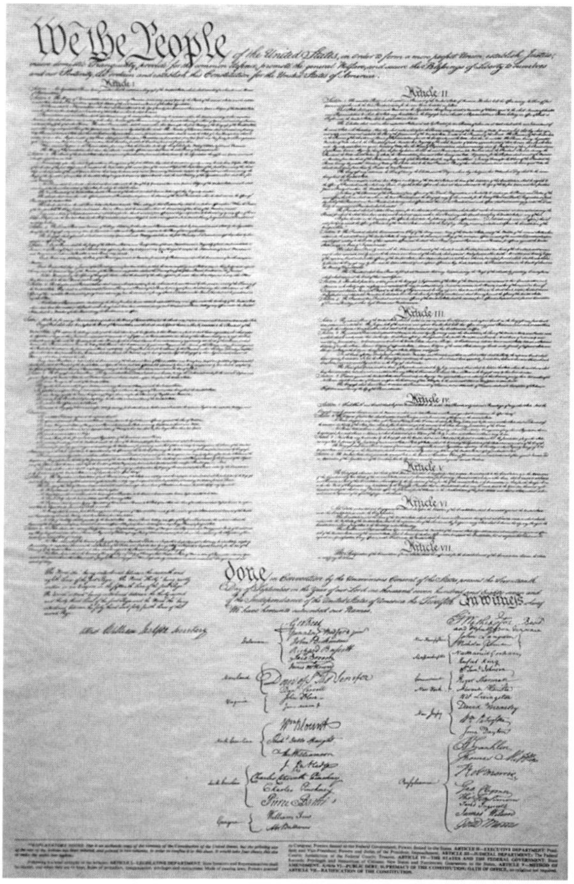

FIG 2.1A The American constitution is an early example of a codified document

US federal powers	US state powers
Economic management	Most criminal law
Currency control	Education
Foreign policy	Property and sales taxes
Defence policy	Most policing
Foreign trade	Industrial development

Both systems, federal and unitary, are popular, as is illustrated by the list of major countries shown below, showing which type of **constitutional government** they use.

Unitary constitutions	Federal constitutions
UK	USA
France	Germany
Italy	Australia
Zimbabwe	Nigeria
Thailand	Malaysia
China	Russia
Pakistan	India
New Zealand	Canada

> **Constitutional government**
> Government that is limited by a constitution and by constitutional principles.

Sources of the UK constitution

So the British constitution is neither codified nor entrenched. Some even suggest that it does not really exist, but is simply 'whatever Parliament says it is at any given time'. It is certainly difficult to define and is constantly evolving; but there is no doubt that there is an 'idea' of the British constitution, so we can attempt to identify what components make it up.

Parliamentary statutes

These are Acts of Parliament which have the effect of establishing constitutional principles. The Human Rights Act has been described above as an example, but we can also add the **Parliament Act** of 1949, which established limitations to the power of the House of Lords, and the **Scotland** and **Wales Acts**, which devolved power to those countries. Further examples of constitutional statutes are shown in the next table.

Constitutional conventions

A convention is an unwritten rule that is considered binding on all members of the political community. Such conventions cannot be challenged in law, but have so much moral force that they are rarely, if ever, disputed. Many of the powers of the prime minister are governed by such conventions. It is, for example, merely a convention that the prime minister exercises the monarch's power to appoint and dismiss ministers, to choose the date of the general election and to grant various answers. It is also a convention (known as the Salisbury Convention) that the House of Lords should not block any legislation that appeared in the governing party's most recent election manifesto.

Historical principles and constitutional writings

Similar to conventions, these principles have become effectively binding because they have been established over a long period of time. The most important is the **sovereignty of Parliament**. We could add a similar concept, which is **parliamentary government**, the principle that the authority of the government is drawn from Parliament and not directly from the people. The **rule of law** is a more recent development, originating in the second part of the nineteenth century. Among other things, the rule of law establishes the principles of equal rights for citizens and that government is itself constrained by legal limitations. On the whole, historical principles are attributed to important constitutional theorists, such as Sir William Blackstone (**parliamentary sovereignty**) and A.V. Dicey (rule of law).

Common law

The term 'common law' is a largely Anglo-Saxon principle. It refers to the development of laws through historical usage and tradition. Judges, who occasionally must declare and enforce common law, treat it as any rule of conduct that is both well established and generally acknowledged by most people.

The most important application of common law has concerned the protection of basic rights and freedoms from encroachment by government and/or Parliament. The right of people to free movement and to gather for public demonstrations, for example, are ancient freedoms, jealously guarded by the courts. So too was the principle that the Crown could not detain citizens without trial. For the most part, common law principles have been replaced by statutes and by the European Convention on Human Rights, which became UK law in the year 2000. But from time to time, when there is no relevant statute, the common law is invoked in courts by citizens with a grievance against government.

Examples of such cases in recent times have included the 'right to die' for the terminally ill or the rights of couples to be able to use frozen or donated embryos to help them to have their own children.

Customs

Similar to common law, constitutional customs govern many of the rituals of parliamentary government. The procedures of both Houses of

Parliamentary sovereignty The British principle that Parliament is the source of all political power (with the exception of the prerogative powers of the prime minister) and that all enforceable laws must be approved by Parliament.

Parliament are traditional in nature, as are some of their rituals. The practice of allowing the monarch to announce the legislative programme for the coming year (the so-called 'Queen's Speech') is such a custom, as are many of the rules of debate.

The table below summarises the main sources of the British constitution.

The Influence of European Union Treaties and Statutes

To some extent, parts of the British constitution have been moulded and altered by treaties with the European Union and some of the directives which apply to the British government. Most importantly, the division of sovereignty between the UK parliament and the EU is defined in agreements such as the Maastricht Treaty (1992) and the Single European Act (1986). Such treaties and directives also define the relationships between UK and EU courts. The European Communities Act of 1972 stated that all EU laws automatically become UK laws. This is perhaps the most fundamental constitutional principle of all.

Type of source	Examples
Statutes	Human Rights Act 1998 incorporates the codified European Convention on Human Rights into UK law.
	Equal Franchise Act 1928 established full and equal voting rights for women.
	Scotland Act 1998 established a Scottish Parliament with legislative powers.
	Life Peerages Act 1958 introduced the appointment of life peers to add to the hereditary peerage.
	House of Lords Act 1999 abolished all but 92 of the hereditary peers in the House of Lords.
	Freedom of Information Act 2000 introduced the right of citizens to see all official documents not excluded on grounds of national security.
Conventions	Salisbury Convention states that the House of Lords should not block any legislation which appeared in the governing party's most recent election manifesto.

Continued on next page

Type of source	Examples
Conventions	Prerogative powers are the powers remaining to the monarch, but which are exercised, by convention, by the prime minister. These include appointment and dismissal of ministers, commanding the armed forces and negotiation of foreign treaties.
	Collective responsibility means that all members of the government must support official policy in public or resign or face dismissal.
	Government formation is based on the rule that, following an election, the monarch must invite the leader of the largest party in the Commons to form a government.
Historical principles	The sovereignty of Parliament establishes the supremacy of Parliament in legislation.
	The rule of law states that all, including government itself, are equal under the law.
	Constitutional monarchy is a principle that the role of the monarch is limited and permits no active role in politics.
Common law	Freedom of association implies that all are free to form political parties, pressure groups and any other lawful organisation.
	Freedom of movement establishes the ancient right of people to move across public land.
	The principle of equity asserts that all are entitled to be treated equally and justly by public bodies.
Customs	The practices and traditions of Parliament.
EU Treaties and Directives	Treaties which define the relationship between UK and EU sovereignty and which define the relationships between UK and EU institutions.

Main characteristics of the UK constitution

Having established how the various parts of the British constitution have come about historically, and how it continues to develop, we can examine its main characteristics.

Constitutional monarchy and royal prerogative

Britain is a monarchy and has been for most of its history. Since 1688, however, it has been a constitutional monarchy. Until then, the monarchy enjoyed almost absolute power. Parliament only restrained the king or queen's ability to raise taxes. All other powers, known as the **royal prerogative**, were effectively arbitrary. However, when William of Orange was invited to take the throne with his wife, Mary, in 1689, following the largely peaceful Glorious Revolution, the price of the invitation was that he should accept the supremacy of Parliament in lawmaking.

Since that time the prerogative powers of the monarchy have been gradually eroded. Though no constitution has ever been enacted, there is a sense that the monarch is constrained by fixed constitutional principles. This erosion has taken place from two directions. First, all lawmaking power has passed to Parliament. The monarch must give Royal Assent to make bills laws, but it is accepted that s/he must never refuse such assent. Not since 1707, when Queen Anne attempted to block the Act of Union, which abolished the separate Scottish Parliament, has Royal Assent been withheld. She was brought quickly into line, the Act was passed and no monarch since has tried to defy Parliament.

Second, since the development of the idea of a separate head of government in the 1720s, the remaining prerogative powers of the monarch have been gradually taken over by the prime minister. By the 1870s Queen Victoria had to accept that she and her successors would never again have discretion over the appointment of ministers. Nor would they be able to dissolve Parliament and call an election, negotiate foreign treaties, command forces in combat, create peerages or interfere in any significant way in policy making. The constitutional monarchy thus means that many actions are taken *in the name* of the monarch, but s/he is not *actually* making any decisions. So we still speak of 'Her Majesty's forces', 'Her Majesty's ministers and government', the 'Crown courts', and so on, but in fact we know that these are all under the control of the government and/or Parliament.

In practice, the monarch remains head of state, but since the head of government (the prime minister) carries out most of his/her functions, it is the prime minister who *appears* to be the head of state. It is the prime minister who negotiates with other heads of government and heads of state, and represents the nation abroad. In other words, the British prime minister is *effectively* head of state and behaves in that way. The monarchy, now playing a largely ceremonial role, is limited by firm constitutional rules.

Parliamentary government and parliamentary sovereignty

Writing in 1867, in his famous work, *The English Constitution*, the great English political journalist, Walter Bagehot (1826–1877), declared that he understood the 'efficient secret' of the British political system. This was the 'fusion' of executive and legislative power. What he meant was that Britain did not recognise a separation between Parliament and government. In most modern political systems, especially that of the USA, there is a strict separation between the power and membership of government and legislature. This is practised in order to ensure that each branch controls the other. No such separation existed in Britain in 1867 and it does not to this day.

The so-called separation of powers is usually praised for keeping governmental power under democratic control. But it can also hinder the effectiveness of strong government. In the UK, government members are drawn from Parliament (all ministers must, by convention, be Members of either Commons or Lords). Furthermore, we expect the government to control the legislature by manipulating its majority in the House of Commons. Parliament grants authority to government ministers and then expects them to be accountable to it. In return, Parliament allows ministers to dominate it. This system of parliamentary accountability, combined with executive supremacy, is known as **parliamentary government**.

Though the government is politically dominant, as Bagehot had pointed out, this does not make it legally sovereign. **Legal sovereignty** – the ultimate power to make laws that will be enforced – lies only with Parliament. This means that government has to accept the final word of Parliament when proposing legislation. Of course, we expect Parliament to approve most government proposals because government has a mandate from the people. But Parliament retains a reserve power to veto such proposals. In extreme circumstances, Parliament can even dismiss a government, normally forcing an election, through a vote of no confidence. This was last done in 1979, when James Callaghan's Labour Government was defeated on the floor of the House of Commons and was forced to resign.

This principle of parliamentary sovereignty must not, however, deflect our attention away from the fact that *most* political power still normally lies with the government. Some describe this as political sovereignty to distinguish it from legal sovereignty.

> **Legal sovereignty**
> The location of ultimate power to make laws, together with the location of the source of all legal power within the political system. In the UK legal sovereignty lies in Parliament.

Party government

The British constitutional system can only operate in the context of party control. In particular, the arrangements concerning the operation of both Cabinet and the House of Commons depend upon the fact that a single party is in control of the executive branch and is usually able to control its majority in the Commons. The principles of collective responsibility, mandate and manifesto, government and opposition, and patronage all depend upon the reality that one party wins an election outright and forms a government alone.

If government lay in the hands of shifting coalitions and unstable governments, there would no longer be a central decision-making body – the Cabinet – which would be invariably unified and present a united front to Parliament. It would no longer be clear to the electorate what manifesto commitments they were voting for, and the way in which ministers are appointed and dismissed would have to placed on a more formal basis. Above all, the whole relationship between the executive and Parliament – which the former dominates – depends upon the dominance of parties and party control.

Unitary government

Finally, it should be re-stated that the UK is a unitary political system. Legal sovereignty is located at the centre, in one body – Parliament. Though a great deal of power has been decentralised through devolution, and much sovereignty has been delegated to the European Union, ultimately Parliament has the final say in all political and constitutional matters.

Sovereignty in the UK

Before considering this issue we need to remind ourselves of what we mean by the term 'sovereignty'.

Legal sovereignty is the ultimate power to make laws which will be enforced within the state.

Political sovereignty is where political power lies in reality. Whoever may possess legal sovereignty, *real* power lies with those bodies which are able to determine what political decisions are made.

Legal sovereignty in the UK lies firmly with Parliament. This means that no other body has the power to make laws or to overrule laws made by Parliament. This second point needs to be qualified, however, in the light of the UK's membership of the European Union. This is explored further below, but at this stage it is sufficient to say that Parliament can restore all its legal sovereignty at any time by withdrawing from the European Union.

It is also true that statutory powers can only be granted to a subsidiary body or a minister by Parliament. In such cases, Parliament is *delegating* its legal sovereignty – it can take it back at any time. Thus the Scottish Parliament has *primary* legislative powers under the Scotland Act 1998, but the Act could be repealed.

When we use the term, 'a parliament', it means the group of MPs which has been elected at each general election (together with the House of Lords over the same period). Thus each parliament normally exists for about four or five years between elections. Each successive parliament is legally sovereign. It is not bound by the laws made by previous parliaments. In theory, a new parliament can undo all the laws in existence (not that it would have the time to do so, of course)! Similarly, no single parliament can entrench any laws; it cannot prevent future parliaments from repealing or amending them. This is in contrast with New Zealand and Canada (neither of which has a codified constitution), where their parliaments can pass *Basic Laws*, which cannot be repealed in future without a special procedure.

Political sovereignty is a more difficult matter. We can certainly say that, at an election, the people become politically sovereign. They determine who shall make up both government and Parliament. They also choose between the competing manifestos of the parties. But between elections the people lose control of the decision-making process.

In general terms, we can say that it is the government which is politically sovereign. We expect that ministers will control the decision-making process. The executive branch dominates Parliament, and that is generally what we expect to happen. It is the government which has a mandate from the people and it is a tight-knit group of ministers from the same party that can provide firm political direction. Parliament may have the ultimate power to pass or veto proposed laws, but it is not normally expected that it should be a decision-making body.

At this stage, the question of the constitutional status of the monarch needs to be addressed. Confusingly, the monarch is sometimes referred to as the 'Sovereign' or as 'His/Her Sovereign Majesty'. But this is misleading. It refers to a historical reality that no longer persists. The monarch is certainly *technically* a part of Parliament and so shares its legal sovereignty, but this is only because Royal Assent is required to make bills into laws. As the monarch cannot realistically refuse such assent, this aspect of legal sovereignty is purely ceremonial. The status of the royal prerogative is a different matter, however.

As we have seen above, the prime minister, by convention, exercises the prerogative powers of the monarchy. These include the following:

- appointing and dismissing all government ministers;
- dissolving parliament and thereby calling general elections;
- creating peerages;
- granting honours such as knighthoods;
- appointing ambassadors;
- final appointment of senior judges and bishops of the Church of England;
- commanding the armed forces and declaring wars;
- agreeing foreign treaties;
- conducting relations with foreign powers;
- declaring a state of emergency and thus suspending normal government;
- granting pardons to convicted persons.

This represents an impressive amount of power. So the prime minister can be said to have a great deal of political sovereignty that is not controlled directly by Parliament. However, we need to add a word of caution here. It is conceivable – only *just* conceivable – that the monarch could take back his/her prerogative powers under exceptional circumstances. If, for example, a prime minister or government acted in a totally unconstitutional manner (e.g. taking powers not granted to it by

Parliament), it is possible that the monarch could dismiss them. More likely, if an election failed to produce a decisive result, the monarch might have to take it upon him/herself to appoint ministers in the absence of a clear candidate for the post of prime minister.

So the monarch could restore to him/herself political sovereignty in highly unusual circumstances. But for the most part (and certainly for the past century), the monarch is politically passive and powerless.

The EU and the constitution

Britain joined the European Community (now known as the European Union) on 1 January 1973. Parliament had passed the European Communities Act in 1972, allowing this to happen. It has had a profound effect on the UK's constitutional arrangements.

We should note at the outset that there are some areas of government jurisdiction which are virtually unaffected by membership of the EU. On the other hand, some policy areas are very deeply affected, so much so that they are largely controlled by the EU. In between these two extremes are a number of policy areas which are certainly influenced by membership of the EU, though they do not fall under European control. These are shown in the table below.

Areas where jurisdiction has passed largely to the EU	Areas where EU membership influences but does not control government policy	Areas where virtually no jurisdiction has passed to the EU
Trade	Economic policy	Education
Agriculture	Environmental protection	Health provision
Fishing	Defence	Social security
Employment law	Foreign policy	Law, order and justice
Consumer law	Overseas development	Moral legislation
Competition control	Asylum and immigration	Local government services
Regional economic development		Personal taxation
		Internal political system

So we can certainly say that the question of where political and legal sovereignty lie has been clouded. We can summarise the situation as follows:

- EU laws are superior to UK law. This was established in 1990 in the Factortame case (*Regina* versus *Secretary of State for Transport*) in the appeal court of the House of Lords. It was ruled that the Merchant Shipping Act, a UK law, was inferior to the EU fisheries regulations. In this case, Spanish fishing vessels were given rights to operate in British waters against the wishes of the UK Parliament.

- British courts must implement EU laws.
- Where an interpretation of EU law is required, it must be referred upwards to the European Court of Justice. Thus the House of Lords has ceased to be the highest court of appeal in all cases. This principle was established in the 1993 case, *Regina* versus *International Stock Exchange*, by Lord Bingham.
- For proposals that require a unanimous vote in the EU Council of Ministers to become EU law, the UK does not sacrifice sovereignty as it has an effective veto. For example, the UK has consistently vetoed any attempts to harmonise taxation throughout Europe.
- However, where proposals can become EU law with only a qualified majority vote (about 71 per cent) in the Council of Ministers, the UK must submit to the shared sovereignty of the EU.
- Parliament should not pass any statute which conflicts with existing EU law (for example, removing workers' rights guaranteed by the EU Social Chapter). If it does so, the courts will not enforce such a law.

Thus the constitutional status of the UK Parliament and the courts has been significantly altered by British membership of the EU.

A codified constitution for Britain?

The Liberal Democrat Party and the pressure group Charter 88 are the main proponents of a fully codified constitution for Britain. Elsewhere there is little appetite for such a major undertaking. But in some ways the question may have become irrelevant.

Arguably, Britain is in the process, particularly since 1997, of creating a codified constitution bit by bit. True, it may not be contained in a single document for the foreseeable future, but, increasingly, large parts of the constitution are now both written and, effectively, entrenched. The aspects of the constitution which conform to this analysis are as follows:

- The European Convention on Human Rights, brought into law by the Human Rights Act, is effectively a bill of rights. Though it could be fully or partly repealed in the future, it seems politically unlikely.
- The devolution Acts codify the powers enjoyed by the Scottish Parliament and the Welsh, Northern Ireland and Greater London Assemblies.
- The UK's relationship with the European Union is codified in the various treaties which Britain has signed, such as Maastricht and Nice.
- The public's right to see public information is codified in the Freedom of Information Act.
- The status and conduct of political parties is now codified in the Political Parties, Elections and Referendums Act.
- Important constitutional changes are effectively entrenched by the fact that they have been approved by referendum and can therefore only be repealed by referendum.
- The Electoral Commission has now created a codified set of rules for the conduct of elections and referendums.

So the old boast – or perhaps criticism – that the British constitution simply evolves and remains in the control of the Parliament of the day is out of date. Labour's stated intention to modernise the constitution has been substantially achieved in the sense that Britain's constitutional arrangements bear a closer resemblance to those of the rest of the democratic world than ever before. There is still no codified constitution, but the vast majority of Britain's constitutional arrangements are now certainly written.

The Arguments for a Codified Constitution

Those who argue that the British Constitution, though now largely written, should be properly codified cite the following arguments:

- A codified document would have an educative function in that it would clarify the nature of the constitution, which currently remains a mystery to large sections of the citizenry.
- Liberals, especially, argue that the lack of clarity has led to a gradual drift of power to the executive and to the prime minister. If the powers of parliament, the executive and the judiciary were clearly stated, there would be less opportunity for power to be transferred in an unplanned way.
- There are many recent developments in the political system, say critics, that have created confusion; a problem that would be solved by codification. The indistinct role of the growing number of political advisers in government is an example of this, as is the changing constitutional position of the cabinet (given that cabinet meetings have become less frequent, shorter and less meaningful).
- By codifying the constitution, it is suggested, we would also make it more difficult to change. Such entrenchment would prevent temporary governments trying to manipulate indistinct powers (such as the prime minister's uncodified prerogative powers) to their own advantage. The same is true of the rights of citizens. If these were part of a broader codified document, they would be less vulnerable to attacks by parliamentary legislation.
- Because there is no codified constitution, no action by parliament can be declared 'unconstitutional'. In other words the sovereignty of parliament means that government in general has unlimited competence. All modern democracies, it is pointed out by liberals, limit the power of government and parliament. The British constitution does not do this.
- Finally, there is a general feeling that, if Britain is to be considered a modern European state, it should conform to the 'normal' practice of being governed by a codified constitution.

The Arguments against Codification

■ Conservatives, in particular, argue that the current flexibility of the constitution is a good thing. It allows the constitution to adapt *naturally* to changing circumstances. So, for example, we have been able to adapt to the changing role of the monarchy and membership of the EU, without the need for major constitutional upheaval.

■ It can be suggested that codification will over-simplify the UK's constitutional arrangements. The very complex nature of relationships between government and parliament, between prime minister and government, between ministers and civil servants and so on cannot be codified accurately.

■ Again, conservatives often argue that codification is simply not necessary. The system works well and has done for centuries. Why, they say, should we create unnecessary problems when a solution is simply not required.

■ Britain, say many, is a unique political system and so does not need to conform to a European 'model'. The enduring stability of the British political system (in comparison to many European neighbours) suggests that current arrangements work well enough.

Problems of the British Constitution

Notwithstanding the arguments about codification, there are a number of problems associated with the British constitution which have been identified by critics, as follows:

■ As we have seen above, lack of codification creates a number of difficulties.

■ The flexibility of the constitution has allowed an unacceptable amount of power to drift towards the executive in general and the prime minister in particular.

■ Although the principle that human rights need to be protected has been accepted by all British parties, the Human Rights Act does not prevent parliament setting aside such rights. This has been done, for example, in much of the recent legislation to deal with the threat of terrorism.

■ The importance of unwritten conventions is often criticised. Such conventions govern many of the powers of the prime minister, for example, and this is seen as a dangerous situation, causing both confusion and excessive executive power. The Salisbury convention, which limits the power of the House of Lords, is also seen as uncertain and has caused a number of problems in disputes between the Commons and the Lords.

■ The independence of the judiciary has been called into question. The Lord Chancellor, head of the courts system, has been a member of the cabinet, giving rise to claims of political interference (there are current proposals to end this anomaly). The prime minister also retains a veto

over which individuals should be promoted to the senior judiciary, again giving rise to fears of political influence.

- The principle of parliamentary sovereignty means that there are no limits to what government can do if it can secure parliamentary consent. This, say liberals, is extremely dangerous and should be addressed by establishing firm constitutional limits to the power of the state.
- In more general terms, the lack of a real separation of powers – notably between the government and parliament – is seen as undemocratic. Without a system of 'checks and balances' (as they are described in the USA) to regulate the system, there are fears that power will continue to drift towards the executive.

KEY CONCEPTS

Constitution

A set of principles, which may be written or unwritten, that set out the distribution of power within a political system, relationships between political institutions, the limits of government jurisdiction, the rights of citizens and the method of amending the constitution itself.

Constitutional government

Government that is limited by a constitution and by constitutional principles.

Parliamentary sovereignty

The British principle that Parliament is the source of all political power (with the exception of the prerogative powers of the prime minister) and that all enforceable laws must be approved by Parliament.

Legal sovereignty

The location of ultimate power to make laws, together with the location of the source of all legal power within the political system. In the UK legal sovereignty lies in Parliament.

Revision topics and examination questions

Revision topics

- Nature and functions of constitutions
- Nature of codification and entrenchment
- Sources of the British constitution
- Main features and characteristics of the British constitution
- Federal and unitary constitutions
- Sovereignty and parliamentary sovereignty
- Impact of the EU on the British constitution
- Arguments concerning codification
- Problems of the UK constitution

Short answers (approx. 50–100 words)

- What are the functions of a constitution?
- What is a codified constitution?
- Distinguish between a federal and a unitary constitution.
- What is parliamentary sovereignty?
- Identify any THREE sources of the British constitution.
- Identify any THREE features of the British constitution.
- What is meant by constitutionalism?
- What is the rule of law?

Medium answers (approx. 250 words)

- What are the sources of the British constitution?
- Where does sovereignty lie in the UK?
- Which parts of the British constitution are written?
- What are the main features of the British constitution?

Long answers (approx. 500 words)

- What has been the impact of the EU on the British constitution?
- What are the advantages of an uncodified constitution?
- What are the advantages of a codified constitution?
- Where does sovereignty lie in the UK?
- What are the main problems associated with the UK constitution?

Resources and Web Guide

Books

The classic work on the British constitution was written in 1867 by journalist Walter Bagehot. Though clearly dated, it is an interesting insight:
Walter Bagehot, *The English Constitution*, various editions.
A very detailed account (perhaps too detailed for all but the most committed students) is given by:
Peter Hennessy, *The Hidden Wiring*, Gollancz, 1995.
Perhaps the single chapter on the constitution from Gillian Peele's work is best for modest further reading:
Gillian Peele, *Governing the UK*, Blackwell, 2004.
A book that covers both the current state of the constitution and some reform issues is:
Robert Hazell, *Constitutional Futures: A History of the Next Ten Years*, OUP, 1999.

Useful websites

The best site for comprehensive information is:
www.ucl.ac.uk/constitution-unit/ (accessed 11 November 2005)
The government service on the constitution is published by the department for constitutional affairs:
www.dca.gov.uk (accessed 11 November 2005)
The main campaign group for reform is Charter 88:
www.charter88.org.uk (accessed 11 November 2005)

2.2
Parliament

Introduction

Parliament is normally known as the 'legislature'. This suggests that it is mainly concerned with making law (from the Latin *legis*, meaning 'of the law'). This is undoubtedly appropriate, but it would be a mistake to assume therefore that lawmaking is Parliament's primary function. It is not. As we shall see below, most laws certainly do have to pass through parliamentary procedure, but this is not to say that *making* law is what Parliament does. It is more accurate to say that it makes laws *legitimate.*

So if Parliament is not primarily a lawmaking body, we will have to ask what its main purposes are. This chapter will explore the functions of Parliament, explain how it carries them out and evaluate how well it performs them.

It is perhaps worth examining briefly the historic role of Parliament, as such a perspective can help us to understand many of its current activities and procedures.

From the Middle Ages onwards it became the practice of English monarchs to call together representatives of the aristocracy (a council which became the House of Lords) and of the boroughs (towns) and the counties (a gathering that became the House of Commons). It is immediately interesting to note that early parliaments were called by the monarch him/herself, not by the people. Thus Parliament existed to assist the monarch rather than as an expression of democracy.

Parliaments up to the latter part of the seventeenth century had two main functions: one was to give legitimacy to laws that the monarch wished to see enacted; the other was to give consent to taxation (taxation also implied expenditure on a war or a public building, etc.). There have been lengthy periods when monarchs attempted to govern without Parliament, but these became increasingly brief as time went by. Indeed, it was Charles I who paid the ultimate price for attempting to govern without Parliament (he was executed in 1649). King Charles' successors certainly learned the lesson!

In other words, the role of Parliament was to *support* the monarch, not to *control* his/her power. Though Parliament insisted on being consulted, its role was subordinate to the monarchy through most of its history. To some extent this legacy remains to this day, except that we have replaced the monarchy with the elected government of the day.

Parliament did demand something in return for its support. This was the 'redress of grievances'. The Commons, in particular, expected that the monarch would listen to the complaints of the representatives on behalf of the inhabitants of their boroughs or counties. Many such disputes were

about tax, of course, but there would also be problems of land tenure, inheritance and military service, for example.

It was only after the Glorious Revolution of 1689, when the Stuart monarchy was replaced by William and Mary, that we can say that Parliament began to assume its current role. At that time, responsibility for legislation began to pass decisively from the monarch to Parliament. But even then it was not expected that Parliament would actually *initiate* any legislation. This function was gradually transferred from the monarch to the leaders of Parliament, that is, the most prominent Members of both Houses. It was this leadership group which eventually was to become the more formal *Cabinet*, and the Cabinet's most senior figure became known as prime minister in the 1720s. By the end of the nineteenth century, Cabinet also came to be exclusively made up of leading members of the dominant party in Parliament.

If we look back at this brief parliamentary history, we can see that the basic functions of Parliament remain the same as they always were. Parliament exists to make government legitimate, to give consent to legislation without actually making that legislation, to approve the government's financial arrangements and, in return, to expect to raise grievances against the government and thus make it accountable. On the whole, therefore, Parliament's key role – or at least the role of the governing majority – is to support government, not to threaten it. But one additional major function has been added. This is Parliament's ability to dismiss a government through a vote of no confidence. This reserve power, a constant reality that governments are aware of, means that every government must make itself responsible to Parliament.

Parliamentary and presidential government

Before proceeding, it is important to make clear the constitutional basis of parliamentary government. At the same time, it can usefully be contrasted with presidential government, as it operates in the USA, to bring into focus its important elements.

Parliamentary government implies the following features:

- Parliament is the main (in the UK the *only*) source of political authority. That is, political power may only be exercised if it has been authorised by Parliament.
- The government must be drawn from Parliament – either the Commons or the Lords. In other words, all members of the government must also be Members of one of the two Houses.
- Therefore, there is no strict **separation of powers** between the legislature and the executive.
- Government must be accountable to Parliament.

As we can see, these principles place Parliament at the very centre of the British political system.

Parliamentary government

A system of politics where government is drawn from Parliament and is accountable to Parliament. In other words, the government has no separate authority from that of Parliament.

Separation of powers

A constitutional principle, that the three branches of government – legislature, executive and judiciary – should have separate membership, separate powers and should be able to control each other's powers. It is largely absent in the UK.

Presidential government

In contrast to parliamentary government, a president normally has a separate source of authority from that of the legislature. This means that the executive (president) is accountable to the people directly, not to the legislature.

Presidential government (the American model mainly) is quite different. These are its main features:

- The legislature and the executive (in the form of the presidency) have separate sources of authority. They are elected separately.
- The president is not part of the legislature.
- The president (and therefore executive government as a whole) is accountable directly to the people, not to the legislature.
- There is a clear separation of powers between the executive and the legislature.
- This implies that there must be a codified constitutional arrangement which separates those powers.

Parliamentary sovereignty

This is perhaps the most important reality in the whole of the British political system. The general meaning of the term 'sovereignty' is explained in the introduction to this book, but it is important to place this concept in the context of Parliament itself.

Parliament in the UK is aid to be *legally sovereign*. This means the following:

- Parliament is the source of all political power. No individual or body may exercise power unless it has been granted by Parliament. In effect, of course, Parliament does delegate most of its powers – to ministers, to devolved governments in Scotland, Wales and sometimes Northern Ireland, to local authorities and to the courts of law.
- Parliament may restore to itself any powers which have been delegated to others. For example, in 2003 it was decided to suspend the powers of the Northern Ireland Assembly and return them to Westminster.
- Parliament may make any laws it wishes and they shall be enforced by the courts and other authorities. There are no restrictions on what laws Parliament may make. In this sense, Parliament is said to be *omnicompetent* (literally, capable of any act). For example, it may take away rights or add to our statutory rights.
- Parliament is not bound by its predecessors. In other words, laws passed by parliaments in the past are not binding on the current parliament. Existing laws may be amended or repealed at will.
- Parliament cannot bind its successors. This means that the current parliament cannot pass any laws which will prevent future parliaments from amending or repealing them. In effect, therefore, we can say that laws cannot be *entrenched* against future change. For this reason, Britain cannot have a fixed, entrenched constitution as long as the current principle of parliamentary sovereignty endures.

If, on the other hand, we consider another type of sovereignty – **political sovereignty** – we can certainly say that Parliament has lost much of its sovereignty. Political sovereignty refers not to strictly *legal* power, but to

where political power lies *in reality*. It is the practical rather than theoretical location of power.

In reality, most political power lies with government. Normally the government of the day enjoys a majority in the House of Commons and can therefore virtually guarantee that its proposals will be passed by Parliament. It is sometimes said, therefore, that *the sovereignty of parliament is, in reality, the sovereignty of the majority party*. It is generally understood that the government has an electoral mandate to carry out its manifesto commitments and Parliament should not thwart that authority. We expect Parliament to block government plans only if government is seen to be abusing its mandate or operating beyond it. In addition, of course, at a general election, political sovereignty returns to the people, who are both electing a new parliament and giving a new government a fresh mandate.

Before we dismiss Parliament as the sovereign body in theory only, we must remember that Parliament retains enormous *reserve* powers. In some circumstances it can block legislation (in modern times the House of Lords does this quite frequently), and in really exceptional circumstances (as discussed above) Parliament can dismiss a government by passing a vote of no confidence. This rare event last occurred in 1979 when James Callaghan's Labour government was dismissed by a majority of just one vote. More recently, in 2005, the Commons voted down a proposal to allow security forces to hold terrorist suspects for up to 90 days without charge or trial.

In summary, therefore, we can say that Parliament in the UK is legally sovereign, but that political sovereignty is less clearly located. It lies with the people at elections, with the government between elections, but with the proviso that Parliament can ultimately overrule the government.

The erosion of parliamentary sovereignty

There are four main senses in which it can be said that parliamentary sovereignty has been eroded. These are:

1. Clearly, a great deal of legislative power has moved to the European Union. European law is superior to British law, so if there is any conflict, European Union law must prevail. At the same time, Parliament may not pass any law that conflicts with European Union law. There remain large areas of policy which have not passed to Brussels, including criminal law, tax law, social security, health and education, but there are also significant shifts of legislative authority – over trade, environment, employment rights and consumer protection, for example.
2. As we have seen above, executive power has grown considerably in recent decades. This involves a transfer of political, but not legal sovereignty.
3. It is increasingly the practice to hold referendums when important constitutional changes are being proposed, such as devolution or the election of city mayors. Although the results of such referendums are

not technically binding on Parliament, it is almost inconceivable that Parliament would ignore the popular will of the people. So, in effect, sovereignty in such cases returns to the people.

4. Finally, there is devolution, especially to Scotland. As with referendums, Parliament can restore to itself all the powers that it has delegated, but it is difficult to imagine circumstances in which the powers granted to the Scottish Parliament and the Welsh Assembly would be removed. Here again, sovereignty has been transferred in reality, though not in constitutional law.

So we could say that parliamentary sovereignty is now something of a myth. But before we jump to such a conclusion we must remind ourselves again of Parliament's reserve powers. Britain can, at any time, leave the European Union and so restore all her sovereignty. Parliament can thwart the will of the government, devolution could be cancelled – bear in mind that the Northern Ireland Assembly has been suspended and direct rule from London restored on several occasions. Parliament could, under exceptional circumstances, decide not to accept the verdict of a referendum. Furthermore, if there comes a time when the government does not enjoy a secure parliamentary majority, it could be that the balance of power – both legal and political – could return to Parliament, much as it did in the middle part of the nineteenth century.

The structure of Parliament

Parliament is divided into three parts. These are the House of Commons (known as the *Lower House*), the House of Lords (known as the *Upper House*) and the King/Queen-in-Parliament. The House of Lords is known as the Upper House, not because it is senior or more important, but as a reflection of its more illustrious history. In practice, and paradoxically, the House of Commons is considered the senior chamber, even though it remains the Lower House in name.

One aspect of this triple personality – the monarchy – is immediately puzzling, especially as the monarch is not welcome at the Palace of Westminster except when s/he is performing the ceremonial opening of the new session of Parliament, normally in the autumn. Indeed, the monarch is never allowed in the House of Commons. This is a relic of past occasions when the monarch's presence in the chamber was seen as a direct threat to the independence of its Members. So the Queen must deliver her annual speech in the Lords. The only reason, today, why the Queen is considered part of the legislature is that proposed legislation requires her signature (the Royal Assent) to become legitimate. But the monarch plays no *active* role in parliamentary politics and Royal Assent has not been refused since 1707 (as described above).

The following table shows the make-up of the House of Commons as of September 2005.

Party	Male MPs	Female MPs	Total
Labour	257	98	355
Conservative	181	17	198
Liberal Democrat	53	9	62
Democratic Unionist Party*	8	1	9
Scottish Nationalist Party	6	0	6
Sinn Fein*	4	1	5
Plaid Cymru	3	0	3
SDLP*	3	0	3
Independents	2	0	2
Respect Party	1	0	1
Ulster Unionist Party*	0	1	1
The Speaker (neutral)	1	0	1
Totals	519	127	646

Government majority = 165

*Northern Ireland parties

FIG 2.1A The House of Commons at work

We can now examine Parliament in more detail.

Plenary sessions

Neither the House of Lords nor the Commons meets very often in full, or plenary, session. Indeed, there are not nearly enough seats for all the Members! The occasions when the Houses are full are normally for Prime Minister's Question Time (PMQT) in the Commons every Wednesday, or when a great issue of the day is to be debated. In recent years the debates on the banning of hunting with dogs, the 2003 war in Iraq, the 2001 Anti-terrorism Act and student tuition fees have all attracted full Houses. But for the most part the two chambers are only part filled. It is true that all loyal party Members are expected to *vote* on government legislation, but this does not mean that Members of either House have to be present during debates.

Standing committees of either House

The term 'standing' committee is misleading. In fact, these committees are specially formed for each separate bill. They are, in reality, temporary. They normally contain between 15 and 50 members (depending on the impor-tance and complexity of the legislation under consideration). All MPs and peers have to take their turn at sitting on these committees. A relevant govern-ment minister sits on each committee, together with specialist spokespersons from the other main parties. The committees' role is to examine each piece of legislation as it passes through the House. Proposed amendments to bills are debated in committee and inserted if a majority on the committee votes in favour. Amendments vary from attempts merely to clarify the wording of a bill, to fundamental changes which will alter the application of the law.

Before we assume that this role grants much power to MPs and peers, we must be aware that these committees are not free from party discipline. The governing party is always granted a majority on the committees (that is, positions are allocated in rough proportion to party membership in the two Houses as a whole). Party loyalty is expected to apply in committee. Members of the governing party are required only to vote for amendments that are approved by the government (indeed, many amendments are proposed by ministers as a result of consultations with pressure groups or other interested parties). Similarly, governing party members normally vote against any amendment that is not approved by government. It is rare for an amendment to succeed against government wishes.

The government does have a further precaution against unwanted amendments. Any changes proposed in the House of Lords committees must also be approved by the House of Commons. It is normal that Lords' amendments that are hostile to government intentions will be overturned in the Commons. However, as we shall see below, the Lords can make such a nuisance of itself, holding up important legislation in standing commit-tees, that the government will sometimes be forced to concede. Unwanted amendments from House of Commons standing committees can also be overturned when the *Report Stage* is reached. The whole House in plenary session is invited to vote on proposed amendments and the party whips can get to work at this point, reversing unwanted changes.

Membership of standing committees can be a frustrating experience and it is not a particularly popular role for Members. Of course, MPs and peers who have a special interest in and/or experience of a particular issue will be keen to be on a particular committee and will request to be allocated accordingly. It should also be pointed out that pressure groups tend to be very active at this committee stage of a bill's progress through Parliament. They seek to persuade both committee members and relevant ministers to include amendments that are supportive of their cause. It is in committee that any changes can be made.

Committees of the whole House

In the House of Lords it is often, though not always, the case, that the committee (amendment) stage of a bill is considered by plenary session of the whole House. In the Commons, however, such 'committees of the whole House' are rare. When a bill is of special significance, and if it is of constitutional significance (i.e. it is about the structure and powers of government), a committee of the whole House of Commons will be called. But here again, party discipline applies.

Departmental select committees in the House of Commons

There are 18 such committees, each one of which is concerned with a specific area of government responsibility (i.e. they mostly shadow a government department).

The following 18 departmental select committees existed in September 2005:

- Constitutional Affairs
- Culture, Media and Sports
- Defence
- Education and Skills
- Environment, Food and Rural Affairs
- Foreign Affairs
- Health
- Home Affairs
- Housing, Planning, Local Government and the Regions
- International Development
- Northern Ireland
- Scottish Affairs
- Science and Technology
- Trade and Industry
- Transport
- Treasury (Finance)
- Welsh Affairs
- Work and Pensions

Select committees are normally made up of 11 members, chosen by the parliamentary liaison committee. Although this selection committee has a degree of independence, a great deal of pressure is applied by party whips to get their own choices nominated. The chairperson of these committees is a significant parliamentary personality, with a good deal of influence. Such positions are, therefore, much sought after. Although the governing party has a majority of its members on select committees, all members are expected to behave in a non-partisan, neutral fashion. Indeed, when the select committees produce their reports, the chair will normally attempt to achieve unanimous support for their conclusions. If the members simply split along party lines, reports have little interest for Parliament as a whole. A unanimous report, on the other hand, carries significant weight.

The select committees have considerable powers. They can call for ministers, civil servants, external witnesses and official papers in their investigations. Their role is multi-faceted and includes the following tasks:

- To investigate the work of government departments to determine whether they have acted efficiently and effectively.
- To consider major departmental policies, determining whether they are well considered and have taken into account relevant opinions.
- To consider proposed legislation, not with a view to blocking it, but to decide whether it is likely to be effective.
- To consider matters of major public concern which fall within the remit of the committee and the government department which it shadows.
- To investigate any serious errors or omissions made by the department, making recommendations to correct the problem.
- Occasionally to propose future legislation where there is an overwhelming need.

This is a wide range of responsibilities and their work is taken seriously. In addition, they tend to adopt an adversarial style of questioning which can, on occasions, be aggressive. Indeed, many ministers and civil servants have admitted to approaching select committee hearings with some trepidation.

The committees have a small research staff to assist them, and, after years of service, the MPs can develop a high degree of knowledge and experience. Most select committee members end up serving for more years than the ministers they are investigating.

There is no equivalent of departmental committees in the House of Lords.

The following extract shows the programme of activities of the Select Committee on Defence for 2005–06.

At its first meeting on Tuesday 19 July 2005, the Foreign Affairs Select Committee:
- elected Mike Gapes MP (Labour) as its Chairman;
- agreed to carry out a continuing inquiry into Foreign Policy Aspects of the War against Terrorism, with a particular focus in the Autumn of 2005 on the Middle East and on the Arabian peninsula;

- agreed to inquire into the Foreign and Commonwealth Office's Departmental Annual Report for 2004–05, including the work of the British Council and the BBC World Service;
- agreed to inquire into Human Rights, basing its inquiry on the FCO's Annual Report on Human Rights for 2005;
- agreed to conduct a continuing inquiry into Developments in the European Union.

Further announcements of oral evidence sessions to be held in October and of deadlines for receipt of written evidence will be made in due course.

Source: House of Commons

Other select committees of either House

There are a number of committees in Parliament as a whole that deal with domestic issues with which we need not concern ourselves here. However, a number of committees are of political significance.

The most important select committee is the **Public Accounts Committee** (PAC), the oldest in Parliament. It is a highly independent body, so much so that its chairperson is, by tradition, a Member of the Opposition. The PAC is charged with the task of investigating the financial arrangements of the government. In particular, it checks that public spending has been used for the purpose intended by Parliament. In this respect it is also searching for any possible examples of corruption (mercifully very rare in British politics), but its main work has proved to be investigations of how efficiently public money has been used. Its reports often highlight examples of government wastefulness and inefficiency. Membership of the PAC is much sought after by MPs.

The **Standards and Privileges Committee** is concerned mainly with standards of public life. It deals with disciplinary matters against MPs and comments on the way in which ministers and other public officials have conducted their relationship with Parliament. The **Statutory Instruments Committee** exists to check the government's use of 'secondary legislation' (Acts of Parliament are known as 'primary legislation'). Parliament grants wide powers to ministers to make detailed legislation without recourse to parliamentary debate. The device used by ministers for this purpose is known as a 'statutory instrument'. Though Parliament does not debate these, it is important that a check is kept on the use of such powers. This committee looks at statutory instruments and alerts Parliament to any that might be contentious.

Both Houses of Parliament have **European Scrutiny Committees**, whose role it is to examine proposed legislation or regulations coming from the European Commission. They may alert Parliament as a whole to any concerns they have. In particular, they attempt to guide ministers in their negotiations with the Commission and their European partners. Finally, the **Liaison Committee** of the Commons determines which Members shall sit on which committees. The committee is heavily lobbied by the party whips, so a good deal of negotiation has to be undertaken.

It would be a mistake to overemphasise the power and influence of these committees. They are a vital part of the process of making government accountable, but they suffer from the problem of lacking any powers of enforcement. They can criticise, publicise and recommend action, but there is no guarantee that their conclusions will result in action. That said, a sample of some recent reports of important action made by select committees demonstrates that they do sometimes find themselves at the centre of major controversy.

Committee	Report	Detail
Foreign Affairs	Pergau Dam, 1994	Revealed apparent connection between a decision to fund a new dam in Malaysia with an arms deal with that country. Its criticisms seriously embarrassed the government.
Treasury	Barings Bank, 1996	A report which was highly critical of the Bank of England in its failure to discover the financial plight of a major bank which subsequently collapsed.
Culture, Media and Sport	National Lottery, 2000	Critical of the operation of the National Lottery.
Public Accounts	Passports, 2000	A critical report when the Passport Office's new computer system caused major delays in the granting of passports.
Education and Skills	Literacy, 2005	Critical of government's literacy strategy in schools and urging a full-scale inquiry.

The Speakers

Both Houses have a Speaker, whose role it is to oversee the debates, select speakers from the floor and to arrange the business of their House with party leaders. They are expected to be entirely neutral and even-handed.

The Speaker of the Commons is a senior MP who is elected by the House. It is someone who has no political ambitions and so is prepared to retire from party politics. The current (2005) Speaker, Michael Martin, was a Labour MP, but has a high reputation for his fairness. He has three deputies who sit in for him on occasions, drawn from the main parties.

The Speaker of the Lords is the Lord Chancellor (who sits on the famous Woolsack). Unlike his Commons counterpart, the Lord Chancellor is a political figure, who has a place in Cabinet. When he presides over the proceedings of the Lords, therefore, he must ensure that he remains neutral. When he wishes to contribute to a debate, he leaves the Woolsack and is replaced by a deputy.

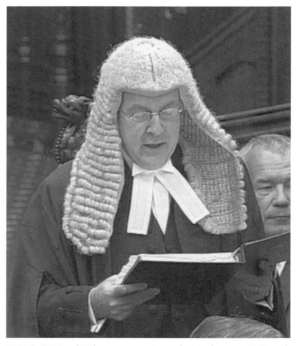

FIG 2.2B Lord Falconer, secretary of state for constitutional affairs, was charged with the task of setting up the new supreme court

The functions of Parliament

As we have seen above, it would be wrong to see Parliament as primarily a legislature in the strict sense of the word. Parliament does *pass* law, but it does not usually *make* law. Professor Philip Norton, a leading constitutional expert, has classified parliaments in various countries into three main types:

1. Policy-making legislatures.
2. Policy-influencing legislatures.
3. Weak legislatures.

Norton suggested that the British Parliament falls into the second category, though many might argue it belongs in the third. In order to make such a judgement, we need to examine the role of Parliament in more detail.

Legitimation

Our brief history of Parliament demonstrated that a traditional role was to provide consent for the monarch's legislation. This remains a key function today. Although any government enjoys a mandate from the electorate, it is still important that its authority to legislate is underpinned by Parliament. For any law or executive action to be implemented and respected, parliamentary sanction is required. This is effectively granting popular consent *indirectly*. In short, Parliament is making legislation legitimate. In this sense, Parliament is supporting government, not challenging it.

As Parliament is acting on behalf of the people, it is clear that the House of Commons plays the leading role in this regard as it is elected. The unelected House of Lords cannot claim the same authority.

We can also employ the term 'promulgation' to describe this function. The formal procedures by which laws are passed (see details below) serves the purpose of proclaiming the law and announcing its legitimacy.

Scrutiny

Though Parliament does not normally make law, it has the important function of scrutinising proposed legislation. Scrutiny involves close inspection, and where it is seen as necessary, amendments may be proposed. Detailed scrutiny is carried out by standing committees of both Houses (see above) and more generalised consideration by plenary sessions of each House.

In this respect, Parliament is representing various interests in society, ensuring that unnecessary discrimination does not take place, that minorities are not unfairly discriminated against and that laws will be clear in their application. Scrutiny does not normally involve blocking legislation, but important changes can be proposed and accepted.

It is not only major, or primary, legislation which is scrutinised. Parliament also looks at secondary legislation – decisions made by ministers under statutory powers granted by Parliament – and at proposed European laws or regulations. It is not expected that Parliament will make substantial changes to such legislation, but it does warn and inform government as far as it can.

Opposition

This function only applies to the parties which do not make up government. In other words, the opposition parties. Governments virtually always enjoy a majority in the House of Commons. So opposition does not imply that any proposals will be defeated on the floor of the House. The government does not command a loyal majority in the Lords, but it is understood that occasions when the Lords can defy the government and the Commons will be rare and exceptional. Opposition is more of a ritualised process, but one which nevertheless plays an important role.

It is expected that parliamentary politics in Britain will be *adversarial* in nature. That is, whenever government makes a proposal, it normally expects it to be robustly challenged in Parliament. This process ensures that the government is forced to explain and justify its policies. The opposition parties do not expect to overturn the government majority, but they do hope to expose any weaknesses in the government's position. It is often said that *the role of the opposition is to oppose.* This apparently bland expression suggests that all proposals have to be challenged as a matter of course. It is a process which ensures that government prepares its case effectively.

Accountability

In a modern democracy the accountability of government is essential. At election times, of course, government becomes directly accountable to the people. Thus, in 2005, when the Labour Government saw its popular support fall, from 41 per cent of the voters in 2001, to just over 36 per cent, the people were delivering something of a negative verdict on Labour's performance (even though the government survived). But continuous accountability is not yet feasible, so Parliament must act on behalf of the people between elections.

Accountability implies a number of activities:

- It means forcing the government, its ministers in particular, to justify their policies, explaining why they were developed and what their effects are likely to be.
- It may mean criticism of those policies. Obviously it is mainly the role of opposition parties to criticise, but MPs representing the government party itself may also have their say.
- For opposition parties, accountability can also imply the presentation of alternatives to the government's proposals. This represents a more positive form of criticism.
- Where it is believed that serious errors have taken place, it is largely the role of Parliament to expose such mistakes. The doctrine of **individual ministerial responsibility** is particularly relevant here.

Individual ministerial responsibility

This doctrine suggests that every minister is individually responsible for *all* the activities of his/her department. Ministers are also responsible for their own personal conduct, quite naturally. Responsibility means that they must be prepared to face criticism from Parliament, including its select committees, and in extreme circumstances it is expected that they should resign.

The issue of when ministers are expected to resign is a contentious one. It used to be the case – perhaps until the 1970s – that *any* serious mistake made within a department, whether or not the minister knew anything about it, should result in ministerial resignation. In other words, ministers were considered to be responsible for the actions of their own senior civil servants. It was, in fact, considered a matter of honour that the minister was responsible. The principle has been considerably eroded in recent decades, however.

Perhaps the most celebrated example of the doctrine at work occurred in 1982, when Foreign Secretary Lord Carrington resigned. He accepted responsibility (it has never been clarified whether his department was *actually* responsible) for the fact that British forces were unprepared for the Argentine invasion of the British Falkland Islands in that year. More recently, Estelle Morris (Education Secretary) resigned in 2002 over the generally poor performance of her department, and in the same year Stephen Byers was forced to resign as Trade and Industry Secretary, when his own personal advisers had been accused of behaving unprofessionally.

But ministers today are more likely to hang on to their jobs when serious errors are revealed. Michael Howard, for example, suffered a number of embarrassing criticisms over his running of the prison service when he was Home Secretary in the 1990s, but he survived. Similarly, Defence Secretary Geoff Hoon refused to resign, despite a number of problems relating to the inadequate equipping of British forces in the 2003 Iraq war. In practice, it is up to the prime minister whether a minister takes the rap. Once a minister has lost the confidence of the prime minister, s/he is likely to be undermined by excessive errors.

Where personal conduct is concerned, however, ministerial resignations are more common. In 2004, for example, Home Secretary David Blunkett was forced to resign following a major parliamentary and media campaign against him. His error was to be discovered to have interfered with a visa application for a member of his mistress's domestic staff (interestingly enough, the demands for his resignation did not concern his having a married mistress in the first place!). But it was during the 1990s that resignations over personal conduct reached their height. In the so-called era of 'Tory sleaze', a succession of ministers were forced out of office as a result of sexual or financial scandals. Perhaps the best known of these was Neil Hamilton, a junior minister who became involved in the 'cash-for-questions' scandal. Outside interests were found to be paying MPs and junior ministers to ask parliamentary questions to bring their interests to the public attention. This is against parliamentary rules and Hamilton, who had to admit his role in the practice, resigned in a blaze of publicity.

It is more difficult for ministers to resist calls for their resignation over personal conduct than over political errors. In essence, Parliament has more influence over the former than the latter. It has become difficult, therefore, to assert that individual ministerial responsibility is effective. What we can say is that it is often the case that an individual minister is required to accept responsibility for problems so as to save the embarrassment of the government as a whole.

It should be pointed out that Parliament does not have the power to remove an individual minister from office. Only the prime minister can do that. Parliament can only apply pressure for a resignation and often MPs do not succeed. Conversely, however, Parliament can remove the government as a whole. But as we shall see below, the removal of the whole government, through a vote of no confidence, will normally result in a general election. MPs, especially from the governing party, are naturally reluctant to precipitate a general election in which many of them may lose their seats. Turkeys, as they say, do not vote for Christmas!

So accountability normally stops short of forcing resignations and involves investigation and criticism. There are a number of ways in which Parliament can call government to account.

Questions to Ministers

Questions to Ministers is the best-known device for calling government to account. Every minister is expected to appear regularly in the House (ministers who are peers will also face questions in the Lords). They will face many questions from MPs, some of which are expected (notice must be given), some of which are unexpected (notice is not needed for

FIG 2.2C Government ministers must be accountable to parliament

supplementary questions). Questions may be relatively gentle, being designed merely to obtain factual information. Others, however, may be hostile and can create a good deal of discomfort. Ministers must face criticism and be prepared to answer it. Many questions are also written, in which case the minister (in fact, his senior civil servants) has time to frame an answer. Written questions are much less hostile than oral questions.

MPs relish the opportunity to question ministers, especially in areas of special interest to them. It is one of the rare occasions when they feel they may be able to make an impact, freed from the discipline of the party whips. It is also vital that ministers know that, whatever their department does, they may be subject to parliamentary scrutiny at some stage. But it also has to be said that the ministers have a great advantage in such exchanges. They have an army of civil servants to prepare answers for them. MPs do not have access to this kind of help. Clever ministers are also able to deflect attention away from their shortcomings and are notoriously difficult to pin down with sensitive material.

Prime Minister's Question Time (PMQT) used to be an occasion for making the head of government accountable. For many years, however, it has taken on the form of an occasion which has been reduced to a ritualised contest between party leaders. It is designed more as a media show than an attempt to shed light on the activities of the government. It is entertaining to the public and to MPs, but does little to support accountability.

The following is an extract from the proceedings of the House of Commons on 14 July 2005. A junior minister, Bill Rammell (on behalf of his boss, Ruth Kelly), is being questioned about sixth-form colleges. It can be seen in the extract that not only are MPs concerned with sixth-form

colleges in general, but they are also seeking to publicise the plight of colleges in *their own constituencies.*

Kelvin Hopkins (Luton, North) (Lab): If she [the Secretary of State for Education and Skills – Ruth Kelly] will ensure that successful sixth-form colleges are not closed.

The Minister for Higher Education and Lifelong Learning (Bill Rammell): The Secretary of State considers proposed changes to 16-to-19 provision, including to sixth-form colleges, in the light of the needs and interests of young people in a given area. There may be instances where local plans include the closure of a sixth-form college as part of a reorganisation that is intended better to meet the needs of local learners. Individual cases are decided by the Secretary of State on their merit.

Kelvin Hopkins: I thank my hon. Friend for his answer, but I am not fully reassured about the future of sixth-form colleges. I should declare an interest, in that I am vice-chair of the governors of Luton Sixth Form College. As he will know, it recently received a grade 1 rating following its inspection, and it has beacon status. Permitting feeder schools to establish sixth forms will completely undermine entrance to sixth-form colleges, and their future could be in doubt. Such colleges are among the best institutions in our education system, and I hope that my hon. Friend can reassure me that they are guaranteed a future, and that we will have more of them, rather than less.

Bill Rammell: I certainly think that sixth-form colleges can contribute to raising standards in the locality. I am aware of my hon. Friend's concerns; indeed, he has written to Ministers about this issue. The reality is that the area-wide Ofsted inspection of 16-to-19 provision in the Luton area concluded that it was poor, and I welcome the fact that Luton colleges and schools are now working together to respond to that. However, I am not aware of any proposals to close a college within Luton as part of that process. Should any such proposals be submitted, they would be looked at on their merits. However, it is right for us to look towards the expansion of sixth forms within 11-to-16 schools, particularly where it can increase choice and drive up standards. Further to our commitment given during the general election, we will shortly be producing guidelines setting out how best to achieve that.

David Lepper (Brighton, Pavilion) (Lab/Co-op): To support successful sixth-form colleges such as Varndean and Brighton, Hove and Sussex sixth-form colleges in the city of Brighton and Hove, will the Minister undertake to look again at the inequalities in funding between sixth-form colleges and school sixth forms? Will he also consider, in particular, liability for VAT on the part of sixth-form colleges and capital allowances for the development of extensions?

Bill Rammell: I thank my hon. Friend for that question. I accept that there is a funding gap between schools and colleges and I have to admit that that is a direct result of the Government's extra investment in schools – and I am not going to apologise for that. In 2002–03, we estimated the funding gap at 10.5 per cent. Since then, we have brought up the overall funding levels for sixth-form colleges and further education colleges, which has resulted in that gap shrinking significantly. We want to make further progress, but we can do so only if the resources are available.

Source: Hansard

Select committees

Select committees, especially departmental select committees of the House of Commons, are a different matter altogether. Committees of 9–11 MPs have the power to question, and indeed cross-examine, ministers, their civil servants and any witnesses they may call from external organisations. Unlike Questions to Ministers, there is no ritual, and questioning may go on for some time. Furthermore, MPs usually spend several years on the committees and so develop a good deal of knowledge and expertise. The examples of important select committee reports shown above demonstrates how significant they have become since they were introduced in 1979.

The extract below shows some of the main recommendations in the report of the Select Committee on Defence of March 2005 into the post-war situation for British forces in Iraq. It can be seen that this part of the report is both critical and congratulatory of British forces. We can also be impressed by the detailed information that is contained in the report's conclusions. Such detail is the result of the extensive questioning of witnesses that took place during the investigation.

CONCLUSIONS AND RECOMMENDATIONS
Pre-war Planning for the Post-Combat Phase

1. The post-conflict situation with which the Coalition was faced did not match the pre-conflict expectations. The strategic centre of the Coalition in Iraq was inevitably the Coalition Provisional Authority in Baghdad. To some extent this complicated the task of British forces in the south. Taken together these factors contributed to delays in post-war stabilisation. It is not difficult to understand how mistakes could have been made in planning and executing Iraq's post-conflict reconstruction. No post-conflict mission in the last 60 years has been as challenging as that which faced the Coalition in June 2003.
2. The considerable success that has been achieved in Iraq – especially in the areas controlled by the UK – can, in large part, be traced to the British forces' ability to adapt to changing circumstances. Suppleness and pragmatism are at the heart of the British forces' professionalism.

The Insurgency

3. It is difficult to avoid concluding that the Coalition, including British forces, were insufficiently prepared for the challenge represented by the insurgency. A wide range of predictions for the post-conflict situation in Iraq were made in advance of the conflict. We are concerned that there is some evidence that the extensive planning, which we know took place in both the US and the UK, did not fully reflect the extent of that range. We also believe that the Coalition should have foreseen that its presence would be resented by some Iraqis, particularly Sunni Arabs and some Shia nationalist elements, and portrayed as cultural and economic imperialism.

4. We note that there is not one anti-Coalition insurgency in Iraq, as frequently portrayed in the media, but several, anti-Coalition, anti-Iraqi Government movements. These different movements are conducting operations with very different objectives.

5. We note that the scale of the anti-Coalition, anti-Iraqi Government insurgency movements was underestimated by the Coalition. At the same time, we acknowledge that a fixation simply on the number of insurgents does not necessarily, by itself, provide insight into their effectiveness and resilience.

6. We are concerned at the continued influx of foreign fighters into Iraq through neighbouring countries, particularly Syria and Iran, and note that this was probably facilitated by the inadequate attention paid to border security by the Coalition immediately following the invasion. More broadly, it appears to us that the Coalition failed to appreciate the potential for an insurgency in Iraq to attract foreign fighters, both from the Middle East and further afield (e.g. Chechnya).

7. We note that the various insurgency movements have been structured, motivated and resourced to inflict significant military and civilian casualties. They have employed a range of tactics from assassinations to suicide bombings depending on their motivations and goals, but foreign fighters, such as Musab al-Zarqawi and other Islamic extremists, have been particularly skilled at using psychological operations such as kidnappings and beheadings. In the foreseeable future, MNF-I and the Iraqi Government will continue to be attacked, but the various insurgency movements have not developed into a genuine national war of liberation and are unlikely to do so in the future.

We commend British forces for their approach to counter-insurgency in their areas of operations. We are convinced that their approach has been a contributing factor in the development of the more permissive environment in southern Iraq, which has resulted in relatively little insurgent activity. We do, however, remain concerned about a number of tactics employed by the MNF-I generally. We urge MoD to use its influence to affect MNF-I's posture and approach. We also encourage MoD to ensure that the Iraqi civilian powers are given

a prominent role in the counter-insurgency campaign. Finally, we emphasise and endorse the need to combine politico-economic and military strands of the counter-insurgency campaign. We have been told that this approach was adopted following the appointments of General Casey and Ambassador Negroponte, but we are concerned about the state of civil-military cooperation in the counter-insurgency campaign preceding their appointments, i.e. from May 2003 until June 2004 when Ambassador Bremer was head of the Coalition Provisional Authority.

Source: House of Commons

Debates on legislation

These are further occasions when accountability can be achieved. Every proposed piece of legislation must be fully debated at least twice. Here again, ministers must justify the proposals. It is extremely rare for the government to lose a vote on a major bill, but the procedure ensures that every aspect of legislation is carefully examined in a public forum.

The extract from Hansard shown below refers to the introduction of the London Olympics Bill by the Secretary of State, Tessa Jowell. We can see the degree to which MPs were concerned by a number of issues, including the impact on the area, the environment and the country's finances.

LONDON OLYMPICS BILL

The Secretary of State for Culture, Media and Sport (Tessa Jowell): I beg to move, That the Bill be now read a Second time.

I wish to take this opportunity to place on the record the warmest congratulations of – I hope – the whole House to Seb Coe, Keith Mills and the whole 2012 bid team, including Barbara Cassani, who chaired the bid for the first year, on the excellence of their campaign and the result of which we are all so very proud.

Two weeks have passed since we were awarded the games and we know that our focus now has to be on delivery. There is no time to waste. Much of the effort and a substantial share of the resources spent on bidding for the games were focused on preparing for delivery. I am delighted to announce today that the Government have already taken the first major step in the development of the best ever Olympic park in Stratford. I have today given the London Development Agency the go-ahead to start the massive construction and regeneration programme that will shape the Olympic park to be ready in seven years' time. The first step is the undergrounding of the power lines that currently blight the Olympic park and the lower Lea valley.

Mr. Eric Forth (Bromley and Chislehurst) (Con): Now that the Secretary of State has introduced the subject of money, can she give us – as she develops her argument on the Bill – her estimate of the total cost of the entire project and some idea of the cost to London council tax payers per year, and for how many years?

Tessa Jowell: The answers to both parts of that question have already been clearly set out in the submissions to the IOC and before the House. We have before us a once in a lifetime opportunity, not just to develop excellent Olympic facilities, but – working closely with my right hon. Friend the Deputy Prime Minister – to deliver sustainable communities and a powerful legacy for one of the most deprived areas of Britain. I pay the warmest tribute to the Deputy Prime Minister for the imagination that he has shown in understanding the potential of the Olympic development for the east end of London.

Richard Ottaway (Croydon, South) (Con): I apologise to the Secretary of State if she was planning to discuss this point, but when she addresses regeneration will she consider the several hundred businesses that will have to be displaced? Many of them feel that the level of compensation they are being offered is inadequate. Will she give an undertaking to look at the issue and ensure that no one loses out in that process?

Tessa Jowell: I believe that the figure is lower than 700.

Richard Ottaway: Several hundred.

Tessa Jowell: It is about 350. The matter is one for negotiation between the LDA and the businesses concerned, and I am aware of the progress of those negotiations.

The Government were clear and consistent in their support for London's bid, and I also pay tribute to all the major political parties in the House who were such strong and consistent supporters of the bid.

Pete Wishart (Perth and North Perthshire) (SNP) *rose.*

Tessa Jowell: With the exception of the hon. Gentleman.

I underline the importance of cross-party support and consensus in securing the bid but it is absolutely clear that we cannot bid for, win or stage the Olympic games without clear and unequivocal Government support.

Mr. Sadiq Khan (Tooting) (Lab): I am slightly concerned about the magnanimity shown by my right hon. Friend. The hon. Member for Twickenham (Dr. Cable), who is not in the Chamber today, is the shadow Chancellor for his party. He said:

> "London badly needs better transport and more police. It does not need the Olympics."

He also objected to people in Twickenham paying for facilities in the east end of London, some of which will be used for only 18 days and then demolished. Does my right hon. Friend agree that we do not mind everyone jumping on the bandwagon as long as they can eat some humble pie?

Tessa Jowell: I can assume only that the hon. Member for Twickenham (Dr. Cable) was not speaking for his party, but it would not be the first time that we have heard a chorus of different voices from that party – the flexible approach to policy.

Several hon. Members *rose.*

Tessa Jowell: I shall allow more interventions later but I want to make some progress, as many people want to speak in the debate.

I may be counting my chickens but I believe that the Bill is evidence of cross-party support for the games and of our determination to get moving with their staging, to set up the structures to deliver them and to make sure that the public interest is protected and that public money is properly spent, so that the 2012 Olympic and Paralympic games are delivered on time and within budget.

Mr. Clive Betts (Sheffield, Attercliffe) (Lab): Investigations by Robert Booth, a freelance journalist, showed that towards the end of 2003 a heads of term agreement was reached between the London Development Agency, acting on behalf of the bid team, and Stratford City Developments that neither would frustrate the planning applications of the other. At the time, Sir Stuart Lipton was a director of Stratford City Developments and also chairman of the Commission for Architecture and the Built Environment, which was conducting a design review of the Olympic bid team's proposals. There is no evidence that Sir Stuart took part in the design review, but does not it show the need for complete transparency in all the many public–private sector arrangements that will be needed to deliver the project? There should be proper parliamentary scrutiny of such arrangements.

Tessa Jowell: I have noted my hon. Friend's intervention and I shall be happy to write to him further. The important thing is that substantial sums of public money and, through the lottery, of the public's money will be invested in the games.

Mr. Forth: How much?

Tessa Jowell: The public sector undertaking in relation to the staging and to building the infrastructure is £2.375 billion. There will be additional investment arising from regeneration in the area immediately surrounding the Olympic park and further investment in London's transport structure, so the long-term benefits for London will be considerable. No one could deny that transparency has already been established in setting out the costs of the games.

Several hon. Members *rose.*

Tessa Jowell: I shall give way to the hon. Member for Shrewsbury and Atcham (Daniel Kawczynski), but that is the last intervention I shall take for quite some time.

Daniel Kawczynski (Shrewsbury and Atcham) (Con): I am grateful to the Secretary of State for allowing me to intervene. I am extremely pleased to see Lord Coe in the Gallery this afternoon.

Mr. Deputy Speaker (Sir Michael Lord): Order. May I explain to the hon. Gentleman and to the House generally that we do not normally refer to people outside the Chamber during debates?

Daniel Kawczynski: I apologise, Mr. Deputy Speaker.

The Secretary of State is talking about London, which is the key part of the Olympic bid, but places throughout the country want to take part in our great success, and in Shrewsbury we hope that we can host a rowing event on the River Severn, so will the right hon. Lady discuss how Shrewsbury and Shropshire can take part?

Tessa Jowell: I thank the hon. Gentleman for that question. I note that he joined the tribute that I made to Lord Coe and his colleagues at the beginning of my remarks. If he can contain himself, I shall come back to the point about the importance of the whole UK benefiting from London's hosting the games.

I want to set out for the House the shape of the Bill. The Bill does three things: it creates the public body that will get London ready to stage the games – the Olympic Delivery Authority; it provides the powers needed to meet IOC requirements for the way that the games and the Olympic environment are managed; and it provides the Mayor with an Olympic-specific power so that he can meet his obligations as the signatory to the IOC's host city contract. I shall provide an outline of the scope of the legislation in each of those areas, before describing in more detail how some of the clauses will work.

The Olympic delivery authority will be the body that manages the Government's interest in the Olympic construction project and the public money going into it. It will make sure that the necessary infrastructure is in place by 2012, and that all the venues are built. Clauses 3 to 6 and schedule 1 allow for the authority to be created, grant it the necessary powers and functions and specify how it will be structured, organised and funded. Clauses 8 to 16 deal with transport, and establish the ODA as the co-ordinating authority for the Olympic transport plan. Existing transport authorities will be under a duty to co-operate with the ODA in order to implement the plan and to deliver Olympic transport services.

The Bill also provides for the creation of an Olympic route network and the ODA will be able to issue traffic regulation orders on that network; for example, to establish Olympic lanes or parking restrictions. Obviously, the authority's role will need to evolve over time. Before 2012, the ODA will focus on acquiring land – 80 per cent of which is already under public control – constructing venues and planning transport.

Ian Lucas (Wrexham) (Lab): Will the authority have an obligation to pursue sustainable development in its operations? This is a huge opportunity for a low-carbon games. In my constituency, we have a major manufacturer of solar cells. We have a vital opportunity to develop a showcase for that industry, and to catch the imagination of the general public and deliver a low-carbon games.

Tessa Jowell: I am grateful to my hon. Friend for his intervention. Sustainability was one of the key characteristics of the bid when it was presented to the IOC back in February and it is certainly a very clear criterion that the Deputy Prime Minister will be looking to address in all the regeneration investment that will be going into the Olympic park.

Source: Hansard

Financial control

Although the approval of the government's financial arrangements is one of Parliament's oldest functions, dating back to the Middle Ages, it is also an area where it is seen at its weakest. Governments depend on their ability to collect taxes and to spend money on their key functions. These financial powers have to be renewed every year, while any changes to the tax system or to spending allocations must also be approved in Parliament. If Parliament were to withhold consent, government would cease to function very rapidly and would almost certainly be forced to seek a fresh popular mandate by calling a general election. As the position is so critical, it is customary for Parliament to renew financial powers with relatively little obstruction.

The House of Lords has long since lost any powers over financial affairs. The 1911 Parliament Act took away the Lords' ability to vote on financial matters. Having attempted to block the Liberal Government's annual budget in 1909, it was clear that the unelected House of Lords could no longer be allowed jeopardise the position of the elected government. Meanwhile, in the Commons, the MPs representing the governing party tend to be at their most loyal when the annual budget is being voted.

When we consider the operation of the Public Accounts Committee (PAC), however, the picture changes. This committee considers the *effectiveness* of government expenditure. Its members feel that they represent the interests of the taxpayers, trying to ensure that they get value for

money. Some of their reports can be highly critical and can result in remedial action by government. It should be stressed that the PAC does not consider the way in which public funds are allocated among different functions – that is the role of Parliament as a whole. Its task is to root out waste and inefficiency, to raise awareness of examples of poor administration within government departments and agencies.

Representation

The role that Parliament undoubtedly has, of representing the people, is a difficult one to grasp. The problem for MPs is that they are required to represent so many different sections of society and ideas. We can identify the following areas of responsibility:

- They are elected to represent their party and its manifesto. Therefore, we normally expect an MP to toe the party line. An exception to this occurs when an MP, during the general election campaign, declares openly that he does not support a particular aspect of his party's official policy. In 2005, for example, a large number of Labour candidates openly stated that they did not support British military involvement in Iraq. Conversely, a smaller number of Conservatives asserted that they supported British withdrawal from the European Union.
- MPs must represent the interests of their own constituency whenever they are involved in government policy or a ministerial decision. For example, when it was proposed to set up a number of centres for asylum seekers in rural areas in 2004–05, the MPs involved set up an ultimately successful campaign to reverse the policy. It is very typical for local MPs to become active, for example, in decisions to build (or not) road bypasses, nuclear power stations, airport terminals, and the like.
- There are times when the national interest can be at stake and MPs or peers will take this into account when parliamentary debates are held. Here our representatives in both Houses must weigh up their party's attitude to the issue against *what they perceive* to be in the nation's best interests. The 2003 war in Iraq, Britain's relations with the European Union, how we should deal with suspected terrorists (in particular, whether we could suspend civil liberties in the fight against terrorism) and whether identity cards should become compulsory are all examples where our representatives step out of traditional party allegiance and consider the country as a whole on non-partisan lines.
- It is currently estimated that about 75 per cent of MPs are either paid a retainer to represent an outside group or regularly support the interests of a group without payment. Many peers fulfil a similar role in the House of Lords. This is considered normal and part of the democratic process. As a safeguard, any representatives who are paid to represent groups must declare their interest and so avoid any possibility of corrupt practices. It is well known, therefore, that many trade unions, professional associations, industrial organisations, large companies and campaign groups have friendly representatives in both Houses. They will

alert the groups to any hostile policies, promote their interests and attempt to gain publicity for their aims.

The main occasions when this process occurs are during debates, committee hearings, Questions to Ministers and three special types of parliamentary opportunities for MPs to raise such issues: *adjournment debates, early day motions* and *ten minute rules*. They are gaps in normal procedure which have been protected to give MPs the chance to raise a matter of constituency interest or which concerns an external group which they represent. In all these cases, no direct response from government is expected, but at least the issue becomes a matter of public record and may be used for later campaigns.

In the House of Lords, external groups are particularly active when legislative amendments are being considered. Most peers are not strongly tied down by party discipline, and many see their role in terms of protecting minority interests. The Lords' amendment process – when the government is at its most vulnerable in Parliament – is where representation of interests can be seen at its most intense.

Redress of grievances

Along with consent to finance, the redress of citizens' grievances is an ancient parliamentary function. It is necessarily carried out by individual MPs on behalf of their constituents.

Where a constituent feels they have been unfairly or unjustly treated by the government or by one of its agencies, such as the NHS, the police, immigration authorities, the social security system or the taxation authorities, that constituent may well complain to their local MP. This privilege remains part of an unwritten contract between MPs and the government. It is that Parliament will normally support the government in its key functions, in return for which MPs will be given special access to ministers.

The degree to which MPs undertake such work varies a good deal. Some are known as dutiful constituency workers, others are less enthusiastic. Ministers find the constituency role particularly difficult (remember that most ministers are also constituency MPs, including the prime minister), but their role is usually performed by friendly neighbouring MPs or by their own paid constituency agent. MPs will raise issues either on the floor of the House or will see ministers and civil servants directly.

Private Members' legislation

Most legislation is presented by the government. Opposition parties are not permitted to do this. However, a few lucky MPs, who win an annual ballot, are allowed to present their own private legislation. Though such proposals are nearly always blocked by the government, occasionally – very occasionally – a so-called **private Member's bill** does find its way through to law. This requires an enormous effort by the MP concerned, who must convince a large number of his/her colleagues to support it, and persuade the government to keep their hands off it.

In effect, therefore, private Members' legislation can only succeed if the government either supports it or has its own reasons for not opposing it. Thus, successes are rare. Yet one of the most significant pieces of legislation in modern history was a private Member's bill. This was David Steele's Abortion Act of 1967, which legalised abortion for the first time. In the same era, private acts between homosexuals were also legalised under such legislation. More recently, since 1997, private Members' legislation has been less momentous. It has concerned such issues as dog breeding, energy conservation in private homes, guide dogs in taxis and employee share-owning schemes.

Deliberation

Occasionally – and it is only occasionally – Parliament is given the opportunity to hold a great debate on a vital issue. Such debates can form part of a national process of deliberation. These are moments in history when a nation must take a moment to draw breath and make a critical decision which will affect its future. The debates on the war with Iraq in 2003 were such an example. So too were the debates in the House of Lords on the issue of detention without trial for terrorist suspects.

Delving further back into history we can find many examples of where Parliament has made a significant contribution to national debate. Independence for India, Britain's imperial future, the 1956 invasion of the Suez Canal Zone, the Falklands crisis of 1982 and Britain's reaction to the 9/11 atrocity in New York in 2001 were all occasions when Parliament played a full role.

Reserve powers

Parliament enjoys two powers which it rarely uses (hence the term 'reserve powers'), but which nevertheless give it great authority. These are the ability to veto government legislation and to dismiss a government.

The House of Lords has voted down legislation on a number of occasions, but such decisions will normally be reversed by the House of Commons in the next session. If the Commons rejects a bill, however, that is normally the end of the matter, at least until after the next general election. As we have seen above, it is not the role of Parliament to defy the will of the elected government, but merely the threat of action faced by any government which attempts to act in an arbitrary way remains an important discipline.

The 1986 Second Reading defeat of the Sunday Trading Bill, intended to allow more stores to remain open on a Sunday, occurred because a determined coalition of MPs from all parties were opposed on the grounds of either religion or the need to protect workers' rights. The government whips miscalculated the level of opposition and were too late to withdraw the bill before the embarrassing defeat. The rarity of such defeats disguises the reality that government does face such a threat from time to time, and usually responds by making concessions to head off opposition. Just because government defeats on the Second Reading come once in a blue moon does not mean that Parliament is toothless. Indeed, John Major's

second administration, from 1992 to 1997, was beset by such threats from a House of Commons in which he enjoyed only a narrow majority.

The threat to remove a government by a vote of no confidence in the Commons is also constant. Of course, when a government enjoys a large majority it remains a distant threat, but the people can be comforted by the fact that there is an ever-present safeguard against arbitrary government. The last time this happened was when James Callaghan's Labour Government was removed in March 1979. He had lost his Commons majority, but tried to continue too long. The impatient Conservatives, led by Margaret Thatcher, could not wait for the impending election and organised a no confidence vote, which they won by a majority of one.

Specific Lords powers

Although it is the junior House, the Lords does have two specific powers not necessarily enjoyed by the Commons. One is the power of delay. The Parliament Act of 1949 states that, if a bill is rejected in the Lords, it will automatically become law if the Commons passes the same piece of legislation in the next session (year) of Parliament. This effectively means that the House of Lords has the special power to delay a proposal for a year. The Commons does not do this because MPs are whipped to support the party and so government defeats are, as we have seen above, very rare. The Lords, on the other hand, is more free to defy the government in the knowledge that, if it is determined enough, the government will have its way in the long run. The purpose of delay is twofold. First, it forces the government to think again and so ensure that there is sufficient support for a proposal. The second is that the threat of delay is often enough to obtain important concessions by way of amendments.

FIG 2.2D The House of Lords at work

The 1991 defeat of the War Crimes Bill – passed under the Parliament Act rule in the following year – was an important example of the use of the power of delay. So too was the Hunting with Dogs Act, which was passed twice in 2004 and 2005. On that occasion, attempts to compromise failed, but the Lords succeeded in ensuring a full debate on the issue. Similarly, the Lords' rejection of the bill to outlaw incitement to religious hatred in 2004 provoked a full debate on the issue. This kind of obstruction, negotiation and compromise is a luxury which the strictly controlled House of Commons does not enjoy.

The Lords also has slightly more opportunity for amending legislation than the Commons. Here again, the greater political independence of peers plays its part. But, perhaps more importantly, Lords' amendments have the effect of delaying legislation. Every Lords' amendment must be confirmed by the Commons. If there is a disagreement between the two Houses, a bill will simply pass backwards and forwards between the two Houses (a process known, not surprisingly, as ping-pong) much to the frustration of the government. The result is often important compromises. In 2004–05 a most important example of ping-pong created critical changes to a key piece of legislation.

The 2001 Anti-terrorism Act had been declared unlawful under the European Convention on Human Rights. This forced the Government to return the legislation to Parliament in a modified form. But the Lords decided to add some critical amendments, preventing the Home Office from detaining suspected terrorists without trial or process of law. The Lords' amendment was passed back and forth along the long, straight corridor which leads from the Commons to the Lords. Eventually, the Government, running out of time and patience, was forced to concede the point to the determined peers.

We can now summarise the principal functions of Parliament, noting the main limitations of each.

Functions	Limitations
Legitimation	The House of Lords is not elected.
	The Commons is seen to be dominated by the executive and therefore not independent.
	The electoral system means the Commons is not politically representative of the electorate.
Scrutiny	Both Houses lack enough time to consider bills thoroughly.
	Standing committees are whipped, so fall under government control.

Functions	Limitations
Opposition	Collective government responsibility makes it difficult to examine government decisions.
	The Opposition lacks the administrative back-up of the government.
Accountability	Skilful ministers and civil servants can evade questioning by MPs and peers.
	MPs and peers may lack expertise and knowledge.
	The power of patronage prevents governing MPs and peers being hostile or too inquisitive.
	There remains a good deal of government secrecy, especially in the fields of defence, security and foreign policy.
Financial control	Traditionally, Parliament is not expected to challenge government seriously in this area.
	House of Lords has no jurisdiction at all.
Representation	The electoral system makes the Commons highly unrepresentative.
	The House of Lords is not elected.
	Both Houses are socially unrepresentative, especially in terms of women or social and ethnic background.
Redress of grievances	MPs lack time to deal with many grievances of constituents.
Private Members' legislation	Little time is devoted to private Members' legislation.
	Government is easily able to 'kill' any bills it opposes.
	It is difficult for MPs and peers to gather enough support to force bills through.
Deliberation	Lack of parliamentary time.
Reserve powers	MPs of the governing party are especially reluctant to use reserve powers for fear of precipitating a general election in which they might lose their seats and/or their party might lose power.
Delaying (House of Lords)	The Parliament Act limits this power to one year.
Amending (House of Lords)	Proposed Lords' amendments must be approved by the House of Commons where the government dominates.

The Legislative Process

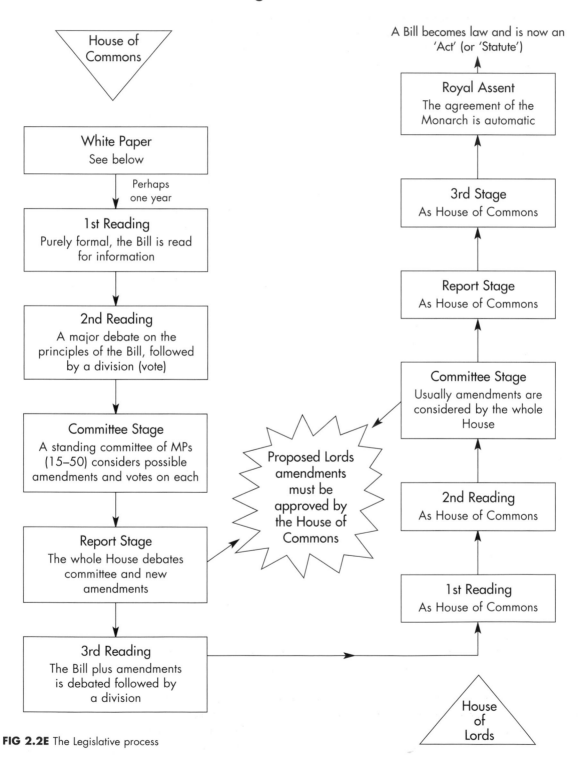

FIG 2.2E The Legislative process

Notes:

1. A white paper sets out government proposals in some detail but is not yet a 'bill'. The House debates a white paper and votes on it. If there is significant opposition, the government will normally drop the proposal or make significant changes. There is normally a year between a white paper appearing and the final bill being considered to allow for wider consideration and consultations.
2. Most bills are considered by the Commons first, but a significant minority appear first in the Lords.
3. If a bill receives a negative vote at second or third readings, it is lost and must be re-introduced or abandoned.
4. If the Lords rejects a bill, it may be re-introduced next session (parliamentary year) in the Commons. If passed a second time in the Commons, the bill becomes law despite Lords opposition (under the terms of the 1949 Parliament Act).

If an amendment is proposed in the Lords, it is immediately passed to the commons for approval. If there is no agreement on the amendment, three outcomes are possible:

1. The government may accept the Lords amendment.
2. A compromise may be negotiated.
3. The bill is abandoned and may be re-introduced in the next session (see note 4 above).

Agencies supporting Parliament

Parliament is assisted in its work by a number of specialist agencies, which have the task of investigating various aspects of government work and reporting back to Parliament on their findings. The departmental select committees have a particular interest in their work. Some of the key organisations are described below.

The Parliamentary Ombudsman

Despite the name – of Scandinavian origin – it is not necessarily a man. Nor is it a single person, but in fact an extensive office staffed by experienced officials.

The Parliamentary Ombudsman investigates complaints – claims of what is known as maladministration – which are routed through MPs from constituents or groups of constituents. These are cases where a government department is accused of not dealing fairly or thoroughly enough with a member of the public. It may be that standard procedures have not been followed, or that a civil servant has been negligent, if there has been undue delay or citizens have not been granted equal treatment. The Ombudsman cannot deal with all complaints, but normally concentrates on matters which are likely to affect large numbers of people. In the past it was a role carried out by constituency MPs, but they no longer have enough time to deal with them thoroughly enough.

The Parliamentary Ombudsman receives about 2000 complaints per year (the number varies considerably) and decides to investigate about half of them. Where a complaint is upheld, the Ombudsman makes a report to a special select committee which deals with the work. The committee for the Parliamentary Ombudsman or Parliament as a whole may order that compensatory action be taken by the department concerned. Over the years, the role of the Ombudsman has expanded and has now become a key element in Parliament's role in the redress of grievances.

Several other industries in the private sector have also set up ombudsman systems and these should not be confused with the Parliamentary Ombudsman, which deals only with central government. The banking and insurance industries are examples of private ombudsman systems. There is also an ombudsman for local government.

The Comptroller and Auditor General

This extensive office works directly for the Public Accounts Committee. It has two main functions. One is to ensure that government revenues are spent on the purposes for which Parliament has given approval. In other words, the government is not permitted to shift expenditure from one use to another without seeking parliamentary sanction. Second, it checks the government accounts to ensure that money has been spent carefully and effectively. Therefore it forms part of the wider role of Parliament in trying to ensure that government is run efficiently. Major criticisms are reported to the Public Accounts Committee, which may then summon ministers and/or civil servants to account for the problem.

National Audit Office

Closely connected to the role of the Comptroller, the much expanded National Audit Office provides a service both to government itself and to parliamentary select committees. It looks at various aspects of the work of government departments to check for efficiency, guard against wastefulness and ensure that services serve the public effectively. It looks especially at what are known as frontline services – those where the service deals directly with the public, such as the NHS, the social security system and the tax authorities. Its reports, often highly critical, are used by government to improve its performance, and by select committees as a basis for their own investigations.

Audit Commission

Like the National Audit Office, the Audit Commission serves both government and Parliament. It investigates the operations of local government specifically. All local authorities are expected to provide services on the

basis of *best value*. This means that they should combine value for money with the best possible standard of service within the financial constraints. Audit Commission reports are used by central government to control the activities of local government, but may also be used by Parliament to monitor the quality of services at local level.

Membership of the House of Lords

The nature of the membership of the House of Lords is essential to an understanding of how it behaves. The immediate thing to notice in the table below, of the House of Lords in 2005, is that the government (Labour), does not enjoy a majority in the Lords. Indeed, as a result of historical circumstances, Labour had fewer Members than the Conservatives in 2005 (a circumstance that will change in the near future).

Categories of membership	Number
Life peers	600 (approx.)
Hereditary peers	92
Bishops	24
Archbishops	2
Law Lords (Lords of Appeal in Ordinary)	12

Party strengths in the House of Lords (March 2005)

Party	Number
Conservative	203
Labour	202 (including the Lord Chancellor)
Cross-benchers (no party)	183
Liberal Democrat	69
Bishops/Archbishops (no party)	26
Law Lords (1 Labour, 11 no party)	12 (including the Lord Chancellor)

The **life peers** are appointed mostly on political grounds, with each of the main parties having the privilege of regularly nominating a number of new life peers each year to replace those who have died. The parties are able to nominate new peers in proportion to their representation in the Commons. This means that the Conservatives were able to nominate more peers between 1979 and 1997, but since then Labour has had an advantage. The Liberal Democrats naturally have a limited number of nominations. Most – but not all – party nominations are either retired politicians, such as Lord Coe (former MP and athlete) and Lord Lawson (former Chancellor of the Exchequer), or current professional politicians who do not wish to be constituency MPs, such as Lord Adonis (Junior Education

Minister and prime ministerial adviser) and Baroness Amos (Cabinet Minister).

In order to prevent total domination by the parties, a number of life peers are nominated each year who have no party allegiance. They become cross-benchers and represent a large presence in the Lords which is extremely independent. They also guarantee that the government can never enjoy an overall majority. The neutral life peers can be nominated by anyone, though they are normally nominated by existing peers, and are ultimately appointed by the independent Appointments Commission. Most of them are prominent citizens who are 'life achievers', such as Lord Hastings (former TV executive) and Lord Ramsbotham (prison reformer).

The 92 **hereditary peers** are a legacy of the time before 1999 when the Lords was dominated, in terms of numbers, by hereditary peers who owed their position to being the eldest son of a hereditary peer who had died. Though many of them rarely (if ever) attended the debates, the minority who were active created a permanent inbuilt Conservative majority. The Labour Government that came to power in 1997 was determined to abolish the right of hereditary peers to sit and vote in the Lords. In the event, the House of Lords was extremely obstructive and so a compromise was reached, allowing 92 hereditary peers to retain their seats. It is intended (and now widely accepted) that even these hereditary peers will lose their right to vote in the near future. So their political significance will be short-lived.

The **bishops and archbishops** are all members of the Church of England. They represent the fact that the Church of England remains the 'established' religion of the UK. Their position is controversial for two reasons. One is that the majority of citizens in the UK do not regularly observe *any* religion. The second is that they no longer represent the religious traditions of the UK. Why, many ask, are the Catholic, Muslim, Jewish and Hindu religions not represented formally in the same way? This, among other membership issues, is discussed in the final unit of this book. Though a small group, the bishops can be influential when moral and religious issues are at stake. They are politically neutral and therefore form a kind of pressure group within the Lords.

Finally, we turn to the **law lords**. Their formal title is Lords of Appeal in Ordinary. There are 12 of these law lords, 11 of whom are politically independent. It is a matter of considerable controversy that these law lords are members of both the judiciary and the legislature. This violates – so the argument goes – the principle of an independent judiciary. But yet more controversial is the position of the **Lord Chancellor**.

The Lord Chancellor is an ancient office and it has always been the case that the holder is a representative of the government (in the past this meant the monarch). The same is true today. The Lord Chancellor is a member of the Cabinet, manages the Department of Constitutional Affairs, which means that he runs the legal system, and has the major say in appointments to senior positions in the judiciary. If this is not enough, the Lord Chancellor is also the Speaker of the House of Lords, effectively its chairman. So, the position of the Lord Chancellor has also become the

subject of political debate. Reform is under way and, again, this is discussed in the final unit of this book.

We can now summarise the significance of the membership structure of the Lords:

- The government is prevented from enjoying an absolute majority.
- Even peers who have a party allegiance tend to be more independent than MPs because politics is not their principal occupation, so the whips have little leverage over them.
- Because most peers have had a previous occupation, they have a wider variety of experience than MPs and so represent a wide range of interests in society.
- The Church of England is strongly represented, as is the legal profession and the judiciary.
- Despite its greater independence, the House of Lords is subject to the political patronage of party leaders.
- The position of the most senior members of the judiciary in the Lords calls into question the constitutional principle of the separation of powers and the independence of the judiciary.
- It is likely that the membership structure of the House of Lords will be significantly reformed in the years after 2005.

Why the House of Lords is becoming more significant

Until the 1980s the House of Lords was considered to be of relatively little significance in the British political process. It contained a large majority of hereditary peers, many of whom did not attend at all or had only a passing interest in its proceedings. More importantly, there was a permanent inbuilt Conservative majority, largely because the bulk of the hereditary peers were, as one might expect, Conservatives. These two realities meant that the Lords simply could not be allowed to wield any great influence as it was so clearly undemocratic in nature. Furthermore, before 1983, it was the norm for the government to enjoy relatively modest majorities in the House of Commons. The lack of a comfortable majority meant that there was a reasonable amount of effective opposition to the government among MPs. So much was the Lords held in modest esteem, indeed, that its complete abolition remained a well-supported proposal, mainly among Labour Members of the Commons.

But there has been a remarkable change in both the prestige and the influence of the Lords since that time. There have been a number of factors at work in this process, among them:

- Large government majorities in the Commons became normal. Governments enjoyed majorities of over 100 following the elections of 1983, 1987, 1997 and 2001. This meant that opposition in the Commons was weak. Members of the House of Lords therefore felt it their duty to bolster parliamentary opposition to make up for Commons' weakness.

- At the same time, the House of Lords began to develop a new 'professionalism'. An increasing proportion of its membership began to take their role more seriously, attending regularly and making themselves specialists in certain fields of policy. To some extent, this is the result of party leaderships selecting professional politicians for the Lords to a greater degree.
- The reform of the Lords in 2000, removing all but 92 of the hereditary peers, gave the Lords greater authority. It was still not a democratic body, but at least it was seen as more politically and socially representative of the country.
- There is now a stronger 'rights culture' in the UK, especially since the incorporation of the European Convention on Human Rights into British law in 2000. The Lords, which contains many lawyers and human rights experts, has taken upon itself the role of guardian of individual rights against governments which have been accused (whether justifiably or not) of being too dictatorial.

The following table sets out prominent examples of the House of Lords' defiance of the will of government and Parliament.

Issue	Detail	Outcome
House of Lords Reform, late 1998–99	The Lords objected to the complete abolition of the voting rights of hereditary peers.	The government was forced to compromise, allowing 92 hereditary peers to retain their rights.
The legal age of consent for homosexual males, 1998–99	The Lords voted twice, in 1998 and 1999, against lowering the age of consent to sex for homosexual males from 18 to 16.	In November 2000, the government forced the measure through by using the 1949 Parliament Act. The legislation had been passed in two consecutive sessions of the Commons.
Anti-terrorism legislation, 2001	The Lords defeated the government on ten occasions, proposing key amendments.	The government compromised, removing incitement to religious hatred as an offence from the legislation.
Hunting with dogs, 2001	The Lords blocked the proposal to ban hunting with dogs (mainly fox hunting). Time ran out for the bill because of the 2001 general election.	The ban was postponed, but did pass both Houses by 2004.

Issue	Detail	Outcome
Reform of the Judiciary, 2004	The Lords voted down a measure to create a separate Supreme Court to hear major legal appeals.	The measure remains in doubt in 2005.
Anti-terrorism legislation, 2004–05	The Lords insisted that the Anti-terrorism Act 2001, following a successful appeal to the law lords by several Belmarsh prisoners, was unacceptable on the grounds that it allowed suspects to be detained without trial.	The government was forced to accept amendments, ensuring that terror suspects could have movements restricted with permission of a judge, but could not be detained in prison.

The Commons and Lords compared and contrasted

On the face of it, the Commons and the Lords appear to be remarkably alike. The procedures of each House are similar and both spend a high proportion of their time passing legislation. Even the shape of both chambers are similar – rectangles, with the Speaker at the end and government and opposition benches ranged opposite each other on either side. But when we scratch the surface, crucial differences appear.

If we stay for a moment with the shape of the chambers, there is an immediately noticeable contrast. In the Lords there are benches – known as cross-benches – that sit in the middle, facing towards the Speaker. These are absent in the Commons. The cross-benches seat a large number of peers who are politically independent. They are said 'not to take a party whip'. The cross-benchers are in a minority, but there are enough of them to ensure that the governing party can never enjoy an overall majority. So, when the House of Lords divides on strict party lines, the fate of a bill or an amendment lies with the independent cross-benchers.

Even those peers who do 'take the party whip' and declare themselves members of one party or another are far more independent-minded than their counterparts in the Commons. A relatively small number of party supporters in the Lords have political ambitions. Many are retired from their professions (a large number are former professional politicians, often ex-ministers) or have other major roles in society (for example, as lawyers, journalists, pressure group leaders, university professors or business men and women), which means they are effectively very much part-time politicians. Such individuals may well have strong party allegiances, but they are no longer subject to prime ministerial patronage and do not have to submit themselves to the discipline meted out by the whips. Nor do they have a constituency to worry about if they decide to defy their party leadership.

Perhaps the most important distinction lies hidden behind the apparent likenesses. That is, that the House of Lords simply lacks the legitimacy of the Commons. While it remains unelected (as we shall see later, there are proposals for a partly elected Lords in the future), it is an undemocratic body. Its Members are fully aware of this and therefore do not even *claim* to enjoy the same degree of authority as the Commons. The following restrictions on the Lords therefore apply:

- It can only delay the passage of bills for one year under the terms of the Parliament Act 1949.
- It has no power over the financial arrangements of the government under the terms of the Parliament Act of 1911.
- Its Members agree voluntarily that they will not block any legislation which clearly appeared in the government's previous election manifesto. This is under the unwritten Salisbury Convention.
- Any amendments proposed by the Lords must be approved by the Commons (although the Lords can delay legislation simply by repeatedly passing the same amendments over and over again, until a compromise with the government is reached).

As a result of these restrictions, we can identify a much more traditionally limited role as played by the Lords. It looks like this:

- To delay any legislation where peers felt it was desirable for the government to think again and perhaps consult more widely. This was certainly the case with the legislation to ban hunting with dogs in 2004–05.
- To make helpful and friendly suggestions for amendments to bills, often to protect minority interests or to improve the quality of the legislation. This was done with the proposals to introduce top-up tuition fees for university students in 2003–04.
- Sometimes to make hostile suggestions for amendments in the hope that constant obstruction will force the government to compromise. This tactic worked with the amendment of the Anti-terrorism Act of 2004–05.
- To debate some of the great issues of the day in order to ensure that the government and the House of Common hear representations from a wide variety of different groups in society and from experts in the Lords who have great experience of the issue concerned. Such issues as mercy killing, abortion, in-vitro fertilisation and embryo research have been debated in this way in recent times.

The relationship between government and Parliament

The domination of the legislature by executive government in the UK is one of the key features of the political system. Indeed, it could be considered to be its most important feature. The nineteenth-century political journalist, Walter Bagehot, called the 'fusion' of executive and legislative power the 'efficient secret' of the British system. We refer to this fusion as a lack of the **separation of powers**. The separation of powers refers to an idea developed by the seventeenth century French philosopher Montesquieu. He stated that the three branches of government – executive, legislature and judiciary – should be strictly separated so that they could balance each other's power. This would also prevent the accumulation of too much power in one branch. In Britain, this separation between parliament and government is largely absent (unlike in, for example, the USA) so the danger of excessive executive power is always present, as Montesquieu had warned. Certainly the power of government creates two important realities:

1. It means that governments are rarely removed from office prematurely. Most governments last the full legal maximum of five years in office or decide to call an election before that on a voluntary basis. The stability of government in the UK is certainly envied by countries whose governments are much less secure and often shorter-lived.
2. It also means that governments are generally able to carry out virtually all of their manifesto commitments, with relatively little obstruction. The electorate is therefore able to vote for a party, confident in the knowledge that they are granting them a solid mandate.

Of course, these are the advantages of executive domination. There are also two very striking problems that arise:

1. Governments may become dictatorial in nature. Legislation may not be properly scrutinised and may survive with undesirable features contained in it.
2. There may be times when the government has lost the confidence of the public. The public cannot remove a government, but Parliament can. However, as long as the government whips can maintain control, the government will survive, even with a small majority in the House of Commons.

So the question of whether executive dominance is desirable is a balanced one. When governments appear to be popular and successful, the weakness of Parliament is of little concern. But when the opposite is true, the public bemoans the fact that MPs do not seem willing to exercise their considerable reserve powers.

'Revolting MPs', 2001–05

Although the executive dominates Parliament and although the Labour Government of 2001–05 did not suffer a major defeat in the House of Commons, there were a number of examples of significant revolts by its MPs against the whip. The government was not defeated on these occasions, either because the revolt was too small, or because it was supported by MPs from other parties. The following examples demonstrate this:

MPs who often defied the whip	Number of occasions they defied the whip
Jeremy Corbyn	148
John McDonnell	135
Lynne Jones	103
Robert Wareing	97
Alan Simpson	96
Kelvin Hopkins	87
Dennis Skinner	76
Mark Fisher	74
Kate Hoey	73
Diane Abbott	68
Glenda Jackson	64

Examples of major revolts	Year	Number of MPs defying the whip
Anti-terrorism Bill	2001	32
Immigration and asylum	2002	42
Iraq war	2003	121
Foundation hospitals	2003	63
University top-up fees	2004	72
Gambling Bill to allow more casinos	2004	30
Children Bill to outlaw smacking	2004	49
Prevention of Terrorism Bill	2005	62

Source: Philip Cowley and Mark Stuart, www.revolts.co.uk (accessed 11 November 2005)

Why government dominates Parliament

We should now examine the reasons why the government is able to control Parliament so effectively. The following factors are important:

■ The electoral system almost guarantees that one party will win an absolute majority in the Commons. Furthermore, the government's parliamentary majority tends to be very large. Here again the electoral system is the cause. It tends to exaggerate even a modest lead in the popular vote. For example, Labour's 3 per cent lead over the Conservatives in the 2005 election was translated into a majority of more than 60 seats.

■ Party loyalty in the UK is traditionally strong. Political parties are normally ideologically unified, so the number of dissidents is usually low. Governments can therefore rely on their parliamentary majority with some confidence.

■ Prime ministerial patronage is extremely important. There is virtually only one career path for a professional politician and that is to achieve ministerial office. Since all posts in the government are controlled by the prime minister, he can demand loyalty from a high proportion of his party's MPs. There are over 100 Members of both Houses who are already ministers and therefore bound by collective majority. They will always support the government. Of the others, the majority retain hopes that they will one day be promoted to ministerial office. One of the important qualities which an aspiring minister must enjoy is loyalty.

■ The ultimate sanction a whip can use against a dissident MP is to suspend or remove them permanently from the party. This will have no short-term effect, but if an MP loses the nomination of his/her party at the next general election, s/he will almost certainly lose his/her seat.

■ Even if the whips do not remove an MP's party membership, the constituency party of the MP in question may well 'deselect' him/her if they feel that there has been excessive disloyalty. Deselection means that s/he will not be the official party candidate any more, with the effect described above.

■ The prime minister can also bring dissident MPs into line by threatening to resign the government and call an election. This was a tactic used twice by John Major when he was faced by a divided and rebellious party in the 1990s.

■ The House of Lords can be a thorn in the government's side, but its lack of authority and powers means that the government can often sidestep its attempts to be obstructive. As we have seen above, there is no doubt that the Lords is stronger and more obstinate than it used to be, but ultimately it will nearly always have to bow to the authority of the government and its majority in the House of Commons.

We can now summarise the relative strengths and weaknesses of the Commons and the Lords.

Commons strengths	Commons weaknesses
■ The Commons has the ultimate power to remove a government from office. ■ Under exceptional circumstances the MPs can veto legislation, or threaten to do so, and thus force compromises. ■ Also under exceptional circumstances MPs can force legislative amendments from the government. ■ MPs can call ministers to account. This is particularly effective when conducted by select committees. ■ Every constituency can be effectively represented by its own MP, who can raise grievances in the Commons. ■ Various interest and cause groups are represented by MPs.	■ Governments normally have a comfortable majority and so can dominate MPs through patronage and discipline in general. ■ The legislative standing committees are largely controlled by the party whips, so the amending function of the Commons is weak. ■ MPs have insufficient time and support to be able to call government to account effectively. Ministers are also very adept at avoiding intrusive questioning. ■ MPs have a very limited role in developing legislation. ■ The Commons is not socially representative, lacking women and members of ethnic minorities especially. ■ Governments are increasingly ignoring Parliament and consulting groups and the public directly.

Lords strengths	Lords weaknesses
■ Many Members of the Lords are more independent from party control than MPs. They can therefore be more effective in controlling government. ■ Peers represent a wide variety of interests and expertise, being largely prominent citizens with considerable specialised experience. ■ The Lords can delay legislation and so force compromises by government. ■ The Lords has more effective time to conduct debates and to scrutinise legislation.	■ In its unreformed state, the Lords lacks democratic legitimacy. ■ The powers of the Lords are limited by law. It has no power over financial matters and cannot veto legislation in the long term. ■ Its proposed amendments can be overturned by the Commons. ■ Like the Commons, the Lords has a very limited role in developing legislation. ■ Peers face the same problems as MPs in calling government to account.

KEY CONCEPTS

Parliamentary government A system of politics where government is drawn from Parliament and is accountable to Parliament. In other words, the government has no separate authority from that of Parliament.

Separation of powers A constitutional principle, that the three branches of government – legislature, executive and judiciary – should have separate membership, separate powers and should be able to control each other's powers. It is largely absent in the UK.

Presidential government In contrast to parliamentary government, a president normally has a separate source of authority from that of the legislature. This means that the executive (president) is accountable to the people directly, not to the legislature.

Representative government A form of government where political power is largely exercised by elected representatives, through individual MPs, Parliament as a whole and through parties.

Revision topics and examination questions

Revision topics

- The main functions of Parliament
- Differences in functions between the House of Commons and House of Lords
- Meaning of parliamentary government
- How Parliament calls government to account
- Strengths and weaknesses of Parliament
- Factors that prevent Parliament controlling executive power
- Extent to which Parliament is representative
- Nature of parliamentary sovereignty

Short answers

- Outline THREE functions of Parliament.
- Outline THREE functions of the House of Lords.
- What is meant by the term 'parliamentary government'?
- What is meant by 'parliamentary sovereignty'?

Medium answers

- Distinguish between parliamentary government and presidential government.
- What are the main distinctions between the House of Commons and the House of Lords?
- To what extent is Parliament truly sovereign?
- How does Parliament bring government to account?
- How representative is Parliament?

Long answers

- How effective is Parliament in calling government to account?
- What factors prevent Parliament being effective?
- Why has the House of Lords become more significant in recent years?
- In what ways, and to what extent, does the executive dominate Parliament?

Resources and Web Guide

Books

The classic modern work, and still very relevant, is:
Philip Norton, *Does Parliament Matter?*, Harvester Wheatsheaf, 1993.
A full description is given in:
P. Silk and R. Masters, *How Parliament Works*, Longman, 1998.
A more journalistic account, but very readable, is:
P. Riddell, *Parliament Under Blair*, Politico's, 2000.
A very authoritative discussion of the current state of Parliament, as well as possible reform is:
Hansard Society, *The Challenge for Parliament: Making Government Accountable*, Hansard, 2001.

Useful websites

The official website is:
www.parliament.uk (accessed 11 November 2005)
The other useful site is the Hansard Society:
www.hansard-society.org.uk (accessed 11 November 2005)
Acts of Parliament can be viewed at the website for the Office of Public Sector Information:
www.opsi.gov.uk (accessed 11 November 2005)

2.3
The executive

How governments are formed

Before looking at how governments come into existence in the UK, we need to be clear about what is meant by the term 'government'. Essentially, there is a broad and a narrow definition. The broader meaning of 'government' includes elected ministers, together with the army of civil servants, advisers, committees and other bodies, involved in the formulation of policy and the implementation of decisions and services. The narrow definition includes only the hundred plus ministers and senior party officials who are appointed by the prime minister and thus form the 'inner circle' which governs the country. It is this narrow definition with which we are concerned here.

There are no codified rules operating in the UK to state how a government is formed. Instead it is the natural consequence of the outcome of general elections. In theory, we do not need rules because the choice of government – both which party will govern and which members of that party will make up that government – is in the hands of the reigning monarch. Up until the nineteenth century, indeed, this was largely a reality. The monarch would choose his/her preferred ministers and, as long as it was felt they could command the support of Parliament, they would form a government, which ran the country on behalf of the monarch. Of course, the monarch no longer plays any active role in this process. Fortunately, the way elections usually turn out in Britain makes the intervention of the monarch unnecessary.

There are also two (very rare) circumstances when a new government could be formed without a general election being held. One, when a government might resign and be replaced by a completely fresh government (possibly even one made up of a different party). Such a new government might be able to take over if it felt it could command the regular support of a majority in Parliament. The other occurs when a prime minister is replaced by a different party leader. This occurred in 1990 when Margaret Thatcher was replaced by John Major as Conservative leader. She had to resign as prime minister and Major formed a new Conservative administration without the intervention of a general election. A similar situation will arise if, and when, Tony Blair chooses to resign as prime minister and Labour leader some time before 2009, as he has promised to do.

As long as one party has won an absolute majority of the seats in the House of Commons after a general election, its leader will be invited by the monarch to form a government. There has only been one occasion since 1945 – in February 1974 – when this was not the outcome of an election. We will examine how that problem was resolved below. So the near inevitability that it will be clear which party has won the election means that rules have never been needed. There are, however, two circumstances that could cause a problem:

1. It may be that the winning party does not have an acknowledged leader. For whom would the monarch send if such a party won the election? There is no answer to this question, largely because such a circumstance has not occurred since the nineteenth century. All the main parties have formal procedures for electing their leader, so there is unlikely to be any confusion. For the time being, therefore, we can discount this problem.
2. More likely, however, is the possibility that no single party wins an absolute majority in the Commons. The term 'absolute majority' means that a party wins more seats than all the other parties put together. It is important because, without such an overall majority, the government would find it very difficult to pass legislation and secure consent for its financial arrangements. As we saw above, this has only occurred once since the Second World War. The aftermath of that election is shown below.

The events of February 1974

At that time there was a Conservative Government, led by Prime Minister Edward Heath. He decided to call a general election unexpectedly at a time when there was considerable industrial unrest, especially among the miners, over his economic and industrial policies. He hoped that, by securing a victory, he would obtain public support for his policies and so quell the disturbances.

Heath's gamble failed. Labour won more seats than the Conservatives at the election. However, no party secured an absolute majority. It was expected that Heath would resign, but he sent a message to the Palace, saying that he was going to attempt to form a coalition government with the small Liberal Party. Such an arrangement would give the coalition a narrow overall majority. For several days there was confusion. The Labour leader, Harold Wilson, claimed that this was unconstitutional and that Labour should be invited to form a government.

Ultimately, Heath failed to reach agreement with the Liberals. He therefore suggested to the Queen that she should indeed summon Wilson and ask him to try to form a government.

A crisis was thus averted. Labour formed a minority government. That is, all the opposition parties put together had a majority of 33 seats over the government. There was no coalition with the Liberals. Clearly a government that has no majority in the Commons is unlikely to last long, and so it proved. A second general election was called in October of the same year. Labour secured a tiny three-seat absolute majority. Despite the narrow win, the government that took office survived for four and a half years.

We should not dismiss the 1974 incident as a mere historical curiosity. The decline in support for the two major parties and the rise in the number of seats being won by the Liberal Democrats since 1997 means that such an outcome – known as a **hung Parliament** – is becoming increasingly likely in

the future. Furthermore, if the electoral system were to be reformed in ways described in Unit 1 of this book, it would be almost inevitable that no party could secure an absolute majority.

After we have examined the 'normal' way in which governments are formed, therefore, we will return to speculation about the future under a hung Parliament.

'The government'

Bearing in mind that we are still using the narrow definition, we can look at a typical structure of a modern British government. The exact structure of every government may change, but the following figures are normal.

Type of member	Typical number	Role
Cabinet members	23	These include the prime minister, the heads of large government departments, plus a small number of other senior party members. They are the ultimate source of official government policy.
Senior non-Cabinet posts	15	The holders of important offices, such as Attorney General, who are not quite senior enough to be in the Cabinet.
Junior ministers not in the Cabinet	60	These are subordinates of those Cabinet ministers who run departments. Most are known as Ministers of State.
Whips	17	The Chief Whip sits in Cabinet. All other whips do not. They have the task of ensuring party discipline among MPs and peers, running the administration of debates and votes in Parliament and keeping MPs and peers informed.
Total	115	The complete 'government'.

Because government must have a substantial presence in both Houses of Parliament, it always contains a number of peers. Again, the proportion will vary from one administration to another, but it is typical for 25 members of the government to be Members of the House of Lords. The other 90 are all MPs.

We can now establish a number of characteristics of the body we know as 'the government':

- All members of the government must sit in Parliament as well as being ministers, and so on. As we have seen above, most, but not all, are MPs in the Commons. It can therefore be noted that members of the government who are MPs – 90 or so – also have a constituency to look after, even the prime minister.
- MPs from the party which is in government are NOT members of the government. It is a common misconception that they are. They are known as *backbenchers*, while government members are known as *front-benchers*. Backbenchers from the party in government are not bound by the same rules as frontbenchers.
- All members of the government are appointed by the prime minister. Though s/he may seek advice from trusted colleagues, the decision is hers/his alone. This also means that only the prime minister may dismiss a member of government.
- All members of government are bound by the principle of **collective responsibility**. This means that they must all take public responsibility for all policies of the government, even if they disagree privately or had nothing to do with the formulation of policy. If a minister, however junior, publicly disagrees with government policy, they are expected to resign or face rapid dismissal. In fact, it is the prime minister and Cabinet that make virtually all policy, so the 90 or so government members who are not Cabinet members are required to support policies in whose formulation they may have played no direct part.
- The full government – a hundred plus members – would never normally meet together in one body. The Cabinet, usually of 22–23 members, does meet regularly, however.

Ministerial selection

The next question to be posed is, how does a prime minister decide whom to put in his/her government? This is a complex issue, mainly because there are two considerations that may well conflict with each other. One concerns the competence of the individual in question. This may be simple enough. But there are also political considerations. The best person for the job may have unorthodox views, may be considered to be something of a 'rebel' and may well have clashed with the prime minister in the past. Therefore, the prime minister must weigh up the qualities of individuals against the political consequences of appointing them.

Nevertheless we can identify a number of qualities which ideal ministers should possess:

- They must be politically reliable. This does not necessarily mean that they should agree with the prime minister on every issue, but it does mean that they will be willing to accept collective responsibility and support the government, at least in public. Well-known dissidents are occasionally appointed. Tony Blair, for example, appointed such characters as Mo Mowlam (Northern Ireland Secretary), Robin Cook (Foreign Secretary) and Clare Short (Overseas Development Secretary), knowing that they were potentially difficult to control. He chose them for their personal qualities and because they had a substantial following in the party. In the event, all three left the government: Short and Cook over policy in Iraq, and Mowlam because she became disillusioned with politics in general. Tony Benn, however, Labour's best-known left-winger, was not considered for government office as it was highly unlikely that he would ever accept collective responsibility.
- Junior ministers, on the first rungs of the promotional ladder that leads to Cabinet office, must have potential. Prime ministers are always looking for younger MPs who will be able to fill senior posts in the future. 'Potential' generally means an ability to cope under pressure, to be a good debater in Parliament and to be a good 'politician'. This means displaying such skills as negotiation, persuasion and a general feel for how opinion is moving.
- Political leaders like Tony Blair and Margaret Thatcher, who have a strong political philosophy and wish to put that philosophy into practice, normally will try to recruit a team of ministers who share their political views. This creates a united and dynamic government. Dissension within government can hold back progress towards specific political goals. Sometimes, of course, as was the case with John Major from 1992 to 1997, this is not always possible. Major had to accept a number of colleagues who were not his political allies. This was because, in his position as prime minister, he was constantly undermined by having a small parliamentary majority and by serious political rifts within the Conservative Party.
- Finally, potential ministers must have managerial skills. Those who will head a government department, or a section of a department, will have a large number of civil servants, advisers and other bodies to manage. If they cannot do this they will inevitably fail.

Other forms of government

So far we have looked at the conventional form of government seen in the UK. That is, a government made up of members of the same party and which is able to command an absolute majority in the House of Commons – where it really matters. However, we should also look at two other forms of government, for two reasons. First, the British model of dominant,

single-party government is unusual in most other so-called liberal democracies. The proportional representation and majority electoral systems that are used almost everywhere in the democratic world would rarely throw up a single party with an absolute parliamentary majority. Therefore, they have to form other types of government. Second, it could well be that we will have to adapt to new forms of government formation in the future, either if we change our electoral system or if the Liberal Democrats continue to make progress and create a three-party system.

The two types we will consider are minority and coalition governments.

Minority government

Minority governments are unusual, unstable and normally short-lived. But they are not unheard of and have been known in the UK. It is a situation where a party forms a government without a parliamentary majority. This was the case in Britain from February to October 1974 (see above), and also occurred in the 1920s. Usually a minority is a caretaker government, waiting for a fresh general election in the hope that it will produce a decisive result.

A minority government can never rely on getting its legislation or its financial budgets passed. Therefore, it must take each issue separately and try to build a coalition of support from other parties, or sections of other parties. It cannot hope to pass legislation without such a consensus of support. In effect, minority governments cannot attempt to do anything radical. They can keep government ticking over, but little more.

Coalition government

A coalition government is one in which two or more parties take part. There are two conditions which must be met:

1. Ministerial posts are shared between two or more parties. In the British system this would also have to mean shared Cabinet posts. Which posts are given to which parties would be the subject of considerable negotiation.
2. There would need to be agreement on which policies can be accepted by all the coalition partners. All the parties would need to be willing to give up some policies and perhaps agree to some of their rivals' proposals.

Coalitions can be remarkably stable, as has been the case in countries such as Germany, Japan and Sweden. There coalitions are the norm and have tended to last for many years. But they can also be very unstable and are typically short-lived. Italy and Israel are notorious for such instability. We will consider the relative merits and drawbacks of coalition government in Chapter 3.1 on electoral reform.

There has been no coalition government in Britain since 1945, and it is certainly a kind of administration which is considered to be unnatural, to be avoided at virtually all costs. But we have now seen coalition government at work in Scotland, where Labour and the Liberal Democrats have worked together since devolution was introduced in 1998. There was also a brief agreement between the same two parties in the Welsh Assembly. In local government, coalitions are very common, with all combinations of parties being possible. So the British are coming round to the idea that coalitions are not a disaster. As we have said, either the introduction of proportional representation for general elections or the rise of the Liberal Democrats may mean they will become common.

There are a number of different types of coalition, any one of which might be seen in the future:

- **Majority coalitions**: Normally formed by just two parties, such coalitions are formed simply to create a parliamentary majority.
- **Grand coalitions**: This is a coalition between two major parties, formed to create an overwhelming majority. They would normally be considered in times of national emergency or crisis.
- **Rainbow coalitions**: These are agreements between a larger number of parties, often of greatly varying philosophies. It would normally be one large party and several other smaller parties.
- **National coalitions**: A coalition where all parties (or sections of parties) are invited to participate. They occur at times of national crisis and are designed to create unity. Britain used such a coalition in the 1930s, when there was a major economic depression, and in the Second World War.

Before leaving coalitions, we can consider a scenario in which coalition government might be used in the UK. Let us assume the following general election results and the possible coalitions that might be formed.

Party	Seats won
Conservative	290
Labour	250
Liberal Democrat	75
Scottish Nationalist	10
Welsh Nationalist	4
Others	17
Total	646

Possible coalition	Seats controlled	Majority
Cons./Lib. Dem.	365	84
Lab./Lib. Dem.	325	4
Cons./Lab.	540	434
Lab./Lib. Dem./Nationalists	339	32

This decision tree represents the likely range of outcomes following a general election

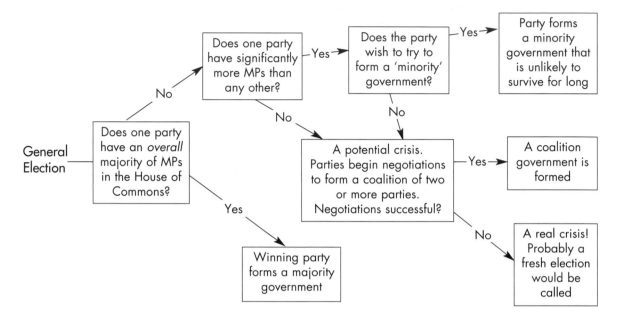

FIG 2.3A Government formation in the UK

Cabinet government

Until the 1960s, most (if not all) textbooks would describe the British system of government as **Cabinet government**. Since then, however, the concept of Cabinet government has been gradually eroded and replaced by the notion of **prime ministerial government**. We will consider the conflict between these two ideas below, but before doing that it is necessary to consider the traditional idea of Cabinet government.

The following realities used to be taken for granted:

- The Cabinet represented the collective identity of the government.
- All important domestic and many foreign policy decisions were made within the Cabinet.
- In order for a policy to be official, it would need full Cabinet approval.
- Any disputes within the government would be resolved within the Cabinet.
- The prime minister was considered *primus inter pares* (first among equals), meaning that he had a higher status than his colleagues, but also implying that he could be – and often was – outvoted within the Cabinet.

In summary, the Cabinet was considered to be the centrepiece of the government and its supreme policy-making institution.

It was during the premiership of Harold Macmillan (Conservative, 1957–63) and, more particularly, the first administration of Harold Wilson (Labour, 1964–70) that commentators began to realise that the days of Cabinet government, as described above, were numbered.

The changing UK Cabinet

What began to happen in the 1960s was that the prime minister came to become increasingly dominant within the government. Two of Wilson's Cabinet colleagues, Richard Crossman and Barbara Castle, began to speak and write openly of 'prime ministerial government'. This was not because they were Wilson's political opponents within the Labour Party, but because their experience of Cabinet government was not what they had expected. It certainly did not correspond to the textbook descriptions they had read. So Wilson started a process of degradation of Cabinet government that continues to this day. What were the changes that constituted this process?

Prime ministerial domination

Harold Wilson soon learned how he could dominate the whole governing process, the Cabinet especially. With the help of a small, close-knit team of allies, the Cabinet secretary (the most senior civil servant, who came to serve the prime minister almost exclusively), a few trusted private advisers (known in Wilson's day as the *kitchen Cabinet*, from where it often met to discuss strategy in Downing Street) and his own force of personality, he could control the political agenda from Number 10.

Wilson manipulated the agenda of Cabinet meetings, reached private agreements with ministers before the meetings so as to control the probable outcome and even, it was reported, had the accounts of the meetings (the secret Cabinet minutes) written to suit his own conclusions. So even senior Cabinet colleagues began to feel that matters were outside their control, even though they sat at the apparent centre of power.

In the same period – the 1960s and early 1970s – the role of the media was becoming increasingly important. TV, radio and the press were taking over from Parliament as the main forums within which political issues were being presented. Wilson was perhaps the first prime minister who understood the power of TV in particular. Meanwhile, the media were choosing to focus on the prime minister alone as the spokesman for the whole government. It was almost inevitable, therefore, that the prime minister would increasingly be both the presenter and the maker of government policy.

Margaret Thatcher (1979–90) took prime ministerial domination to a new level. By 1983, when she had removed most of her political opponents from the government and had won decisive victories over Argentina in the Falklands War (1982) and in the general election which followed it, Thatcher appeared to dominate the whole government machinery. Even more than Wilson, she possessed great strength of purpose and came to be either feared or respected by her colleagues. The Cabinet seemed to operate as it had always done, but it was packed with her own supporters and she controlled its meetings just as Wilson had done. She was respected abroad, almost as much as Churchill had been, and the media concentrated their attention on her almost exclusively. Even the most senior of her colleagues in Cabinet felt marginalised by her and most of them left government in angry circumstances at one stage or another. Nevertheless, it was ultimately her own Cabinet that removed her in 1990. Tired of her unshakeable support for the highly unpopular local poll tax, they replaced her with the mild-mannered and apparently reasonable John Major.

Excited political commentators heralded Thatcher's removal with talk of the 'return of Cabinet government'. Indeed, John Major himself promised to restore 'collective' decision making, and for most of his period in office he had to put up with a quarrelsome Cabinet which contained some of his deadliest enemies. Surviving close votes of confidence in the House of Commons and a leadership challenge in 1994, he held on in power for seven years. But Major's period in office was not the return of Cabinet government, as many thought it was. The Cabinet certainly did not operate as it had done in pre-Wilson days. Rather it proved to be an obstacle in the path of Major's attempts to solve the country's economic difficulties and to adopt a coherent policy towards the European Union. It was less a collective decision-making body and more a battleground in which warring factions within the Conservative Party played out a damaging war of self-destruction. It has taken more than a decade for the Conservatives to begin the process of repairing the damage wrought during that period.

To prove that prime ministerial government had not disappeared, Blair set about restoring personal control. Combining Wilson's manipulation of the government machinery with Thatcher's media supremacy, and adding his own brand of domination by controlling the flow of information to the governing community, he has taken prime ministerial control to new heights. This reality has been barely disputed by commentators and politicians alike.

Cabinet committees

Although Cabinet committees have existed since the 1920s, their full use did not emerge until the 1960s. Since then they have taken over increasingly from the full Cabinet in terms of policy and decision making. A Cabinet committee is a small group – around five – of Cabinet ministers who meet regularly to discuss a specific area of government policy. Of course, a decision that is not considered of great strategic importance and that does not affect more than one government department will be made within the department itself, but most important decisions need wider approval.

Some committees are permanent, dealing with such matters as the economy, defence or foreign affairs, but some are temporary in nature, dealing with policy areas which may not be long-lasting, such as the Olympic Games or the terrorist threat. The larger areas of policy making also require highly specialised subcommittees, which report back to the full committee. Below follows a list of the Cabinet committees in operation in May 2005:

- Antisocial Behaviour
- Asylum and Immigration
- Civil Contingencies
- Constitutional Affairs (three subcommittees)
- Intelligence Services
- Defence and Overseas Policy (four subcommittees)
- Domestic Affairs (five subcommittees)
- Economic Affairs
- Energy and Environment (one subcommittee)
- European Policy
- European Union Strategy
- Housing and Planning
- Legislative Programme
- Local and Regional Government
- National Health Service Reform
- Public Services and Expenditure (one subcommittee)
- Public Services Reform
- Regulation, Bureaucracy and Risk (two subcommittees)
- Schools Policy
- Science
- Serious and Organised Crime and Drugs
- Welfare Reform
- Restructuring of the European Space and Defence Industry
- Animal Rights Activists
- Universal Banking
- Olympics
- London
- Efficiency and Relocation

Over many decades, as the business of government had broadened and become more technical and complex, Cabinet committees increasingly have taken over the work of the full Cabinet. Decisions are often taken in committee only and, even if a recommendation is passed up from committee to full Cabinet, approval tends to be automatic. The Cabinet in full session simply has neither the time nor the information to be able to deal with most matters. It is therefore an unusual occurrence when the full Cabinet makes its own decision following discussion or decides to overrule the recommendation of a committee.

The growth in number and importance of the committees has had the effect of increasing prime ministerial control. The prime minister controls the creation of the committees and who sits on them. He also has a great deal of influence over their agendas. It is much easier for a prime minister to control a small group of ministers than the whole Cabinet. Of course, under Blair, the management of the economy remained the personal empire of Chancellor Gordon Brown, but in all other areas the committee system allowed the prime minister to exercise some control.

Marginalisation

During the 1960s, 1970s and 1980s Cabinet government *appeared* to operate in the traditional way. However, behind the scenes, important rivals to Cabinet power were emerging. Some of these were as follows:

■ As we have seen above, the personal authority and power of the prime minister alone has grown in contrast to the collective power of Cabinet.
■ There is a growing tendency for the great departments of state – the Treasury, Home Office, Foreign Office, Department for Constitutional Affairs, Department for Education and Skills, and so on – to see themselves as separate 'kingdoms' or 'baronies', as they have sometimes been described. At their head, ministers jealously guard their own empire and resent any attempt at interference by the Cabinet. Of course, they must retain allegiance to the prime minister and s/he may influence what they do, but there is less and less inclination to bring matters of importance to full Cabinet.
■ As we have seen above, a great deal of policy making now takes place within Cabinet committees. It is, therefore, perhaps best to think of Cabinet as a system or network, rather than a single body. In other words, meetings of the full Cabinet are almost ceremonial. The real work goes on elsewhere.
■ Not only have Cabinet functions moved to the prime minister, to departmental ministers and to committees, but there has also been a shift in policy-making functions to 10 Downing Street itself. Again, since the 1960s, but particularly under Tony Blair, there is a growing army of private political advisers, think tanks and policy units doing the work previously undertaken by the Cabinet and its committees. This has both extended prime ministerial control and has tended to reduce Cabinet importance.
■ Finally, we should remember that the prime minister still conducts much government business on a *bilateral* basis, that is, by discussing policy with an individual minister, reaching agreement with him/her and then presenting the decision to the rest of the Cabinet as a fait accompli.

The Cabinet today

We can see now that the nature of the British Cabinet is much changed since the 1960s. So we need to ask, what functions does it perform today? The short answer is to say 'far fewer than 50 years ago', but this does not explain its position in the executive branch of government today. It still meets normally every week and it is still a requirement for the prime minister and his colleagues to attend unless they have pressing, unavoidable business elsewhere. But the meetings now tend to be short, lasting as little as 45 minutes, and they attract relatively little publicity. Nevertheless, the endurance of the Cabinet has some significance; we can identify the following current functions:

1. On rare occasions, when a dispute between ministers cannot be resolved elsewhere, by the prime minister, the Cabinet secretary or other advisers, the matter may be brought to the full Cabinet. In this way, the ministers who are in conflict are forced to accept the decision under the doctrine of collective responsibility. The most common kind of dispute concerns public spending, usually when one minister finds his/her proposed budget is being cut and s/he feels that the cut should fall elsewhere.

2. There may also be circumstances when the prime minister decides that an issue should be resolved by a full Cabinet session. This may be because s/he has no personal interest, or because s/he would prefer not to commit to a decision which may later cause her/him personal embarrassment. Perhaps the best-known example of such a decision was the commitment to build the notorious Millennium Dome in Greenwich in 1997. Though Blair wanted it built, despite claims it would fail and be a waste of public money, he chose to seek a full Cabinet decision to head off the opposition. But there may also be less sinister reasons for seeking Cabinet approval, for example, when it was decided in 2005 to press ahead with plans for the introduction of identity cards. As fierce opposition was expected in Parliament and among the public, it was felt that the commitment needed collective government approval.

3. Similarly, in times of national emergency, it is often seen as desirable that the whole Cabinet should back government policies. This was the case with plans to deal with the terrorist threat after the attack on New York's Trade Center on 9/11, and following terrorist atrocities in London in July 2005.

4. It has become increasingly important for government to present a united front to the media and Parliament, and to ensure that policy is seen in the most favourable light possible. Cabinet therefore has the task of making decisions about the *presentation* of policy. This may be little more than a set of instructions by the prime minister on how s/he would like policy presented.

5. Just as Parliament must legitimise all proposed legislation, so too must Cabinet legitimise policy proposals and key decisions. If the political community, especially members of the governing party, are to accept policy as 'official', it needs the Cabinet stamp of approval. This is largely a formal process – some call it little more than rubber stamping – but it remains necessary for the effective working of government.

We can now summarise the current state of Cabinet government.

Remaining functions of Cabinet	Main weaknesses of Cabinet
■ Settling ministerial disputes. ■ Making decisions which cannot be made elsewhere. ■ Dealing with domestic emergencies. ■ Determining presentation of policy. ■ Legitimising decisions made elsewhere.	■ Prime minister is now dominant. ■ Most decisions are made in committee. ■ Meetings are shorter and are stage-managed. ■ Large departments have become more independent. ■ More decisions are made in bilateral meetings. ■ Much decision-making has moved to the 10 Downing Street organisation.

Cabinet formation

It is one of the key roles of every prime minister to select a Cabinet. It is an important role because it can both shape the political direction of the government and, to some extent at least, determine how successful it will be. It is also a vital instrument of power for the prime minister. The power to make senior government appointments and, indeed, to dismiss office holders, is known as *patronage*. The power of patronage is a key element in the prime minister's ability to control the top levels of his party. Every minister, in and out of the Cabinet, owes their position to the prime minister and may, in theory at least, lose it at any time on his/her say-so. Added to these office holders, there are hundreds of MPs and a smaller number of peers who are hoping to be promoted by the prime minister. But it is appointments to the Cabinet itself that a prime minister considers to be the most important component in his/her powers of patronage.

On first coming to power, a prime minister has to start afresh in forming a new Cabinet. There are two initial decisions to be made:

1. Will s/he choose a balanced Cabinet, containing all shades of political opinion in the ruling party, or will s/he choose a team which is ideologically united? The former option may appear easier because it will please all sections of the party. John Major was forced to do this when he found himself with a reduced majority in 1992 and a divided party. However, to do so runs the risk of internal dissension, as Major was to find to his cost. The second option – the united team – may alienate some sections of the party, but is likely to give the prime minister an easier ride. This was Margaret Thatcher's choice in 1983 and Tony Blair's in 1997. Of course, even the united Cabinet option may contain one or two dissidents if they have great personal qualities and might cause too much trouble if left outside on the back benches.
2. Which individuals should fill the 22 or so posts which are available in a modern Cabinet.

We can offer the following list of criteria which a prime minister might take into consideration when choosing individuals. Beside each consideration is an example of a choice made by Tony Blair:

- He may have close political allies from the past who have been guaranteed a post if the party gains power (Gordon Brown).
- There may be an individual who can represent an important section of the party (John Prescott and the trade unionists).
- He may decide that a potential rebel who has great ability and is widely respected is best placed in the Cabinet, where they will be silenced by the discipline of collective responsibility (Clare Short).
- He may identify some individuals who are thought to have great potential to be successful ministers, that is, who will manage a department well (Alan Milburn).
- He may even have old personal friends whom he wishes to have close by him (Derry (Lord) Irvine).
- Some individuals may be popular figures with the public and the media (Mo Mowlam).
- A number of choices will be based on a desire to retain the political identity of the new government, individuals who symbolise the ideology of the ruling group (Jack Straw).
- Some may achieve their position simply because they are thought of as extremely able people who will do a good job (Stephen Byers).

Of course, as time goes by, some of these ministers will fall by the wayside. Some may find the pressures of high office too much for them, as was the case with Labour's Education Secretary, Estelle Morris. Others may find themselves isolated from government, out of step with its policies and therefore unable to continue to support the party line. Foreign Secretary Robin Cook found this to be the case and resigned in 2003 over the Iraq war. Some are not considered to be doing a good enough job by the prime minister and are removed during one of his regular Cabinet reshuffles. Occasionally there may be a scandal which forces a minister to resign. This was an all-too-common occurrence under John Major, but also happened when Ron Brown resigned from Tony Blair's first Cabinet over his personal life. Finally, there is the doctrine of **individual ministerial responsibility**, which requires that a minister should consider resignation if a serious mistake is made within his/her department. Trade and Industry Secretary Stephen Byers lost his job in 2002 in such circumstances, when one of his private political advisers made a serious error of judgement. David Blunkett resigned twice under the doctrine – in both 2004 and 2005. He had been reinstated to Cabinet between his two resignations.

Collective Cabinet responsibility

When a minister joins the government s/he is immediately bound by the principle of collective responsibility. Members of the Cabinet are bound especially tightly by it. The doctrine declares that all ministers, in and out

> **Individual ministerial responsibility**
> The convention that a minister should resign if s/he or his/her department makes a serious political or personal error. In practice, this usually means that a minister is responsible to Parliament and must face questioning and criticism.

Collective responsibility

In the UK all Cabinet decisions must be collectively supported by all members of the government, at least in public. It also implies that the whole government stands or falls as one on the decisions made by Cabinet.

---

of Cabinet, must publicly support all decisions made within Cabinet. It also implies that Cabinet decisions are considered to be *collective* decisions for which they are collectively responsible. Ministers may disagree with policy in private and in Cabinet meetings, but once a decision has been reached, it must be supported by all.

This can be illustrated by what happens at the end of most items of Cabinet business. The prime minister is unlikely to ask whether all members of the Cabinet agree with a decision. What s/he will ask is whether they are all prepared to defend that decision in public. If an individual is not prepared to do so, they are expected to resign, as former Foreign Secretary Robin Cook did over the decision to commit troops to the invasion of Iraq in 2003. (Interestingly, Clare Short, who was also known to disagree, did not resign and survived for a few months. However, she did eventually go under great pressure and over the government's handling of the post-war situation in Iraq.)

Collective responsibility can be seen as something of a sham. Political journalists, for example, who are in the know, understand perfectly well that many Cabinet decisions have been bitterly contested, but, once announced, all members of the government will line up to support those decisions in public without a murmur. On the other hand, it is argued, if collective responsibility did not apply, governments would regularly fall apart. Parliament and the public would soon lose respect for a group of ministers who regularly failed to agree on policy and said so in public.

Everyone in the political community, including the opposition parties, understands the workings of collective responsibility, and most accept it as a necessary reality. It gives government its unity and creates stability. The great disadvantage of collective responsibility, however, is that it stifles public debate, and it is difficult for Parliament and the media to understand how government reaches its decisions. If ministers are not prepared to debate government policy in public it becomes difficult to make them accountable for those decisions.

The following table shows the make-up of the British Cabinet in January 2006.

Post	Holder
Prime Minister	Tony Blair MP
Deputy Prime Minister	John Prescott MP
Chancellor of the Exchequer	Gordon Brown MP
Secretary of State for Foreign Affairs	Jack Straw MP
Secretary of State for Work and Pensions	John Hutton MP
Secretary of State for the Environment, Food and Rural Affairs	Margaret Beckett MP
Secretary of State for Transport and Scotland	Alistair Darling MP
Secretary of State for Defence	John Reid MP
Leader of the House of Commons	Geoff Hoon MP
Secretary of State for Culture, Media and Sport	Tessa Jowell MP
Secretary of State for Health	Patricia Hewitt MP
Chief Whip in the Commons	Hilary Armstrong MP

Post	Holder
Home Secretary	Charles Clarke MP
Secretary of State for Wales and Northern Ireland	Peter Hain MP
Minister without Portfolio (Labour Party Chairman)	Ian McCartney MP
Leader of the House of Lords	Baroness Amos
Secretary of State for Constitutional Affairs (Lord Chancellor)	Lord Falconer
Secretary of State for International Development	Hilary Benn MP
Secretary of State for Trade and Industry	Alan Johnson MP
Secretary of State for Education and Skills	Ruth Kelly MP
Minister for the Cabinet Office	Vacant
Treasury Chief Secretary (Deputy Chancellor)	Des Browne MP
Minister for Communities and Local Government	David Miliband MP

FIG 2.3B The cabinet in 2005

The role of the prime minister

It is worth pausing at this point to consider how the office of prime minister came about. All monarchs, of course, have had their close advisers and generally there has been one who has been closest of all. However, during the seventeenth century, the political authority and power of the monarchy began to wane. It was also true that the early Hanoverian kings – George I and George II – had relatively little interest in British politics. As a result, the Cabinet began to assume independent powers of its own, effectively running the country on behalf of the king.

Naturally, one member of the Cabinet would come to be thought of as the most senior member and the most trusted ally of the king. In the 1720s, when Robert Walpole filled such a role, the position came to be known as 'prime minister'. But there was still no formality about the position and it was never acknowledged in British law. Walpole happened to be First Lord of the Treasury and it has come to be that the prime minister has held this honorary position ever since. This is despite the fact that the Treasury is in fact run by the Chancellor of the Exchequer. But this is the nearest to the formalisation of the post that has ever occurred. In effect, prime ministers were declared to be so by the monarch. Since the late nineteenth century, however, the prime minister has automatically been the leader of the largest party in the House of Commons. As we saw above, in the section on government formation, the prime minister is the individual who is called upon to form a government by the monarch. This is where we are today.

The functions of the prime minister

The post of prime minister has been evolving constantly, but we can identify a clear list of functions carried out by today's office-holder:

1. **Chief policy maker**. Although this role is clearly shared to some extent with other ministers, with Cabinet and with the party, there is no doubt that the prime minister is completely pre-eminent in making the government's policy. The fact that he must seek wider approval for much of what he decides does not alter this political reality.
2. **Head of government**. This is a function that covers a number of roles. The prime minister is in charge of the machinery of government. He can create new posts and new departments as well as abolish them, establish committees and policy units and amalgamate existing ones. It also means he is head of the civil service and can seek advice from its vast machinery. As we have seen above, too, he chairs Cabinet meetings, determining their agenda and controlling the system of Cabinet committees, which underpins the Cabinet itself. But above all, it includes the task of determining which individuals should hold posts as ministers, senior judges and senior bishops and archbishops of the Church of England.
3. **Chief government spokesperson**. It is now expected that the prime minister must be the ultimate source of the official version of government policy to the media. Though other ministers may be called upon to represent the government on TV, radio and in the press, the definitive expression of policy must come from the prime minister. To some extent this can create an illusion that the prime minister makes *all* policy. This would be wrong. But it certainly does mean that he can place his own interpretation on policy, whoever has made it. Often this is described by the media and opposition politicians as 'spin'.
4. **Commander-in-chief of the armed forces**. This is a role which is exercised on behalf of the monarch, who is no longer permitted to become involved with such matters except on a purely ceremonial level. It is the decision of the prime minister alone whether or not to commit British troops to battle or to any other role. S/he may seek much advice, of course, but s/he has the final say.

In recent times it is a function which has often had to be carried out. Margaret Thatcher ordered a military task force to the Falkland Islands in 1982 to oust the Argentine invaders. John Major decided to support the USA and other forces in the liberation of Kuwait from Iraqi invaders in 1990–91. Tony Blair has committed British forces to action in Kosovo in 1998 to protect the Muslim population from ethnic cleansing; in Afghanistan in 2001 to oust the Taliban regime; in Sierra Leone in 2002 to protect the democratic government from a rebellion; and, most famously, in Iraq in 2003 to topple Saddam Hussein.

We can add to this impressive list of responsibilities the task of maintaining national security. This means directly controlling the intelligence and counter-terrorism services, as well as assuming emergency powers in a time of emergency, such as war.

5. **Chief foreign-policy maker**. Again, this is a function carried out for the monarch. This can mean anything from negotiating with foreign powers, negotiating and signing treaties, to chairing international meetings. Tony Blair, in particular, has concentrated on this role. As well as chairing meetings of the G8 group of leading nations, he has chaired the British presidency of the European Union in 2005 and taken a leading role on such issues as global warming and the relief of poverty in less developed countries. The prime minister today must also conduct British relations with the European Union.

6. **Parliamentary leader**. Although government ministers play a substantial role in debates and parliamentary questioning, it is the role of the prime minister to lead his party in Parliament. As we have seen above, he must decide who shall be a minister, but he is also in overall control of the government's strategy within both Houses.

The sources of prime ministerial power and authority

As we have shown, the British prime minister today completely dominates the political system. This accords him/her tremendous power and huge responsibility. It is therefore an important question as to how one single office can have accumulated so much authority, allowing the prime minister to exercise so much power. The answer lies in the fact that the office stands at the junction of a number of different sources of authority. Authority is turned into power and so we have an extremely potent combination. The prime minister draws authority from these main sources:

1. **The ruling party**. Although it is possible for the prime minister not to be the leader of the governing party, it would be highly unusual, and, arguably, unworkable, if s/he were not. So it is safe to assume that the prime minister has the support of his/her party, both in Parliament and in the country in the form of the ordinary members. Since that party has won the right to govern at the last general election, the prime minister carries all the party's elective authority with him/her.

2. **The royal prerogative**. The reigning monarch retains, in theory and in law, the power to carry out functions as head of state. This means

commanding the armed forces, conducting relations with foreign powers or international organisations and generally maintaining the security of the state. It also bestows the right to appoint and dismiss ministers, decide the date of the general election by dissolving parliament, making key appointments of peers, judges and Church of England bishops, and controlling the civil service machinery. Of course, in a democracy, we cannot allow the unelected monarch to employ any of these powers in reality. The traditional authority of the monarch to exercise these so-called prerogative powers is therefore delegated to the prime minister of the day.

3. **Popular mandate**. Although technically the electorate is choosing MPs and a party when they vote at a general election, it is undeniably true that they are also conscious of the fact they are electing a prime minister. Indeed, research suggests that the leader of each party has become a more significant factor in voting choices than ever before. In this sense, therefore, the victorious prime minister can claim, in some degree at least, to enjoy the authority of the electorate, the popular mandate.

4. **Parliament**. Finally, we should remind ourselves that the prime minister is a parliamentary leader. As long as s/he enjoys the support of the majority in the House of Commons, s/he can claim to have parliamentary authority.

What we see here are four different sources of authority, providing us with an explanation of why the prime minister can exercise so much power. We could perhaps also add the effects of the office holder's own personal qualities. These too can be converted into yet more power. Margaret Thatcher certainly enhanced her inherited authority by becoming such a dominating personality, who was admired and respected, at least in conservative circles. Tony Blair, at least in his first term from 1997 to 2001, was also seen as a charismatic figure and was therefore able to enjoy greatly increased authority and power.

Prime ministerial power

We are now in a position to summarise the prime minister's powers. At the same time, we can establish the ways in which these powers may vary, depending on circumstances. This can be done by dividing powers into formal and informal powers, or, put another way, by identifying the powers which *all* prime ministers enjoy, whatever the circumstances, from those which vary according to circumstances.

The powers enjoyed by all prime ministers (formal powers) are as follows:

- appointment and dismissal of ministers;
- granting peerages and other honours;
- head of the civil service;
- appointing senior judges and senior bishops;
- determining the date of the general election;

- commanding the armed forces;
- conducting foreign relations;
- maintaining national security;
- chairing Cabinet meetings.

The powers which vary according to circumstances (informal powers) are as follows.

Powers	Circumstances
Making government policy	How united is the ruling party? How secure is s/he as party leader? How forceful is his/her personality? How much does s/he wish to dominate the political agenda? How ideologically united is his/her party?
Parliamentary leadership	How large is his/her parliamentary majority? How united are his/her party's MPs?
Controlling Cabinet	Does s/he have powerful adversaries in the Cabinet? How politically united is the Cabinet? How much is s/he inclined to prevent collective decision making? How secure is s/he as party leader?
National leadership	How much personal popularity does s/he enjoy? How high is his/her media profile? How high is his/her standing abroad?

Limitations on prime ministerial power

Having reviewed the circumstances within which a prime minister operates, we are able to establish and summarise what the main limitations to his/her power must be.

- The size of the parliamentary majority is critical. Margaret Thatcher enjoyed huge majorities of over 100 following the 1983 and 1987 elections. So too did Tony Blair after 1997 and 2001. But when the majority is low or non-existent, the prime minister can never rely on parliamentary approval. Therefore, they must take into account forces within both Parliament in general and their own party in particular before taking any initiatives.

This was the case with John Major from 1992 to 1997. Starting with a majority of 21, he soon found this whittled away by by-election defeats and the defection of his MPs to other parties. He therefore found himself governing with his hands almost tied behind his back. There were even times when he had to rely on the support of a handful of Ulster Unionist MPs to survive – a fact that disabled his ability to conduct the policies he wanted in Northern Ireland. James Callaghan faced similar circumstances in 1976–79. In his case, it was economic and industrial policy which suffered. Left-wing, union-sponsored MPs in his own party proved to be major obstacles. As a result, the economy and industrial relations gradually deteriorated.

■ The unity or otherwise of the ruling party is also critical. A prime minister who leads an ideologically united leadership group can achieve a great deal more than one who is constantly forced to try to maintain some kind of cohesion. Margaret Thatcher's premiership illustrates this well. From 1979 to 1983 she was confronted by a divided party. Many were supportive of her proposals for a new free market economy and reduced state intervention in industry. There was also, however, a substantial group (known by her as 'the wets') who were traditional conservatives and opposed her radical ideas. This meant that too much of her attention was taken up by the need to keep the party together and so preserve her own leadership. By 1983, however, she had removed most of the dissident wets from the Cabinet. This left her with a more tight-knit group that shared her convictions. Her power increased dramatically and there followed seven years of the most dynamic leadership Britain had known in the twentieth century.

Tony Blair had no such problems in 1997 when he took power. New Labour, as his allies were known, was an exceptionally united group. This meant that Blair enjoyed several years of almost total domination. This contrasted with his predecessor, John Major. Between 1992 and 1997 Major led a Conservative Party completely split over the issues of Britain's relationship with Europe and over the state's relationship to the economy. This gave him the reputation of being one of Britain's weakest prime ministers of modern times.

■ Similarly, the public and media profile of the prime minister is important. When a leader loses the confidence of the public and of the media they become an electoral liability. In such circumstances, the ruling party will become unwilling to accept their leadership. This is what eventually happened to Margaret Thatcher in 1990, when she was removed.

■ Prime ministers can only survive if they enjoy the confidence of the Cabinet and Parliament. This is the ultimate limitation on their power. If the Cabinet overrules the prime minister, there is nothing s/he can do, as Cabinet is the ultimate source of government policy. Similarly, the policies of the prime minister are meaningless if s/he cannot secure parliamentary approval for his/her proposals.

■ Finally, there is the party of which the prime minister is the leader. Today, parties are undoubtedly less important than they used to be. Little policy is made within parties and the members have little

influence over the leadership. But, as we have seen above, the prime minister draws much of his/her authority from the ruling party. It is not the norm for parties to remove a sitting prime minister (with Thatcher a notable exception), but prime ministers must always be careful not to lose the confidence of their own party.

It would be wrong to assume that prime ministers always lose office against their will, but, as can be seen below, they usually do. The following list describes how prime ministers in recent times have ended their period in office.

Prime minister	Period in office	Reason for loss of office
Harold Macmillan	1957–63	Resigned through ill health.
Alec Douglas-Hume	1963–64	Lost election.
Harold Wilson	1964–70, 1974–76	Retired voluntarily.
Edward Heath	1970–74	Lost election.
James Callaghan	1976–79	Lost vote of no confidence in the Commons.
Margaret Thatcher	1979–90	Lost leadership of the Conservative Party to John Major.
John Major	1990–97	Lost election.

Thus, of the seven prime ministers shown, two resigned for personal reasons, three were removed by the electorate, one by her party and one by Parliament. This gives a good idea of what the main limitations on prime ministerial power are.

The debate concerning prime ministerial and presidential government

The arguments which used to take place among political academics about prime ministerial government have now largely disappeared. Few, if any, now doubt that the office of prime minister dominates the British political system. As long as the holder of that office is not faced by too many limiting factors, such as a small parliamentary majority or a divided party, the British system has moved away from the traditional Cabinet government model to a prime ministerial model.

A somewhat different question has emerged concerning the role and importance of the prime minister. This asks whether the system has now become 'presidential'. This term implies a number of things:

- That the prime minister has come to be, effectively though not legally, the head of state, the leader of the nation, irrespective of party allegiance. It should be stressed that this is not the same as national popularity. Rather it means that, in times of difficulty, emergency or crisis, such as war or terrorist threats, the country can unite behind its head of government. Nothing new in that, you may say, and certainly it has always been true to a great extent. But it can be argued that there has been a long-term drift towards seeing the prime minister of the day, rather than the monarch, as national leader.

- That the prime minister now has an extensive network of personal advisers, think tanks, policy units and working groups that serve him/her alone and are not available to the rest of the government unless s/he wants them to be so. Just as the US president has his own White House staff and large executive office, so too does the prime minister have his/her own 'government department', mostly in Downing Street. It used to be the case that the prime minister was at a disadvantage when negotiating with ministers because they had huge departments of civil servants to assist them, while the prime minister had very little.

- The growing importance of the media in politics has contributed to the greater concentration on the individual holder of the office of prime minister, rather than the government as a whole. Prime ministers now have large groups of advisers whose sole task is to enhance their media image and to control the flow of information coming out of Downing Street. Perhaps as a result of this, or perhaps coincidentally, the general public has also come to see government in terms of its leading member, rather than as a collection of ministers and MPs. This is a double-edged sword for the prime minister, who can often claim credit for the successes of the government in general, but also takes personal blame for their failures, whatever his/her own role may have been.

- The undoubted growth in the importance of foreign and military affairs has contributed to a presidential feel for the office of prime minister. When the head of government has to negotiate with foreign powers, attend international conferences, negotiate treaties, conduct wars and meet visiting dignitaries, s/he is bound to appear presidential. Indeed, at large conferences s/he will be seen rubbing shoulders with the presidents of France and the USA who represent their countries on these occasions. Margaret Thatcher (with Reagan), John Major (with Clinton) and Tony Blair (with Clinton and Bush junior) all forged close links with US presidents. Standing on the White House lawn after one of their many bilateral meetings, who could say that both did not appear equally presidential? Furthermore, all these three prime ministers led the country into important foreign wars.

- Finally, we turn to the concept of spatial leadership. This is a relatively new theory of prime ministerial power (and indeed of power in general). It suggests that political systems are increasingly led by leaders who consider themselves to be distinctly *separate* from the rest of the government. This separateness gives rise to the term *spatial*. Presidents are naturally spatial leaders, largely because they are elected separately from the rest of the government and therefore have a different source of authority and are accountable directly to the people. This has not been the case with the British prime minister. Nevertheless, as the role has become more dominant, there has been a tendency for the office holder to see him/herself as separate from government and, to some extent, to have his/her own mandate directly from the people.

We will now examine three of these phenomena in more detail.

The growth of 10 Downing Street

There has long been a body known as the Cabinet Office situated in Downing Street. A relatively small organisation, the Cabinet Office was originally largely administrative, existed to serve the whole Cabinet and did not become directly involved with policy making. That was until the 1960s. Since then there has been a steady growth in the Downing Street machine. Furthermore, it has shifted from serving the government as a whole, to serving mainly the prime minister. In addition, it has become far more concerned with the development of policy. This means that, wherever policy needs to be coordinated between different departments, the Downing Street organisation is in a position to develop strategy. Measures to combat youth crime, terrorism, drug abuse, child poverty and homelessness in recent times are all examples of such coordinated action. This enables the prime minister to play a pivotal role and so appear to be dominating government.

The list below shows the main individuals and bodies that make up the sources of advice available specifically to the prime minister:

- Chief of Staff
- Deputy Chief of Staff
- Principal Private Secretary
- Director of Communications
- Director of Events, Visits and Scheduling
- Director of Political Operations
- Head of the Policy Directorate
- Chief Adviser on Strategy
- Director of Government Relations.

All these individuals also have sizeable offices to support them. The two most important units are the **Policy Directorate** and the **Strategy Unit**.

Spatial leadership

This concept was developed by Michael Foley in his important work, *The Rise of the British Presidency* (MUP, 1993). In it he looks at leaders such as US President Ronald Reagan and Margaret Thatcher. Above all, he suggests these leaders deliberately make themselves into *outsiders* within government. They separate themselves from its other members and so are able to act independently, but also to remain part of government itself.

Thatcher and Reagan took this a step further. They even criticised governments of which they were the head, suggesting that they tended to be inefficient, wasteful and, simply, tried to do too much. On taking office in 1981, Reagan expressed the issue thus: 'Government is not the solution to our problems. Government is the problem.'

Meanwhile, Margaret Thatcher was promising to 'roll back the frontiers of the state', roundly criticising the civil service for its conservatism and wastefulness and not averse to openly opposing her own ministers. Both Thatcher and Reagan were popular leaders who commanded great public support. This enabled them often to appeal to the people above the heads of their own party leadership. Most famously, Thatcher eventually decided to use her own advisers on economic policy and to bypass her own Chancellor of the Exchequer, Nigel Lawson, a tactic which ultimately led to his resignation in 1989 and contributed to her own demise a year later.

John Major was also a spatial leader, though this was not necessarily through choice. He had to separate himself from large parts of his government simply because they were his political enemies. He was not powerful enough to remove them and so had to try to govern without them. He was also something of an outsider in that he was generally more popular in the country than the government as a whole. He was trusted; the rest were not.

Foley's analysis pre-dates Tony Blair, but Blair very much fits the same mould. He has chosen to adopt certain areas of policy as his own – foreign affairs, Northern Ireland, education and health – and attempted to dominate the political agenda by introducing his own policy initiatives above the heads of the relevant ministers. In areas where he does not choose to become involved – the economy, poverty relief and the environment, for example – he leaves matters very much to his ministers. In this way, he too had become an outsider. When we add this to his total domination of foreign policy, we see a prime minister who is indeed very separate from the rest of government.

Foley argues that all recent US presidents have been spatial leaders. As British prime ministers have followed their lead, they too appear to be presidential in style.

Labour MP Graham Allen has taken this analysis a stage further. He accepts the general thesis of a 'separate leadership' and suggests that we should embrace the reality of it and make changes to the constitution to accommodate the 'British presidency'. He suggests that the prime minister (who is a quasi-president anyway) should be elected separately from Parliament, just as occurs in the USA and in Israel. In this way we would acknowledge the inevitable truth and would give the prime minister his own source of authority. The electorate would then be in a position to distinguish between the performance of the prime minister and that of the government as a whole.

'President Blair'?

Although, arguably, Margaret Thatcher was a more dominant prime minister than Blair, there is little doubt that Blair has brought presidential style to new heights. As we have seen, he dominates some parts of the domestic political agenda, but his real preference lies in foreign and international affairs.

Here he has taken a world lead in supporting US Middle East policy, as well as showing a close interest in global environmental issues (though not domestic ones), world poverty (along with Gordon Brown, his closest political rival) and the reform of European Union finances and its political structure. He has also made periodic attempts to solve the Northern Ireland problem. He appears more comfortable in these roles, is certainly more popular and has gained a good deal of respect abroad. In short, on the world stage, Blair looks like a president. To some extent this rebounded on him at home, where he became less popular in his second and third terms. Furthermore, the British resented his presidential style, especially after the failure to find the much promised weapons of mass destruction in Iraq. Thus respect abroad was countered by lack of trust at home.

There is, of course, a counter-argument to the thesis that Blair became, effectively, a president. This is that the political opposition to him and his governments was weak. He saw off four different Conservative leaders and the Liberal Democrats failed to make the major impact they had hoped for after 1997. It could therefore be said that Blair dominates, not through his own efforts, but through the failings of others. But this counter-analysis does not alter the fact that Blair has become a major international statesman. It will be of great interest to see if Blair's successors, whether Labour or Conservative, will attempt to emulate his personal style.

The counter-arguments to the presidential thesis

So far we have looked at the evidence which suggests that the British prime minister is indeed effectively a president. But there are some important arguments against this thesis:

- Perhaps the most compelling argument has been provided by Professor Peter Hennessy. He suggests that the office of prime minister is an extremely flexible one. In other words, it is what the holder wishes to make of it. Some prime ministers will therefore seek to dominate, while others will be either unable or unwilling to do so. The actual powers and limitations of the office have not, he argues, changed a great deal in modern times. What has happened is that Britain has seen two very dominant individuals – Thatcher and Blair – who have been able to squeeze as much power from the office as possible. The weaker premierships of Edward Heath, John Major and James Callaghan prove that presidential style is not inevitable.
- A second critique is that there has indeed been a change in recent decades, but that it has been a change of style rather than substance. In other words, prime ministers now *seem* to be more presidential – largely as a result of media attention and the importance of foreign policy – but in fact they are subject to the same constraints that have always existed. This was most clearly seen with Margaret Thatcher, who, ultimately, was

reined in by her own party leadership when she attempted to implement a policy (the introduction of a local poll tax) against their wishes.

■ A third analysis has been offered in the past by Professor George Jones. This is the 'elastic' theory. It suggests that, as a prime minister tries to stretch the powers of the office further and further (a tendency among prime ministers who have been in office for a long time), the forces of constraint become increasingly strong. Again, this analysis fits well with the experience of Margaret Thatcher, who gained increasing numbers of enemies as she sought to exercise more and more control. Eventually, the enemies turned on her when they felt they had enough strength to remove her. There are those who suggest that Tony Blair will go the same way.

Is the Prime Minister Now Effectively a President?

Arguments for the proposition

■ Prime ministers perform most of the functions of a head of state.

■ Prime ministers now have extensive sources of advice of their own. 10 Downing Street increasingly resembles the inner circle in the presidential White House.

■ The media tend to concentrate on the prime minister as personal spokesman for the government rather like a president.

■ Foreign and military affairs have become more important. The prime minister dominates these.

■ The importance of spatial leadership in the UK increasingly looks like the president's style of leadership.

Arguments against the proposition

■ There has been no permanent change. The dominant role of the prime minister constantly ebbs and flows.

■ There has been a change to a more presidential *style*, but in substance the role of the prime minister has not changed.

■ There are important forces which will rein in prime ministerial power. Most of these forces are absent for a true president.

■ It should not be forgotten that, though the prime minister may appear so, he is not actually the head of state.

Now that we have considered the positions at the apex of power in Britain, we can study the rest of the machinery of government.

Ministers and departments

The machinery of British government is divided into departments. The precise nature and responsibilities of these departments lies in the hands of the prime minister and is constantly evolving. The following list shows the main departments of state in 2005:

■ Treasury
■ Department of Health
■ Foreign and Commonwealth Office

- Department of Constitutional Affairs
- Department of Work and Pensions
- Home Office
- Department of the Environment
- Department of Culture, Media and Sport
- Food and Rural Affairs
- Department of Transport
- Department of International Development
- Scottish Office
- Department of Trade and Industry
- Welsh Office
- Department of Defence
- Department for Education and Skills
- Department of Communities and Local Government.

Each department effectively has two heads. One is a minister, the other is a civil servant. The normal title for the minister is Secretary of State, and for the civil servant it is Permanent Secretary. The precise nature of the relationship between ministers and civil servants is examined further below. However, at this stage we can establish that the department has a *political structure* standing alongside an *administrative structure*.

The political structure is comprised of the Secretary of State, who is normally also a Cabinet minister, along with junior ministers, below him, who are normally known as Ministers of State. Ministers of State do not sit in the Cabinet, but are bound by the same political rules. To assist these ministers there will also be a number of private political advisers. Their role is to give political advice, conduct research and help ministers deal with Parliament, the media and the public in general. It is expected that political advisers will give advice which is sympathetic to the political aims of the government in general. Indeed, many such advisers go on to become elected politicians themselves. All Secretaries and Ministers of State are appointed by the prime minister. Political advisers are appointed by the ministers themselves.

The Permanent Secretary is the administrative head of a large number of civil servants. The men or women who take on this role will normally have worked their way up through the ranks of the civil service, will possibly have worked for two or more different government departments and will be considered highly skilled and experienced managers and administrators. As we shall see below, they must be politically neutral and should not attempt to change official government policy. All their work is expected to take place within the constraints of existing policy, as declared by the prime minister, Cabinet and the minister him/herself.

The top two levels of the civil service in each department are appointed from a short list by the prime minister in consultation with the minister concerned. A short list is drawn up by the Senior Appointments Selection Committee, which is made up of a number of senior civil servants. They normally choose individuals who are well established in the civil service, but increasingly they are allowed to consider applicants from outside the civil service, for example, from universities or the world of business and commerce.

In 2005, there were 16 government departments, staffed by 114 ministers. If we count only those civil servants who are close advisers to the minister (i.e. are in regular contact and involved in key decisions), there are about 4000 very senior civil servants. In addition, departments may form task forces or policy units from outside the structure of the civil service, staffed largely by outside experts to assist in policy making.

As an illustration, the ministerial structure of the senior levels of the Department for Education and Skills (September 2005) is shown below:

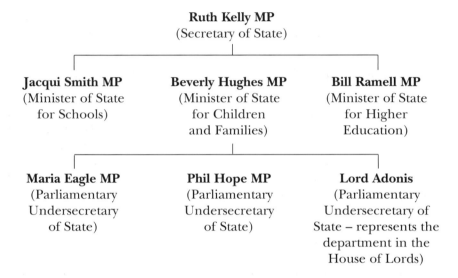

We can see that the department is divided into three sections, each headed by a junior minister. The lowest level of minister is Undersecretary of State. They report to Ministers of State, except for Lord Adonis, whose role in the Lords means that he reported directly to the Secretary of State, Ruth Kelly.

Each level of minister is shadowed, or served, by civil servants of appropriate rank.

Ministers and civil servants

The differences between ministers and civil servants is critical to an understanding of how government works in the UK. Unfortunately, there is a certain amount of blurring of the distinction between the roles of ministers and civil servants, and this confusion has been compounded by the growth in the number and use of private political advisers. However, we can identify the key distinctions.

Essentially, ministers are appointed for political reasons – because they are leading members of the ruling party – while civil servants are appointed because they have specialist or administrative skills, and they are expected to be politically neutral. Ministers are essentially temporary. They hold

office as long as the prime minister wishes them to do so. Civil servants are permanent in that they can expect to retain their position, and hopefully climb up the ladder of promotion if they are good enough, whoever is in government. In short, ministers are politicians who come and go, civil servants are administrators and managers who are expected to stay.

This is relatively straightforward. The confusion arises when we seek to identify their separate roles. Ministers are expected to hold political views and they may have a very specific political agenda. They are, after all, representatives of a government which was elected on a popular mandate to carry out certain stated policies. Civil servants, on the other hand, must have no political agenda, whatever their private views might be. The information and advice given to ministers by civil servants should be free of any political bias.

The following scheme will help to distinguish the roles in policy.

Tasks of ministers	Tasks of civil servants
■ Set the political agenda.	■ Gather information for policy making.
■ Determine priorities for action.	■ Provide alternative courses of action.
■ Decide between political alternatives.	■ Draft legislation.
■ Obtain Cabinet and prime ministerial approval for policies.	■ Advise on consequences of decisions.
■ Steer proposals through Parliament.	■ Provide briefings for other ministers.
■ Be accountable to Parliament for policies and their implementation.	■ Advise on implementation methods.
■ Account to Parliament for the general performance of their department.	■ Organise implementation of policy.
	■ Draft answers to parliamentary questions.

We can see from these tasks that it is only ministers who make political decisions. Civil servants have the task of facilitating decision making and ensuring the successful implementation of those decisions.

Of course, it would be naive to believe that civil servants never influence ministers. When they prepare alternative courses of action and when they advise on the consequences of each possible decision, there may be a possibility that the advice could be manipulated to steer the minister in a particular direction. If the civil servants are acting strictly in the national interest, there may be little harm in this. It only becomes a dangerous – and therefore forbidden – practice if the motives of the civil servant are political in nature.

The following extracts from the Civil Service Code of 1999 give a strong sense of how civil servants are expected to behave:

> The constitutional and practical role of the Civil Service is, with integrity, honesty, impartiality and objectivity, to assist the duly constituted Government of the United Kingdom, the Scottish Executive or the National Assembly of Wales ... whatever their political complexion, in formulating their policies, carrying out decisions and in administering public services for which they are responsible.

> **Accountability**
> A political principle which suggests that an individual or an institution has to account for what it does and for its policies. Thus, in the UK, MPs are accountable to their constituents, and the government is accountable to Parliament.

Civil servants must recognise their **accountability** to ministers, and their duty to discharge public functions reasonably and according to law.

Civil servants should conduct themselves with integrity, impartiality and honesty. They should give honest and impartial advice to the minister ... without fear or favour, and make all information relevant to a decision available to them. They should not deceive or knowingly mislead ministers, Parliament, the National Assembly or the public.

Source: Cabinet Office, 1999

There is one other aspect of the relationship between ministers and civil servants which is important. This is the anonymity rule. Civil servants are expected to be anonymous. This means that they should keep a low public profile, never make public statements about policy, unless required to do so by Parliament or a parliamentary committee, and avoid revealing their *precise* role in policy making. They are allowed to reveal what department they work for and their rank. What they should not do in public is to reveal exactly what kind of advice they are giving.

This rule presents a problem in a democracy. How are civil servants, who are contributing very often to key decisions, to be made accountable for what they do if they are anonymous? The answer lies in the doctrine of ministerial responsibility which has been described above. Briefly, it is expected that the minister will answer for his/her civil servants to Parliament or to the public. In other words, the minister is accountable *on their behalf*. It used to be the case that ministers were expected to resign or face demotion if their civil servants made serious errors, but this principle has now all but disappeared. Nevertheless, where there is criticism circulating, the minister is the one who must take the flak. Disciplining of civil servants takes place strictly in private.

We are now in a position to summarise the respective status of ministers and civil servants:

Ministers	Civil servants
■ Are politically committed to one party.	■ Must display no political allegiance.
■ Are temporary – they only hold office as long as the PM wishes them to.	■ Are permanent, or at least will spend a long time in the civil service.
■ Are expected to make political decisions.	■ May only suggest alternatives in a neutral way.
■ Have to use judgement about the outcome of decisions.	■ Identify possible outcomes in a neutral way.
■ Have a high public profile.	■ Are expected to be largely anonymous.
■ Are publicly accountable for the performance of their department.	■ Cannot be held publicly accountable for what they do.
■ Will lose office if their party loses power.	■ Will remain in position even if there is a change of government.

Civil service neutrality has been an important principle of government in the UK since the latter part of the nineteenth century. It is considered essential that ministers have access to advice that is free from political bias. Since the 1870s the principle of neutrality has included the following 'rules':

- Civil servants must not be politically active. The lower ranks of the service may join a political party, but not be active. Senior civil servants should not be party members.
- They should not express politically biased views either in public or in the course of their professional duties.
- Although they are expected to understand government policy and to facilitate such policy, they must separate their service to the government from any political service to the ruling *party*. In other words, they serve a government minister, but not his/her party.
- The advice they give should be free of political bias. It should conform to what the civil servant considers to be in the national interest within the constraints of official government policy.
- They must avoid any situations that might lay them open to external political pressure.
- In giving evidence to a parliamentary committee, they must only express views that conform to official government policy; they may not express personal opinions outside their department.

> **Civil service neutrality** The constitutional principle in the UK that civil servants must retain political neutrality, must give neutral advice to ministers and should not become involved in party politics.

Political advisers to ministers are not expected to be neutral. They serve the interests of both the government and the ruling party. It is expected that they be politically sympathetic to the aims of the ruling party. This causes tension within government circles. While civil servants are attempting to give neutral advice, they may feel that their position is being undermined by the political advisers. It is almost inevitable that rivalry has grown between civil servants and advisers as to who can gain the ear of the minister. There may also be considerable blurring between the roles of the two. Ultimately, it is up to the relevant minister to distinguish between neutral and political advice.

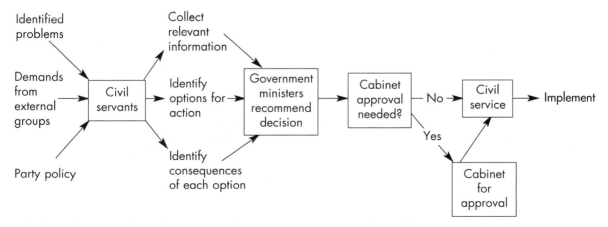

FIG 2.3C Ministers and civil servants and decision making

228

Open government
A principle and an aspiration that the processes of government should be made as open to public and parliamentary scrutiny as is possible and reasonable.

Open Government

The term, open government, refers to a policy of attempting to allow more access by the media and the public to decision making processes in government. In particular, the relationships between ministers, civil servants and private advisers remain shrouded in some mystery. The Freedom of Information Act, which came into force in January 2005, has gone some way to opening up the processes of government, but progress has remained limited. Successive governments since the 1970s have promised to open up government, but relatively little has been done.

The requirement for civil servants to be neutral and anonymous has led to a great deal of secrecy in government. Indeed, it is said to be an established part of civil service culture to be secretive. This culture has made it difficult for members of parliament to obtain relevant information from government. So the concept of 'open government' remains more an aspiration than a reality.

KEY CONCEPTS

Collective responsibility

In the UK all Cabinet decisions must be collectively supported by all members of the government, at least in public. It also implies that the whole government stands or falls as one on the decisions made by Cabinet.

Cabinet government

A system of government where the Cabinet is the central policy-making body.

Prime ministerial government

Political circumstances in which the prime minister dominates policy making and the whole machinery of government.

Individual ministerial responsibility

The convention that a minister should resign if s/he or his/her department makes a serious political or personal error. In practice, this usually means that a minister is responsible to Parliament and must face questioning and criticism.

Accountability

A political principle which suggests that an individual or an institution has to account for what it does and for its policies. Thus, in the UK, MPs are accountable to their constituents, and the government is accountable to Parliament.

Civil service neutrality

The constitutional principle in the UK that civil servants must retain political neutrality, must give neutral advice to ministers and should not become involved in party politics.

Open government

A principle and an aspiration that the processes of government should be made as open to public and parliamentary scrutiny as is possible and reasonable.

Revision topics and examination questions

Revision topics

- The main powers of the prime minister
- Limitations to prime ministerial power
- The functions of the prime minister
- The sources of prime ministerial power
- Role of the Cabinet
- Nature of Cabinet government
- Factors in appointment of ministers and the Cabinet
- Collective and individual ministerial responsibility
- Nature and growth of prime ministerial government
- Extent to which the prime minister has become presidential
- Differences between ministers and civil servants
- Relationship between ministers and civil servants
- Neutrality of the civil service

Short answers

- Outline THREE powers of the prime minister.
- Outline THREE functions of the prime minister.
- Outline THREE sources of prime ministerial power.
- Outline THREE functions of the Cabinet.
- What is meant by the term 'party government'?
- Outline the main role of a civil servant.

Medium answers

- What are the main limitations on prime ministerial power?
- Distinguish between Cabinet government and prime ministerial government.
- What factors does the prime minister take into account when appointing a Cabinet?
- What factors does the prime minister take into account when appointing ministers?
- Why do ministers resign?
- Distinguish between collective and individual ministerial responsibility.
- Distinguish between the roles of a minister and a civil servant.
- In what senses is the civil service neutral?

Long answers

- To what extent is British government prime ministerial government?
- Why do some prime ministers appear to be more powerful than others?
- Is the British prime minister now effectively a president?
- Assess the importance of the Cabinet in British government.
- What problems exist in the relationship between ministers and their civil servants?

Resources and Web Guide

Books

A concise account of PM and Cabinet is:

N. McNaughton, *Prime Minister and Cabinet Government*, Hodder and Stoughton, 1999.

Modern developments are covered in:

D. Kavanagh and A. Seldon, *The Powers Behind the Prime Minister*, HarperCollins, 1999.

Presidential government issues are covered excellently in:

M. Foley, *The British Presidency: Tony Blair and the Politics of Public Leadership*, MUP, 2000.

Another very good update is:

G. Thomas, *Prime Minister and Cabinet Today*, MUP, 1998.

A modern history of the office of PM, full of useful examples, is:

P. Hennessy, *The Prime Minister: The Office and its Holders since 1945*, Penguin, 2001.

A huge book on the civil service (probably too big) is:

P. Hennessy, *Whitehall*, Fontana, 2001.

More manageable is:

K. Theakston, *The Civil Service since 1945*, Blackwell, 1995.

Useful websites

There are a number of official government sites:

www.cabinet-office.gov.uk (accessed 11 November 2005)

www.number-10.gov.uk (accessed 11 November 2005)

www.civil-service.gov.uk (accessed 11 November 2005)

Information about recent prime ministers can be found on:

www.margaretthatcher.org (accessed 11 November 2005)

www.johnmajor.co.uk (accessed 11 November 2005)

www.number-10.gov.uk (accessed 11 November 2005)

2.4
The judiciary and civil liberties

The nature of the judiciary

It is important at the outset to distinguish between two definitions of the judiciary. The first is a wide description that includes all those officials who are concerned with the dispensation of justice within the legal system. The other, narrower definition deals only with those judges who are directly involved with the process of lawmaking and politics. When we refer to the three branches of government – the executive, the legislature and the judiciary – it is this second, specific definition to which we are referring.

Therefore, we can first describe the complete judiciary of England and Wales, including those who have no direct political significance.

Post	Type of post holder	Main roles
Lay magistrates	Part-time, non-legally qualified members of the public.	Hearing minor criminal cases, giving verdicts and setting punishments. Deciding whether to grant bail to arrested persons. Conducting committal hearings to decide whether more serious suspects should be sent for trial at a higher court. Granting licences to pubs, entertainment places, etc. Deciding whether children should be taken into local authority care.
Stipendiary magistrates	Full-time lawyers.	As above, but usually in larger cities.
Circuit and Crown court judges	Full-time judges and recorders ('junior judges') who are mostly former barristers. They sit in Crown courts or county courts.	Hearing more serious criminal cases. Giving verdicts and determining punishments. Hearing disputes such as cases of negligence, commercial issues, divorce.

Post	Type of post holder	Main roles
Tribunal officials	Lawyers or experts in a particular field, sometimes part-time, who staff special administrative tribunals which are not courts of law but have a judicial function.	Deciding on disputes over issues such as unfair dismissal, taxation, social security payments, compulsory purchase of property by local government.
High Court judges	Senior judges.	Hear appeals from county courts. Hear cases involving matters and disputes over large sums of money. **Hearing cases where citizens or organisations have a dispute with some part or agency of government, known as judicial review.**
Appeal courts	Very senior judges.	Hearing appeals from criminal courts and the High Court. **Dealing with disputes from lower courts over the accurate meaning of the law.** **Dealing with appeals involving human rights.**
House of Lords (only the Appellate Committee of 12 judges, not the whole House) also known as the 'Law Lords'	The most senior judges – 12 in number. All these judges also sit as ordinary members of the House of Lords and are therefore also peers who deal with proposed legislation. They have to be neutral and so sit as cross-benchers.	Hearing appeals from the appeal courts in England and Wales. Hearing appeals from Scottish and Northern Ireland Courts. **Settling major disputes over human rights and judicial reviews.** **Dealing with major problems over determining the accurate meaning of law.** **Settling disputes over conflicts between British and EU law.**

Notes:

■ The roles shown in bold have greater political significance.

■ Court systems in Scotland and Northern Ireland differ slightly, but major appeals and political cases end up in the House of Lords in London.

■ The table above does not show the **Judicial Committee of the Privy Council**. This is a highly specialised committee of the otherwise largely ceremonial Privy Council. This committee is the highest appeal court for a few British Commonwealth countries and also deals with any disputes over whether matters are under the jurisdiction of the British government and Parliament or should fall under the jurisdiction of the Scottish Parliament, Welsh executive or Northern Ireland government (when the latter is not suspended).

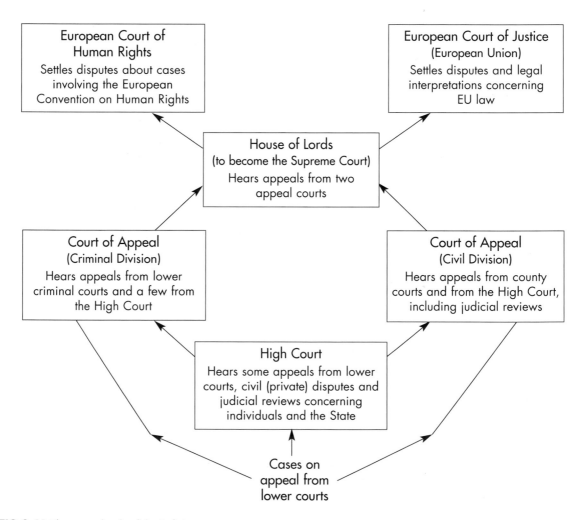

FIG 2.4A The upper levels of the judiciary

The political role of the judiciary

We can now see that the role of the vast majority of the judiciary has no great political significance at all. Its overall task of administering justice is just that – administration. But a minority of the total judiciary is certainly involved with cases of 'political' significance. What do we mean by this? The kind of issues which we can consider to be political in nature are explored below.

Dispensing justice

Though not of directly political importance, the lower courts – Magistrate's, Crown and County courts – do have a vital role in ensuring that legal justice is delivered. This implies that all citizens should be treated equally under the law and that the law is applied to them in a fair way. Trials and hearings should all be conducted in such a way as to ensure that all parties gain a fair hearing and that the law is applied in the spirit intended.

Interpretation

The precise meaning of a statute is not always clear. However well the drafters of legislation have done their job, and however much parliamentary standing committees may have tried to make the law easy to understand, there will always be circumstances where those in court – disputants in a civil case, defenders and prosecutors in a criminal case – come into conflict over what the law is supposed to mean. In such cases it is for judges to interpret the meaning of law. In cases involving the powers of government or its agencies, or the rights of citizens, such interpretations may be of great public significance.

Creating case law

Similarly, it is not always clear how the existing laws are to be applied in a particular case. For example, there are laws relating to racial prejudice, discrimination against women and against actions which are likely to incite people to commit crime or to indulge in race hatred. This is all very well, but how should the law operate in *specific circumstances*? It is for judges to decide this. Furthermore, when such a decision is made, it is expected that any similar cases which arise in the future should be dealt with in the same way (the concept of judicial precedent – see below). Once the application of law in specific kinds of cases is established, the precedents are known as **case law**. We also refer to such law, including the interpretation of law described above, as **judge-made law**, because it is judges, rather than Parliament, who are effectively making new law.

Declaring common law

Not all law is made by Parliament. Some law is known as **common law**. These are rules of behaviour which have developed solely by tradition. In other words, they are common ways of dealing with disputes of various kinds. It typically relates to such matters as inheritance, commercial practices and, very occasionally, the rights of citizens. Much common law is well enough established for judges to be able to apply it relatively easily. However, from time to time there may be problems in settling disputes for which there is no relevant statute law (made by Parliament) and no clear common law. When this happens a judge must take evidence and decide what the common law is. This is the third example of judge-made law. Once again, the rule of judicial precedent applies.

Judicial review

Judicial review

A process whereby the courts review decisions by the state or any public body in relation to its citizens. Where a review finds that a citizen has not been treated fairly, or that their rights have been abused, or that a public body has exceeded its legal powers, the court may set aside the decision.

The quantity of cases involving **judicial review** has grown dramatically since the 1960s. The landmark case of *Ridge* versus *Baldwin* in 1964 established the principle that citizens could appeal against decisions by government that appeared to be against 'natural justice'. Natural justice simply suggests that citizens have not been treated fairly, as we generally mean by that term. Typically, these are cases where a citizen, a group of citizens or an organisation believes it has been mistreated by the government or an agency of government. In such cases they will ask for a judicial review of their case, normally in the High Court. Typical examples of judicial review are cases where a minister or civil servant has not dealt equally with different citizens, or where there has been a clear injustice or where government or a public body has exceeded its statutory powers. Judicial reviews increased still further after 1977, when the procedures for citizens who wished to call for a judicial review of a decision by the courts were considerably simplified.

Judicial review is clearly a critical role because it helps to achieve two democratic objectives: one is to ensure that government does not overstep its powers; the second is to assert the rights of citizens. The courts were given an enormous boost in this area when the Human Rights Act came into force in 2000. This meant that courts could review actions by government and public bodies which might contravene the European Convention on Human Rights. At the same time, the Freedom of Information Act, which came into force in January 2005, gives citizens and the courts a right to see a much wider range of official documents than before. In this way there is considerably more scope for discovering whether injustice has been done and whether rights have been abused.

A number of examples of judicial review and the general political work of the courts are shown below.

Public inquiries

Though it is not necessarily the case, judges are often called up to conduct public inquiries into matters of widespread public concern. The reason for

using judges is twofold. First, as experienced judges they are used to handling such issues. Second, they are independent of government, so an inquiry led by a judge can be seen to be politically neutral. The following table shows a number of such inquiries held in recent times. In each case the chair was a current or former judge.

Public inquiry	Detail
Bingham Inquiry, 1992	The collapse of the Bank of Credit and Commerce International (BCCI) raised concerns about the failure of the Bank of England to regulate foreign-owned banks.
Scott Inquiry, 1996	The British government apparently changed the rules on the sale of arms to Iraq without making the matter public. This caused a number of embarrassing legal cases and ministerial errors.
Phillips Inquiry, 1998	Into the government's handling of the crisis over the outbreak of BSE (mad cow disease) in the UK.
Macpherson Inquiry, 1999	Into the killing some years earlier of black teenager, Stephen Lawrence, by a group of young white men. Conducted into the handling of the case by the police and the implications for race relations in the UK.
Hutton Inquiry, 2003	Into the circumstances surrounding the apparent suicide of David Kelly, a civil servant and weapons expert, who had been criticised for his role in the issue of Iraq and the search for weapons of mass destruction there.

External jurisdiction

The activities of government are now further constrained by relations with political and legal systems outside England and Wales. First, there is devolution. The courts have to settle any disputes concerning the jurisdiction of the Scottish Parliament and the Welsh or Northern Ireland Assemblies. The Devolution Acts which established devolution could not possibly deal with every single eventuality. It is therefore the role of the courts (especially the Judicial Committee of the Privy Council) to decide who has power in particular cases – London or one of the devolved administrations.

Second, there is the European Union. When there is a dispute over whether a matter falls under the power of British government and courts, or whether it is a matter for the European Court of Justice, the case will first be

FIG 2.4B Lord Phillips who became Chief Justice in 2005

referred to one of Britain's appeal courts – the Court of Appeal or the House of Lords. If there is a further appeal, or more consideration needs to be given to the case, it will pass to the European Court of Justice for a final decision.

Sentencing issues

Finally, we need to turn to the contentious issue of sentencing in criminal cases. In the past this has not been a political issue. Judges were given a very free hand in deciding what sentences to give out. The only major restrictions on this power were homicide cases of various kinds – where a life sentence was mandatory – or the general use of maximum sentences determined by Parliament.

Since the mid-1990s, however, when growing crime rates became a major political issue, politicians, mostly Home Secretaries, have sought to take control out of the hands of judges and to try to force their hand in various ways. The judges have resisted this very strongly on the grounds that they should be independent from government and that they are the best judges of each individual case and should decide them on their own merits. Politicians counter this by saying that judges are not accountable to the public. The public have shown a clear preference for more severe sentencing in general, so judges should be forced to respond to public opinion. The dispute goes on, but politicians appear to be winning, by introducing *minimum sentences* for certain offences and for repeat offending. This takes away most of the flexibility which judges formerly enjoyed.

Now that we have established the nature of the judiciary's role, we can review some UK court cases of political importance which illustrate that role.

Cases of political importance	Detail
GCHQ, 1985	Prime Minister Margaret Thatcher announced that no member of General Communications Headquarters (GCHQ) – the government's international radio surveillance centre – could be a trade union member. The decision was challenged on the grounds of freedom of association. The House of Lords ruled that the PM had such a prerogative power in the interests of national security.
Factortame, 1991	European Court of Justice ruled that the UK Merchant Fishing Act was in conflict with European Union Fisheries directives. The UK law was set aside, establishing the principle that EU law is superior to UK law.

Cases of political importance	Detail
Michael Douglas v. *Hello Magazine*, 2001	Court ruled that Michael Douglas and Catherine Zeta-Jones had a right not to allow unauthorised photos of their celebrity wedding to be published. This established a right to privacy, under the Human Rights Act, for such celebrities.
Mental Health Act, 2002	The UK Mental Health Act required that a person detained with a mental illness had to prove their own fitness to be released. The Court ruled this contradicted the Human Rights Act's individual right to freedom. Instead such detainees have a right to freedom unless it can be proved to be against the public interest.
Belmarsh, 2004	House of Lords ruled that detainees held against their will under the anti-terrorism legislation contradicted the Human Rights Act on the grounds that citizens have a right not to be detained without trial. This forced the government to amend the anti-terrorism legislation to ensure safeguards for suspected terrorists.
Herceptin Case 2005	Breast cancer sufferer, Anne Marie Rogers, won the right to a judicial review over her NHS Trust's decision to refuse her treatment with a new drug, Herceptin. This case created a precedent – that NHS patients will be able to use judicial review over their treatments.

FIG 2.4C The British judiciary is renowned for its neutrality and independence

The legal and constitutional environment of the judiciary

The judiciary does not operate in a vacuum. There are a number of limitations, principles and safeguards within which it operates. These are as follows.

The sovereignty of Parliament

Since Parliament is the source of all political authority, it cannot be overruled by the judiciary. In particular, this means that the judges cannot legally defy the legislative will of Parliament. Even if judges believe that a law is an offence to human rights or discriminates unfairly against a particular group within society, they do not have the power to set that law aside. They are obliged to enforce it. They may, of course, give a critical opinion and suggest a change in the law, but that is as far as it goes (see Belmarsh case, above). The advent of the Human Rights Act in 2000 has given the courts a great deal of ammunition in its defence of individual rights, but, even so, they cannot overturn a statute that has been properly passed by Parliament.

The rule of law

It is a firm principle of the British constitution that all citizens are considered to be equal under the law. This also applies to the government itself. The judiciary must always apply this principle. All citizens are also entitled to a fair trial. If the courts do not provide this, they leave themselves open to appeal to a higher court.

Judicial precedent

As we have seen above, when a judge makes an interpretation of law, creates new case law or declares common law, all courts in the future must abide by that interpretation. Only a higher court is able to overturn an interpretation made by a lower court. Ultimately, most disputed interpretations will end up in the House of Lords for a final decision. Of course, if a judge's interpretation of the law causes a problem for the government, ministers are at liberty to ask Parliament to clarify the law by passing a new statute or amending existing legislation.

The primacy of EU law

In areas of policy where jurisdiction has been transferred to the European Union, British courts must accept the fact that Union law takes precedence over domestic law (see Factortame case, above). In other words, it is the duty of the British courts to enforce Union law. Only when there are problems of interpretation of Union law will British courts pass a case up to the European Court of Justice.

The independence of the judiciary

An essential feature of any healthy democracy is that the judicial branch should be independent of the government. There are a number of reasons why this is so:

- If judges are not independent, there is a danger that the government will exceed its powers without legal justification. Without any effective check on government power, tyranny may result.
- Citizens need to feel certain that any legal cases with which they may become involved will be dealt with on the basis of justice and the rule of law. It may suit government to discriminate against individuals or groups in society for its own benefit. An independent judiciary can prevent such discrimination. The citizens of a democratic state must feel that their rights will be effectively protected.
- In some political systems the judiciary may appear to be independent, but in practice the judges are specially selected by the government to ensure decisions which are friendly to that government. Independence, therefore, also implies that judges are selected on a neutral basis to prevent collusion between the judiciary and the government.

How is independence maintained?

There are four main ways in which **judicial independence** is guaranteed in the UK. These are: first, security of tenure; second, rules of *sub judice*; third, the system of appointments; and, finally, the background of senior judges.

The first and key principle that attempts to ensure the political independence of the judiciary is **security of tenure**. This principle says that judges cannot be removed from office on the grounds of the kind of decisions they make. The only reason a judge can be removed is if s/he can be shown to be corrupt as a result of personal conduct incompatible with being a judge. It follows, therefore, that judges are free to make decisions without fear of dismissal, even if such decisions offend the government. For the same reason, judges are appointed on the understanding that their salaries cannot be reduced if they make contentious decisions.

Second, it is a **contempt of court** for any servant of the government to attempt to interfere with the result of a court case or even to comment on such a case in public or in Parliament. This rule is designed to prevent any political pressure being placed upon judges. Any such interference would be strongly criticised in Parliament and could result in legal action against the government member concerned.

The issue of **appointments** to senior positions in the judiciary is less clear. The final decision on the appointment of senior judges is in the hands of the Lord Chancellor (now the Secretary of State for Constitutional Affairs) and the prime minister. This appears to open the door to political interference in the composition of the judiciary. On the other hand, there are two constraints to such a possibility. One is that any

> **Judicial independence** The principle that members of the judiciary should retain independence from any influence by government or parties or other political movements.

obvious political bias in appointments would be noticed in Parliament and cause great controversy that would damage the government. Second, there is a Judicial Appointments Commission, which can object if it feels an appointment has been made on political grounds.

Finally, it should be pointed out that all senior judges must have enjoyed a lengthy career as courtroom **lawyers**. This means that they are accustomed to the principle that cases must be judged on the strict basis of law and not according to their own personal opinions. Indeed, junior judges who gain a reputation for lack of impartiality are most unlikely to be put up for promotion.

In case one is tempted to be sceptical about these safeguards there is a great deal of evidence to suggest that the UK judiciary is indeed politically independent. Under both Conservative and Labour administrations, senior members of the judiciary have made a large number of judgements that have been clearly contrary to government interests. This has been especially true since the implementation of the Human Rights Act in 2000. Indeed, it is significant that politicians of *both* the main parties have criticised the judiciary on the grounds that it is politically biased. This certainly implies that there is little or no political bias among the judges.

How independence may be threatened

Although the British judiciary has a reputation for political independence, it remains true that threats still exist. These include:

- The fact that the Lord Chancellor, who is head of the court system, is a major political figure who sits in the cabinet. This gives rise to a danger that he might interfere with appointments of judges and may manipulate which judges hear which cases. It should be pointed out that this remains a *theoretical* danger. There is no hard evidence that the Lord Chancellor administers the legal system in a political way. We must also bear in mind that this anomaly is likely to have been reformed by 2008.
- In recent years there has been an increasing tendency for politicians to enter into open political dialogue with judges over such issues as sentencing and the protection of rights. Though this does not constitute *direct* interference, it may result in indirect pressure being placed on the judiciary.
- Though the appointment of senior judges is now handled by an independent judicial appointments committee, the prime minister (on the advice of the Lord Chancellor) has a final veto over such appointments. Again, this remains a *theoretical* problem which may or may not be grounded in reality.
- Finally it must be noted that the twelve senior law lords and a number of other senior members of the judiciary sit in the House of Lords. Though they cannot be active members of political parties, it is still true that they are involved in the legislative – therefore *political* – process in the Lords so their political independence cannot be guaranteed.

The reforms to the judicial system which have commenced after 2005 are described further in Chapter 3.2. below. However, it can be pointed out at this stage that the proposed reforms are largely designed to ensure greater independence for the judiciary. In particular, removing the law lords from the House of Lords to a separate Supreme Court and removing the Lord Chancellor from the cabinet can be seen as movements in the direction of greater independence.

The neutrality of the judiciary

This may seem to be the same as independence, but there are crucial differences. Independence implies that judges are kept free from political pressure. **Judicial neutrality**, on the other hand, suggests that judges themselves are free from political or any other bias. The principle of the rule of law insists that every citizen should be treated equally under the law. This makes it essential that judges who preside over cases should conduct them without any personal favour to one side or the other.

Until the 1990s there was a widespread view that the British judiciary was not neutral, however much they claimed to be so. Since then, however, there is a great deal of evidence to suggest that the senior judges in the UK do indeed dispense justice in a politically neutral fashion. Each of these arguments can be examined in turn.

Judicial neutrality is important for a number of reasons. First, it helps to give confidence to citizens that justice will be dispensed in a fair manner. Second, minority groups need to believe that they will be given a fair hearing. Third, and perhaps most importantly, judicial neutrality is a key feature of any system that wishes to describe itself as 'democratic'. Democracies must protect the rights of citizens and groups in society. A neutral judiciary can go a long way to ensuring that this is the case.

> **Judicial neutrality**
> The principle that members of the judiciary should avoid allowing their political ideas to affect their decisions in cases. It also implies that judges should not show any systematic bias towards or against any groups in society.

The case for lack of neutrality

The main argument here is that judges come from a narrow social and professional background. The majority are from middle- and upper middle-class backgrounds. They are almost exclusively male and the majority have been educated at independent schools, and often are graduates of Oxford or Cambridge.

Professor John Griffith, writing in 1997, produced an important argument claiming that judges could not be consistently neutral. Their social background, he suggested, inevitably would affect the kind of judgements they make. In cases concerning the rights of women, gays or trade unionists, for example, the gender and social background of the judges might be decisive. More importantly, he argued that judges are all lawyers, by definition, and this affects the way they think and act. He believed that judges were naturally inclined to favour the interests of the state and/or public order against the interests of individuals and minorities. In other words, they were likely to be conservative rather than liberal. In cases where the rights of individuals were in conflict with a public order issue, therefore, it was likely that a judge would favour public order. This might not apply to *every* judge, of course, but he argued that there was a general tendency in this direction.

Up to the time of Griffiths' writing there was a good deal of evidence to suggest he was right. During the 1980s, in particular, there had been a succession of cases concerning trade union rights (see the GCHQ case above) and activities, conflicts between central and local government, and issues about the powers of the police, where judgements seemed to run consistently in favour of the centralised state.

Many of the senior judges also have seats in the House of Lords. Up to the late 1990s this was seen as a particularly conservative institution, and the judges, it could be argued, were heavily influenced by their colleagues.

The case for neutrality

The main argument in favour of the view that the British judiciary is effectively neutral arises from hard evidence. An increasingly large number of judgements in recent years has fallen in favour of individuals and minorities against the government. Indeed, in the mid-1990s, Conservative Home Secretary Michael Howard lost a string of judicial review cases brought against him by prisoners in custody, who claimed his prison regime abused their human rights. The Mental Health Act and Belmarsh cases, described above, also provide evidence of the changing attitude of the judiciary.

The implementation of the Human Rights Act in 2000 has given further ammunition for judges to use against the power of the state in favour of individual rights. Indeed, so active have the judges been in this area that Conservative politicians have begun to talk of repealing the Human Rights Act and the Labour Government has spoken of amending parts of it. The old charge that the judiciary normally favours the powers of the state against individuals seems no longer to be true. Indeed, the situation seems to have been largely reversed.

Civil liberties
The rights and freedoms that citizens enjoy in relation to the state and its laws. These include, for example, the right of all to vote or stand for office, freedom of expression, freedom of association and the right to a fair trial.

The social composition of the judiciary has changed little. There is still only one female member of the law lords and members of ethnic minorities on the senior bench remain rare. The independent school and Oxford and Cambridge bias is gradually disappearing, but it remains true that senior judges are largely middle class in origin. Nevertheless, there has been a succession of independent-minded, 'liberal' judges appointed to senior positions. Lords Woolf, Hoffman and Bingham are good recent examples. All of these individuals have been quick to criticise government for threatening **civil liberties**. As we have seen above, when the senior judges are being criticised by politicians from both main parties, it suggests they may indeed be largely neutral.

Civil liberties in the UK

We need first to define the term 'civil liberties' precisely. These are those freedoms and rights which the citizen of a state may enjoy at any particular time. They are freedoms seen in relation to the state itself and to its laws. In other words, they are the freedoms that are guaranteed by the state and its constitution (assuming the state has a constitution).

Until the passage of the Human Rights Act in 1998 (implemented in 2000), the UK had no codified set of civil liberties. Freedom was, up to 2000, 'negative' in nature. That meant that the citizens of Britain were considered to be free to do anything up to the point where the law limited their actions. In other words, citizens only knew the extent of their freedom in terms of the *limits* to those freedoms. For example, there was freedom of expression up to the point where that freedom was limited by the laws of libel, slander, pornography, incitement to crime, blasphemy, and so on. Similarly, there was freedom of movement up to the point where the laws of private property, trespass, public order, and so on, limited the citizens' right to go wherever they pleased. There was no specific *statement* of what civil liberties were. This was for two reasons.

The first was that Britain enjoyed a particularly strong common law tradition of liberty. The Magna Carta, drawn up in 1215, was indeed an expression of those traditional rights and freedoms, even though it was largely ignored by monarchs for centuries afterwards. The traditional enjoyment of liberties made the creation of a statement of rights apparently unnecessary. The second reason is the principle of the sovereignty of Parliament. Because Parliament is *omnicompetent* – can pass any legislation it wishes – it is not possible to establish a set of civil liberties (usually referred to as a bill of rights) that will be protected from future erosion. When we put these two realities together – the common law tradition and the sovereignty of Parliament – we have a state of affairs whereby citizens are completely free up to the point where Parliament places limits on that freedom.

The people of the UK have considered themselves to be largely 'free' – arguably freer than most peoples in the world – because Parliament has been unwilling, traditionally, to erode those liberties. Whenever governments proposed any measure that might threaten British liberties, Parliament had normally been reluctant to allow them to do so. Put another way, we can say that the instinct for civil liberty has always been very strong in the British political culture, strong enough not to need the creation of a binding bill of rights. But in the 1990s the situation changed.

The threat to civil liberties

In the 1990s there was growing concern in the UK that civil liberties were under serious threat. This was the result of a long-term accumulation of developments that seemed to add up to a dangerous growth in the powers of the state. The principal elements of this threat seemed to include the following:

- Increases in police power, notably as a result of the Police and Criminal Evidence Act of 1984 and the Criminal Justice and Public Order Act of 1994. In general terms, the growth in crime rates gave rise to growing calls for even more powers to be granted to law enforcement agencies.
- Legislation, passed in the 1980s, limiting trade union activities.
- Increasing quantities of information about individual citizens being held by the state and its agencies, such as the police, social security system and National Health Service.
- Increasing tension between governments and the media concerning the right of the government to limit what they printed and broadcast.
- There was a general fear that executive power was growing and the ability of Parliament to limit that power was weakening. This presented a generalised fear that civil liberties might be threatened by over-powerful government.

Citizens did have some ability to challenge the apparent erosion of civil liberties. They could appeal to the European Court of Human Rights (ECHR) – a body set up by the Council of Europe in 1950, *not* by the European Union (a common misconception) – on the grounds that the actions of the state contravened the European Convention on Human Rights. However, this was far from being a satisfactory safeguard. It was slow and extremely expensive – facts that put off most potential appeals. More importantly, the European Convention was not binding on British government. For these reasons, appeals to the ECHR have remained relatively rare.

The perceived threat to liberties and the unsatisfactory status of the ECHR in the UK led the Labour Party leadership to include proposals to safeguard civil liberties more effectively in its 1997 manifesto. Two measures were included. One was the introduction of a **Freedom of Information Act**, and the other was to incorporate the **European Convention on Human Rights** into British law. These two measures have transformed the status of civil liberties in the UK.

Freedom of information and open government

The Freedom of Information Act was passed in 2000, but did not come into force until January 2005. It was intended to be the main stage in a longer-term process of creating more open government.

During the 1970s there was increasing concern that government in the UK was too secretive. Citizens were denied access to information about the institutions and processes of government. This was felt to be detrimental to democracy. Furthermore, other political systems, notably that of the USA, were in the process of opening up government to public scrutiny. Britain was looking out of step with the rest of the democratic world.

The first major development was the introduction of departmental

select committees in the House of Commons. These committees (which are described in more detail above) had powers to question ministers and civil servants, as well as calling for official papers. The committees have had their limitation, but they were an important step on the road to more open government.

Next came the **Data Protection Act**, in 1984. This gives citizens the right to see the contents of any computer file that contains information about themselves. There are exceptions, of course, notably police records, but in general they have helped to ensure that citizens can check that important details about themselves are accurately kept.

The Data Protection Act recognised the growing importance of computers in society. The development of the internet accelerated this process. It is increasingly true, therefore, that government – central, regional and local – has used the internet to provide increasing amounts of information about themselves for public scrutiny. It has become possible to discover what agencies are serving government, what is their role, how government itself is organised and who is being employed to advise government. Indeed, civil servants and other public officials are now encouraged to publicise their work rather than hide it, which used to be their natural instinct.

The original **Freedom of Information Act** was designed to give considerable powers to citizens to see government papers. However, under pressure from the civil service itself and from Conservative politicians, especially in the House of Lords, the final version was watered down.

In essence, the Act gives all citizens the right to see all public documents. However, the exemptions to this general principle have become very extensive. Understandably, matters referring to national security and to private communications within government (such as the minutes of Cabinet meetings) cannot be open to the public. But there is a also a general rule attached to the legislation. This says that government can withhold information if it is felt that publication will cause damage to the public interest. This is considered by critics to be too wide an exemption. It means, effectively, that government retains the opportunity to maintain a good deal of secrecy about its processes.

Nevertheless, the Act is an important extension to civil rights in the UK. The media, in particular, are beginning to find that they can obtain more background information on government than ever before. Individual citizens also now have access to papers relating to their own dealings with the state. It is, perhaps, too early to determine how significant the Freedom of Information Act will prove to be.

The Human Rights Act

As we have seen above, the European Convention on Human Rights has been in existence since 1950, but it had relatively little impact in the UK as governments have not considered it binding on them. All this changed when the Labour Government of 1997 decided to incorporate the Convention into British law. This was done in 1998, with the passage of the Human Rights Act.

The Act stated that all legislation, actions and decisions made by government, its ministers, regional parliaments, assemblies and governments, local government or by any agency engaged in public business (which includes schools and the media) had to conform to the European Convention on Human Rights. If it did not, the courts could strike down the action or legislation if it were successfully challenged. So, at first sight, the Act seems to be extremely powerful. But it contained one crucial exemption.

The government (and Parliament itself) was unwilling to set aside the principle of the sovereignty of Parliament. It was decided, therefore, that the Westminster Parliament would not be subject to the Convention. If the government does introduce legislation which will conflict with the Convention, it must alert Parliament to the fact by making a declaration of incompatibility. In doing this, Parliament becomes aware that there is an important rights issue at stake and may wish to refuse to pass the legislation. If, however, the government can persuade Parliament that the legislation is important enough to set aside the Convention, the new law will stand.

There is one other safeguard, however. If a citizen or group of citizens challenges a law on the basis that it conflicts with the European Convention, the court may agree and declare the law to be incompatible. This does not mean that the law is invalid, but it does mean that the government and Parliament will be made aware of the opinion of the court. This is what occurred in the case of the Belmarsh detainees in December 2004.

Eight citizens were being detained without trial in Belmarsh prison, suspected of being Islamic terrorists. Their detention was legal under the Anti-terrorism Act of 2001. In a ground-breaking decision, eight of the nine members of the House of Lords who heard the appeal declared that the detention of the suspects without trial contradicted the European Convention. As we have seen above, the verdict did not invalidate the Anti-terrorism Act (it had been properly passed by Parliament), but the political fallout from the ruling was immense. The government came under pressure to amend the Anti-terrorism Act to make it compatible with the Convention. After much political wrangling, this was achieved, and a considerable number of additional legal safeguards were built in to the amended Act. This demonstrated the fact that, although Parliament remains legally sovereign, it will find it difficult to resist the pressure of an adverse court decision.

In other areas the European Convention is all-powerful, and all bodies other than the Westminster Parliament must conform. The development therefore represents an enormous extension in the protection of rights in the UK. It is likely to have far-reaching effects in years to come.

The list below shows the main areas covered by the European Convention on Human Rights and, therefore, the Human Rights Act:

1. The protection of property.
2. The right to life.
3. Prohibition of torture.
4. Prohibition of slavery and forced labour.

5. Right to liberty and security.
6. Right to a fair trial.
7. No punishment without law.
8. Right to respect for private and family life.
9. Freedom of thought, conscience and religion.
10. Freedom of expression.
11. Freedom of assembly and association.
12. Right to marry.
13. Prohibition of discrimination.
14. Restrictions on political activity of aliens.
15. Prohibition of abuse of rights.
16. Limitations of restriction of rights.

For the first time in its history, the UK has a positive set of rights that is fully codified. They are not entrenched, as Parliament can repeal all or part of the Human Rights Act, but it is hard to imagine that Parliament would allow such a development in the foreseeable future.

Human rights in the UK

Having examined the issue of civil liberties, the question of human rights in general can be considered. When we refer to human rights *in general*, we are including civil liberties, but also adding two other categories of rights. One is the prevention of discrimination against certain groups in society, notably women, members of ethnic and religious minorities, gays and the disabled. The other is usually described as economic and social rights (as opposed to civil rights).

Economic and social rights concern our status as citizens in relation to employment and to welfare benefits, including health and education. Thus, for example, citizens in the UK are entitled to some protection from unfair dismissal from work, have a legal right to join a trade union and to take industrial action (as long as it is legally approved), and have an equal right to benefits under the welfare state, provided they have contributed.

The most important development in the field of economic and employment rights in the UK occurred when the UK signed the EU Social Chapter in 1997. This effectively extended such rights to all workers and citizens in Britain.

We can now put together all the various kinds of rights that are protected in some way in the UK, and the ways in which they are safeguarded.

We can see, therefore, that human rights are protected in a number of ways in the UK. In each case, it is the courts, or perhaps a tribunal, that is involved in the enforcement of laws, conventions and European Union directives. In each case, appeal procedures can be undertaken and, ultimately, cases may appear in the House of Lords or one of the European Courts – the Court of Justice (EU) or the Court of Human Rights – if they are considered to be of great importance and to have wider implications.

Type of right	Examples of main methods of protection	Enforced by
Civil Liberties	European Convention on Human Rights Common law rights	Judicial Review European Court of Human Rights Appeal to common law in the High Court
	Parliamentary statutes such as the Habeas Corpus Act	Judicial Review
Anti-discrimination	Race Relations Acts Equal Opportunities Acts Equal Pay Acts (for women)	Courts and tribunals Courts and tribunals Courts and tribunals
Employment and Union right	Employment Protection Act Trade Union Acts EU Social Chapter	Industrial tribunal Civil cases EU European Court of Justice
Rights to Welfare	Welfare State Legislation	Judicial Review

The government and the judiciary

In theory, the executive and the judiciary in the UK should be kept entirely separate. This also implies that the government should not interfere with judicial independence, while, at the same time, judges remain totally aloof from political issues. In recent years, however, this reciprocal arrangement has begun to break down. A number of issues have emerged which have brought government ministers and senior judges into serious conflict. There have been four main areas in dispute:

1. As ministers, especially Home Secretaries, have sought to gain more control over sentencing in serious crime cases, they have encountered opposition from judges who believe that the issue of sentencing in criminal cases should remain in their hands. Specifically, judges have resisted the introduction of legally binding *minimum* sentences for some categories of crime. More generally, the judges have also expressed a strong view that they would prefer to reserve longer prison sentences to the most serious of crimes. Lord Woolf, the Lord Chief Justice (Britain's most senior judge until 2005), declared that judges reserved the right to use alternatives to prison when sentencing in less serious cases. In other words, judges resent political interference and believe they should be free to conduct cases as they wish in their own courts.

2. Many senior members of the judiciary, including Lords Woolf and Hoffman, publicly criticised the erosion of civil liberties that would occur if the government introduced ever tougher anti-terrorism measures. As we have seen above, indeed, eight of the law lords declared the 2001 Anti-terrorism Act unlawful on these grounds. Judges also criticised the Criminal Justice Bill of 2003. This bill proposed that accused persons could be tried twice for the same crime in some circumstances (so-called double jeopardy), that many types of cases would be heard without a jury and that accused persons' past conditions could be used as evidence against them. Many judges believed these changes would endanger the rights of accused persons and lead to miscarriages of justice. Judges sitting in the House of Lords have been increasingly active in obstructing legislation that threatens individual rights. The anti-hunting bill of 2004, for example, was opposed by many judges on the grounds that it would oppress a minority – hunters.

   The outgoing Conservative leader, Michael Howard, waded into the controversy in August 2005, commenting on the behaviour of the senior judges in insisting that individual rights were more important than measures to protect the public against terrorism: 'aggressive judicial activism could also put our security at risk', he said (*Daily Telegraph*, 9 August 2005).

3. The general tendency of judges to become publicly involved in political controversies of the kind described above has angered government ministers, who insist that the judiciary should be seen to be politically neutral. Home Secretaries Blunkett and Clarke, in particular, criticised judges for being too politically active. Their argument was that ministers are elected and accountable, whereas judges are neither. They therefore have no right, the politicians assert, to obstruct the political process. Judges counter that they are guardians of individual rights against the power of overmighty government.

4. The Labour Government which was elected in 2005 is set on a course to reform the nature of the British judiciary. In particular, they wish to separate the highest court of appeal from the House of Lords. This would create a Supreme Court that would not be involved in the political process. The House of Lords – largely influenced by the judges – voted against the change in March 2004, forcing the government to reintroduce amended proposals. There are also plans to take the position of Lord Chancellor out of politics and replace it with a post that is purely legal in nature. Most members of the senior judiciary are opposed to these reforms. This is partly from a general sense of conservatism, and partly from fear that the judiciary will lose political influence and so be at the mercy of elected politicians. As we shall see in Unit 3, the battle continues.

Finally, we can now summarise the position of the judiciary in relation to government by identifying its main strengths and weaknesses.

Main strengths	Main weaknesses
■ The Human Rights Act has given the judiciary a codified set of rights upon which to judge whether executive and legislative action threatens civil liberties. As it is binding on all but Parliament, the Act is a key weapon available to judges. ■ The judiciary can justifiably claim to be independent. In recent years, they have shown themselves willing to defy government, especially in the field of civil rights. ■ It has become considerably easier for citizens to seek judicial review so that judges now hear many more cases of political importance. ■ Many senior judges sit in the House of Lords and so have some legislative influence.	■ The sovereignty of Parliament means that judges are forced to accept legislation made at Westminster. ■ The Human Rights Act is not binding on Parliament. ■ Judges do not have the power to undertake 'pre-legislative review', that is, they cannot take positive action to influence legislation before it is presented to Parliament. ■ Judges are neither elected nor accountable, and so lack democratic legitimacy. ■ Where judges are believed to be obstructing government, the law can be amended to force them to comply with government wishes.

KEY CONCEPTS

Judicial review A process whereby the courts review decisions by the state or any public body in relation to its citizens. Where a review finds that a citizen has not been treated fairly, or that their rights have been abused, or that a public body has exceeded its legal powers, the court may set aside the decision.

Judicial independence The principle that members of the judiciary should retain independence from any influence by government or parties or other political movements.

Judicial neutrality The principle that members of the judiciary should avoid allowing their political ideas to affect their decisions in cases. It also implies that judges should not show any systematic bias towards or against any groups in society.

Civil liberties The rights and freedoms that citizens enjoy in relation to the state and its laws. These include, for example, the right of all to vote or stand for office, freedom of expression, freedom of association and the right to a fair trial.

Revision topics and examination questions

Revision topics

- Nature of civil liberties
- Nature of human rights
- Various roles and functions of the judiciary
- Independence of the judiciary
- Neutrality of the judiciary
- Ways in which the judiciary can protect rights
- Importance of the Human Rights Act
- Nature of the rule of law
- Limitations to the power of the judiciary
- Ways and extent to which the judiciary can control the power of the executive
- Reasons for disputes between the judiciary and governments

Short answers

- What are civil liberties?
- Outline any THREE examples of civil liberties.
- What is meant by the term 'human rights'?
- Explain TWO ways in which the judiciary can protect human rights.
- What is the rule of law?
- What is the independence of the judiciary?
- What is meant by the neutrality of the judiciary?

Medium answers

- How is the independence of the judiciary maintained?
- To what extent are judges neutral?
- How do judges protect civil liberties?
- How can the judiciary attempt to control the power of government?

Long answers

- In what ways, and to what extent, are judges independent and neutral?
- To what extent can judges control the power of the government?
- In what ways are civil rights protected in the UK?
- In what ways are human rights protected in the UK?
- What limits the judiciary's power to control government?
- Why have judges increasingly come into conflict with governments?

Resources and Web Guide

Books

The best-known work on the political role of the judiciary is:
J. Griffiths, *The Politics of the Judiciary*, Fontana, 1991.
Another important work, if now a little dated, is:
R. Stevens, *The Independence of the Judiciary*, OUP, 1993.
Perhaps the best general reader is:
P. Joyce, *Law, Order and the Judiciary*, Hodder and Stoughton, 1999.
On rights:
F. Klug, *Values for a Godless Age: The Story of the UK's New Bill of Rights*, Penguin, 2002.
Though it pre-dates the Human Rights Act, the whole issue is covered very well in:
M. Zander, *A Bill of Rights?*, Sweet and Maxwell, 1997.

Useful websites

Official information and news on both the judiciary and human rights can be found on the government site:
www.dca.gov.uk (accessed 11 November 2005)
For information and a full account of the European Convention on Human Rights:
www.echr.coe.int (accessed 11 November 2005)
The pressure group Liberty has a useful website on human rights:
www.liberty-human-rights.org.uk (accessed 11 November 2005)

3

The Changing UK System

3.1
The party system and electoral reform

Introduction

The **party system** which characterises any democratic state is closely associated with the electoral system that underpins it. It is not necessarily true that the electoral system actually *determines* the party system, but there is no doubt that it is *one* of the determining factors. It is important, therefore, to study party and electoral systems together.

Before we investigate them individually and together, however, we need to define the two terms.

Party system

A party system describes the typical number of important parties that compete in a political system, the way they relate to each other and the part they play in the formation of governments. Thus we speak of *two-party systems* (for example, in the USA), *three-party systems* (Spain) or *multi-party systems* (Italy). This does not mean that the USA has only two parties, or Spain three, but it does mean that the system is *dominated* by two or three parties, while in a multi-party system a significantly large variety of parties have some political influence.

Allied to these descriptions is the question of how governments are typically formed. Many systems are essentially *one-party governments*. This is certainly true of the UK. Others are typified by coalitions where more than one party shares government – a situation that is extremely common in Europe. Occasionally, systems have minority governments, as occurred in the UK in the 1920s (Labour minority government), but these are usually temporary circumstances.

The two-party system

Politics in Britain is often described as a two-party system. This does not mean, of course, that there are only two important parties. What it does mean, however, is that the system is *dominated* by two parties and its character is determined by the conflict between government and opposition. The main features of the so-called two-party system in the UK include the following:

■ Only two parties have a realistic chance of winning an election outright and therefore forming a government alone. This is partly because the British electorate is reluctant to give their support to small parties and

> **Party system**
> Refers to the typical structure of parties within a political system. It describes the normal number of parties that compete effectively. Thus we may speak of two-, three- or multi-party systems. It also refers to the typical party make-up of governments – for example, single-party government, coalitions, and so on.

partly because the electoral system discriminates against them, especially the Liberal Democrats. The table below demonstrates the dominance of the Labour and Conservative parties in elections since 1979.

Election	Total seats won by Labour and Conservatives	% share of the vote won by Labour and Conservatives
1979	608	80.8
1983	606	70.0
1987	605	73.1
1992	607	76.3
1997	584	74.0
2001	578	72.4
2005	554	67.6

- The two parties dominate the **political agenda**. This means that the business of Parliament is largely determined by the two main parties and that the general debate over policy tends to be determined by them. In particular, the proceedings of Parliament tend to assume that there is an interplay of conflict between two parties – the one that forms the government and the other that is described as 'Her Majesty's Opposition'.
- **Finance** plays an important role in modern party politics. Naturally, donors, who today provide most of the funding, will concentrate on the parties that are likely to win power. This means just two parties, because the Liberal Democrats, despite their revival since 1997, do not have a realistic chance of gaining or sharing power. As an example of the financial domination of the two parties, we can view the donations received by the three political parties during the three months around the elections (April–June 2005).

Party	Donations (£)
Conservative*	12.4 million
Labour	5.3 million
Liberal Democrat	0.8 million
*Including one donation of £5 million from oil billionaire, John Paul Getty	

Source: Electoral Commission

We can see the extent to which the two parties completely outscore the Liberal Democrats in their ability to attract revenue.

Other party models

There is case for suggesting that Britain has become a **three-party system**, certainly since 1997. In that year the Liberal Democrats more than doubled their parliamentary representation, from 20 in 1992, to 46. The party sustained its recovery by winning 52 seats in 2001 and 62 seats in 2005. Voting for the third party has also picked up, standing at 22 per cent by 2005. Were Britain to adopt any form of proportional electoral system, the Liberal Democrats would be a significant third force. These numbers were not enough to threaten the dominance of the two parties and did not threaten Labour's hegemony sufficiently to influence policy, but they are an indication of considerable progress that may continue into the future.

It is possibly true that the Liberal Democrats did cooperate with Labour over constitutional reform in the late 1990s, and there was, for a short period, a Cabinet committee on such reforms which contained Liberal Democrat representation (a unique example of the voluntary introduction of an opposition party into a part of the governing process), but the experiment was very short-lived. Similarly, some consensus policies have seen consultations between the leaders of the three parties – over Northern Ireland, national security and anti-terrorism measures, for example. But these examples are exceptions rather than signs of a developing three-party system.

It is more compelling to say that local government, especially in England and Wales, is shared very evenly between the three main parties. Indeed the Liberal Democrats have control, or shared control, over many large councils. In Scotland and Wales, too, the Liberal Democrats enjoy an elevated status. The party was second (albeit a distant second) to Labour in terms of seats won at the 2005 general election in Scotland and Wales. In the Scottish Parliament the Liberal Democrats have prevented Labour winning an overall majority and so have been in coalition with a Labour administration there. In Wales the Liberal Democrats were also in coalition with Labour for a short time after 1999, and have enough representation to make a significant impact on policy there.

Finally, we could say that, in parts of the UK, there is a **multi-party system**. In Scotland and Wales, four parties are in competition for seats in the devolved Parliament and Assembly – that is Labour, Liberal Democrats, Conservatives and Nationalists (with some representation also by Greens and Scottish Socialists). The same is true in many local councils, where even small parties such as the BNP have won seats. Northern Ireland is a special case. Its party system is unique and contains none of the conventional 'British' parties. It is very much a multi-party system, with four large and several small parties winning seats in Assembly elections.

For a few years there were suspicions that Labour may have become the **dominant party** in British politics, having captured the political consensus and maintained complete control over the political agenda. But its poor performance in the 2005 election, when its majority was slashed to 66 and its share of the vote fell to only 35.2 per cent, has discredited such a theory. Indeed, the same theory was suggested when the Conservatives won four successive elections between 1979 and 1992, but the demise of the Conservatives in 1997 demonstrates that it was a premature analysis.

Though parties in Britain may be less significant than they used to be, party conflict appears to be as competitive and meaningful as it ever was.

Electoral system

An electoral system is a method by which votes are converted into seats in the legislature, or sometimes into the election of a single leader, such as a president or a mayor. It is connected to the party system in that certain types of electoral system normally (but by no means always) will produce a particular party system. Thus, UK and US elections reinforce the two-party system, while German electoral arrangements have produced a three- or four-party result. As we shall see, there is a general rule that the more proportional an electoral system is, the more parties with political significance it will produce. But we need to beware. While there is a close causal link between electoral systems and party systems, it is not a totally predictable relationship.

So when we consider the possible effects of reform in the electoral system, we must not assume that we can predict the outcome of such reform. In other words, the party system is determined by a number of different factors, not just the electoral system.

The UK party system

Until the 1980s the UK was undoubtedly a two-party system. This had been broadly true since the 1870s. The term 'two-party system' implied a number of realities:

■ General elections tended to produce a result which demonstrated the dominance of only two parties – at least in terms of the seats won in the House of Commons. There was a brief period in the 1920s when three parties were effectively competing for power, but this only occurred because the Labour Party was replacing the Liberals as the main opposition to the Conservative Party. As Labour was overtaking the Liberals, there was a short-lived three-party system. But it was clear that the two-party system was reasserting itself very quickly. The following table, showing elections in the UK since 1945, demonstrates the dominance of two parties very clearly.

Election	Cons. seats	Labour seats	Liberal (or Lib. Dem.) seats	% of seats won by largest two parties
1945	210	393	12	94.2
1950	298	315	9	98.1
1951	321	295	6	98.6
1955	345	277	6	98.8
1959	365	258	6	98.9
1964	304	317	9	98.6
1966	253	364	12	98.0
1970	330	288	6	98.1
1974 (Feb.)	297	301	14	94.2
1974 (Oct.)	277	319	13	93.8
1979	339	269	11	95.8
1983	397	209	23	93.3
1987	376	229	22	93.0
1992	336	271	20	93.2
1997	165	418	46	88.4
2001	413	166	52	87.8
2005	198	356	62	85.6

While it is true that the dominance of the two parties has begun to subside since 1997, it is still very plain to see that it remains the 'normal' situation in the UK.

■ It is a less clear question whether Britain is a two-party system in terms of *votes*. Here again, up to the 1980s, the two main parties dominated the voting, but since then the third party – now the Liberal Democrats – has gained considerable ground. This is shown in the table below.

Election date	% votes won by Labour and Conservatives	% votes won by third party
1979	80.8	13.8
1983	70.0	25.4
1987	75.1	23.2
1992	77.5	18.3
1997	75.5	17.0
2001	72.4	18.3
2005	67.5	22.0

The two tables shown above, therefore, suggest that Britain remains very much a two-party system in Parliament, but that in terms of popular support, it is a three-party system.

- More clear is the near certainty that the government will be formed by one of the two main parties, and that the third party is therefore habitually excluded from power. There has been no coalition government in the UK since 1945, and there was only a brief period (1976–78) when a second party had any significant influence on the governing party. At that time, Labour had lost its parliamentary majority and so had to rely on parliamentary support from the Liberals. This was known as the Lib-Lab Pact, but it was not a coalition; rather it was a formal parliamentary arrangement, and it was an exception to the rule.
- Because it has been a certainty that governments would be formed only by either Labour or the Conservatives, the two parties have also dominated the political agenda, both in terms of election campaigns and during parliamentary business. Though Liberal Democrats and others have occasionally succeeded in bringing new issues to the public's attention, on the whole, political conflict rests between the two major parties.

Now that we have established that Britain is largely a two-party system, but that this status is becoming less certain, we can turn to the electoral system and its possible reform to understand what the likely effects of such change might be. We must also examine the experience of the devolved systems of Scotland, Wales and Northern Ireland for clues as to how *national* reform might unfold.

Electoral systems

As we have said, an electoral system exists to convert votes into seats in the legislature (we will ignore, for now, systems in the UK that are used to elect mayors or presidents). In order to evaluate systems and their effects we must first examine what we are trying to achieve through the electoral system. We will concentrate for now on general elections because it is these that determine who shall govern the country.

So the possible aims of any electoral system *might* include the following:

- To ensure that representation in Parliament accurately reflects the range and strength of political opinion among the voting population.
- To ensure that people will feel they are effectively represented within the political system.
- To ensure that every vote is of equal value.
- To give voters a fair choice in their preferences.
- To ensure that an effective government can emerge from the result of the election.

The problem is that there is no electoral system in the world that can deliver *all* these objectives, except in highly unusual circumstances. A system can produce some of them, but not all. For example, the UK system does tend to produce governments that can rule effectively – that is, they are highly stable once elected – but this is achieved at the expense of a truly representative House of Commons, where the Conservatives and Liberal

Category	Electoral system	Main characteristics
Plurality system	First-past-the-post	Single-member constituencies. Winners need only a **plurality** of the votes. Distorts results in favour of larger parties. Individuals and parties are often elected on a minority of the votes. Normally produces single-party government.
Proportional systems	List systems Single transferable vote (STV)	Is accurately proportional. Tends to produce multi-party systems. Gives representation to small parties. Eliminates constituencies. Preserves large constituencies. Highly proportional result. Voters have wide choice. Favours small parties.
Mixed system	Additional member system (also known as a mixed member system)	Gives voters two choices. Preserves constituency representation. Helps small parties. Creates a reasonably proportional result.
Majority systems	Second ballot or alternative vote	Preserves constituencies. Gives voters a second choice. Favours small parties, but not very small parties.

Democrats are severely underrepresented.

A detailed account of the nature of different electoral systems is included in Unit 1 of this book. However, a brief review of electoral systems should remind us of the main alternatives that exist.

The problem of first-past-the-post (FPTP)

If reform of the electoral system is to be contemplated, it is first necessary to understand the problem, as it is perceived by the proponents of reform. The problems, as stated, are as follows:

- Governments are being elected on a minority of the votes cast in a general election. In the last two elections this problem has worsened, to the extent that the Labour victory of 2005 was secured with a mere 35.2 per cent of the total vote.
- The fact that governments are claiming a mandate on a minority of the votes calls into question the democratic legitimacy of a government. This lack of legitimacy may lead increasingly to sustained and violent dissent.

> **Plurality**
> A description of an electoral system that awards a position or a seat in the legislature to a candidate who has achieved more votes than any other, even if this does not represent an absolute – 50+ per cent – majority. The British FPTP system that operates in general elections is an example of plurality at work.

- The House of Commons does not represent the range of political opinion in the UK. Support for both the Conservatives and the Liberal Democrats is seriously underrepresented.
- Too many votes are wasted. Those who support small parties, such as the Greens or UKIP, together with those who support parties which are inevitably going to lose in a 'safe' seat, know that their votes are wasted.
- Voters are given a very narrow choice. They have only one vote and no say in which candidates shall be put forward from each party.
- Because so many voters feel their vote is wasted, they are forced to vote tactically, that is, to vote for their second-choice party in order to have some say in the result in their constituency.
- The discrimination against the Conservatives and Liberal Democrats effectively means that votes are of unequal value. It needed, on average, 27,000 votes to elect a Labour MP in 2005, but 44,000 for a Conservative and 96,000 for a Liberal Democrat.
- It is almost impossible to establish a new party from modest roots. This creates political atrophy, that is, a stagnant situation where new political ideas or movements are stifled by the big parties who have such a huge advantage.
- Though there are several reasons for declining voter turnout, it is believed that disillusionment with an electoral system which is widely perceived to be unfair may be one of the causes of political disengagement.

The consequences of reform

As we have said, the consequences of changing the UK's electoral system from FPTP to one of the alternatives is uncertain. We can only speculate as to what would happen, using such evidence as we can find from experience elsewhere. The result of reform also depends upon which electoral system might be adopted.

Under AMS

If we begin by considering the additional member system (AMS), it may be instructive to look at what has happened in recent times in Germany and Scotland, both of which use a form of AMS.

AMS in Germany operates so that half the parliamentary seats are based on a FPTP constituency system, as in the UK, but the other half of the seats available are based on a regional list system, where seats are awarded in proportion to the votes cast for each party. For many years after 1969 this system produced a parliament where no single party had an overall majority, but where one of the two main parties – the right-of-centre Christian Democrats or the left-of-centre Social Democrats – was always able to form a government in coalition with a smaller party. These coalitions, either with the Greens or the liberal Free Democrat Party, were remarkably stable and

usually lasted for the four-year term of parliament. But in 2005 all this certainty suddenly collapsed. In that year the election produced a totally inconclusive result, as shown below.

Party	% of the vote	Seats won
Christian Democrats	35.3	226
Social Democrats	34.3	222
Free Democrats	9.8	61
Left Socialists	8.7	54
Greens	8.1	51

We can see that neither of the large parties enjoyed an overall majority and, more importantly, neither could form a majority coalition with only one of the small parties. The result was virtually a dead heat! Furthermore, it was not clear which of the two main parties should provide the chancellor (prime minister). The political deadlock that resulted created major problems for a country which desperately needed strong leadership to deal with its serious economic problems at the time. Ultimately, a grand coalition – of the two major parties – was formed, but it proved to be an uneasy alliance. The CDU leader, Angela Merkel, became Germany's first female chancellor, but she led a Social Democrat-dominated government.

By a strange coincidence, the largest party (by a whisker), the Christian Democrats, secured exactly the same proportion of the total vote – 35.2 per cent – as Labour had done in the UK. But Labour came home with a 66-seat majority in Britain! This demonstrates very clearly how different the result can be under FPTP. It also suggests that a move to AMS in the UK might create the same problems experienced by Germany.

Turning to the elections to the Scottish Parliament in 2003, where a slightly modified form of AMS is used, we see a rather different outcome, as follows.

Party	Seats won
Labour	50
Scottish Nationalist	27
Conservative	18
Liberal Democrat	17
Greens	7
Scottish Socialist	6
Independents	4

If we apply the effects of AMS in Scotland to the UK general election result in 2005, we find the following predicted outcome.

Party	% of vote	Estimated seats*
Labour	35.2	320
Conservative	32.3	190
Liberal Democrat	22.0	105
Others	10.5	31

*This predicted outcome was calculated by the author, by applying the same statistical method of converting votes into seats used in the Scottish election of 2003 to the UK general election of 2005.

The estimated (and it is only an estimate) results, as shown above, suggest that Labour would remain the dominant party under AMS, but that it would probably be forced to enter a coalition with one of the other two parties, likely to be the Liberal Democrats. As we can see, Labour would just fail to secure an overall majority, winning just under half of the 646 seats. The effect of AMS is to reduce Labour seats, but not by a great amount, and also to reduce Conservative seats. The main gainers would be the Liberal Democrats. This predicted result also clearly indicates that Britain would become a three-party system. In Scotland in 2003, where the Scottish Nationalists also enjoyed a strong showing, there was clearly a four-party system.

The devolved Welsh Assembly uses the same electoral system as Scotland. In the 2003 election to that assembly, Labour won 36.9 per cent of the vote and exactly half the seats. In the 2005 general election, under FPTP, Labour's 42.7 per cent of the vote secured them 29 of the 40 seats available. Meanwhile, the Tories won 11 of the 60 seats in 2003, having won no seats at all in 2001. As in Scotland, AMS produces a four-party system in the Welsh Assembly, whereas in a general election, the results are totally dominated by one party – Labour.

In both Wales and Scotland, the use of AMS has had important consequences. Because Labour has won an overall majority in neither political system, it has been forced to enter a coalition agreement with the Liberal Democrats. This has had two immediate effects. One is that members of the Scottish Parliament and Welsh Assembly have considerably more influence than their counterparts at Westminster. This is because the executive branches in Scotland and Wales are inevitably weaker, being coalitions, rather than single party groups. The other is that a relatively small party – the Liberal Democrats – has a significant share in power. In Scotland especially, the Liberal Democrats have influenced policy in such areas as university tuition fees, care of the elderly and the local government system. Were a similar system to be introduced for UK general elections, therefore, we might expect very similar consequences.

Under proportional list

The result of a proportional list system is easier to predict. This can be estimated by taking the proportion of the total vote won in 2005 by the three main parties and awarding seats to each in the same proportion, as follows.

Party	% of vote won	Seats won (predicted)
Labour	35.2	227
Conservative	32.3	209
Liberal Democrat	22.0	142
Others	10.5	68

Under these circumstances, the UK would undoubtedly be a three-party system. The only feasible structure of government would be a coalition between one of the major parties and the Liberal Democrats.

Under STV

The outcome of the single transferable vote system in the UK cannot be estimated with any certainty. However, we can certainly say that a number of consequences would be discernible:

- The Liberal Democrats would do well from STV and win a substantial proportion of the seats.
- Smaller parties, such as the Greens and UKIP, would be able to win a significant, though not very large number of seats.
- The nationalist parties in Scotland and Wales would gain considerable ground.
- Independents and representatives of very small parties would win a handful of seats.

Coalition governments would also be inevitable under STV. But the nature of Parliament might also change, as a large number of MPs from very small parties would probably gain seats. This would perhaps persuade more voters to support them in the future (as votes for them would no longer be wasted). As a result, some of the small parties might gain a good deal of ground.

In the Northern Ireland Assembly election of 2003, STV certainly produced a multi-party result, as follows.

Party	Seats won
Democratic Unionists	30
Ulster Unionists	27
Sinn Fein	24
Social Democratic Labour Party	18
Alliance	6
Others	3

Under the alternative vote (AV)

This system gives voters a second choice. It might very well be, therefore, that the Liberal Democrats would gain considerably. Many voters see the Liberal Democrats as their second choice, so there could be wins for the party in seats where neither Labour nor Conservative candidates are able to dominate. The smaller parties would probably not win many, if any, seats.

So AV would create a genuinely three-party system and would offer the chance for the Liberal Democrats to become as significant as the two traditional main parties.

Some overseas clues

If we look at the results of recent elections among the 15 members of the European Union (before the 2004 enlargement), we can also find some indications of the relationship between electoral systems and party systems in Europe.

Country	Electoral system	Form of government
Belgium	PR list	Multi-party coalition (2003)
Austria	PR list	Two-party coalition (2002)
Luxembourg	PR list	Two-party coalition (2004)
Finland	PR list	Three-party coalition (2003)
Netherlands	PR list	Three-party coalition (2003)
Greece	PR list	Single-party majority (2004)
Portugal	PR list	Single-party majority (2005)
Spain	PR list	Single-party minority (2004)
Sweden	PR list	Single-party minority (2002)
Denmark	PR list	Single-party minority (2005)
Germany	AMS	Two-party coalition (2005)
Italy	AMS	Multi-party coalition (2001)
Ireland	STV	Two-party coalition (2002)
France	Second ballot	Two-party coalition (2002)
UK	FPTP	Single-party majority (2005)

Source: Electoral Reform Society

It can be seen immediately that PR list systems are the most popular and that this system normally produces coalition governments. The main alternatives are minority administrations, though, in two countries, the list system has produced a single-party majority (Greece and Portugal). Whatever system is used, however, coalitions are the most common type of party system. The UK, meanwhile, looks like the odd one out, with its unusual electoral system and its clear, single-party majority government.

The forces of reform

The movement for **electoral reform** consists of a number of groups. The Liberal Democrat Party (and its predecessor, the Liberal Party) has supported electoral reform for many decades. Of course, cynics claim that they support reform because it is in their own interests. This is true, but Liberal Democrats argue that their case is based on democratic principles and is held in the interests of good government for the UK.

There is also a substantial group within the Labour Party that supports reform. This movement has declined in influence since Labour's three successive victories in 1997, 2001 and 2005, but it remains significant. Small parties such as the Scottish Nationalists, Plaid Cymru and the Greens also support change, partly because they are discriminated against and partly because they feel Britain is not democratic enough with its current system in operation. There is little support for reform within the Conservative Party, but after 2005, there were signs that support for change might be growing, albeit in a modest way.

Two significant pressure groups campaign for reform. The Electoral Reform Society is the prime example, especially as it is concerned with this one issue alone. The Society publicises the faults in the current system and the benefits of alternatives. It campaigns both among the public and within Parliament itself. Charter 88 is concerned with democratic reform in general, but places electoral reform near the centre of its campaign for constitutional reform.

> **Electoral reform**
> A process whereby the electoral system is changed or where there is a campaign for such change.

The positive arguments for reform

Having considered the main problems of FPTP that have been identified by its opponents, we can look at some positive benefits that reformers believe would come about if the system were changed. On the whole, the benefits described below would occur *whichever alternative* system were adopted. These include:

- Voters would be given more choices. This may be an increase from one to two, as with the alternative vote, second ballot or additional member system, but it could also be extremely wide, as with STV.
- The value of votes would be largely equalised. This would be especially true if a proportional list system were adopted.
- If STV or an open list system were adopted, voters would also have the opportunity to choose between candidates *of the same party*.
- Any alternative system would produce a result which was more accurately representative of the political views of the electorate. A proportional list system would be the most accurate, but it is argued that any change from FPTP would be more representative.
- It is argued that the current system places too much power into the hands of a single party which does not enjoy majority support. This is

seen as undemocratic at best, and dangerous at worst. Electoral reform would almost certainly result in *no* party winning an overall majority in Parliament on its own. This would force the big parties to compromise and probably enter into coalitions with other parties. Such circumstances would prevent the accumulation of too much power in too few hands. Furthermore, if the winning party were no longer guaranteed a majority in the Commons, MPs themselves would gain influence and so make government more accountable.

- A 'fairer' electoral system may restore some respect for the political system and so reduce disengagement and encourage higher levels of voting and political participation in general.
- The political system would become more dynamic, with smaller and newer parties having more opportunity to establish themselves.
- Every other country in the European Union uses a different electoral system, either proportional, mixed or majority. Britain is therefore out of step with most of the rest of the democratic world. Of course, many argue this is irrelevant and that special circumstances prevail here, but the reformers suggest that other European countries do have a superior democratic record to Britain's.

The arguments against reform

Though electoral reform is a popular issue among the general public, there is probably a minority of support within the political community itself. The Conservative Party has staunchly resisted change – not surprisingly, as the party is generally suspicious of change where the constitution is concerned. The Labour leadership is largely (though not unanimously) opposed. This is also not surprising, given the fact that, since the mid-1990s, FPTP has favoured Labour heavily. The rest of the Labour Party is divided on the issue, and even those who favour reform have been mostly silent in recent times.

Labour was elected in 1997 with a mandate to hold a referendum on the issue. After 18 years of uninterrupted rule by the Conservatives it was to be expected that the electoral system would be partly blamed. In the event, the startlingly decisive victory for the party in 1997 changed the situation drastically. The leadership lost interest and stalled on the issue. Eventually, apathy in the Labour ranks turned into opposition to reform. Now that it was clear that the old system could produce governments from either party, there was less impetus for change. Furthermore, the prospect of either party being forced into coalition with the Liberal Democrats under a proportional system concentrated the minds of the party leaders on opposition to reform.

A number of arguments have been deployed against reform. These have included:

■ The FPTP system has successfully delivered decisive, single-party government, with comfortable working majorities in the House of Commons, for over 60 years. Whatever the arguments in favour of reform, this simple fact cannot be denied. The classic conservative argument, therefore, is that we should beware of exchanging what we know for the unknown consequences of a different electoral system.

■ The current system also delivers government which has a clear mandate to govern, based on its election manifesto. Electoral reform will probably lead to coalition governments. This would involve many compromises on policy. This in turn would destroy the mandate system since voters would not be able to know what policies an unpredictable coalition might adopt.

■ The predictable outcome of reform, as we have seen above, is likely to be that no party would win an overall majority in the House of Commons. This would result in either minority or coalition governments. Coalitions, it is often claimed, are inherently unstable. Critics point to the experience of Italy and the Netherlands, for example, where governments come and go frequently, to demonstrate how difficult it can be to establish permanent governments under **proportional representation**.

■ One argument against reform is more subtle. This suggests that the UK is naturally a two-party system. The conflict between government and opposition, between the two traditional parties, is part of the political culture. The people are used to it and it gives them a sense of security and stability. The FPTP system underpins the two-party system and so maintains the political traditions of the country. This, say many conservative thinkers, is worth preserving. By contrast, reform threatens this firmly established tradition.

> **Proportional representation**
> Describes any electoral system that converts votes into seats in a broadly proportional way.

The future of electoral reform

The alarmingly distorted result of the 2005 general election has put reform back on the political agenda. There is likely to be great pressure to reconsider reform, especially if a substantial proportion of the Conservative Party decides it is time for a change.

Which alternative system would be adopted is anybody's guess. The Jenkins Committee, which investigated the issue for the Labour Party in the 1990s, suggested a mixed system. This would see half the seats contested in constituencies using the alternative vote, and the other half of the seats being awarded on a proportional list system. This proposal is known as AV plus. It remains a popular option in both the Labour and Liberal Democrat parties. But there are also supporters for both AMS and STV.

On the other hand, it seems very unlikely that a Labour government will allow time for Parliament to debate reform in a serious way, let alone hold a referendum on the issue, as it had promised to do in the 1997 election campaign. Despite its many faults, FPTP still has many friends in the political community.

KEY CONCEPTS

Party system

Refers to the typical structure of parties within a political system. It describes the normal number of parties that compete effectively. Thus we may speak of two-, three- or multi-party systems. It also refers to the typical party make-up of governments – for example, single-party government, coalitions, and so on.

Plurality

A description of an electoral system that awards a position or a seat in the legislature to a candidate who has achieved more votes than any other, even if this does not represent an absolute – 50+ per cent – majority. The British FPTP system that operates in general elections is an example of plurality at work.

Electoral reform

A process whereby the electoral system is changed or where there is a campaign for such change.

Proportional representation

Describes any electoral system that converts votes into seats in a broadly proportional way.

Revision topics and examination questions

Revision topics

- The link between FPTP and the party system
- The arguments in favour of electoral reform
- The arguments for retaining the current system
- The probable effects of reform
- The attitude of parties and pressure groups towards reform
- Reasons why alternative systems have been adopted in devolved systems.

Sample questions

Study the following data and answer the questions that follow.

Year	Winning party	% of vote	No. of seats	% of seats	Third party	% of vote	No. of seats	% of seats
1979	Cons.	43.9	339	53.4	Liberal	13.8	11	1.7
1983	Cons.	42.4	397	61.1	Alliance	25.4	23	3.5
1987	Cons.	42.3	376	57.8	Alliance	22.6	22	3.4
1992	Cons.	41.9	336	51.6	Lib. Dem.	17.8	20	3.1
1997	Lab.	43.3	418	63.4	Lib. Dem.	16.7	46	7.0
2001	Lab.	40.7	412	62.5	Lib. Dem.	18.3	52	7.9
2005	Lab.	35.2	356	55.1	Lib. Dem.	22.0	62	9.6

Source: Chapter 1.2 of this book

Party	Seats won	% of seats won	Gain or loss over 2001	% of vote	Gain or loss over 2001	No. of votes won (millions)
Labour	355	54.9	−57	35.2	−5.5	9.55
Conservative	198	30.7	+32	32.4	+0.5	8.79
Lib. Dem.	62	9.7	+10	22.0	+1.8	5.98
Respect	1	0.2	n/a	0.4	n/a	0.11
Others	2	0.3	+1	5.8	+1.2	1.08
Scots Nats	6	0.9	+1	1.4	−0.4	0.41
Plaid Cymru	3	0.5	−1	0.6	+0.1	0.17
Democratic Unionist	9	1.4	+4	0.8	−0.1	0.24
Sinn Fein	5	0.8	+1	0.6	+0.1	0.17
SDLP	3	0.5	0	0.4	−0.6	0.13
Ulster Unionist	1	0.2	−5	0.4	−0.4	0.13
Speaker*	1	0.2	0	n/a	n/a	n/a

*Elected unopposed

Source: Electoral Reform Society

1. From the data, describe one indication that the electoral system in British general elections is 'unfair'. (5 marks)

   Guidance: *Look at any of the examples of how the proportion of seats won by a party is much less than the proportion of votes. Describe it clearly. For example, in 1983 the Alliance won 25.4 per cent of the total vote, but only 3.5 per cent of the seats.*

2. Using the data from both figures, explain how and why the electoral system favours a two-party system. (10 marks)

   Guidance: *Describe why FPTP discriminates against small parties. At the same time, show why it has favoured the larger parties, especially Labour. Use a variety of data from both tables to illustrate the points.*

3. Using the data and your own knowledge, explain the main arguments against electoral reform for general elections. (15 marks)

   Guidance: *The data shows that the system almost inevitably guarantees single-party government with an overall majority. Use examples from the data to illustrate. Explain the advantages of single-party government as opposed to less decisive results that might occur with a more proportional system. This should include the advantages of strong government with a clear electoral mandate.*

4. What are the main arguments in favour of electoral reform? (20 marks)

   Guidance: *Though the question does not require use of the data, examples should be used to illustrate the main points. Describe the faults in the current system and the possible advantages of change. Discuss such issues as reducing executive power, voter choice, coalition government, improved political representation, and so on.*

Resources and Web Guide

Books

A detailed analysis of the 2005 general election is:

D. Butler and D. Kavanagh, *The British General Election of 2005*, Palgrave, 2005.

For an analysis of the electoral system in general, look at:

R. Blackburn, *The Electoral System in Britain*, Macmillan, 1995.

For a discussion of electoral reform as an issue, there is:

M. Drummet, *Principles of Electoral Reform*, OUP, 1997.

Reform is also fully discussed in the 1998 Jenkins Commission Report:

Report on the Independent Commission on the Voting System, HMSO, Cm. 4090, 1998.

Useful websites

Issues concerning elections, parties and results can be found on the website of the electoral commission:

www.electoralcommission.gov.uk (accessed 11 November 2005)

The Constitution Unit at University College London discusses the issues:

www.ucl.ac.uk/constitution-unit/ (accessed 11 November 2005)

There is a full, though one-sided, discussion on the website of the Electoral Reform Society:

www.electoral-reform.org.uk (accessed 11 November 2005)

Another campaign group is Make Votes Count:

www.makevotescount.org.uk (accessed 11 November 2005)

3.2
Constitutional reform

Constitutional reform before 1997

Attitudes to reform

The attitude of most governments towards **constitutional reform** during the twentieth century was essentially conservative. This was, of course, partly the result of the dominance of the Conservative Party for most of that period. But when liberals or the Labour Party have been decisively in power there have always been other policy issues which have tended to dominate. There are few votes in successful constitutional reform, so it has often been squeezed off the political agenda. At the same time, liberals and socialists in Britain have rarely been able to agree *among themselves* on what reforms are desirable. So the conservatives have had a relatively clear field in the constitutional arena.

The dominant conservative view can be described in the following terms:

- There has been a reluctance to make changes to the constitution on the grounds that this is likely to be disruptive to the political process.
- Change has largely been the result of a breakdown of the system, rather than any conscious policy decisions. For example, the powers of the House of Lords were reduced as a result of the Liberal Government budget crisis in 1909; Ireland was partitioned in 1921 in order to avoid a civil war; the institution of life peers was developed in 1958 to head off growing demands for the abolition of the House of Lords. In all these cases, reform was *forced* on government.
- It has always been assumed that the uncodified, flexible nature of the British constitution has allowed it to adapt *naturally* to the need for change. So, for example, the non-political role of the monarchy has gradually evolved for over a century. Similarly, Parliament has rarely experienced any dramatic changes to its powers and procedures, but has adapted itself to the nature of modern government cautiously and gradually.

Reform before 1997

Before 1997, therefore, constitutional change in Britain was mostly both modest and gradual. However, the main change came about when the UK joined the European Community in 1973. This was, by contrast with most of the evolution of the constitution, a rapid and decisive change, challenging

> **Constitutional reform** A process whereby the fundamental nature of the system of government (as well as the relationships between governing institutions) is changed, or where change is proposed. In the case of the UK, this may also involve the process of codification.

the whole notion of parliamentary sovereignty. But it was also a rare event. For the most part, the constitution evolved gradually through a series of relatively minor developments. The main changes were:

1. Without any legislation, the political role of the monarchy was gradually eroded. Of course, this process has its origins in the eighteenth century, but it has been in the last hundred years that we have seen its final demise. It is now accepted that the monarch plays no active part in policy making, even in times of war, and will only become involved in government formation if all other systems have failed. Outright republicanism is weak in Britain, so there have been only limited calls for abolition. But it is true that the monarchy has little more than a symbolic role in Britain today.

2. The role of the House of Lords has been eroded gradually since 1911. Its delaying power was set at two years in 1911 and reduced to one year in 1949. It was not allowed to interfere in the financial affairs of government after the 1911 Parliament Act. In the 1940s the Salisbury Convention was developed – a classic example of how the constitution has evolved without legislation. The convention (first put forward by a Conservative peer after whom it was named) declares that the House of Lords cannot challenge a manifesto commitment of the elected government. In essence, the convention accepts that the unelected Lords has a much weaker degree of political authority than the elected Commons. The decline in the influence of both the House of Lords and the monarchy represented important examples of how *traditional* authority has been replaced by *elective* authority.

3. Particularly after 1979, there has been a steady drift of power away from local government and towards the centre. This has been achieved by the transferring of powers and responsibilities, both through legislation and central executive dominance. There has also been a huge increase in the amount of financial control that central government exercises over local authorities. The fact that Britain has no codified and superior constitution has meant that the process has occurred gradually, through individual pieces of legislation and other developments. No individual statute caused a major change, but the accumulated effect of many has caused a significant change in the distribution of power. By 2001, local government in England and Wales had been reduced to mere local administration, with very few powers of its own.

The sum total of these changes is not very great. When we think of how much change there has been in the constitutions of other European powers during the twentieth century, we realise how conservative Britain has been over the period. This comparison can be viewed in two ways: either it is symptomatic of the deep-seated conservatism of the British political establishment, which has contributed to Britain's relative economic decline; or it is a powerful demonstration of the stability of the British political system. Perhaps it demonstrates both.

Labour's agenda in 1997

Why Labour came to support radical constitutional reform

Significant constitutional reform was a key element in the New Labour 'project', which was developed by Neil Kinnock, John Smith and Tony Blair in the 1990s. The party, which had been transformed by the three leaders and their allies, was essentially a modernising force. It was committed to reforming economic policy making, industry, foreign and defence policy, and the public services. Partly for its own sake, and partly to pave the way for pushing through reforms, it was seen as necessary to make significant constitutional reforms. Three factors made a constitutional reform programme possible and desirable when Labour took power in 1997:

1. The Labour Party has always wished to promote constitutional reform, but has rarely had sufficient political control to be able to do so. To some extent, it has always been something of an ideological commitment among socialists and social democrats. As a party, Labour has always sought to promote popular democracy, equal rights and the reduction of traditional Establishment powers. The ancient constitution was seen by many to be the embodiment of traditional privilege and inequality. The undemocratic status of the House of Lords was a particularly powerful example. By the mid-1990s it was clear that the party was going to win the next general election comfortably and, what is more, had the prospect of at least two consecutive terms in office. Reasonably secure in this knowledge, the party could include constitutional change in its political programme.
2. Despite the prospect of power, the Labour Party had experienced two long periods of Conservative government (1951–64 and 1979–97), during which they had felt totally excluded from influence. The constitutional reforms proposed, therefore, were partly designed to prevent a situation where one party would be able to dominate the political agenda so completely. It is, of course, ironic that Labour's hold on power had become, by 2005, so secure that the constitutional changes it proposed could be directed against themselves when they had in fact been developed to break Conservative hegemony.
3. There was clearly considerable public support for reform. Public opinion polls had long since indicated that a majority would be in favour of change, but this support had always been considered soft. In other words, it was not high on anybody's list of concerns. By the mid-1990s, however, it was becoming obvious that demands for reform were strengthening. This was demonstrated by growing support for the Liberal Democrats, who strongly advocated reform; for campaign groups such as Charter 88; and for Scottish and Welsh Nationalists.

4. It could be said that New Labour felt, in 1997, that it was not distinctive enough from the Conservatives. This was especially true of its economic policies, which were not very far from those pursued by their predecessors. Thus, by proposing a radical constitutional reform programme, they appeared to be a reforming, modernising party in contrast to the Conservatives' attachment to tradition.

The principles of Labour's reform

We can divide Labour's reform programme into the following processes:

1. **Democratisation**. Too much of the British political system was seen as undemocratic. The prime targets were the unelected House of Lords and the notoriously unrepresentative electoral system.
2. **Decentralisation**. As we have seen above, Labour had been scarred by the experience of watching powerlessly as successive Conservative administrations gathered increasing amounts of power into the centre. Part of the programme, therefore, was designed to disperse power away from central government to the regions and localities.
3. **Restoration of rights**. During the 1980s there had been sustained fears that the rights of citizens in Britain had been consistently eroded. In fact, the process could be traced back to earlier periods, but Labour concentrated on what had occurred under the Conservatives. In addition, Labour wished to bring Britain more into line with European practice in constitutional matters. Therefore they proposed the incorporation of the European Convention on Human Rights into British law. In addition, a Freedom of Information Act was seen as essential in the drive to create more open and accountable government.
4. **Modernisation**. As we have seen above, the Conservative Party had done much to modernise the civil service during the 1980s and 1990s. The Labour Party wished to extend this programme further, but also turned their attention to **parliamentary reform**. Changes in the composition of the House of Lords were a key element in this, but there were also hopes that reform of the House of Commons could be undertaken, to make it more efficient and effective.

> **Parliamentary reform** A process whereby reforms in the membership, powers or procedures of either or both Houses of Parliament are made or proposed.

We can now see how extensive the Labour proposals were in 1997. Of course, experience tells us that the new government fell some way short of implementing the whole plan. However, in order to evaluate the process, it is important to be able to compare Labour's original aspirations with its subsequent actions.

Before moving on to examine the detailed changes, however, it is worth summarising the totality of constitutional reform that had occurred between 1997 and the time of the general election of 2005.

Reform	Detail
House of Lords	Stage 1 – Abolition of voting rights of most hereditary peers. Stage 2 – Abolition of voting rights of all hereditary peers; decision by Parliament on whether to introduce elected peers. To be determined by the 2005 Parliament.
House of Commons	Limited changes to the committee system.
Human Rights Act 1998	Inclusion of the European Convention on Human Rights into British law. Effective from 2000.
Electoral reform	The introduction of new electoral systems for the Scottish Parliament, Welsh and Northern Ireland Assemblies, elections to the European Parliament, for the Greater London Assembly and for elected mayors.
Freedom of information	Introduction of freedom of information, effective from 2005. Public right to see official documents.
London government	Introduction of an elected mayor and assembly for greater London.
Local government	Introduction of a cabinet system in local government and the opportunity for local people to introduce elected mayors by initiative and referendum.
Devolution	Transfer of large amounts of power from Westminster and Whitehall to elected bodies and governments in Scotland, Wales and Northern Ireland.
Referendums	Introduction of the principle that any proposal to transfer power within the UK should be approved by a referendum.
Party registration and the electoral commission	A new electoral commission was set up to regulate elections and referendums, including the funding of parties. This reform also required the first ever registration of political parties.

Devolution

The details of the devolution settlement are described in Chapter 3.3, below. Labour had attempted to introduce devolution in the late 1970s, but had been foiled by a combination of two factors. First, the government of the day did not have a parliamentary majority and so could not push through the legislation. Second, forced to rely on **referendum** approval, with more than a simple majority in favour required, the government could not summon enough support in either Scotland or Wales for the proposals. The Welsh voted decisively against in 1979. The Scots did vote yes, but the turnout and majority were too low to satisfy Parliament.

By 1997, however, the political tide had turned decisively in favour of devolution. Labour had a huge majority and so enjoyed a clear field. The Scots were very much in favour and voted for devolution in 1997 by a large margin. Support was lukewarm in Wales, but a narrow referendum vote in favour was enough to persuade the new government to go ahead.

Though falling well short of the aspirations of Scottish and Welsh Nationalists (who want either full independence or at least a federal arrangement, with extensive sovereignty transferred from London), devolution represents a huge shift in power away from London. The Scottish Parliament became a centre of power away from London, which had not been seen in Britain since it had last been abolished in 1707. The Welsh, meanwhile, had never had a true government of their own, so this was a unique political development for them.

Devolution of power to Northern Ireland was part of the wider Belfast (also known as Good Friday) Agreement of 1998. It was essential for the possibilities of a long-term peaceful settlement there. All the sectarian groups needed some political representation and this was provided. At the same time, it was important for the British government to withdraw from most Northern Ireland affairs, as it had come to be seen as a mistrusted element in the sectarian conflict.

The House of Lords

The jewel in New Labour's constitutional crown was undoubtedly devolution. However, the introduction of a codified set of rights and reform of the House of Lords followed closely behind. Over many years, Labour governments had suffered from obstruction from a House which had always had an inbuilt Conservative majority. In the past, attempts at abolition and reform had failed, so it was not surprising that, when the party did have a decisive majority and time to spare, it should decide to take the opportunity while the going was good. Reform has occurred in two stages, as follows.

Stage 1

Immediately after taking office, the Labour Government took steps to remove the voting rights of hereditary peers. These 800 or so members of the nobility were either permanent absentees or were invariably committed to the Conservative cause. The number of Labour or Liberal Democrat

> **Referendum**
> A popular vote in which the people, rather than their elected representatives, resolve a political issue. It is used as a way of gaining consent for constitutional reforms.

hereditary peers was extremely limited. The party had also been severely affected by an incident in 1988 which was to herald the ultimate demise of the political role of the hereditary peerage. This incident entered the collective memory of the Labour Party, so when they returned to power, it was hardly surprising that it should occupy their immediate attention.

In 1988 Margaret Thatcher's government was trying to force through legislation to introduce the poll tax into local government. The poll tax was extremely controversial, being seen in many quarters as unfair as it was not based on ability to pay. The whips forced the bill through the House of Commons with relatively little difficulty. The Lords, on the other hand, was threatening to thwart the government's will. It was at this stage that the government, with its back to the wall, decided to persuade large numbers of hereditary peers to come to London to vote through the new tax. Many of these peers – sometimes known as backwoodsmen – never normally voted. Some did not even know where to go to vote. However, the plan worked and the legislation was passed through. Labour, as we have said, never forgot these events. The days of the hereditary peerage were numbered, though no one knew it at the time.

At first, the legislation to remove the voting rights of hereditary peers was held up. Not surprisingly, the large Conservative majority there was unhappy with the proposals. Many meetings were held behind closed doors to find a compromise. Conservative leader William Hague feared that the obstruction would lead Labour to even more radical reform. Therefore, he persuaded his colleagues in the Lords to accept a limited reform: 92 hereditary peers – less than an eighth of the total – were to remain on a temporary basis. These peers were to be elected by the rest of the hereditaries. They were still a Conservative majority, but the government now had the opportunity to redress the political balance by creating many new Labour-supporting life peers.

It was always asserted that this was only the first stage of reform. The next stage was initiated with the appointment of a commission to consider a long-term solution. By appointing a Conservative peer – Lord Wakeham – Tony Blair signalled the fact that he did not expect any radical change. Wakeham obliged with a moderate report. Its main principles were as follows:

- The powers of the Lords were to remain substantially unchanged. It was to be clearly subordinate to the House of Commons.
- A minority – possibly as small as 20 per cent – was to be elected by proportional representation on a regional basis.
- There were to be no more hereditary peers in the House.
- The rest of the House was to be appointed.
- An independent Appointments Commission would ensure that appropriate people were appointed and prevent the excessive use of political patronage by party leaders.
- The political balance of the House would prevent domination by any one party. Independent cross-benchers would hold the balance of power.

The Wakeham Report was not implemented, but it formed the basis for the debate on reform that was to follow.

Stage 2

After a second decisive election victory in 2001, the Labour Government was encouraged to complete its reforms. However, attempt after attempt failed. Between 2001 and 2004, the political forces lined up as follows:

- **The prime minister and senior colleagues** wanted an all-appointed House of Lords. The fact that it was not elected would prevent it gaining too much authority and, therefore, too much influence. Thus executive power would not be seriously threatened by reform.
- **Most Labour MPs** supported either a fully elected House of Lords or one with a large elected element.
- **Liberal Democrats** insisted that the second chamber should be fully elected by proportional representation. It could then act as a counter-weight to the power of government and the House of Commons.
- **Conservatives** after 2001 hoped that the issue of reform would either simply fade into obscurity or would be blocked once again by the peers themselves. They watched with satisfaction as successive proposals to introduce a fully or partly elected second chamber failed though lack of consensus. By 2004, however, the party had made a complete u-turn and decided to support the idea of a chamber that was to be half elected and half appointed.

The Arguments Concerning Further House of Lords Reform

For

- The Lords still lack sufficient political authority. This can only be gained if it is wholly or partly elected.
- An elected second chamber would act as a more effective check on the power of the executive which many consider to be excessive.
- An unelected second chamber could be freer of political control and so act in a more independent way.
- If Britain is to claim to be a genuine democracy, it cannot be partially governed by unelected institutions.
- The appointments system to the Lords gives too much patronage power to the prime minister. Introducing elected members would reduce such power.
- An argument for a wholly appointed chamber is that its membership could be manipulated to create a more socially representative chamber.

Against

- The classic conservative argument is that the Lords currently performs its role well and so does not need further reform.
- An elected second chamber would have *too much* authority and so would thwart the will of the elected House of Commons and the government.
- Though undemocratic, the remaining hereditary peers should be retained because they are genuinely independent.
- An elected second chamber might simply replicate the House of Commons and therefore be pointless.

By the time of the 2005 general election, no progress had been made. However, the Labour leadership reluctantly agreed to allow the House of Commons a free vote (i.e. the whips would not try to influence voting) on the issue. It was hoped that a final solution was imminent if compromises could be made on all sides. One thing seemed certain – that the final 92 hereditary peers would ultimately lose their voting rights.

House of Commons

New Labour also pledged to make reforms to the House of Commons in order to modernise it. In the event, however, this proved to be one area of reform that appeared to be stillborn, despite widespread and growing concern that the Commons was becoming, at best, ineffective and, at worst, impotent and irrelevant. It was in need of streamlining certainly, though whether it needed more power was problematic.

A modernisation committee was set up early in Labour's administration, but it had little effect. A few cosmetic changes were made, including the reduction of Prime Minister's Question Time from two short sessions to one longer one. The facilities for MPs have been improved, with a new office block, and there are increased allowances for secretarial and research backing. But nothing *substantial* has altered. Indeed, after 1997, most commentators saw the Commons as declining in importance, especially as Labour won two thumping majorities in succession.

Robin Cook, who took over as Leader of the House in 2001, showed some willingness to promote change, but he could make little headway. The one major change which Cook made, in fact, was forced on him by his own backbenchers. They insisted that membership of the departmental select committees should be placed in the hands of MPs rather than the party whips. In the long term this may prove to be a significant reform, but as long as the government has a large majority, the balance of power is likely to remain firmly with the executive. When Robin Cook left office in 2003 (over his opposition to the war in Iraq), the impetus for reform seemed to be lost.

Prime Minister Blair also promoted one other change which, again, may become significant in the future. Blair decided to submit himself to a twice-yearly questioning session at the hands of a liaison committee comprised of the chairs of all the departmental select committees. It is a small step in the direction of more government accountability, but nobody can claim it is of great significance.

Ironically, it has been the Conservatives who have made most of the running on Commons reform. It was Margaret Thatcher herself who had backed the creation of departmental select committees in 1979, perhaps the most important parliamentary development of the twentieth century. These committees certainly improved the Commons' ability to call ministers to account, and are still the main way in which our representatives are able to scrutinise the work of government. In fields such as foreign policy, defence spending, health administration and police matters, they have been especially effective in throwing extra light on official or unofficial policies.

More recently, the Norton Committee, headed by a Conservative peer, has led the calls for further changes. Its report, published in 2000, contained many recommendations, the most important of which included:

- The restoration of two sessions of Prime Minister's Question Time.
- Longer ministerial question time sessions, with more in-depth questions.
- More opportunities for backbench MPs to raise issues.
- Shorter speeches in debates so that more people can participate.
- More research resources available for the opposition parties.
- More research facilities for select committees.
- MPs to control their own select committees, rather than the party whips.
- More time to use outside witnesses for standing committees which consider legislation (along the model of the US Congress).
- More resources for the Commons to consider European Union legislation.
- Select committee chairmen to be paid a minister's salary, so that there is an alternative career option for MPs to being a minister. This would break much of the influence of the prime minister and the whips.

These recommendations represent something of a consensus on how the Commons' work could be made more effective. However, Blair's government showed no enthusiasm for them, especially as it had been too busy struggling with a rebellious House of Lords to worry about the Commons. We may also reflect on the comments of former Cabinet Secretary Lord Butler in a 2001 lecture to the Politics Association. He suggests that only the reform of the electoral system could bring about any truly meaningful change in the role and influence of the Commons.

The new parliament which assembled in 2005 certainly did not expect to find itself the subject of many of such reforms.

Human rights

A more detailed analysis of the **human rights** issue in Britain is contained in Unit 2. However, a brief description of the events surrounding the introduction of the Human Rights Act needs to be included here.

Why the Human Rights Act was proposed

A number of factors led the Labour Party to incorporate the European Convention on Human Rights into British law. These were:

- A general desire to bring the British constitution into line with the rest of Europe, all of whose states have special arrangements to protect individual rights.
- The increase in the powers of the police and the courts which had occurred in the 1980s and 1990s were now seen as a major threat to our rights.

Human rights
Basic rights that all citizens can expect to enjoy. Key examples include freedom of expression, freedom of association, freedom of worship, right to privacy and freedom from imprisonment without trial.

- The British government had been brought before the European Court of Human Rights (which seeks to enforce the Convention) over 50 times since 1966 and had lost most of the cases. Although the decisions of the court are not legally binding, these cases had been an embarrassment to the government.
- New Labour stressed the idea of active citizenship. This concept included the principle that citizens have responsibilities to their communities and to the country as a whole. In return for these responsibilities, it was believed that rights should be better understood and safeguarded.
- It was part of the devolution settlements that the Welsh and Northern Ireland Assemblies and the Scottish Parliament should be bound by the Convention. This was designed to reassure the citizens of these nations that devolution would not threaten their rights.

So it was that the Human Rights Act (passed in 1998) made the European Convention part of British law in 2000.

How the Human Rights Act works

The Human Rights Act states that the European Convention on Human Rights is binding on virtually all public bodies in virtually all circumstances. Furthermore, it can be enforced by any British court of law. In essence, therefore, the following individuals and bodies are bound by the Act:

- the Welsh, Scottish and Northern Irish political systems in their entirety;
- local authorities;
- government ministers, civil servants and their departments;
- all government executive agencies;
- all quangos (non-government public bodies);
- any other organisation engaged in 'public business' – this includes the media, all schools and colleges, charities, and so on.

Any regulation or action by any of these bodies can be scrutinised in a court of law and may be declared unlawful. This will result in the action being cancelled and may result in compensation.

The main exception to this law concerns parliamentary legislation. In order to preserve the constitutional principle of parliamentary sovereignty, the convention cannot be considered superior to Parliament. A minister who introduces proposed legislation in Parliament must make a declaration. This declaration will state whether the government believes the proposal to be either compatible or incompatible with the Convention. If it is thought to be *incompatible*, the fact will be taken into consideration when Parliament debates the bill. However, if a bill receives parliamentary approval, it will be enforced by the courts.

The European Court of Human Rights may still hear appeals against UK national legislation and may declare an Act to be in breach of the Convention, but its judgements are still not binding in Britain.

The Human Rights Act in context

In some senses, the Act can be considered to be an extremely radical example of constitutional reform. Indeed, some commentators have suggested that it is the most important development since the Great Reform Act of 1832, when Parliament began the road to democratisation.

Certainly it is the first example of the **codification** of rights in British history. What is familiar to most Europeans and all North Americans – a clear statement of enforceable individual rights – has not been seen here since Magna Carta in 1215. It also represents a huge advance in the protection of individuals against the power of the state.

On the other hand, critics suggest that the Human Rights Act does not go far enough. By preserving parliamentary sovereignty and making parliamentary legislation an exception to its jurisdiction, the Act fails to deal with a fundamental problem in the British constitution: that is, the enormous power of central government and its almost complete control over Parliament. Had the Human Rights Act been binding on parliamentary legislation, it would have represented a major check on governmental power. But it stopped short of this.

Nevertheless, an incident late in 2004 seemed to contradict the criticisms that the Act was too weak. Under the anti-terrorism legislation of 2001, the security services were granted power to detain, without trial, British citizens who were suspected of planning or carrying out terrorist acts. Eight such detainees were being held in Belmarsh prison, but decided to appeal on the grounds that their detention contravened the European Convention on Human Rights. Their appeal was upheld in the House of Lords. Parliamentary sovereignty dictated that the government did not need to obey this judgement. The European Convention is not binding on Parliament and the legislation had been lawfully enacted. But the political repercussions of the judgement were so great that the government felt it had to act. The legislation was amended so that a number of safeguards were added to the Anti-terrorism Act.

The Belmarsh case suggested that the passage of the Human Rights Act represents a more dramatic constitutional change than had been envisaged. Furthermore, in 2005, the rules on the deportation of foreign terrorist suspects also had to be amended. The European Convention forbids the use of torture. This also implies that the UK should not deport any individual to a country where s/he is likely to be tortured. This appeared to tie the government's hands in the fight against terrorist infiltration. In this case, the government had to gain assurances from other countries that deportees would not suffer torture. Here again, the force of the Human Rights Act has been demonstrated.

> **Codification** The process of setting out a constitution in an organised way in a single document.

Electoral reform

The relationship of electoral systems to the party system is analysed in section 3.1. The operation of electoral systems in the UK is also described in Unit 1. Here we examine the political background to reform.

Background

Both the Labour and Liberal (now Liberal Democrat) parties have long since espoused the cause of electoral reform in the UK. The Liberals have been more consistent in their support and, by the 1960s, it was firmly at the centre of their political beliefs. The Labour Party's interest in such reform, on the other hand, has ebbed and flowed.

Cynics suggest that the interest of both these parties has been fundamentally self-interested. The decline of liberalism after the 1920s meant that they could not hope to recover their strong position under the FPTP system. Once the party had lost most of its seats in the House of Commons, a vote for them was seen as a wasted vote. Furthermore, the Liberals have always had very dispersed support. The lack of any concentration of voting power has also meant that the traditional electoral system works against them. With a more proportional system, the party believed that it could reverse its fortunes and challenge for at least a share of power again.

Similarly, Labour has watched while the electoral system has tended to exaggerate the support for the Conservatives. The tendency in the past was to convert votes into parliamentary seats more generously for the Conservatives than for Labour. Three election defeats in a row, from 1951 to 1964, and an even longer period in opposition, from 1979 to 1997, resulted in renewed interest in electoral reform within the Labour Party. Certainly after their 1992 defeat, many in the Labour Party began to believe they might never win again under the FPTP system.

Of course, both parties have refuted these criticisms, arguing that their support for electoral reform is, in fact, *principled*. In other words, they argue that FPTP is unfair, undemocratic and unrepresentative. The Liberal Democrats add that it results in governments which have large parliamentary majorities and, therefore, are able to dominate the policy agenda excessively. It also means that the House of Commons fails to make government properly accountable.

Two groups have maintained implacable opposition to electoral reform. These have been the Conservative Party and most elements of the traditional left wing of the Labour Party. The Conservatives take a pragmatic view. FPTP guarantees a two-party system and governments with decisive parliamentary majorities. This means stability and certainty – key aspects of Conservative philosophy. Traditional sections of the Labour Party have set great store by the power of the state. This power, they have argued, has been essential to make the necessary reforms to create social justice. A multi-party system, which would result from electoral reform, would weaken state power and so jeopardise any future socialist programmes.

New Labour and electoral reform

In truth, the Labour Party which prepared itself for power in the 1990s was completely split on the issue of electoral reform. From a pragmatic, self-interested point of view, a change looked attractive. The dominance of the Conservative Party since 1951 showed no signs of disappearing, especially after their against-all-odds victory at the 1992 general election. If this hegemony could not be broken by political means, argued many in Labour, perhaps electoral reform would do the trick. But this was not the only factor.

As we have seen, New Labour was committed to modernising elements of the British constitution. The old electoral system was beginning to look out of date, whatever the consequences of reform. There were powerful voices in the party who suggested that Britain had become fundamentally undemocratic.

The doubts within Labour were demonstrated by the party's indecisive approach to possible reform. In opposition, they had commissioned Lord Plant to recommend a course of action. The Plant Committee did opt (albeit unenthusiastically) for reform, suggesting something like the German additional member system as an alternative. Still unconvinced, Tony Blair offered the electorate a referendum on the issue if Labour won power in 1997. Labour duly won, but no referendum was forthcoming. Instead, another Commission was appointed, this time under Liberal Democrat Lord Jenkins.

Jenkins reported in 1998. He strongly advocated a more radical system than Plant had done. This was known as AV plus. Its basic operation is described below. The party leadership demonstrated little enthusiasm for the Jenkins proposals and they have been shelved, effectively. Labour continued to delay and, having won again in 2001, was far from ready to consult the electorate. However, this did not mean that electoral reform was a dead issue. On the contrary, various forms of proportional representation were steadily creeping into the political system.

Electoral reform since 1997

While little progress has been made by the electoral reform movement in terms of *general elections*, there has been great progress in other forms of election. Indeed, Britain since 1997 has resembled a great experiment in how different electoral systems can work. The details of these systems is described in section 3.1 above.

The future of electoral reform

One word can sum up the prospects for future reform. That word is 'uncertain'. The Labour leadership has gone cold on the issue as far as general elections are concerned. There are a number of reasons for this:

■ New Labour in the mid-1990s assumed it would need the cooperation of the Liberal Democrats to be able to govern effectively. To secure their future collaboration, the party had to be prepared to entertain electoral reform – the likely price for Liberal Democrat support. This turned out to be a correct assumption in the case of Scotland and Wales, but not at Westminster. So Labour duly delivered on electoral reform for the devolved governments, but has prevaricated in the case of general elections.

- Two enormous election victories in a row, followed by a third, more modest win, exaggerated Labour's success by converting votes into seats extremely generously. In 2001, for example, a 40.7 per cent share of the vote netted 62.6 per cent of the seats; more dramatically still, the 2005 election saw a popular vote of only 35.2 per cent converted into a 66-seat majority for Labour. Therefore, the party was unenthusiastic about changing a system which was now working so obviously to their advantage.
- Conversely, the FPTP system, which used to favour the Conservatives, was now working against their interests. In the 2001 general election, the Conservatives' 31.7 per cent share of the votes yielded only 25.2 per cent of the seats. The party closed the gap with Labour in 2005, but the system still consigned them to opposition. Furthermore, Conservative representation for Wales and Scotland at Westminster had been all but wiped out. The desire to defeat Conservatism in the long term runs deep in Labour mythology, so these figures strengthen the resolve not to change the system which is helping to keep them out.
- Above all, perhaps, the leadership of the Labour Party is largely opposed to reform. No matter how many MPs want to see change, without the support of the majority of the leadership, especially Tony Blair and Gordon Brown, their hopes are in vain.

The result of the 2005 general election led to renewed calls for electoral reform. With Labour winning an overall Commons majority of 66, with only 35.2 per cent of the popular vote, the Conservative Party finally woke up to the fact that the existing electoral system is likely to favour Labour strongly for the foreseeable future. But, although a few voices in the party were raised against FPTP, the issue faded away once again.

The best hope for reformers is that local government will be next in line for a new system (the Scottish Parliament has already made a commitment to introducing STV for voting in local government there). The very low turnout in local elections is causing concern, and some form of proportional representation might go some way to reviving public interest. Many local authorities are already controlled by two-party coalitions, so a change to PR would not cause major disruption, but would give voters more choice.

Proportional representation for UK general elections remains a distant proposition, however.

Freedom of information

The lack of any citizen's right to obtain publicly held information was one of the features of the British constitution which lagged behind the European and North American experience in the 1990s. The Labour Party, supported by the Liberal Democrats, made a firm commitment to introduce such a measure. When it appeared in 1997, however, the legislation proved to be a disappointment to civil rights campaigners.

There are two strands to freedom of information. The first gives the right to citizens to see information which is held about them by public bodies (these include government, schools, medical bodies and other institutions of the welfare state). This has been relatively uncontroversial. Indeed, the right to view records held on computer files had long been established under the earlier Data Protection Act. The main disappointment here was that the right would not come into existence until 2005.

The second strand has caused more problems. This concerns the right to see documents and reports which are held by government and its agencies. In other words, there was to be a public right to see inside the very workings of government. The ability to suppress information would be limited, while the media and Parliament would have much greater access to information. In theory, this represents a major move towards more open government. If implemented in full, freedom of information would have virtually ended the British culture of secrecy in government.

As with electoral reform, the new Labour Government proved to be less enthusiastic about reform once it was in *office* than when it had been in *opposition*. The legislation which appeared in 2000 was very much a watered-down version of similar measures in operation elsewhere in Europe. The security services were completely exempt, while the rest of government was given a key concession. The 'normal' situation is that governments have to justify any reason for suppressing information. The British version, however, gives government the right to conceal information if it feels it might prejudice the activities of government. In other words, the onus is on the outsider to prove that a document or other information should be released.

Civil rights groups see the new Act as virtually useless. It will not be possible to reveal more information than before in any field which the government considers critical. Hopes that there might be a dramatic shift in power over information towards citizens and the media had been dashed. The Act only came into effect in 2005, so (at the time of writing) its full effects are not yet known; it is possible that the widespread pessimism might be misplaced.

London government

The abolition of the Greater London Council (GLC) in 1986 by Margaret Thatcher's government was a bitter experience for the Labour Party and it left a lasting scar. The GLC had been seen as something of a socialist experiment, especially when it had been controlled by its left-wing leader, Ken Livingstone. Its programmes of subsidised education, transport, employment schemes and housing were designed to counterbalance many of the social deprivations, which, it was believed, were largely the result of Thatcherite policies.

When Labour saw the prospect of returning to power, therefore, the restoration of London government stood high on its political agenda. However, there was no prospect of recreating such a powerful body as the

GLC. A strong lesson had been learned – that it was dangerous to create a political institution that could rival central government power in its own heartland. Devolution was all very well, but autonomous government in London was too radical for New Labour. Instead, the Labour Party proposed a limited form of government in the capital.

The most prominent proposal – to elect a mayor for London – was a unique measure. No part of the British political system had ever seen, throughout her history, a single *elected* figure. True, all local authorities had mayors as figureheads for centuries, but these were not elected, but appointed by the rest of the council. The ancient institution of *Lord Mayor of London* was also an appointment: in this case, of the traditional livery companies which control the small City of London. The idea of an elected mayor was imported from the USA and France, and represented a complete break with the past.

The people of London took to the idea with enthusiasm and a 1999 referendum endorsed the measure decisively. Thereafter, however, matters began to take an unpleasant turn for the Labour Government. First, the party's own candidate, Frank Dobson, was thoroughly beaten by Ken Livingstone, who had left the party to stand as a radical independent candidate. Second, the Greater London Assembly, of 25 elected members, was not, as the party had hoped, dominated by Labour candidates. In fact, the Conservatives secured as many seats as Labour – nine each – so Labour's influence in London was extremely weak.

The Labour Government had never intended that independent London government should be strong, but Labour's setbacks at the first elections ensured that it should remain weak, however much Ken Livingstone might try to raise its profile. In effect, the GLA has some control over public transport and traffic management, together with powers to veto major building developments. It started with a small budget – £4 billion – and had little power to raise any of its own funds. It is not allowed to raise local taxes, for example.

But two developments have raised the profile of the office of mayor and may well demonstrate that this was a more significant constitutional reform than had been appreciated at first. The first was the introduction of the congestion charge in central London in 2003. Though widely disliked, it proved successful in reducing congestion and raised funds for the improvement of public transport in the capital. The second was London's securing responsibility for staging the Olympic Games in 2012. Not only was Mayor Livingstone widely praised for his role in the successful bid, but also the prospect of the Olympics, and all its lucrative spin-offs, raised the profile of London government considerably. The government's 2004 approval of the cross-rail project (to create a railway line from east to west London) also placed huge amounts of funding into the hands of *Transport for London*, which is in the mayor's control. By this time, Livingstone had rejoined the Labour Party and was re-elected in 2004. Labour's enthusiasm for reform had certainly been rekindled.

Local government

As with London, the government's enthusiasm for reform of local government in general withered very quickly after Labour was elected to office in 1997. Cities, towns and districts have been given the opportunity to elect mayors following a local referendum. However, in the first few years, very few had held referendums and fewer still had voted in favour of an elected mayor (only 11 by 2005). Furthermore, if the new mayors suffer the same fate as Livingstone in London, it will prove to be an ineffective reform.

Similarly, local authorities have been given the option of changing to a cabinet system of government. This involves the creation of a central cabinet of leading councillors from the dominant party, or from a coalition, who may take over central control of the council's work, making key decisions and setting general policy. This replaces the former system, where the work of the council was divided between a number of functional committees.

As with elected mayors, the take-up for the new cabinet system has been patchy. Moreover, it is generally acknowledged that this kind of internal change does not tackle the real problems of local government. These are seen as threefold:

1. Lack of autonomy from central government.
2. Lack of accountability to local electorates.
3. Largely as a result of the first two problems, very low public interest in local government and politics.

The Labour Government elected in 2001 did promise progress on these fronts. However, reform of local government remains low on the list of priorities and it seems unlikely that any radical change will be forthcoming for some time to come. There was little said about local government in Labour's 2005 manifesto, so fundamental reform remains unlikely.

Referendums

There has not been a piece of legislation establishing the practice of holding referendums to provide popular consent for constitutional changes. Nevertheless, it has now become firmly established that a referendum will be held if any power is to be transferred away from central government in the UK. This transfer could be upwards to the European Union, or downwards to regional or local bodies.

In other parts of the democratic world referendums are often used as a special arrangement for constitutional reform. In the past, Britain has not had special arrangements for constitutional amendments. They have been created either by Act of Parliament or by the emergence of new unwritten conventions. But the referendum is now a regular feature in the UK, so much so that we can describe its use as an important constitutional reform.

The registration of political parties

The Political Parties, Elections and Referendums Act of 2000 was a land-mark in the codification of the party system in the UK. Before then, the existence and conduct of parties was largely conventional and voluntary in nature. Now all parties must be registered if they are to take part in elections. By registering, they subject themselves to a variety of strict rules on finance and conduct.

But behind the legislation there lies a more fundamental change. This is the admission, in a constitutional statute, that elections are about parties rather than individuals. Individuals can still stand for election, but if they are to use a party label, they become subject to a new, stricter set of regulations.

Reform of the judiciary after 2005

Though not originally a part of Labour's 1997 reform programme, important changes to the constitutional position of the judiciary are to be made in the period 2005–08. These proposals are mainly as follows:

- The law lords are to be removed from the House of Lords and to sit separately in a new Supreme Court. It will have the same role as before, but Supreme Court judges will no longer be members of the legislature so there will be less confusion over their roles.
- The office of Lord Chancellor may be abolished or modified. In particular, it is proposed that the holder of this post (whether or not its title is changed) will no longer be a senior political figure sitting in cabinet, but will be a politically independent individual.
- Senior judges will be appointed by an independent Judicial Appointments Commission. This will be subject to a final veto by the prime minister. This will remove most of the suspicions that judicial appointments might be politically motivated.

An assessment of constitutional reform after 1997

The position with regard to constitutional reform in Britain at the start of the twenty-first century is certainly paradoxical. On the one hand, the years after 1997 have seen the greatest constitutional changes in Britain probably since 1832 and, some have suggested, even since Parliament became effectively sovereign in 1688. The list of reforms shown in the table at the start of this chapter is certainly impressive. On the other hand, New Labour's reforms have disappointed many, inside and outside the party.

The Liberal Democrats and constitutional pressure groups, such as Charter 88 and Liberty, see reform as only half completed. They point to the following gaps in the programme needed to make Britain a truly modern democracy:

- The new, largely appointed House of Lords falls well short of being properly accountable, authoritative and representative. Only a fully elected second chamber is acceptable.
- The House of Commons remains ineffective and inefficient. Lack of government accountability is seen as a fundamental problem and only a reformed, revitalised House of Commons can provide this.
- The Human Rights Act, though a vital development, has not been given the political status it needs. The fact that the European Convention cannot overrule Acts of Parliament means that rights can still be trampled on by powerful governments. The anti-terrorism measures which were enacted after the 9/11 terrorist attacks on the USA were seen as a case in point.
- The Freedom of Information Act is too weak and allows government to remain over-secretive.
- Perhaps, most importantly, Labour has failed to deliver electoral reform for parliamentary or local elections. It is this measure which is most often seen as the way in which the political system can be fundamentally changed for the better.

Whether future Labour governments will listen to these criticisms and act upon them remains to be seen.

KEY CONCEPTS

Pluralism
In the context of this chapter, pluralism refers to the idea that different views about reform of the political system can flourish together.

Constitutional reform
A process whereby the fundamental nature of the system of government (as well as the relationships between governing institutions) is changed, or where change is proposed. In the case of the UK, this may also involve the process of codification.

Parliamentary reform
A process whereby reforms in the membership, powers or procedures of either or both Houses of Parliament are made or proposed.

Referendum
A popular vote in which the people, rather than their elected representatives, resolve a political issue. It is used as a way of gaining consent for constitutional reforms.

Human rights
Basic rights that all citizens can expect to enjoy. Key examples include freedom of expression, freedom of association, freedom of worship, right to privacy and freedom from imprisonment without trial.

Codification
The process of setting out a constitution in an organised way in a single document.

Revision topics and examination questions

Revision topics

- Reasons for constitutional reform after 1997
- The details of all constitutional reforms since 1997
- The details of incomplete reforms
- Reasons why some reforms have not been made
- Ways in which executive power may have been weakened

Sample questions

Read the following passage and answer the questions that follow.

When Labour came to power in May 1997 it promised a programme of radical constitutional reform. To an extent this has been delivered, but supporters of Charter 88 and those who campaigned through the years of Conservative dominance in 1979–97 are likely to feel disappointed.

The government has shown a marked reluctance to implement constitutional reform where it is likely to hinder the power of the executive. As the cliché goes, 'turkeys do not vote for Christmas'. Is it fair to accuse Labour of suffering a severe bout of 'executiveitis'?

Labour's record since 1997 is an impressive one and represents the most profound constitutional change since the Great Reform Act of 1832. Yet, at the same time, Labour has fought shy of taking the reform process to its logical conclusions and introducing a constitutional settlement with a written constitution at its heart. For all the reforms that have occurred we still have an uncodified constitution onto which have been bolted various acts of parliament. This means that a substantial part of the British constitution is now written although it still it is still a ramshackle structure that fails either to define the power of the executive and to control it. It is possible to argue that that Britain is now slowly acquiring a written constitution 'through the back door' via such pieces of legislation as the Human Rights Act and the Freedom of Information Act.

Source: Andrew Granath, 'Constitutional Reform, A Work in Progress', in Talking Politics, vol. 14, no. 3, April 2002.

1. Identify and briefly describe any two constitutional reforms referred to in the passage. (5 marks)
   Guidance: *Clearly this refers to the Human Rights Act and the Freedom of Information Act. Very briefly describe what each does. Arguably, the idea of codifying the constitution could also be used.*
2. From the passage and your own knowledge, outline ways in which constitutional reform since 1997 may have produced greater control over the power of the executive. (10 marks)
   Guidance: *Here again, the Human Rights and Freedom of Information Acts apply. Describe how they exercise such control over the executive. But more are needed, as the question implies. Devolution is the obvious example. Briefly describe what powers have been devolved. Strengthening the authority of the House of Lords is a further example. Perhaps quote a couple of examples of how it has made government difficult.*
3. In what senses is Britain now 'acquiring a written constitution through the back door'? (15 marks)
   Guidance: *This refers to the large number of Acts of Parliament of a constitutional nature that have been passed since 1997. A good selection is required. Mention all the Acts you can and describe them briefly, notably those not mentioned in the two previous questions. The prime examples are the Devolution Acts and the Human Rights Act, which effectively created a Bill of Rights.*
4. Describe and explain the proposed constitutional reforms which have either not been made or remain incomplete. (20 marks)
   Guidance: *The reforms referred to clearly are electoral reform, House of Lords reform and English regional devolution. It is important to explain how these reforms are incomplete or unmade, but especially to explain why they have not been completed.*

Resources and Web Guide

Books

Perhaps the best book on constitutional reform in recent years has been:
Vernon Bogdanor, *Power and the People. A Guide to Constitutional Reform*, Gollancz, 1997.
Almost equally good is:
Robert Hazell, *Constitutional Futures: A History of the Next Ten Years*, OUP, 1999.
An interesting and slightly unconventional view can be seen in:
Anthony King, *Does the United Kingdom Still Have a Constitution?*, Sweet and Maxwell, 2001.
Finally, more up to date is:
J. Morrison, *Reforming Britain, New Labour, New Constitution*, Pearson, 2001.

Useful websites

The best site for comprehensive information is the UCL Constitution Unit:
www.ucl.ac.uk/constitution-unit/ (accessed 11 November 2005)
The government service on the constitution is published by the department for constitutional affairs:
www.dca.gov.uk (accessed 11 November 2005)
The main campaign group for reform is Charter 88:
www.charter88.org.uk (accessed 11 November 2005)
Also look at the Liberty site, mainly on human rights:
www.liberty-human-rights.org.uk (accessed 11 November 2005)

3.3
How united is the United Kingdom?

Devolution

Movements that were dedicated to the introduction of greater self-government for Britain's national regions can be traced back as far as the nineteenth century. There has been a Scottish Nationalist movement for over a century, although the Scottish National Party (SNP) did not come into existence until 1928. Welsh **nationalism** is a younger phenomenon, but Plaid Cymru – the Welsh Nationalist Party – does date back to 1925. Both these movements were certainly influenced by the fact that Ireland had been granted virtually full independence in 1921.

The situation in Northern Ireland, quite clearly, has been very different. The full circumstances of nationalist movements are described in Chapter 1.3. It should be emphasised, however, that Northern Ireland was granted devolved government in 1921 and enjoyed a large measure of independence until 1972, when direct rule from London was established. Since 1972, the idea of **devolution** receded in Northern Ireland. The Republican or nationalist communities wanted to see reunification with the Irish Republic. The Loyalists or Unionists were more concerned with resisting nationalism than with re-establishing devolved government.

The origins of devolution

Much of the background to the devolution movement refers specifically to Scotland and Wales, for reasons described above. Despite the long history of nationalism, the modern devolution story really begins in the 1970s. In that decade there was a distinct rise in nationalist feeling. The most obvious symptom was a rise in voting for nationalist parties at elections. The SNP had one only one seat at Westminster up to 1970. By the October 1974 election, however, the party had 11 seats as a result of winning over 30 per cent of the vote in Scotland. Plaid Cymru secured 11.5 per cent of the vote in Wales in 1970, but no seats. However, by October 1974 it had 3 seats and had established itself in Welsh politics.

Why devolution?

The nationalists were, on the whole, interested in full independence. But in the 1970s this was an impossible aspiration. The union of the UK was strong and the people of Scotland and Wales would certainly not have voted for it. Neither of the main parties could have survived politically had they advocated independence. But the challenge of nationalism had to be met. Compromise was, therefore, in the air.

Nationalism
A political sentiment felt by people who believe they have common circumstances of birth. It usually (though not always) also refers to aspirations for a nation to gain political independence, if it is controlled by another dominant nation, or unity, if it has become divided.

Devolution
A process of constitutional reform whereby power, but not legal sovereignty, is distributed to national or regional institutions. In the UK this has meant transfer of power to institutions in Scotland, Wales and Northern Ireland, but not to the regions of England.

Federalism had to be considered. This would have involved the transfer of large degrees of actual *sovereignty* to regional bodies. There were plenty of models to choose from, including the USA and Germany. But again, this looked to be too close to independence for most Westminster politicians to stomach. Granting powers to Scottish and Welsh Parliaments which could not ultimately be controlled or taken back by Westminster was simply too radical to succeed.

The solution was to propose something similar to the Northern Ireland form of government which had existed before direct rule was imposed in 1972. This became known as devolution. Devolution is a kind of regionalism, though the fact that a large amount of power was to be transferred suggested that it could also be described as 'quasi-federalism'. A Royal Commission – the Kilbrandon Commission – had developed the idea for Scotland in 1973. The word 'devolution' was a new one in British politics. It reflected the idea that power could be transferred to a region, without ceding actual sovereignty. In other words, the national governments would be semi-independent, but would always be subject to oversight from London. Devolution was adopted as the compromise. It was hoped that it would satisfy moderate nationalist opinion, but also be acceptable to MPs at Westminster.

The failure of devolution in the 1970s

The Labour Government which was elected in October 1974 enjoyed a very narrow parliamentary majority. It was clear that it would need to rely on the support of smaller parties to survive for long. The small parties in question were the Liberals, the SNP and Plaid Cymru. All three were pressing the government for some transfer of powers to Scotland and Wales. The Labour Party itself was split on the issue. The Scottish and Welsh Labour MPs were mostly in favour (with the notable exception of Tam Dalyell, the West Lothian MP who remained implacably opposed for many years to come and was to play a key part in the devolution story in the 1990s). These MPs saw and feared the rise of nationalist sentiment. Their seats were, after all, in danger from the new movement. Most English Labour MPs were less enthusiastic, but many recognised that support for devolution might be essential.

The new Labour Government had shown a lukewarm commitment to devolution, which was reflected in a series of abortive attempts to push legislation through the House of Commons. By 1976 the position of the government had become critical. It had lost its majority altogether as a result of by-election defeats and was hanging on to a shaky alliance with the Liberals – the so-called Lib-Lab Pact. It was time to press for devolution more decisively.

The Scotland and Wales Bills, which appeared in 1977, revealed a limited set of proposals for the transfer of power to elected bodies in the two countries. However, the Liberals were reasonably satisfied and agreed to support the government. This would secure a majority for the Government in favour of the measure. At this point, however, a group of dissident

Federalism
In contrast to devolution, federalism refers to the division of legal sovereignty (more than mere power) between the central political authority and regional authorities. This means that the powers thus distributed cannot be returned to the central authority, nor can the central authority overrule regional centres of government. The classic example is the USA.

Regionalism
A desire felt by peoples within regions of a country to have some degree of independent power, allowing them to make political decisions on a regional basis, rather than a national one. Regionalism assumes that there are significant economic, cultural and social differences that warrant regional political variations.

Labour MPs (including Tam Dalyell) entered an alliance with the Conservatives which was to deal the devolution movement a mortal blow.

In January 1978 an amendment was passed to the Scotland and Wales Bills concerning the referendums which were required to approve devolution. The original legislation required only a simple majority vote. The amendment, however, required that approval would be needed from at least 40 per cent of the *total electorate*. Given that it was expected that up to one-third of the electorate would not vote, this was a difficult threshold to meet. In March 1979 the Welsh voted decisively against devolution in any case, but the Scots produced a yes vote. However, only 33 per cent of the Scottish electorate had approved, so the Conservative amendment had its desired effect.

The political fallout was dramatic. Apart from the subsequent events, political commentators pointed out how unusual the events of 1978 had been. The House of Commons had defeated the government on a major piece of its legislative programme. This was something which had not been seen since the Second World War. The government was clearly doomed. Shortly afterwards a vote of no confidence was passed and Prime Minister James Callaghan resigned. The election which followed ushered in 18 years of continuous Conservative government.

Apart from a failed experiment with the transfer of power to Northern Ireland during 1982–84, devolution went on the political backburner. Nationalist sentiment declined markedly as prosperity began to rise in the second half of the 1980s.

We can identify three main reasons for the failure of devolution in 1978–79:

1. In the end there was simply insufficient enthusiasm for devolution, especially in Wales.
2. In London there was not sufficient political will within the Labour Party to force the measure through. The small number of MPs who defied the whips and supported the Conservative referendum amendment in 1978 were in fact representative of wider opposition in the party.
3. Devolution was an idea whose day was coming, but 1979 was too early. It would take a more worldwide movement for nationalism in the 1990s to see Scotland and Wales swept along to partial self-government.

As we shall see, by the second half of the 1990s, the conditions described above had been reversed, so the whole devolution picture was transformed.

The demand for devolution in the 1990s

As we have seen, there was a lull in interest in devolution for most of the 1980s. The prosperity of the mid-1980s helped to head off nationalism temporarily, but it re-emerged after the 1987 general election. The reasons for this were very different to the circumstances of the 1970s. Among them were the following:

- Under Margaret Thatcher's three administrations, the Scots and Welsh began to resent the fact that, however dominant the Conservatives might be in England, their mandate in the two countries was weak. In Scotland, where there were 72 parliamentary seats, the Conservatives won only 22, 21, 11 and 10 seats, respectively, in the elections of 1979, 1983, 1987 and 1992. In Wales' 38 seats, the Conservative showing declined from 14 in 1983 to just 6 in 1992. As Conservative support in the two countries declined, demands for self-government grew.
- The Labour Party in Scotland and Wales felt threatened by a new growth in nationalist voting. They feared they may suffer the same fate as the Conservatives. The Scottish Labour Party, in particular, changed its attitude markedly during the late 1980s.
- In Scotland there was huge resentment at the fact that the unpopular poll tax had been introduced there one year earlier than in England and Wales. Many Scots felt they were being used as mere guinea pigs, a trial run for the wider introduction of the tax. It was a hated measure in Scotland and resulted in the collapse of support for the Conservatives.
- The Scottish Constitutional Convention of 1988, which was led by the Labour Party, but also contained a wide range of Scottish political opinion, came out firmly in favour of devolution as a solution to Scotland's problems.
- In 1993 the Welsh language gained official recognition. Signs and documents were to be in two languages, Welsh was to be offered in all schools and individuals could opt to speak Welsh in court cases. This created a fresh impetus for Welsh nationalism.
- On a global level, the end of the cold war saw a huge upsurge in national feelings all over the world. This new spirit of nationalism and the desire for popular self-determination spread to Wales and Scotland.
- John Smith, who took over the Labour leadership in 1992, was a convinced devolutionist.
- As we see in Chapter 3.2, on constitutional reform, in the 1990s the Labour Party believed it would probably need the cooperation of the Liberal Democrats to secure and retain power. Devolution was a key policy for the Liberal Democrats, so it made pragmatic sense for Labour to adopt it as a firm proposal.

So it was that devolution was made a priority by the incoming Labour administration of 1997. It wasted little time in bringing forward the legislation.

How devolution came about

Principles

The Scottish Constitutional Convention, which had reported in 1988, provided the blueprint for a devolution settlement. However, when Labour was constructing its election manifesto in 1997, it adopted three key principles.

First, it differentiated between Scotland and Wales. In Scotland, where it was expected that the people would embrace devolution enthusiastically, there was to be a Parliament with extensive legislative powers. The Scots were also to be offered some control over taxation. In Wales, where approval was not assured, it was decided that legislative power could not be devolved and there was to be much less financial flexibility. This proved to be a wise device. Nothing less than a Scottish Parliament would do for the nationalists there, but the Welsh might be frightened off if too much power were offered.

The second principle was the intention to use a form of proportional representation – the additional member system – when electing the Scottish Parliament and Welsh Assembly. It was essential that devolution was not seen as an attempt to tighten Labour's grip in the two countries. Under FPTP, Labour would probably have won outright majorities, just as it had done in Westminster elections. This would have defeated the object of devolution, which was to disperse power and not centralise it. Much as the Labour Party might have liked to control the new governments, it had to be pragmatic in relinquishing full power. It was part of the price of making devolution acceptable. Furthermore, it was vital that the nationalist parties be given their fair share of the seats. The additional member system was the ideal way of achieving this.

Third, there were to be referendums on the devolution proposals. This was necessary for a number of important reasons:

■ New Labour accepted the general principle that *any* major constitutional change would need popular approval.
■ A positive referendum result would head off opposition from UK Unionists and Conservatives.
■ It was vital to secure popular consent for the measures in Scotland and Wales. Without it, the new institutions might not achieve respect.
■ Referendums would help to entrench the changes. In other words, it would make it very difficult for any future government to unravel devolution, at least without a further referendum.

The programme

The progress towards devolution proved to be relatively smooth. In some ways, the steps (which follow below) can be seen as a model of how constitutional change can be effected in a parliamentary democracy such as Britain's:

1. Of course, Labour had to win the general election with devolution as a clear part of its manifesto. This would provide a mandate for change. It was important for Labour to win decisively to prevent any questioning of its authority to carry through radical changes. This was achieved comfortably.
2. It was not just important for Labour to win. It also needed to win well in Scotland and Wales. A resurgence of Conservative voting there would call the devolution idea into question. If, on the other hand, the nationalists were to make significant gains, it would suggest that the proposals were not radical enough. In the event, the Conservatives failed to win a single seat in Scotland and Wales in the 1997 general election. The

nationalist parties, meanwhile, made little progress. Labour support held up well, suggesting that it had got its devolution plans about right.

3. Before the legislation was to be considered, referendums were held. These took place in 1997, soon after the general election. Two factors were important in these referendums. First, there needed to be a good turnout. In the event, just over 60 per cent of Scots voted – just enough to give the result authority. In Wales, however, the turnout was only just over 50 per cent, and this has certainly had the effect of reducing the effectiveness of Welsh self-government. Second, of course, a yes vote was needed. There were no problems in Scotland, where 74.3 per cent voted in favour of devolution and 63.5 per cent voted separately for the tax-varying powers which had been hotly contested in the general election campaign. In Wales, however, the yes majority was only 50.3 per cent. Nevertheless, the government decided to approve Welsh as well as Scottish devolution.

4. The legislation had to be passed. With a huge parliamentary majority, this was unlikely to be a problem, and so it proved. The only major stumbling block was the proposal to allow the Scottish Parliament to vary UK income tax in their own country by 3 per cent up or down. The Conservatives had dubbed this a 'tartan tax' – a means of raising taxes by stealth (so-called 'stealth taxes' had formed a major element in the Conservatives' 1997 election campaign). The new government, however, was not to be diverted and the legislation – the Scotland and Wales Acts – survived largely intact. The Acts were passed in 1998.

5. The final hurdles were the actual elections to the Scottish Parliament and Welsh Assembly. Would enough people turn out to vote? Would the results be such that it was possible to form viable governments? As with the referendums, support in Wales was lukewarm, with a turnout of 46 per cent. In Scotland, there was a better turnout – 58 per cent – but there was still some concern that too few people were interested in the devolution project. The results by party, however, were more encouraging. Though Labour dominated both elections, the party failed narrowly to win overall majorities in both countries.

So it was that the Scottish Parliament and Welsh Assembly came into existence in 1999. The Scottish executive was formed from a coalition between Labour and the Liberal Democrats. Donald Dewar, the Labour leader in Scotland (who died in 2001), became the country's First Minister. In Wales, Labour formed a minority executive under Alun Michael. Michael was replaced by Rhodri Morgan in 2001, following a kind of *coup d'état* by Labour Assembly Members. In the same year, Labour gave up trying to govern with a minority and formed a coalition with the Liberal Democrats. In both countries the main opposition duties are shared between the Conservatives and the Nationalists.

The arguments for and against devolution are set out in the following table.

For	Against
■ There has been a growing popular demand for more self-government in the national regions. ■ The national regions have different needs to England, which should be reflected in stronger regional government. ■ By conceding devolution, the demands for fuller independence will be headed off, thus preventing the break-up of the UK. ■ It is more democratic because government will be brought closer to the people. ■ It will reduce the workload of the British Parliament and government. ■ It recognises the new idea of a 'Europe of the Regions' rather than separate states.	■ Conservatives, in particular, believe it may lead to the break-up of the UK because demands for independence will be fuelled by devolution. ■ It was argued that demand for devolution was over-exaggerated, especially in Wales, so it was unnecessary. ■ It creates an extra layer of government, which will increase costs to the taxpayer. ■ In Scotland it was feared that taxes there would inevitably rise because Scotland is less prosperous than the UK as a whole. ■ It will lead to confusion because there is an additional layer of bureaucracy. ■ Nationalists have argued that devolution does not go far enough. British government has retained all the important powers for itself. ■ Nationalists also argue they should have a separate voice in Europe, but devolution does not give them this. ■ The West Lothian question (see below).

Three types of devolution

The process of devolution can be divided into three levels, as follows.

Administrative devolution

This is the transfer of limited powers to devolved administrations. This effectively means control over the allocation of public funds, the nature of administration, the way in which laws (enacted elsewhere) should be implemented and the passage of secondary legislation. Secondary legislation refers to the various rules and regulations that can be imposed within the country under powers granted by Parliament in Westminster.

Financial devolution

This is the ability of the devolved administration to raise its own taxes. Most funds available to devolved administrations are in the form of central government grants. This allows relatively little financial independence. Granting taxation powers, by contrast, conveys a great deal of autonomy. The Scottish Parliament was given very limited financial power, restricted to increasing or reducing the level of income tax by 3 per cent either way.

Legislative devolution

This is the transfer of power to make primary legislation. It is this distinction that makes the Scottish representative body a parliament rather than an assembly.

The table below, showing the distribution of devolution, summarises the way in which these three types of devolution were granted to the nations of Britain.

Country	Administrative devolution granted?	Legislative devolution granted?	Financial devolution granted?
Scotland	Yes	Yes	Yes
Northern Ireland	Yes	Yes	No
Wales	Yes	No	No

Devolution in Scotland

The Scottish Parliament

This came into existence, after a gap of 292 years, in 1999. There are 129 seats: 73 of these are elected by normal, FPTP constituency elections; the other 56 seats are the result of voting for party lists, where each party is awarded seats from its list, according to a combination of what proportion of the votes were won by them in both the constituency and the party list elections. In other words, each Scottish voter has two votes – one for a constituency MSP (Member of the Scottish Parliament), the other for a party. The electoral system is known as the **additional member system** (AMS). The Parliament sits in Edinburgh. It has fixed electoral terms. Elections take place every four years.

In the first election, in 1999, Labour won most seats, but not enough for an overall majority. Labour therefore entered a coalition with the Liberal Democrats. The strength of the parties following the second elections to the Scottish Parliament in 2003 is shown below in the allocation of seats.

Party	Seats won
Labour	50
Scottish Nationalist	27
Conservative	18
Liberal Democrat	17
Green	7
Scottish Socialist	6
Independent	4

Once again, Labour was forced into coalition, this time with a total combined number of seats of 67, a bare majority of 5 over the other parties.

The powers and functions of the Parliament

It is important to note that the Scottish Parliament was granted the power to make **primary legislation** in selected areas. The term 'primary legislation' essentially means two things. First, it refers to the laws as we understand them – what is prohibited, how organisations must behave, what responsibilities citizens are expected to carry out. Second, it grants powers to other bodies to make regulations and rules which are as binding as other laws. We call this **enabling legislation**. For example, local authorities, members of the executive and other public bodies will be given powers to make **secondary legislation**. Secondary legislation involves orders which do not need to be passed through the same process as primary legislation. They are simply announced and become law if there is no successful objection to them in Parliament.

The decision to grant powers of primary legislation was crucial to Scottish devolution. It meant that the Scots were given the opportunity to make themselves and their society distinctive. It should also be remembered that Scotland has always had its own laws, especially criminal and civil law, but that after 1707 these laws were made by the British Parliament in Westminster. In other words, the final say on Scottish law rested with the British government. With its own primary legislating powers after devolution, however, Scotland was granted a significant amount of autonomy. As we shall see below, the Welsh Assembly was not granted the power to make primary legislation and so has to consider itself very much an inferior body.

FIG 3.3A The controversial Scottish parliament building

The functions of the Scottish Parliament are as follows:

1. To pass primary legislation in those areas of policy making which have been devolved to Scotland.
2. The main policy areas devolved are:

   - criminal law;
   - civil law;
   - education;
   - social services;
   - local government;
   - building and planning regulations;
   - agriculture;
   - fisheries;
   - health;
   - transport;
   - emergency services.

3. To determine the level of income tax to within 3 per cent higher or lower than the general British rate set in London.
4. To approve the overall Scottish Budget.
5. To call the executive to account for its actions and policies.
6. To elect a first minister to form the executive (i.e. government).
7. To form committees to scrutinise legislation and the work of Scottish executive departments.
8. To oversee and scrutinise secondary legislation produced by Scottish ministers, local authorities and other public bodies.

The constraints on the Scottish Parliament are as follows:

1. It can only pass legislation in areas allowed under devolution legislation.
2. It cannot pass legislation which conflicts with British law.
3. It cannot pass legislation which conflicts with European Union law.
4. Its legislation must conform to the European Convention on Human Rights.
5. It cannot raise its own national taxes, other than a 3 per cent variation in income tax levels.
6. It cannot amend the devolution legislation, that is, it cannot change the system of government in Scotland.

The Scottish executive

The term 'executive' is used in the devolved systems to replace 'government'. This is to avoid confusion with British government in London.

The Scottish executive is headed by a first minister, who is effectively the prime minister of Scotland, without being given that title. The first minister is chosen, in practice, by being leader of the largest party in the parliament. However, he or she must be elected to office by the whole parliament. That is to say, the parliament must confirm the first minister's appointment (in contrast to Westminster, where the appointment of the prime minister is a very private process).

The rest of the executive is formed by the heads of the various departments which make up Scottish government. The role of the executive is as follows:

1. To formulate policy for Scotland and draft appropriate legislation to be presented in Parliament.
2. To negotiate with the British government for funds.
3. To implement policies which have been developed within the executive and approved by the Scottish Parliament.
4. To make decisions under powers delegated to it by either the British or the Scottish Parliament.
5. Liaison with the British government where there are overlapping functions, such as law enforcement, environmental and industrial policies.
6. To negotiate with institutions of the European Union (though Scotland has no seat at the Council of Ministers) for regional funds and favourable policies.
7. To organise and oversee the provision of services by executive departments (i.e. the Scottish civil service), local authorities and other public bodies.

The West Lothian question

This thorny issue is named after the parliamentary constituency of long-term Labour opponent of devolution, Tam Dalyell. Dalyell it was who first gave voice to a particular problem arising from Scottish legislative devolution. In the Westminster Parliament all MPs have a vote on all issues. This means that Westminster MPs representing Scottish parliamentary constituencies can vote on issues which affect England and Wales *only*. To make matters worse, however, English and Welsh MPs have no such voting rights over affairs affecting Scotland, as they are voted on in the new Scottish Parliament. This issue was illustrated well when the Labour government introduced university tuition fees in 2003. The government relied on the support of its Scottish MPs to obtain a majority, even though the fees did not apply in Scottish universities.

It could be argued that MPs representing constituencies in Scotland could be denied a vote on any issues which affect only England and Wales. But this presents another problem. What if the government cannot rely on a majority from MPs representing only Welsh and English constituencies? In such circumstances, it would have to recruit Scottish MPs to support the government. Of course, this only applies to a Labour government, as only Labour holds a significant number of seats in Scotland. In other words, we could be faced with a situation where a government had a working majority for the UK as a whole, but not for England and Wales.

As it happens, this has not yet been a problem. Labour has enjoyed a

large majority of seats in England and Wales since 1997. It has not had to rely on the support of MPs from Scotland. But there could come a time in the future when this West Lothian question could become a constitutional crisis. It used to be a particular problem for any future Conservative government which might be thwarted by Scottish Labour MPs. For now, though, it remains unresolved.

Devolution in Wales

The Welsh Assembly

In Wales, the representative body is known as an assembly rather than a parliament. This reflects the fact that it has considerably fewer powers than its Scottish counterpart. In particular, it has no powers to make any primary legislation. This is a key difference. It means that the British Parliament and government still rule Wales.

The Assembly was elected at the same time as the Scottish Parliament, using the same AMS electoral system. There are 60 seats in all. The result of the first election, in 1999, was as follows.

Party	Seats won
Labour	28
Plaid Cymru (Welsh Nationalist)	17
Conservative	9
Liberal Democrat	6

As in Scotland, Labour failed to win an overall majority, but was the largest party. However, unlike in Scotland, the party decided to try to govern alone, without a coalition. Within two years this proved to be impractical, so they formed a coalition, again with the Liberal Democrats.

In 2003 the election result for the Welsh Assembly was somewhat different, as follows.

Party	Seats won
Labour	30
Plaid Cymru (Welsh Nationalist)	12
Conservative	11
Liberal Democrat	6
Independent	1

Labour won exactly the same number of seats as the other parties put together. However, they again chose to remain in coalition rather than attempt to sustain a shaky single-party government.

The Assembly meets in Cardiff and, like Scotland, has a fixed term of four years.

FIG 3.3B The Welsh assembly was granted limited powers

The powers and functions of the Assembly

The following list indicates the main policy areas devolved to Wales:

- education;
- social services;
- local government;
- building and planning regulations;
- agriculture;
- fisheries;
- health;
- transport;
- emergency services.

The most important element of Welsh devolution is that the Assembly (note again that it is not called a *parliament*) does not have the power to make primary legislation. This means it has to rely on Westminster for all its legislation. This is a considerable limitation. The Assembly can make *secondary legislation*. This involves more minor laws and regulations, under

the general limitations of the primary legislation passed in Westminster. Therefore, the functions of the Welsh Assembly are as follows:

1. It calls the Welsh executive to account by questioning department heads, both in committee and through the full Assembly.
2. It elects the head of the Welsh executive. It can also dismiss him/her.
3. It discusses Welsh affairs and makes resolutions which it hopes will be influential on London and on Cardiff.
4. It discusses the implementation of policy on Welsh affairs.
5. It attempts to direct the Welsh executive in its implementation of policy and allocation of funds to various uses.
6. It debates and requests changes to the Welsh Budget.

The restraints on its powers are as follows:

1. It cannot pass primary legislation.
2. It cannot grant powers to members of the Welsh executive.
3. It cannot call London government to account directly.
4. It cannot raise any special taxes in Wales.

The Welsh executive

This is, to a large extent, the government of Wales. However, because relatively few powers were devolved, it must share this function with London, the Welsh Office in particular. The head of the executive is elected by the Assembly and s/he appoints the heads of the Welsh departments. These department heads are accountable to the Assembly, which can remove them, effectively. As we have seen above, the first Welsh executive was a Labour minority government, but it has since become a Labour/Liberal Democrat coalition.

The functions of the executive are as follows:

1. To allocate funds, which are provided by the British government, among competing needs such as health, education, transport and industrial development.
2. To negotiate with the Welsh Office in London for those funds.
3. To negotiate appropriate legislation for Wales with the Welsh Office.
4. To organise the implementation of devolved policy areas in Wales.
5. To represent the interests of Wales at various institutions of the European Union, even though Wales is not separately represented in the Council of Ministers.

An evaluation of devolution in Wales and Scotland

Before attempting to assess how well devolution is working, it is useful to consider what pieces of evidence we should look for. If we are to judge devolution a success, what are the signs to look for? Here are some suggestions:

1. High turnout at elections.
2. Public opinion surveys indicating high levels of satisfaction with devolved government.
3. A rise in the sense of 'national identity' in the two countries. This may be assessed by surveys, but is generally difficult to judge and the evidence is likely to be uncertain.
4. Whether Scotland and Wales developed significantly different policies to those which apply in England. If we remind ourselves of why devolution was introduced (because it was felt that Scotland and Wales may have different needs and demands to England), and if this assumption is true, it must follow that there will be differing policies. In this respect, it is clear that Scotland, with powers of legislation, is bound to have become more independent.
5. Arguably, we could consider whether demands for federalism or full independence have subsided. If they have, devolution could be said to have achieved one of its objectives – to satisfy demands for more self-government. If not, it could be argued that devolution has failed in its primary objective.

At the time of writing, devolution is only seven years old – too soon to make a valid assessment. However, the early signs are interesting. Overall indications certainly suggest that devolution has been more successful in Scotland than in Wales.

Wales

There are signs of general dissatisfaction with Welsh devolution. The experiment got off to a bad start when the first chief executive – Alun Michael – was seen as merely a puppet of Labour Party headquarters in London. It was suspected that he had been placed there in order to prevent any radical policies emerging from Wales. He was replaced by the more popular Rhodri Morgan, who has proved to be much more acceptable to the people of Wales.

During the foot-and-mouth epidemic, the Welsh executive was heavily criticised (Wales is more agriculturally based than England) for failing to take Wales' different interests into account. Indeed, there has been a general feeling among Welsh farmers that devolution has not fulfilled its promise.

At the same time, surveys indicate low levels of interest in or support for Welsh government. It seems to have made little difference – a reflection of its limited powers. Part of the low public esteem of the Assembly has been the high degree of adversary politics and party infighting that has been seen.

Having said this, there is no sign of growing Welsh demands for full independence. This suggests a successful outcome. The head of the executive – Rhodri Morgan – has proved to be personally popular and has given Wales some sense of independence.

Scotland

The picture here looks brighter for devolution. The first indication is that Scottish government has made a difference in some areas. Five examples are interesting:

1. The bovine foot-and-mouth crisis – when many thousands of cattle had to be slaughtered and beef and dairy farming were severely affected – was handled more successfully in Scotland and it escaped the worst effects.
2. The Scottish Parliament forced through a measure to make all care of the elderly in special homes free on demand (only medical care is free in England and Wales).
3. The extra tuition fees for Scottish higher education students was abolished. It was retained in England and Wales.
4. While the British House of Commons was locked in an exercise of mutual frustration with the Lords over fox hunting, the unicameral (single chamber) Scottish Parliament had little difficulty in responding to public demands for its abolition (though it remains subject to a possible legal appeal).
5. The Scottish Parliament has now introduced proportional representation (STV) for local government elections under its jurisdiction.

While these legislative innovations were taking place, the feared rises in Scottish taxation have not emerged. Surveys indicate reasonable levels of satisfaction with the operation of the Scottish Parliament and executive. As in Wales, there are also few signs that demands for full independence are rising. The Scottish National Party made no progress in the general election of 2001 – a sure sign that nationalism remains quite weak.

On the other hand, there is small evidence of a stronger sense of Scottish identity emerging. There has always been a strong sense of Scottish cultural identity, but there is little evidence that this is turning into patriotism, which involves pride in one's political institutions.

One additional comment needs to be made about devolution in Scotland and Wales. The arrangements are often described as **asymmetrical.** This means that the same amount of power was *not* granted to the two countries. This caused a good deal of resentment in Wales (which received less power). The reasons why the same amount of power was not granted to each country was twofold. First, Wales had no history of independence from England and had few historically *Welsh* political institutions. By contrast Scotland had been independent up to 1707 and had a number of its own institutions, notably its own law courts and education system. Second, there was considerably more support for devolution in Scotland than in Wales. The Liberal Democrats and Welsh Nationalists still campaign for the same powers to be devolved to Wales as in Scotland, but the government has remained unmoved.

Devolution in Northern Ireland

Devolution in Northern Ireland has to be seen in the context of the Good Friday Agreement of 1998. However, we can identify a number of reasons why devolution in Northern Ireland had to be very different in character from the constitutional developments in Wales and Scotland. These are as follows:

- There is a deep sectarian divide in Northern Ireland. This is more fundamental in character than the division between those English people who favour a close union within the UK (largely Conservatives) and those who wish for more independence in Scotland and Wales, mostly nationalists and liberals. The Northern Ireland devolution arrangements had to take into account the fact that, in many policy areas, it would be difficult to find any consensus.
- The normal, 'British' model of parliamentary government tends to ensure that a clear *majority* government emerges. Both the electoral system of FPTP and the practice of forming executives from one single party – or at least *dominated* by one party – have ensured one-party government. In Wales and Scotland, Labour is the dominant party in the new executives and is likely to remain so for some time, even though it has a junior coalition party. In Northern Ireland, the domination of all political life by the Protestant Unionists from 1921 to 1972 was the main source of discontent. A new system which simply restored majority Unionist rule would be unacceptable. Devolution, therefore, had to break the Unionist hegemony.
- The electoral system had to reflect the diversity of the political community in the province. It is too simplistic to think of it as a duopoly of Unionists and nationalists. The two communities have their own internal divisions, largely along the lines of moderates and extremists. There is also a large part of the political spectrum which does not hold dominant views on the relationship with the UK. They are interested in such issues as economic development, relations with Europe, agriculture and fisheries or women's rights. They have, in the past, been swamped by the Unionist–nationalist split. So it was essential to develop a *pluralist* political system where all groups could participate.
- It was clear that a **power-sharing** system was needed, for reasons described above. This meant that there would have to be a great deal of *innovation*. Devising ways of ensuring that political decisions are only made with a *consensus* of support is not easy and requires original thinking. This is especially true when there is a very fundamental division within the community. The Scottish and Welsh settlements were something of a combination of the British parliamentary system and coalition systems which are common on mainland Europe. Such a compromise was not appropriate in Northern Ireland. A unique settlement was therefore forged, not like any seen in the more stable political systems of Europe.

For these reasons, devolution in Northern Ireland is very different from the rest of Britain. Having said that, the actual powers which were devolved to the Northern Ireland Assembly and Executive are not dissimilar from those transferred to Scotland. The main powers are:

- primary legislation;
- education;
- health;
- transport;
- agriculture and fisheries;
- local government;
- environment;
- housing and planning;
- regional industrial development.

This is an extensive list, but the most important functions of the state remain in the hands of the British government, the Northern Ireland Office in particular. These include:

FIG 3.3C Mo Mowlem who helped to negotiate The Good Friday Agreement in Belfast

- defence and foreign policy;
- relations with the Irish Republic;
- security and policing;
- economic policy;
- social policy;
- taxation.

The governmental system has three main features designed to achieve the objectives described above: the electoral system, legislation and power sharing.

The electoral system

This is the **single transferable vote** (STV), as used in the Republic of Ireland. This is a complex system, the essential features of which are as follows:

- There are multi-member constituencies (normally four).
- Each party can put up as many candidates as there are seats.
- Voters can vote for all candidates, placing them in order of preference.
- The result is based on counting, not just of first preferences, but also subsequent choices, right down to near the end of the list.
- The complex counting system ensures that some of the elected candidates are those who have the support of a wide range of the community, not just their own party supporters.
- The system also ensures that those from small parties and independents have a chance of winning seats.

The result of the first election in Northern Ireland in 2003 demonstrates that STV achieved its objectives – to reflect the diversity of the community and to prevent any party winning an overall majority.

Party	Seats won
Ulster Unionist	28
Social Democratic Labour Party	24
Democratic Unionist	20
Sinn Fein	18
Alliance Party	6
Northern Ireland Unionist	3
United Unionist	3
Women's Coalition	2
Progressive Unionist	2
UK Unionist	1
Independent Unionist	1

The result is highly proportional, reflecting very closely the division of political support for parties and candidates. Even the additional member system, as used in Wales and Scotland, does not produce such a proportional result.

Legislation

Normally, lawmaking requires a simple majority of the legislature. If this were the case in Northern Ireland, as it is in the rest of Britain, the various Unionist parties would be able to dominate, just as they had done before 1972. It is a requirement, therefore, that Assembly votes are only successful if there is a majority among parties on *both* sides of the sectarian divide, that is, Unionists and nationalists. This makes lawmaking difficult, but it ensures consensus support.

Power sharing

There is a guarantee in the Belfast Agreement that the government of Northern Ireland must include representatives of both communities in the Cabinet. This prevents exclusion and is intended to ensure stability. Government places are awarded in general proportion to seats won by parties in the Assembly.

English regional devolution

In 2001 the establishment of regional assemblies in parts of England was a Labour policy. It was supported by the Liberal Democrats, but vehemently

opposed by the Conservatives. However, there was also a commitment to hold referendums in the regions (as had occurred in Scotland, Wales and Northern Ireland), to determine whether there was public consent for such a development.

In 2004 a referendum as held in the north-east to ask whether devolution, very much along Welsh lines, was supported. The proposal was firmly rejected by a majority of 77.9 per cent, against 22.1 per cent in favour. This shocked the government and they promptly cancelled all the other proposed referendums. Regional devolution seemed to be a dead duck, and is likely to remain so for the foreseeable future.

Nevertheless, some English devolution has certainly occurred. England is now divided into eight regions (not including London). Since 2001 some of the activities of government departments in London have been transferred to these regions. Thus, civil service planning in such areas as industrial development, transport and the environment is now undertaken at regional, rather than national level. This does not add up to regional devolution, as such, but can be described as devolved administration.

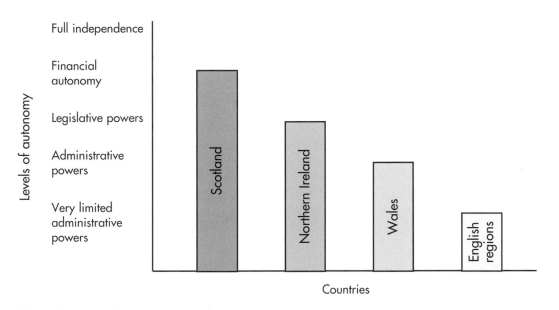

FIG 3.3D Devolution in the UK

London government

In 1985 the Greater London Council (GLC), a powerful local government body with wide powers and responsibilities, was abolished by the Conservative Government. Prime Minister Thatcher was determined to remove from power what she saw as a socialist enclave in the centre of Conservative Britain. Led by left-winger, Ken Livingstone, the GLC was seen by her as a wasteful, over-bureaucratic and excessive burden on London taxpayers. Above all, however, the policies of the controlling Labour group on the GLC were viewed as dangerously socialist in nature. Abolition left London without any central government. Instead, it was divided into 33 boroughs, each with their own powers. Central functions, such as the planning, ambulance, fire and police services were left under the oversight of unelected quangos.

Labour was determined to restore government to London – a measure which has been seen as an extension of local government, rather than devolution – when it returned to power in 1997. In addition, a new innovation was to be introduced. This was the election of a mayor, with a fair degree of executive powers. Elected mayors were unheard of throughout British history. In the past, mayors had been ceremonial offices, appointed by councils, and with no executive power at all.

In 2000, following a decisive referendum in which the people of London approved the introduction of an elected mayor and assembly, elections were held for the two new institutions. However, the legislation seemed to ensure that neither would enjoy a significant amount of political power.

The mayor controls the allocation of funds to different uses in London, funds that are distributed and administered by the elected assembly of 25 members. But, at the same time, the Assembly has the power to veto the mayor's budgetary and other proposals, provided there is a two-thirds majority for such a veto. Similarly, while the mayor has powers of patronage, controlling a variety of appointments, the Assembly again has rights of veto. This was a classic example of the introduction of a system of checks and balances, on the North American model. Furthermore, the electoral system used for the Assembly – AMS, as in Scotland and Wales – meant that there was no possibility of a single party enjoying an overall majority. This ensured that the mayor would always face obstruction for controversial measures. The table below shows the result of the Greater London Assembly election of 2004.

Party	Seats
Conservative	9
Labour	7
Liberal Democrat	5
Green	2
One London	2

Has the mayor made a difference?

The office of London mayor was granted relatively limited power under the legislation. He cannot be said to enjoy a similar position to powerful mayors in New York and Paris, for instance. However, within his limitations, it could be said that Ken Livingstone has been involved in several significant developments in London. Accepting that he possesses influence rather than power, he has been wholly or partially instrumental in the following initiatives:

- The introduction of the congestion charge, together with its extension after 2007, was Livingstone's most decisive action. Motorists must pay to drive in London's centre on weekdays. The revenues from this have been diverted into public transport. The scheme has not been a major revenue earner, but has cut traffic in central London by about a quarter.
- Livingstone lost his battle with central government to prevent the privatisation of the London Underground system, but did gain approval for a huge investment programme from 2004 to 2009.
- He was influential in gaining central government approval of a cross-rail system in London – in effect, the construction of a new east–west rail link.

FIG 3.3E Ken Livingstone, Britain's first elected mayor

- Though he does not control expenditure on the police, he has secured Home Office funding for the increase of police officers in London to their highest ever level. He has also introduced about 2500 community support officers to support the police.
- But it was his part in securing the 2012 Olympic Games for the capital that may prove to be most important in the long run. Livingstone was only one part of a large team which bid for the Games, but his support was certainly critical. Without it, the Games could not have come to London.

So the range of powers available to the mayor and the Assembly that oversees his work is limited, but the impact of this innovation has been considerable and high profile.

Local government (England and Wales)

It is beyond the scope of this book to describe the totality of local government activity in England and Wales. Scotland is also omitted deliberately as it has come under the control of the Scottish Parliament and executive and so does not conform to the normal 'British' model.

The structure of local government is complex and varied. However, the following simple description of the different types of local authorities may be useful:

- **Metropolitan councils**: councils controlling services in large towns and cities such as Liverpool, Birmingham and Manchester. There are 47 of these.

- **The Greater London Assembly**: runs strategic London services in the capital and exercises some control over the mayor.
- **London boroughs**: London is divided into 33 boroughs, each of which has wide-ranging responsibilities.
- **County councils**: 34 large councils, administering most shire counties.
- **County boroughs**: a small number (36) of town councils, with limited powers.
- **Urban district councils**: subdivisions of cities and towns, with limited powers. There are 238.
- **Rural district councils**: subdivisions of county councils, with limited powers. These are now quite rare – there are only 22.
- **Parish councils**: there are thousands of very small councils, dealing with minor local matters, mostly in villages and rural areas.

We can see that the local government structure is far from simple! It is further complicated by the fact that different types of councils have different services to administer.

The following table shows the responsibilities of these various kinds of local authority in England and Wales (excluding the Greater London Authority and parish councils), with 'X' denoting that this level of local authority provides the service.

Service	Metropolitan councils	London boroughs	County councils	Urban and rural district councils	Unitary authorities (boroughs)
Education	X	X	X		X
Housing	X	X		X	X
Minor planning	X	X		X	X
Major planning	X	X	X		X
Transport	X		X		X
Public transport			X		X
Highways	X	X	X		X
Fire			X		X
Social services	X	X	X		X
Libraries	X	X	X		X
Leisure and recreation	X	X		X	X
Waste collection	X	X		X	X
Waste disposal	X	X	X		X
Environmental health	X	X		X	X
Revenue (tax) collecting	X	X		X	X

Note: Some major services, such as fire, police and ambulance, may be provided by joint authorities not included here.

Source: Local Government Associations

How central government controls local government

We are not concerned with the internal workings of the various levels of local government here. What is relevant to us, however, is the relationship between central and local government.

Until the 1980s, local authorities had a good deal of independence. They were relatively free to allocate resources to different services in the way they saw fit. Though there were some controls over the nature and quality of services, these were relatively limited. Of course, there were always major responsibilities, such as education, social services and public transport, which had to be undertaken to a level specified in law, but central government did not intervene to any great extent unless there were obvious failings.

All this changed from the 1980s onwards. Since then, central government has exerted an ever tighter set of controls over local authorities. The main methods by which central control is exercised are described below:

- Central government provides about 75 per cent of all local authority expenditure. The rest must be found from local taxation (council tax). This gives central government an enormous amount of control over how the funding is spent.
- The **standard spending assessment** system specifies how much each authority should spend on its main services. This has two effects. First, it places a straitjacket around the way in which funds are allocated. Second, it means that, if an authority wishes to make additional expenditure, it has to raise the level of council tax, which may cause unpopularity.
- The system of **best value** requires that council services reach a specific standard. Best value includes such targets as satisfaction levels among the consumers of services, improvement levels, target setting and efficiency. Councils which fail to meet best value targets may suffer financial penalties or may find themselves placed under new administration, appointed by central government.
- The **Audit Commission** monitors the quality and efficiency of local services. It can order services to be given to private companies if they are not satisfactory.
- The **Secretary of State** responsible for local government has wide powers to intervene in local authority services, especially when they are not conforming to required minimum standards specified in parliamentary legislation. S/he may also cap the level of council tax charged, if s/he feels a large increase cannot be justified.
- In education, the most significant local service, there is a wide range of controls, such as the **National Curriculum** and a rigorous system of inspection under **Ofsted**. Furthermore, schools are increasingly being given the opportunity to gain independence from local authority control. Failing schools may be brought under outside management control.
- As with all government activities, strict **performance targets** are now in place, with severe sanctions when these are not met consistently.

There are many other controls, but the description shown above represents some of the main methods used today. All this adds up to a situation where local government now has very little flexibility in its service provision. Indeed, it may be better to describe the nature of this level of government *not* as *local government*, but rather as *local administration with a democratic element.* Elected councils are made accountable for what the authorities do, but this places on them an almost impossible burden. The vast majority of what local government does is simply not in their control. Councillors can only have a very limited effect on the nature and quality of local services. It is more accurate to expect that central government ministers and civil servants be made responsible for what is done in our localities.

Reforms in local government

There have been numerous reforms in the nature of local government since 1979, too many to describe fully here. However, four more recent developments are worthy of emphasis:

1. **Best value** now sets standards of service to which all local authorities must conform. Apart from raising standards, best value is also designed to ensure that the quality of service is equal in all parts of the country.
2. In association with best value, there are new **consultative procedures** in local government. It is now acknowledged that **local democracy** is weaker than it has ever been. Elected councillors cannot be held fully accountable for services over which they have declining control. Furthermore, there has been a growing perception that local communities are not aware of who is responsible for their services. Local authorities, therefore, are now required to consult with their communities about the nature and quality of services. This is achieved through the use of questionnaires or meetings of citizens with councillors and officers.
3. A system of **elected mayors** was introduced by the Local Government Act of 2000. Communities were consulted about what political structure they preferred for their authority. In the event, only 40 communities opted for a mayoral system, and in the referendums which followed on the issue only 11 communities chose a system of election. In 2005, therefore, there are only 12 elected mayors in place, including London.
4. In the 2000 Local Government Act, communities were offered alternatives to an elected mayor. This was a **cabinet system**, with a leader chosen by the ruling party or parties. Local government cabinets replaced systems where services were run exclusively by a series of specialised committees. A local cabinet is made up of leading members of the ruling party or coalition. Its role is similar to the Cabinet in central government. The leader and cabinet operate together to manage the overall direction of local policy and coordinate the work of various services. It is hoped that the system of mayors and cabinets will improve the accountability of councils as it is easier for communities to identify with a more familiar political system.

Local democracy

The idea that local government allows members of a community to play a full part in decision making. It also implies that local government institutions should be sensitive to local opinion and should be accountable to their community. The term 'democracy' also implies that local government should have some degree of independence from central government control.

As a result of the consultations in 2000, and the local referendums that followed, the following systems were adopted by large-sized authorities.

System	Number of authorities
Political leader and cabinet	316
Elected mayor and cabinet	10
Mayor without cabinet	1
Other systems	59

Source: Local Government Association, 2003

So local government is beginning to look very different to its traditional structure before 2000. Although elected councillors have considerably less power, and central government exerts a more powerful grip over local authorities, it is argued that there is now more accountability and consultation. Standards in local government are largely determined by central government departments and regulatory bodies, such as the Audit Commission. But local communities are now consulted and, where there are cabinets and elected mayors, have the opportunity to demand greater responsibility.

Sub-central government in the UK summarised

The picture of sub-central government and the relationship between the centre, the regions and localities has become complex and rather confusing. Above all, this aspect of government in the UK can be described as *asymmetrical*. This term refers to the fact that regional and local government arrangements are very different in various parts of the country.

Asymmetry is seen in various ways:

- The powers that have been devolved to Scotland, Northern Ireland and Wales are unequal. Scotland, in particular, has been granted much greater powers, and Welsh devolution is particularly limited.
- The system of local government varies from one part of the country to another. In some communities, such as large cities and counties, there is one major authority which is responsible for all major services. In others, there may be a two- or three-tier system operating the same services. In London, most services are controlled by the boroughs, but there is also a mayor in place who has limited power but retains a high-profile position.
- The internal system of local government also varies from locality to locality. Some have cabinet systems, others do not; some have elected mayors, others have politically appointed leaders.

The varied nature of the system is typical of constitutional arrangements in the UK. They have been developed in a piecemeal way, with no overall structure to act as a guide. This is made possible by the absence of a codified,

entrenched constitution. In federal systems, such as those in the USA or Germany, the constitution demands that the powers granted to regional political institutions are equal in all cases. In France, by contrast, where government is centralised as in the UK, local government systems do not vary to the same extent. There is a uniform system operating throughout France.

But before we are tempted to be overcritical of British arrangements, it can be argued that regional and local variations demonstrate that the arrangements are sensitive to local opinion. The increased use of referendums to give consent to change confirms this view.

KEY CONCEPTS

Nationalism	A political sentiment felt by people who believe they have common circumstances of birth. It usually (though not always) also refers to aspirations for a nation to gain political independence, if it is controlled by another dominant nation, or unity, if it has become divided.
Devolution	A process of constitutional reform whereby power, but not legal sovereignty, is distributed to national or regional institutions. In the UK this has meant transfer of power to institutions in Scotland, Wales and Northern Ireland, but not to the regions of England.
Federalism	In contrast to devolution, federalism refers to the division of legal sovereignty (more than mere power) between the central political authority and regional authorities. This means that the powers thus distributed cannot be returned to the central authority, nor can the central authority overrule regional centres of government. The classic example is the USA.
Regionalism	A desire felt by peoples within regions of a country to have some degree of independent power, allowing them to make political decisions on a regional basis, rather than a national one. Regionalism assumes that there are significant economic, cultural and social differences that warrant regional political variations.
Local democracy	The idea that local government allows members of a community to play a full part in decision making. It also implies that local government institutions should be sensitive to local opinion and should be accountable to their community. The term 'democracy' also implies that local government should have some degree of independence from central government control.

Revision topics and examination questions

Revision topics

- Definition of devolution
- Distinction between devolution and federalism
- Reasons for devolution
- Arguments for and against devolution
- Nature of different powers devolved to different countries
- Effects of devolution
- Nature of central government control over local government
- Nature of London government
- Reforms in local government

Sample questions

Read the following passage and then answer the questions that follow.

An Asymmetrical Settlement

Devolution was not granted on a uniform basis across the UK, but was tailored to meet particular territorial needs. It is not a *federal* settlement, involving a constitutionally guaranteed division of powers between the central government and the regions. In theory it is reversible, although the fact that Scottish and Welsh devolution were supported by referendums (the latter by an admittedly narrow margin), makes this highly unlikely.

It is an 'asymmetrical' settlement: the powers and functions handed over by the centre vary from one region to another, in accordance with local conditions and pressures. Scotland has a long established national identity with, for example, distinctive legal and educational systems. National feeling in Scotland grew during the 18 years of Conservative government from Westminster and resulted in the Scottish National Party increasing its share of the vote. The nature of the devolution arrangements was influenced by the incoming Labour Government's need to head off the SNP as a rival north of the border.

Scotland received a 129 member Parliament with primary legislative powers and the right to vary levels of income tax. In the 1998 Scotland Act certain areas, including UK economic policy, the constitution, foreign and defence policy, were specifically reserved to Westminster, while everything else was devolved. Although the UK Parliament retains a legal right to act in all areas, this is tempered in practice by the Sewel Convention. This means that it will not legislate on devolved subjects without the consent of the Scottish Parliament. The latter has wide scope, its areas of responsibility including health, education, justice, policing, agriculture, the environment and the regional economy. It passed a total of 62 acts in its first session between 1999 and 2003. On a number of issues, it took a position which was distinctive from the rest of the UK. Thus Scottish university students are not subject to tuition fees, and elderly people are entitled to free nursing care. More controversially, land reform has enabled crofting communities in the north to take over the fishing rights and landed property of private owners.

Source: Graham Goodlad, 'Devolution in the UK', in Talking Politics, *vol. 18, no. 1, September 2005.*

1. What does the passage mean by the term 'asymmetric settlement? (5 marks)
   Guidance: *The term is clearly explained so the answer merely needs to summarise the meaning, including one or two illustrations.*
2. According to the passage, what powers do the Scottish Parliament and executive enjoy? (10 marks)
   Guidance: *The passage clearly shows powers of taxation and a list of other areas where Scotland has devolved powers. Also note the legislative changes that have occurred and use them to illustrate these powers.*
3. From the passage and your own knowledge, identify the reasons why devolution was introduced? (15 marks)
   Guidance: *The passage refers to a rise in Scottish national sentiment under Conservative governments and also Labour's need to retain its support in Scotland. Further reasons should be deployed. These might include similar reasons in Wales, general disillusionment with London government, economic factors, and so on. Northern Ireland is a special case – explain how and why devolution was part of the Good Friday Agreement.*
4. What are the main arguments against devolution? (20 marks)
   Guidance: *This is not in the passage so the student's own knowledge is needed. Deploy such issues as lack of real support, additional cost, the additional layer of government, danger of breaking up the UK. Refer to Conservative arguments against radical reform. It should also be included that many nationalists are against devolution because they favour full independence.*

Resources and Web Guide

Books

There is a full account of Scottish devolution in:

Peter Lynch, *Scottish Government and Politics*, Edinburgh University Press, 2001.

The classic general work is:

Vernon Bogdanor, *Devolution in the United Kingdom*, OUP, 2001.

For Welsh devolution, look at:

D. Wigley, *Working for Wales*, Welsh Academic Press, 2001.

Scottish devolution is fully explained in:

Brian Taylor, *The Road to the Scottish Parliament*, Edinburgh University Press, 2002.

For Northern Ireland:

P. Dixon, *Northern Ireland: The Politics of War and Peace*, Palgrave, 2001.

Or:

M. Mulholland, *Northern Ireland: A Short Introduction*, OUP, 2002.

For local government:

D. Wilson and C. Game, *Local Government in the United Kingdom*, Palgrave, 2002.

Or:

J. Chandler, *Local Government Today*, MUP, 2001.

Useful websites

It is worth looking at the websites of two nationalist parties:

www.snp.org (accessed 11 November 2005)

www.plaidcymru.org (accessed 11 November 2005)

Also look at the sites of the various devolved administrations:

www.scottish.parliament.uk (accessed 11 November 2005)

www.wales.gov.uk (accessed 11 November 2005)

www.niassembly.gov.uk (accessed 11 November 2005)

Or look at the sites of the Scottish, Welsh and Northern Ireland Offices:

www.scotlandoffice.gov.uk (accessed 11 November 2005)

www.ossw.wales.gov.uk (accessed 11 November 2005)

www.nio.gov.uk (accessed 11 November 2005)

For issues in local government, the Local Government Association is useful:

www.lga.gov.uk (accessed 11 November 2005)

Or the Local Government Information Unit:

www.lgiu.gov.uk (accessed 11 November 2005)

3.4
How has EU membership affected the political system?

European integration

Post-war Europe

After two world wars, both of which devastated European industry and threatened permanently to sour relations between its states, Europe woke up to the belief that a lasting solution to continental conflict had to be found. The interwar League of Nations had failed and the United Nations was to be a worldwide organisation, which would not solve Europe's problems. Therefore an entirely new kind of arrangement had to be found.

It soon became apparent that there were two rival plans for European integration. One was essentially a cultural, legal and political union. This was promoted by Britain, in particular by Winston Churchill, who had been prime minister from 1940 to 1945. The other was based on the concept of an economic union which would serve a dual purpose in making the states of Europe more interdependent, while at the same time speeding the economic recovery of the continent. This was essentially a French plan, led by one of its most prominent civil servants, Jean Monnet.

These two proposals had the same objective – to remove the fundamental conditions for conflict – but suggested completely different ways of achieving them. Political integration, underpinned by cultural convergence and a unified legal system, would provide institutions within which future disputes could be settled. The cultural dimension would also go some way to preventing extremist movements, notably fascism and communism, from emerging again in Western Europe. The economic plan, on the other hand, would result in the great European powers having such a strong vested interest in peace that war would become unthinkable. Put another way, once there was economic interdependence, the benefits of peace would always outweigh gains to be made through war.

The debates over Europe's future also have to be seen in light of the geopolitics of the time. First, there was an overwhelming desire to prevent a resurgence of German power. Furthermore, any future arrangements would need to ensure that Germany, which was likely to become the strongest economic power after it had recovered from the immediate devastation of war, should not be able to dominate the new Europe. Second, the important continental European states – notably France, Germany and Italy – were extremely wary of any British attempt to dominate a future settlement. Third, it was clear that Europe would have to rely on US aid for many years to come. A new European community could not be allowed to threaten US interests in the region. Therefore, the idea of a military alliance in Europe which did not include the USA was untenable.

It is also worth considering at this stage some of the reasons why Britain became detached from the European project, even at its early stages. The distancing of Britain from Europe was to affect continental relations to the end of the twentieth century.

One issue was undoubtedly Britain's 'special relationship' with the USA. Certainly Winston Churchill saw this as an opportunity for Britain to play a pivotal role in the post-war world. If she was able to position herself as a bridgehead between North America and Europe, with close institutional links with both, she would be able to dominate the future of Europe. Interestingly, this same idea seems to have occurred to Tony Blair after 1997. However, the large European states were suspicious of British motives and were not prepared to consider any plans which would result in excessive US influence.

A second important factor in the estrangement of Britain and Europe was the strong influence of socialism on the early project. Many of the pioneers of a European community were socialists or social democrats. They saw integration as a means to introduce greater equality and social justice throughout the continent. Although Britain had a quasi-socialist Labour Government from 1945 to 1951, it was Conservative-led by the time a more integrated Europe began to emerge in the 1950s. Naturally enough, the Conservative Party was less than enthusiastic in supporting what they saw as a socialist enterprise.

Finally, we should remind ourselves that Britain was still an imperial power. Apart from the difficulties of reconciling Britain's relationship with its colonies with membership of a European economic union, this led the other Europeans to be suspicious of Britain's motives. Could Britain be a truly European partner while its attention lay firmly in the wider world outside Europe? As we have seen above, this feeling also applied to the UK–US axis.

For these reasons, Western Europe in the period after the Second World War was very much prepared to go it alone, at least in the economic sense. They were ready to accept US aid for reconstruction (the Marshall Plan) and to join NATO for collective security after the onset of the cold war, but economic matters were different. There was to be no permanent economic union with the USA as the latter would be too dominant. If an integrated political union was proposed they feared it would be British-dominated.

So the development of a European Community was, therefore, very much a West European affair, with Britain and the USA kept at arm's length. Nevertheless, it is useful to consider the less successful of the two plans – the Council of Europe.

The Council of Europe

In 1948 Winston Churchill, then Leader of the Opposition in Britain, delivered a speech to European leaders at the Hague in the Netherlands. When one considers how Eurosceptic the bulk of the Conservative Party had become by the end of the 1990s, this speech was breathtaking in its radical tone. Churchill not only proposed a new pan-European organisation, but also suggested that each state should be prepared to give up some of its **national sovereignty**.

Most of the states of Europe has recently fought two wars in order to preserve or regain their status as independent nation states. The concept, therefore, that they should be prepared to surrender some of that independence was optimistic, to say the least. In the event, it was indeed unrealistic. Inevitably, the full plan was rejected. In its place, a watered-down version of the Churchill plan was adopted. The Council of Europe came into existence formally in 1949, with an initial 16 member states.

The general idea of the Council was to create a new 'European culture'. It was to emphasise what Europeans have in common and so eliminate their differences. This common culture included such features as:

- emphasis on the importance of the arts and high culture;
- respect for fundamental human rights;
- attachment to democracy and the rule of law;
- stress on the importance of education.

In the event, the Council proved to be a great disappointment to those who hoped for cultural integration. The Assembly of the Council, which contains delegates nominated from member states, does little more than discuss matters of mutual interest. No decisions are binding and no controversial issues are ever adopted by members.

That said, the Council did enjoy one major success. This was the development of the European Convention on Human Rights and the Court which adjudicates on disputes under the Convention. The Convention, which was signed in 1950, has had a profound impact on the status of rights in Europe. Virtually all the members have adopted the Convention, either in its entirety, or as part of their own rights legislation. The last significant member to resist adopting the Convention was Britain. It was not until 1999 that the terms of the Convention were included in the Human Rights Act.

The European Court of Human Rights (which is NOT an institution of the European Union) hears appeals from European citizens who believe their rights have been abused. Britain has been especially affected by the powers of the court, having lost more than 50 cases since the 1960s. These have included issues such as the treatment of prisoners in Northern Ireland, press censorship, the method of trial for juveniles and night flights over Heathrow which deprive residents of sleep.

Apart from the important activities of the Convention and the Court, the Council has had a limited role. It does arrange cultural exchanges, organises educational programmes to improve European understanding,

---

National sovereignty
This refers to the independence of individual nations within the context of an international organisation. In the context of the European Union, it describes the degree to which decision making remains in the hands of member states.

and discusses such concerns as crime, drugs, terrorism and the media, but these are of little political significance. The narrowness of the Council's role demonstrates that, as an experiment in political integration, it is a failure.

The development of the European Union

While the Council of Europe was proving a disappointment to its supporters, the alternative institution – an essentially economic union – moved from one level of integration to the next with relative ease. Most of its members shared a common goal and enjoyed a great degree of unity in achieving it.

Two Frenchmen – Jean Monnet and Robert Schuman – believed that the most effective way of creating an integrated Europe was to pursue an economic union. There is no doubt that they both foresaw a wider political union in the future, but understood that a single economic market would be the first step towards such an objective. The first stage was a relatively modest arrangement and can be seen as something of a prototype for the European Community which was to follow.

The European Coal and Steel Community (ECSC)

In 1951 the Treaty of Paris brought together six countries – France, West Germany, Italy, Belgium, the Netherlands and Luxembourg (the last three named known collectively as *Benelux*) in a single industrial enterprise.

In itself, the ECSC was a limited system. It provided for a single market in coal and steel among the member countries. Fair trade was established between them and a common external tariff established against these goods coming in from abroad. In this way it was hoped that the industries would flourish, encouraged by free competition within the community and some protection from the outside. The Paris Treaty also provided for a central body to regulate production among the member states.

At first sight, this innovation – known as the Schuman Plan – seemed to be a modest one. With the benefit of hindsight, however, we can see how revolutionary it was. The radical measures which brought about the ECSC included the following vital principles:

1. Each member state was prepared to give up some of its national sovereignty to the Community. This idea, of pooled or shared sovereignty in specific functional areas was the first of its kind in the world. It set the tone for all future developments towards the creation of the European Union. All previous supranational bodies (such as the Council of Europe or the League of Nations) had allowed member states to retain their national sovereignty. This meant that they could choose whether to adopt any agreed measures or simply ignore them. The ECSC on the other hand, insisted that, to be members, all states had to agree to conform to all decisions. It was this insistence on shared functional

sovereignty that kept Britain out of the Community. The Labour Government of the day, which had recently nationalised both industries, was not willing to give up one ounce of British independence. This was to set a pattern for the British attitude to Europe for nearly two decades to come.

2. The three branches of national governments – the legislature, the executive and the judiciary – were to be replicated, in an amended form, within the new set-up. Thus the following bodies were created:

- **The High Authority**: a kind of senior civil service which was to develop policy and organise the implementation of decisions.
- **The Council of Ministers**: ministerial representatives from the member countries who would make all important decisions.
- **The Assembly**: nominated members from the six states, who were to give general advice to the High Authority and the Council of Ministers.
- **The Court of Justice**: to deal with disputes between member states; the judges were nominated from the different states and were to be independent.

3. The economic integration which was established in the ECSC was, it was clearly stated, to be the prelude to an even closer political union in the future.

Although the structure of the ECSC was essentially experimental – nothing like this had been attempted before, it proved to be so acceptable that, when the more ambitious successors of the ECSC, leading to the European Union itself, were formed, they followed much the same blueprint.

The Common Market (EEC)

Encouraged by the success of the ECSC, and determined to take integration further, negotiations began among the six members to extend the scope of the market. During 1956 the creation of the Common Market was discussed, and the following year, 1957, the **Treaty of Rome** was signed. This was effectively the founding document of European integration. An additional treaty, for the pooling of nuclear energy resources, was also signed. This was known as Euratom.

Britain did not take part in these early discussions. Both prime ministers of the period – Anthony Eden (who resigned in 1957) and Harold Macmillan (who took over from Eden) – made it clear that political and trade links with the Empire and Commonwealth were more important to Britain than a European system. It was also true that, following the humiliation of the failed Suez episode in 1956, Britain was licking her wounds and certainly not in a position to take part in the great experiment. The other potential members around the fringes of the central six were also less than enthusiastic. Spain and Portugal were still ruled by fascist dictators (Franco and Salazar respectively) and their intense nationalism did not allow them to consider integration. The Scandinavian countries, with their tradition of neutrality, were also far from interested. So it was to be a small exclusive club.

The Treaty of Rome contained five main agreements:

1. To abolish tariffs among member countries.
2. To establish a common external tariff – that is, all members would charge the same tariffs on goods and services imported from outside the Common Market.
3. The removal of all barriers to free competition among all members states.
4. The intention to create the free movement of all goods, services, capital (that is, finance) and labour between member states by 1970.
5. A more general intention to establish a Common Agricultural Policy. This was part of France's price for joining.

It also established the institutions of the Common Market, very much along the lines of what we see today and modelled on the set-up of the ECSC. The functions of these bodies are described and discussed below. Put simply, however, they were:

- **The Commission**: an unelected bureaucracy to develop policies designed to implement the Treaty of Rome.
- **The Council of Ministers**: elected ministers from the member states who would effectively ratify the laws and regulations of the Common Market and discuss future policy.
- **The Assembly or Parliament**: to advise the Commission and Council on policy, but unable to make or amend European law.
- **The Court of Justice**: to handle disputes between members and to deliver interpretations of European law.

We can see how similar this arrangement was to that of the ECSC.

So, in 1957 the great European project was under way. Only six original members had signed up and success was far from assured. By 2002 it had grown to 15 members, with several others queuing up to join. A single market had been established and 12 of the members were using a **single currency**. At first sight, this seems an impressive achievement in 45 years, and so it was in many ways. However, a glimpse at the institutions which were established in Rome tells us that the economic development of Europe has not been matched by political progress.

Towards the European Community (EC)

By 1962 plans for the Common Agricultural Policy were complete. The CAP is a complex system, the basic principles of which are as follows:

1. All agricultural products were to be traded freely within the community. There were to be no tariffs, and any regulations, such as health or content standards, would be common to all members.

> **Single currency**
> The adoption of the same currency by a number of different countries. Each country abandons its own currency, which is abolished. In the EU the single currency is the euro.

2. There would be protection from outside competition in the form of tariffs and subsidies for producers within the community who found it difficult to compete with the outside world.
3. Producers of a wide range of goods would receive guaranteed minimum prices.
4. A system was established whereby the Community would buy up surpluses of goods in order to keep prices up. These surpluses could be used if there were serious shortages in the future, but could be destroyed if necessary.

The CAP was more than merely a free trade system. It was also a device for the protection of key industries and to reap the benefits of specialisation. As such, it represented an important step in the further integration of Europe.

The Common Fisheries Policy (CFP), which had similar aims to the CAP and was also designed to preserve fish stocks, was signed much later, in 1983. It proved as controversial as the CAP, not least because the issue of territorial waters is one where national interest tends to clash with European integration. In some ways, therefore, its establishment was an even greater achievement.

The first phase of integration – the establishment of a tariff- and regulation-free zone, with free movement of goods, labour and finance – had been effectively established by 1968, ahead of schedule. Three years earlier, in 1965, the three European institutions, Euratom, the ECSC and the Common Market had been joined by the **Merger Treaty**. It was therefore time to consider the next phase of development.

In the meantime, the Community was expanding at last. Three countries joined in 1973. These were Britain, Ireland and Denmark.

The Single European Act, 1985–87

By 1985 the Community was ready to take a further step forward. This was movement towards the creation of a single market. This involved three main provisions:

1. There was to be completely free movement of goods, capital and people between member states. There was already such a provision *in theory*. However, in practice, there were still various forms of restriction. For example, members were still preventing some people from moving from one country to another. This inhibited the idea of a free labour market. There were still various forms of restrictions and concessions on the movement of goods through borders. Duty-free concessions were an example, as were variable health and safety regulations. Banking practices also varied, so that there was not a truly free capital market.
2. Each member state was to incorporate the Single European Act into their own laws. This meant that it would be *illegal* in terms of each country's own *domestic laws* to discriminate against any goods, labour or

capital being exchanged within the EC. This meant that each member was fully committed to the single market and would no longer be able to obstruct progress.

3. A target date of 1992 was set for the final completion of the single market.

The Single European Act (SEA) was finalised in 1985, ratified at the Council of Ministers in 1986 and had been incorporated into the law of every member state by 1987. It is, of course, an irony that the SEA was fully supported by Britain's prime minister of the day, Margaret Thatcher. Possibly the most important step in the development of European integration (perhaps with the exception of the single currency) was therefore backed by the leader who was later to become one of the most implacable opponents of the extension of the European Union.

The SEA also gave the European Parliament some additional powers, notably to veto the introduction of new members. More importantly, however, the SEA extended the scope of qualified majority voting. At this stage it may be useful to discuss the issue of qualified voting.

Qualified majority voting (QMV)

When European integration began, and especially when there were only six members, it was assumed that all decisions would require the agreement of *all* the members. This effectively meant that each member would have a veto over all decisions. The importance of this principle cannot be overemphasised.

If a member state can veto decisions, it means that it has not sacrificed its own national sovereignty to Europe. It also means that each state had equal status, since everyone's veto was worth the same. Little Luxembourg could obstruct a decision as easily as Germany, the biggest member. This is all very well in terms of sovereignty. However, it makes decision making extremely difficult. In order to make progress, therefore, the Community had to introduce majority voting.

A straightforward majority vote system, as applies in domestic parliaments, was not desirable, however. This would take away the power of states to an unacceptable extent. Conversely, it would mean that an alliance of the smaller states could thwart the will of the larger members. For example, when there were six members, the four smallest states would have been able to outvote France and Germany together! Clearly a compromise was needed. A system was needed which would take account of the differing size of member states, but would also protect the small states from being bullied by the larger ones. The answer was qualified majority voting.

Each state was given a differential voting power, according to population size. With 25 members after 2004, the voting powers were as follows.

Country	Votes	Population (millions in 2005)
Germany	29	82.0
UK	29	59.4
France	29	59.1
Italy	29	57.7
Spain	27	39.4
Poland	27	38.6
Netherlands	13	15.8
Greece	12	10.6
Czech Republic	12	10.3
Belgium	12	10.2
Hungary	12	10.0
Portugal	12	9.9
Sweden	10	8.9
Austria	10	8.1
Slovakia	7	5.4
Denmark	7	5.3
Finland	7	5.2
Lithuania	7	3.7
Ireland	7	3.7
Latvia	7	2.4
Slovenia	4	2.0
Estonia	4	1.4
Cyprus	4	0.8
Luxembourg	4	0.4
Malta	3	0.4
Total	**312**	
Qualified majority	**232**	

To achieve a qualified majority, and thus ratify any European Union decision, three conditions must be met:

1. There must be a total of 232 votes in favour.
2. There must be a simple majority of countries approving.
3. The measure must be approved by countries whose joint populations account for at least 62 per cent of the total European Union population.

Jacques Delors, 1985–94

Delors, a French socialist, became President of the Commission, and thus the most senior permanent policy maker, in 1985, the year the Single European Act was developed. His election (by the Council of Ministers) marked a new direction for Europe. He wanted to see progress in two areas.

First, Delors recognised that there would eventually have to be monetary union if Europe were to move towards a genuinely single market. His idea was a four-part plan:

1. Prospective members of a single currency system would be required to adhere strictly to the Exchange Rate Mechanism (ERM) which already existed. He understood that this system of fixed exchange rates to bring the economies of Europe closer together had to be supported.
2. The economies of member states would have to converge. Convergence meant that key economic variables, such as inflation, interest rates, government borrowing and unemployment, would have to become similar in all the member states. This would reduce the potentially disruptive effects of adopting a single currency.
3. There would be an interim phase during which the currencies would be absolutely fixed against one another and interest rates would be set for all members by the European Central Bank. This would prevent disturbances in the finance markets of Europe. It would also enable countries to adopt the single currency smoothly in a short period.
4. There would be a rapid changeover to the single currency by all member countries at the same time.

In the event, the Delors plan was adopted and came to fruition on 1 January 2002.

Second, Delors wanted to see progress towards closer political union. It was this intention which infuriated Margaret Thatcher. During the negotiations for the SEA, she had accepted what was seen as an inevitable development. After the SEA, however, Delors wanted to see further progress as quickly as possible. His determination led to Thatcher's speech at a European conference in Bruges in 1988 in which she repudiated the idea of a closer union. This marked a clear watershed in Britain's relationship with Europe. The Conservative Party moved decisively towards a Eurosceptic position. Even so, Britain did join the Exchange Rate Mechanism (a decision which Thatcher agreed to with great reluctance). In theory, therefore, Britain could have entered the single currency system up to the point when she was forced out of the ERM in September 1992.

Delors was undaunted by Thatcher's opposition and moved steadily towards the ratification of his plan. He was finally successful at Maastricht in 1992.

Maastricht Treaty, 1992

Formally known as the **Treaty of European Union**, Maastricht marked a significant step forward. The name of the organisation changed to the European Union. This change was more than cosmetic. The term 'union' suggested that members intended to form a closer, more permanent institution.

Maastricht had a number of facets, making it not only one of the biggest steps forward, but also one of the most extensive. Its main provisions were as follows:

- The future *political* development of the Union was to be based on the principle of **subsidiarity**. This established that government institutions should be as decentralised as possible. The concept of subsidiarity is discussed in more detail below.

- The Single European Act was incorporated into the Treaty of Rome. In effect, this gave the European Union a constitution for the first time.

- A number of further decision-making areas were to become the subject of qualified majority voting rather than unanimity. The significance of this has been described above. By removing national vetoes over a number of functions, national sovereignty was further eroded. It was this measure which caused the British prime minister, John Major, so many problems with his own party.

- A commitment was made to establish in the future a European Defence force and to move towards a common set of foreign policies.

- There was a final commitment to move towards a single European currency, and 2002 was agreed as the target date. Three countries, including the UK, were allowed to opt out of this aspect of the treaty.

- In order to facilitate and maintain the single currency, the principle of **convergence** was developed. It was recognised that it was essential, if the euro was to work, for all members of the system to adopt economic policies which would prevent major disruption of monetary union. Thus, for example, it was recognised that member countries would have to keep control over inflation, public borrowing and unemployment, according to fixed targets. In this way, a single interest rate, set by the European Central Bank, could be applicable to all the European economies.

- It was agreed that there would be movement towards the idea of European citizenship. This implied completely free movement of people between member countries (a process which had already begun as a result of the **Schengen Agreement** of 1985), equal citizenship rights throughout the Union and some progress towards common policing for international crimes. In the longer term, there was an intention to create a European Bill of Rights, which would be binding on all members.

- An attempt was made to reduce the democratic deficit in the Union's political institutions. In particular, the Parliament was given greater powers of legislative amendment and veto. There were also increased powers given to the Court of Auditors, which would better enable them to investigate cases of corruption.

- The **Social Chapter** was negotiated. This established a wide range of rights for workers, such as the Working Time Directive (to prevent excessively long hours of work and short holidays), rights for women workers with or without children, equal treatment for part-time workers and stronger safeguards against unjustified job losses. As with the single currency issue, Britain negotiated an opt-out from the Social Chapter, based on demands from the Conservative Party. It was felt that the protections offered would make the labour market considerably less flexible and make Britain uncompetitive. In the event, the Labour Party made a commitment to sign the Social Chapter, and did so as one of its first acts when it won power in 1997.

The first four clauses of Article B of the Treaty of European Union, 1992 are worth reproducing in full, as they summarise clearly the direction the Union is to take.

ARTICLE B

The Union shall set itself the following objectives:

- To promote economic and social progress which is balanced and sustainable in particular through the creation of an area without internal frontiers, through the strengthening of economic and social cohesion and through the establishment of economic and monetary union, ultimately including a single currency in accordance with the provisions of this Treaty.
- To assert its identity on the international scene, in particular through the implementation of a common foreign and security policy including the eventual framing of a common defence policy, which might in time lead to a common defence.
- To strengthen the protection of the rights and interests of the nationals of its member states through the introduction of a citizenship of the Union.
- To develop close co-operation on justice and home affairs.

So the European Union became wider and deeper. Maastricht was very much the creation of Commission President Jacques Delors, and proved to be his greatest achievement. This is not to say that it was an unqualified success for the supporters of European integration. We can assess the significance of the treaty by comparing its successes and failures.

Successes

- At least 12 of the members did commit themselves to closer union. Indeed, the outcome of Maastricht was entitled 'Ever Closer Union'.
- All signatories to the single currency accepted that they would have to conform to economic disciplines in order to maintain stability under the convergence criteria.
- The Social Chapter represented a major step forward for the rights of workers and for establishing a genuinely open labour market throughout the continent.
- The single currency issue was resolved and, as we now know, the timetable towards union proved to be realistic and achievable.
- By insisting on the concept of subsidiarity, the European Union made some progress towards allaying fears that it was becoming little more than a centralised bureaucracy.

Partial failures

- The treaty failed to establish a firm principle of citizenship. Although there was an intention to move towards common rights and responsibilities, no specific measures were taken.
- Despite committing themselves to the idea of common defence and foreign policies, there was little progress in determining how this might be achieved.
- Schengen had begun the process of establishing free movement, but Maastricht failed to persuade all members, notably the UK, that they should abandon border restrictions.

Failures

- Clearly, the fact that the UK remained determined to opt out of key elements – mainly the single currency and the Social Chapter – can be seen as a failure to persuade John Major to stand up to the rebels in his own party. In the event, this proved to be a disaster for the Conservatives. Britain's uncertain position at Maastricht split the Conservative Party and contributed to its heavy defeat in the 1997 election.
- Attempts to democratise the political institutions were feeble and did little to reduce claims that the Union was not really interested in democracy.

So we can see that Maastricht enjoyed limited success. It is likely that the movement towards a single currency will prove in the future to have been its principal achievement.

Amsterdam Agreement, 1997

Negotiated between 1995 and 1997, the treaty came into force in 1999. If Maastricht had been a series of intentions, Amsterdam was a confirmation of those policies, converting them into commitments. It was also designed to establish and modernise many of the Union's institutions. This was for three purposes. First, the various bodies needed the necessary powers to carry forward the plans which had been agreed at Maastricht. Second, the changes were intended to make the institutions more democratic. Finally, the agreement anticipated the enlargement of the European Union.

The areas covered were:

- The establishment of common rights for all, completely free movement of people, common policies on asylum and immigration. This was to include a common system of freedom of information for all citizens.
- Common standards in the fields of the environment, consumer protection and public health standards.
- A more precise commitment to common defence and foreign policies. A 'High Representative' to express common foreign policy and represent the Union as a whole was to be appointed (in the event, Javier Solana was the first holder of this post).

This diagram shows *basic* flows. In practice further complications may arise

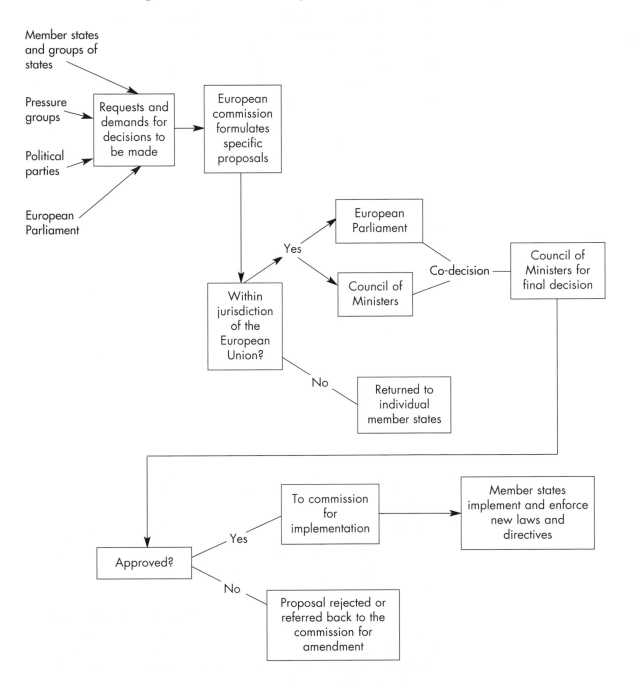

FIG 3.4A The decision-making process in the European Union

■ The voting allocations in the Council were agreed, to take account of the next group of new members.

■ A series of proposals to democratise the institutions of the Union before they were to be enlarged by the addition of new members.

It was especially recognised that future new members might have extremely variable standards of human rights, treatment of immigrants, health and consumer protection arrangements. By establishing these standards, new members would be left in no doubt as to what was expected of them.

Potentially, however, it was the constitutional changes which are likely to have the most profound results. These are described in more detail in Chapter 2.1 of this book.

Nice Treaty, 2001

Nice was required to make the final arrangements for the enlargement of the Union from 15 to 25 members. In particular, it adjusted the voting strengths of the member states to take account of the new entrants. The new voting strengths are shown above (under Qualified majority voting). It also increased the size of the European Parliament to 732.

However, the Nice Treaty was viewed largely as a failure. It was hoped that the procedures of the Union would be streamlined and more democratic, thus answering many of the criticisms that had been levelled at the Union by **Eurosceptics**. In the event, the Union looked even more cumbersome after enlargement. Furthermore, many of the small- and medium-sized member countries appear to have been given too much influence, meaning that decision making was even more difficult. It also failed to introduce a universal declaration of rights within the Union. This last provision was left for the ratification of the constitution in the future. But the constitution failed, having been rejected in France and the Netherlands in 2005, so Europe would have to wait for such a declaration.

> **Eurosceptics**
> Politicians who are opposed to closer European integration; many propose a loosening of British ties with the EU.

Theories of integration

Now that we have reviewed the various stages by which the European Union has evolved and integration has matured, we can examine the various theories of integration which have guided the process and which are likely to inform the debate about future developments.

International cooperation

This is the weakest form of integration. It means that groups of nations may meet regularly to discuss matters of mutual concern. However, if they are unwilling to give up national sovereignty, action can only be taken if they succeed in reaching agreement among themselves. Countries may be legally bound by the resulting agreement if a treaty is signed, but nobody needs to feel coerced.

In such a scenario, each issue must be negotiated in its own right. There is a general commitment by countries to try to reach agreement, but this may not prove possible. If there is no supranational body to which they have given up sovereignty, the organisation need not be threatened if agreement cannot be reached. The North Atlantic Treaty Organisation (NATO) has always operated largely on the basis of such cooperation. Members sacrificed no national sovereignty to NATO, but have agreed from time to time to engage in mutual action, sometimes even committing their own troops to military action under 'foreign' commanders. But in every case the member countries have been free to withdraw cooperation without losing their membership of NATO. The British Commonwealth is a further example of this kind of organisation. It only acts if members can agree (for example, to adopt sanctions against the apartheid regime in South Africa in the 1970s and 1980s). The Commonwealth, like NATO, has never been able to act independently of its own membership.

Had the European Community adopted this form of integration, it is doubtful that it would have made any significant progress towards a single market, and may not even have survived. The steps needed to create a single market and monetary union were so radical that they required members to accept that they had to cede some sovereignty to the Community.

Neo-functionalism

When the European Coal and Steel Community was created, there began a process by which European countries began to transfer national sovereignty to a supranational body. In these early stages it was clear that the way forward was for various government *functions* to be given over by member states. At first it was control over the trade in coal, iron and steel. When the European Community itself was formed, controls over trade in general were transferred. As we have seen in the review which is described above, more and more functions have moved over to Brussels over the past 40 years. Policy and law on agriculture, fisheries, environmental control, consumer issues, working conditions and many others followed trade as functions which member governments were willing to give up.

This approach to integration can be described as **neo-functionalism**. It is a gradualist approach, which is attractive to those of a more conservative disposition. Countries do not have to give up control over a function if they do not wish to. The European Community has always allowed members a veto over any change in functional responsibility. Thus Britain was able to negotiate opt-outs from the single currency and the Social Chapter when Conservative governments felt they were a step too far, involving functions which they were not willing to give up. By the same token, functionalism means that a consensus is always needed if further integration is to take place.

> **Neo-functionalism**
> Can mean a compromise between full-scale federalism in a European context, and the transfer of sovereignty over specific functions of government, such as trade or employment law.

Supranationalism
The principle that different countries should pool their sovereignty and accept the authority of an international body. This applies to some aspects of EU membership, especially where decisions are made through majority, rather than unanimous voting in the Council of Ministers. Both the Conservative and Labour parties are suspicious of tendencies towards greater supranationalism in the EU.

Intergovern-mentalism
A system of international cooperation where countries retain their national sovereignty, but negotiate agreements which are seen as beneficial to all. Both the Labour and Conservative parties prefer this model of European integration.

The alternative to functionalism is to transfer political sovereignty to the supranational body and then allow that body to decide which functions it wishes to take over. The end result may appear similar, but the *process* of transference in functionalism is more cautious and remains in the control of individual members. It is this latter principle which has always governed the way in which European integration has proceeded.

Pooled sovereignty

Opponents of European integration have always stressed the fact that national sovereignty has to be sacrificed if progress is to be made. In other words, the transfer of sovereignty is seen as a *negative* development. In some ways, this is a valid argument. It is undeniably true that members of the European Union have had to give up some of the independent functions of their national governments.

A less sceptical view can be considered, however. This suggests that members are not giving up sovereignty, but simply sharing it with others, or pooling it. The losses of national sovereignty are compensated for, in this way, by *gains* in sovereignty over *other* states in the Union. Thus, for example, when Britain finally signed the Social Chapter in 1997 it lost some national sovereignty over the regulations concerning conditions in the workplace. On the other hand, any future developments in this field have to be negotiated, and Britain will have some say in future working conditions in Germany, Greece, Spain and every other member state.

There are also functions which, by their very nature, represent **supranationalism**. This certainly applies to environmental protection (pollution, for example, does not recognise national borders). Similarly, as an increasing proportion of output is accounted for by multinational companies, national governments become unable to control their operations. Policy on competition (i.e. opposing monopoly power), therefore, must be carried out at supranational level. In such cases, sovereignty has to be pooled.

This notion of pooled sovereignty will not do for its opponents. They have argued that national sovereignty is of a much higher order than shared sovereignty. The domestic government has much more interest in managing its own affairs – after all, national governments are elected primarily to do that – than in interfering in the affairs of others.

Supranationalism or pooled sovereignty stands in contrast to the concept of **intergovernmentalism**. This is largely how the Labour Party under Blair and Brown has seen European integration. Intergovernmentalism implies that decisions are reached following negotiations among independent member states. Such a process involves no loss of sovereignty and the political process is based on compromise and consensus, rather than an imposed settlement.

Federalism

This model of integration has been a common way in which groups of sovereign states have come together to form a larger union – in other words, a new state. Perhaps the most celebrated example of a federal settlement was the creation of the United States of America in 1787. Germany is another prominent example, as are Nigeria, Russia and India.

Federalism is the consequence of a tension which exists between two opposing forces. One is an overwhelming desire to create a new state. The Americans felt that they could not survive in a hostile world as 13 separate countries. In Germany the driving force for union was partly economic, partly cultural, a need to unite the Germanic peoples and restore national pride. The other is the determination of the states which are to be absorbed by the new union to retain some of their own sovereignty.

The result of such a conflict is a federal settlement. All the uniting states agree to give up sovereignty over certain government responsibilities. Furthermore, their decision is permanent. They do not expect ever to repossess these sovereign powers. At the same time, the participants identify which powers they wish to retain for themselves. Here it is understood that the central, or federal, authority will never be able to take over these reserved sovereign powers without the permission of the separate states.

At first sight, federalism seems an attractive blueprint for the constitutional future of the European Union. Member countries would retain their own sovereignty and there would be no way that Brussels would be able to get its hands on that in the future. But problems persist, the main examples of which are as follows:

- A European federal state would be a new state that would stand *above* the member states. In other words, national governments would be downgraded and seen as inferior. This is certainly the experience of other federal states.
- **European federalism** also implies permanence. Under existing arrangements, member states feel they have the opportunity to change their relationship with the centre through negotiation. This is not the case with a federal settlement, which would be entrenched.
- There is a fear that there would be a tendency for the federal authority to gather more and more powers to itself. Until President Reagan began to reverse the process in the 1980s, it was certainly true that the federal government of the United States gained power over the individual states.
- In all other federal arrangements, the most important powers have been given to the centre. These include economic and monetary control, defence, foreign affairs and internal security. The individual states, by contrast, have been confined to less fundamental activities, such as social policy, transport and planning.

Nevertheless, federalism is seen by some as the way forward for Europe.

> **European federalism**
> An aspiration, or a fear among opponents, that the European Union may effectively become a single, federal political system. This would involve a constitutional settlement that would divide legal sovereignty between a central authority and member nations. It implies a permanent loss of some national sovereignty to the EU.

FIG 3.4B Churchill championed post-war European integration

European government

Opponents of complete political integration tend to refer to this vision as the European *superstate*. Supporters see such a development as possibly inevitable and certainly desirable. The latter view is both radical and genuinely internationalist. It is based on the proposition that the independent nation state has had its day. They believe that its survival will hinder progress and argue further that the nation state has been a historical phenomenon which is not appropriate in the modern age of globalisation and interdependence.

Ironically, it was a great Conservative politician, Winston Churchill, who was one of the first post-war statesmen to dare to suggest the idea of a European government. He suggested that a single sovereign government for Europe would be the only way to prevent conflict between the nations of the continent. To those who feared that such a government would destroy cultural diversity, Churchill replied that culture was a European phenomenon in itself, more important than national cultures.

In the event, Churchill's ideas were far too radical for most British politicians. Meanwhile, in continental Europe they were rejected as an attempt to sponsor British domination. There remain a few supporters to this day, but the idea of sacrificing *all* national sovereignty to a European state is unlikely to find widespread favour in the foreseeable future.

Subsidiarity

This principle was adopted for the European Union at Maastricht in 1992. It is fundamentally a liberal idea, but has also been shared by many socialists and even some conservatives throughout the continent.

To understand it, we should be aware that government in Europe can be carried out on four different levels:

1. Supranational (i.e. Europe).
2. National.
3. Regional.
4. Local.

We can now consider what functions of government can and should be carried out at each level. Clearly there are some functions which should be divided between two or more levels, but the principle of subsidiarity suggests that there is normally a rational division of powers. The following table demonstrates a likely scheme of subsidiarity.

Level	Functions
Supranational	International trade
	Environmental protection
	Defence
	Foreign affairs
	Long-distance transport
	Finance
	Some indirect taxation
	Energy planning
	Competition control
	Consumer protection
	Workers' protection
	Agriculture and fishing
National	Health care
	Criminal law
	Direct taxation
	Microeconomic development
	Arts and culture
	Personal taxation
	National transport
	Welfare benefits
	Environment
	Higher education
Regional	Regional transport
	Environment
	Urban planning and regeneration
	Rural affairs
	Economic development
	Some indirect taxation
Local	Education
	Personal social services
	Local planning
	Local transport
	Local environment
	Crime prevention and detection
	Provision for the aged
	Mental health provision
	Local taxation

There are two striking features of such a scheme. The first is that a large number of key functions are shown at supranational level. This may appear alarming to defenders of national interests. However, it should be pointed out that these are issues which do not impact on the everyday lives of citizens, so that European government may not bear down on citizens quite as heavily as may be feared.

The second feature is that most functions in this scheme are *not* placed at national level. To some extent this is a natural process. It is becoming increasingly impractical for nation states to be able to control many issues. Some examples can illustrate this second point:

- **Defence**: traditional wars of invasion and defence are over. Conflicts are increasingly international, highly technical and can only be dealt with through international action. Problems in the Balkans, the Gulf and with terrorism after 2001 are clear examples.
- **Foreign policy**: individual countries have insufficient influence to be able to shape international events. As Europe becomes a single economic bloc, issues concerning trade and economic issues must be conducted collectively.
- **Environment**: environmental problems, such as global warming, emissions control, energy depletion and conservation issues, do not recognise national boundaries.
- **Competition**: since most large corporations are now multinational, control of monopoly power must also be carried out on a supranational basis.

At the same time, the process of European integration itself has taken functions away from nation states. Again, some examples are shown below:

- **Monetary union**: control over finance, interest rates and money supply is now European-based.
- **Single labour market**: uniform regulations concerning working conditions, and so on, are needed.
- **Single product markets**: consumer protection and trade regulations are controlled in Europe.

The single European currency

Twelve members of the European Union adopted the single European currency, the euro, in 2002, following ten years of preparation. The UK had already decided not to join until the economic conditions were favourable. During the late 1990s, the question of whether the UK should join became the key issue in British politics, but it did not figure as a major election issue in 2001 or 2005 because all three parties promised a referendum on the question. Voters could therefore happily support any of the major parties, whatever their attitude to the euro, safe in the knowledge that the people would have the final say at a later date.

If we are to understand the political debate about the euro, it is necessary to review the consequences of joining or not joining. These can be summarised as follows.

The main economic consequences of the euro

- It is no longer necessary for travellers or traders to exchange currencies when operating within the countries which use the euro (the euro zone). This reduces their costs and removes the risks involved in making currency exchanges.
- There is price and cost transparency throughout the euro zone. The price of goods and services, wages and other costs are all quoted in the same currency, so it is simpler to make international comparisons.
- All members of the euro zone must accept a common exchange rate between the common currency and other currencies. This means an individual member country cannot manipulate its own currency exchange rate to its own advantage. However, the common exchange rate does promote more stability in currency markets.
- There must be centralised control over the quantity of money which is allowed to circulate in the euro zone (i.e. money supply). This means that there must be a common basic interest rate set by a central bank. It also means that countries have to accept limitations on the amount of money they may borrow to finance public expenditure, operating a more stable international currency.
- Countries which have traditionally weak currencies, such as Italy and Greece, can now enjoy the benefits of a large, robust, international currency.
- It is assumed that the single currency will promote more trade within Europe. It is also assumed that an increase in international trade will benefit all members of the zone.

The main political consequences of the euro

- Members of the euro zone lose a certain amount of control over the management of their finances and their economy. Countries may not set their own interest rates to suit themselves, cannot manipulate their external currency exchange rate and have some limits on how they manage the public finances. This means granting powers to the European Central Bank, a neutral body staffed by bankers from member countries.
- Members also gain some control over the economies and finances of other countries. In other words, a considerable amount of political sovereignty is pooled or shared.
- Arguably, the large members, notably Germany, France, Italy and Spain, will exert increased domination because their economies are so much larger than other member states and they account for the vast majority of the total money supply.

- Smaller, less prosperous members of the zone do have to accept the dominance of the larger, richer members, but they also gain a share of the euro zone's enhanced influence in world institutions such as the World Trade Organisation and the International Monetary Fund.
- Countries like the UK, which are outside the euro zone, lose a great deal of influence over the economic management of Europe. However, they retain more control over their own economic and financial affairs.

The problem in assessing these arguments in relation to Britain's specific interests is that the economic indicators appear to be favourable (when the time is economically right, that is) for British entry. The political issues, on the other hand, tend to point to much greater caution. It becomes very difficult, therefore, to synthesise and compare the various arguments. This problem is reflected in a good deal of confusion in political circles, especially among those who have no great ideological commitment in either direction.

Enlargement

The most significant enlargement of the European Union occurred in 2004, when ten new members joined. These included a number of countries which had formerly been parts of the communist Soviet Union, including Poland, the Czech Republic and Slovakia. The entry of these countries seemed finally to signal that the old cold-war divisions in Europe were over. But they were significant in other ways too.

The new entrants were largely poorer countries than existing members and so placed a strain on the community's finances, especially those related to the Common Agricultural Policy. They also contained a large workforce, which was ready to migrate to the richer countries in search of work and greater prosperity. It was feared, therefore, that such migrations would cause considerable economic disruption, stresses on communities, with the influx of large numbers of 'foreigners' and, above all, the possibility of unemployment among the existing workforce.

But it is the possible accession of Turkey to the EU, perhaps around 2015 that has caused the most dissension in British politics. The Labour Party has been largely in favour, not least because Turkey is a key member of NATO, an ally of the USA and a bridge to the Islamic world in the East. Conservatives, on the other hand, have been sceptical. They fear the destabilisation of the European Union caused by an extremely large, but essentially poor country joining. Furthermore, the admission of a Muslim country might cause cultural tensions, especially if large numbers of migrants move into Western Europe.

The European constitution

The pressures of enlargement, together with continuing charges that the European Union was undemocratic (the so-called 'democratic deficit') led to the development of a proposed new constitution for the Union. This was created by an international commission led by former French president, Valery Giscard d'Estaing. The constitution was ratified by the European Council in 2004 and set off on a journey to be approved by all the states of the Union.

The constitution was designed to achieve four main goals:

1. To clarify and codify all the past agreements between members into a single document.
2. To introduce a universal bill of rights to which all citizens of the European Union would be entitled.
3. To streamline decision making in the enlarged Union by making more decisions subject to qualified majority voting, rather than the rule of unanimity. In this way, it would be more difficult for individual members to block new proposals.
4. To improve democracy and accountability. This would be achieved by increasing the powers of the Parliament, introducing more openness in decision-making processes and making the executive (Commission) of the Union more accountable to Parliament.

In 2005 the draft Constitution was dealt two mortal blows. Referendums in France and the Netherlands rejected it. As it required the consent of all 25 members, the exercise of ratification ground to a halt. The British Government responded by cancelling its own planned referendum on the issue. Reactions to this setback varied. Optimists in Europe saw it as a temporary problem. A new, amended version could be reintroduced in two or three years' time. British Conservatives and their European allies, on the other hand, rejoiced, seeing this as the end of dreams of further European integration. They claimed that there was no appetite in Europe for what they saw as a failed experiment. So the future of European integration was cast into doubt and will remain so for some time.

FIG 3.4C The French voted against the proposed European constitution as setting back the cause of European integration for years to come

We can now examine political attitudes to European integration in the UK.

European integration and the United Kingdom

The Liberal Democrat view

The Liberal Democrats have been the most consistently enthusiastic of Britain's main parties in supporting European integration. Indeed, they favour further integration, leading to a quasi-federal system where sovereignty would be effectively divided and shared among member states. The Liberal Democrat support is based on a number of beliefs:

- They believe that European integration does not centralise power, but actually disperses most of it downwards to regions and localities. They support the doctrine of subsidiarity – pushing government down to its lowest feasible level – on the grounds that it enhances democracy. For them, government that is close to the people is more accountable to the people.
- Liberals in general, and Liberal Democrats in particular, see the European Union as a means by which rights can be distributed equally to all the peoples of Europe.
- Economic liberals also see Europe as a great free market in which consumers, workers and entrepreneurs are all free to operate.
- The idea of a great European society in which there is a mixing of cultures, nations and peoples is attractive to liberals. They see such diversity as both enriching and promoting progress in all fields, such as economics, technology, culture and intellectual development.

During the 2005 general election campaign, a small minority of Liberal Democrats, including Mark Oaten, showed some dissent by arguing that the adoption of the single European currency was premature and that the party should be less enthusiastic about integration, especially while the Union remains so undemocratic. However, the Liberal Democrats are still the main British party of Europe and are likely to remain so.

The Conservative view

The story of the Conservative attitude to European integration is a long and complex one. A number of distinct phases can be identified.

FIG 3.4D Edward Heath pioneered British membership of the European Community

1970–73

Led by Edward Heath, a convinced disciple of integration, the Conservative Government became determined to bring Britain into Europe. Heath negotiated entry, the treaty was signed in 1972 and Britain became a member on 1 January 1973. At this time most of the party backed Heath. The exception was a group of right-wingers, led by Enoch Powell, who saw membership as a betrayal of the country's sovereignty and national interest.

1974–79

Under Labour governments led by Harold Wilson and Jim Callaghan, the British people voted to remain members in a national referendum in 1975. During this period a divide began to open up within the Conservative Party. Three groups emerged. The anti-Europeans simply wanted Britain out. Economic liberals, such as Margaret Thatcher and Keith Joseph, supported close economic integration, but resisted a closer political union. On the moderate wing of the party, led by Michael Heseltine, there were enthusiasts for European integration who saw close union as essential for the future development of the whole continent.

1979–88

As Margaret Thatcher exerted an ever tighter control on the party, the view prevailed that Britain's best interest lay in closer economic integration. This was confirmed when Thatcher negotiated and signed the Single European Act in 1985–86, which created a single free market. However, there was growing resistance to the French–German plan for a close political union, possibly leading to a federal Europe.

1988–92

Margaret Thatcher became increasingly Eurosceptic. Her opposition to closer integration created a large faction within the party that wished to see a loosening of European ties. This Eurosceptic faction clashed with the pro-European wing, now led by Kenneth Clarke. John Major took over the position of prime minister in 1990, at the head of an increasingly divided party.

1992–97

The party became deeply divided over Europe. John Major fought a battle with the Eurosceptics to accept the Maastricht Treaty and the closer political integration it

FIG 3.4E Bill Cash, a leading Conservative Euro-sceptic in the 1990s

was to bring. He survived a number of critical votes in the House of Commons, but the party was mortally wounded by its split over Europe, and defeat at the 1997 general election became inevitable.

1997–present

Faced by three consecutive election defeats, the Eurosceptic wing of the party gradually took hold and became a majority. When Michael Howard became leader in 2004, he confirmed that the party was now committed to withdrawal from political union altogether, would not join the single currency in the foreseeable future, but would negotiate a separate free trade agreement with the European Union.

This is now the orthodox Conservative view shared by its current leader, David Cameron. It stops short of proposing withdrawal (though some members of the party would prefer that option), but does wish to see a distancing between Britain and the political institutions of the European Union.

The Labour view

As in the Conservative Party, opinions about European integration within Labour have varied considerably over time. As we have seen above, in the middle of the 1970s the party was split on the issue. The left-wing, socialist elements in the party were largely opposed to the European Community, as were most trade union leaders. Tony Benn led this faction at the time.

In the 1980s, the left-wing Labour view (which still persists) was that the European Union existed for the benefit of capitalism, and large business corporations in particular. The interests of workers and consumers, they believed, were not served by the free European market. In the early 1980s this left-wing faction became the dominant force in the party, with Michael Foot at its head. The party's 1983 election manifesto included a commitment to consider withdrawal from the Community.

Towards the end of the 1980s, the new Labour leadership of Neil Kinnock and John Smith changed the party's view of Europe and persuaded their colleagues to support Britain's continued membership. When Tony Blair (closely supported by Gordon Brown and Robin Cook) became leader in 1994, there was a much more positive attitude to integration. By the time of the 1997 election, it was official policy to move towards British entry into the European single currency.

As the European Union economy remained subdued, while British economic fortunes were on the rise, there was no acceptable case for joining the single currency. Chancellor Gordon Brown, in particular, lost faith in the single currency project. The more general attitude to the European Union was that Britain should remain at the centre of Europe, but should resist any movements towards federalism or even closer integration. Brown insisted that taxation powers should never be surrendered, while Tony

Blair was concerned to preserve Britain's independent foreign policy, the close relationship with the USA in particular.

When the European Constitution idea failed, the possibilities of closer integration receded further, as did prospects for the single currency. This was a relief to Labour, who understood that Europe was a potential vote loser for the party. The Labour Party is much more enthusiastic about the European Union than the Conservatives, of course, but its approach has become gradually more cautious and suspicious. This was reinforced by France and Germany's refusal to support the US occupation of Iraq and their lack of enthusiasm for the war on terrorism.

The nationalist parties

Both the Scottish Nationalists (SNP) and Plaid Cymru, their Welsh counterparts, are enthusiasts for European integration. The SNP, which supports full independence for Scotland, recognises that the country is very small and can only be economically successful within the context of the European Union. Scotland would receive generous regional subsidies and would have access to a huge market for its goods and services. They look at the impressive economic renaissance enjoyed by the Republic of Ireland in the 1990s and would expect the same to happen to them.

Plaid Cymru has no immediate aspirations to independence, but still believes that a closer European Union will strengthen their claims for regional aid, especially in the agricultural sector. Wales depends a great deal on its exports, so a free market in Europe is essential.

There is also a longer-term hope shared by both nationalist parties. European integration and the principle of subsidiarity suggest that the continent will become, in the future, a 'Europe of the Regions'. In other words, regional identities and economic structures may become more important than strictly *national* entities. If this occurs, Wales and Scotland will be better placed to reduce their dependence upon England and may be able to compete on an equal basis with the other regions of Europe.

UKIP

The UK Independence Party began life as an anti-EU pressure group in the 1990s rather than a party. However, by the 2001 election it had become a fully fledged party. Though its share of the poll in general elections has been insignificant, it has won seats – ironically – in the European Parliament. In the Parliament its members behave as a faction that seeks to undermine the power of the Commission and to campaign against further integration and loss of national sovereignty.

At home, UKIP wishes to see Britain out of the European Union, though the party accepts the possibility that a special trading agreement could be made that would give Britain access to free European markets, rather as Norway and Switzerland have done.

The arguments against further integration

The main concerns of Eurosceptics and anti-Europeans can be summarised as follows:

- They see integration as a staging post towards a European federal super-state. They fear the loss of national sovereignty that would ensue. Above all, Britain would gradually lose control over its own economy.
- The European Union is seen as fundamentally undemocratic. Should it become more powerful, there would be a further, dangerous erosion of democracy.
- The European Union is seen as expensive and wasteful. Large amounts of funds go to poorer countries and give little benefit to Britain.
- Critics argue that the experiment with the single currency has been an expensive mistake and that it is symbolic of the failure of the European Union as a whole.
- Britain has important alliances elsewhere, notably with the USA and the British Commonwealth. Further integration would place these alliances in jeopardy.

The arguments in favour of further integration

Those who are more enthusiastic about integration point to the following advantages:

- They consider themselves realists. As globalisation increases, they believe a relatively small country like the UK cannot survive outside such an alliance.

FIG 3.4F The 25 national leaders of the European Union (2005)

- They suggest that the economic benefits, in terms of prosperity and stability, far outweigh the loss of political sovereignty involved.
- Many are convinced internationalists. That is, they firmly believe that the world will be enriched and will be more secure if there is greater international cooperation.
- In geopolitical terms, the development of a powerful European bloc is seen as essential to balance out the influence of other powers, such as the USA and China.

The impact of Europe on British politics since 1973

- The issue split the Labour Party (including its leadership) in the 1970s, solved only by the positive 1975 referendum.
- In 1981-88 the Labour Party adopted an anti-European stance which helped to consign it to the parliamentary wilderness for several years.
- The growing Euroscepticism of Margaret Thatcher in the late 1980s contributed to her downfall in 1990.
- John Major's governments of 1990–92 and 1992–97 were dogged by a growing split in the Conservative Party over European integration and the single currency. On a number of occasions his government nearly fell over the issue.
- New Labour was quite enthusiastically pro-European after 1997.
- From 2001 onwards Labour has grown gradually less enthusiastic about integration and the single currency. The issue also contributed to growing rivalry between the pro-European Tony Blair and the less enthusiastic Gordon Brown.
- Also, from 2001, the Conservatives have grown increasingly disillusioned by European integration (fuelled also by the challenge of the UK Independence Party) and has ruled out Britain joining the single currency under any foreseeable circumstances.

KEY CONCEPTS

Intergovernmentalism A system of international cooperation where countries retain their national sovereignty, but negotiate agreements which are seen as beneficial to all. Both the Labour and Conservative parties prefer this model of European integration.

National sovereignty This refers to the independence of individual nations within the context of an international organisation. In the context of the European Union, it describes the degree to which decision making remains in the hands of member states.

Single currency The adoption of the same currency by a number of different countries. Each country abandons its own currency, which is abolished. In the EU the single currency is the euro.

Eurosceptics Politicians who are opposed to closer European integration; many propose a loosening of British ties with the EU.

Neo-functionalism Can mean a compromise between full-scale federalism in a European context, and the transfer of sovereignty over specific functions of government, such as trade or employment law.

Supranationalism The principle that different countries should pool their sovereignty and accept the authority of an international body. This applies to some aspects of EU membership, especially where decisions are made through majority, rather than unanimous voting in the Council of Ministers. Both the Conservative and Labour parties are suspicious of tendencies towards greater supranationalism in the EU.

European federalism An aspiration, or a fear among opponents, that the European Union may effectively become a single, federal political system. This would involve a constitutional settlement that would divide legal sovereignty between a central authority and member nations. It implies a permanent loss of some national sovereignty to the EU.

Revision topics and examination questions

Revision topics

- Various party attitudes to European integration
- Main British arguments against further integration
- Main British arguments in favour of further integration
- Arguments for and against the single currency
- Probable consequences of greater integration
- The nature of supranationalism and intergovernmentalism
- Terms and significance of the various treaties and the proposed constitution

Sample questions

Read the following passage and answer the questions that follow.

As things stand it is unlikely that a referendum [on a European constitution] in the UK would produce a positive result. A recent YouGov poll conducted for the *Sunday Times* concluded that, if a referendum were held now [April 2005], 23% of those polled would be in favour of the European Constitution, while 49% would be against. However, those polled were also asked what they considered were the most important areas that Britain should keep control of. 60% believed that the power to keep control of tax rates was very important, while 52% believed that the right to keep the pound was very important. Nowhere in the constitution does it suggest that it is mandatory for member states to accept the euro, and independent control of tax rates was one of Blair's famous 'red lines' that he managed to protect … However, it is foolhardy to try to predict the result, especially when other factors such as media campaigns would come into play.

Source: Adapted from Chris Lawes, 'The Referendum on the European Constitution', in Talking Politics, *vol. 17, no. 3, April 2005.*

1. What does the passage suggest are the factors most likely to cause the British electorate to oppose a European constitution? (5 marks)
   Guidance: *The straightforward answer is fears of loss of control over tax and the single currency. However, it might be worth mentioning the possible media campaign referred to at the end.*
2. From the passage and your own knowledge, what was Labour's attitude to the proposed constitution? (10 marks)
   Guidance: *Clearly Tony Blair would not allow any loss of control over tax rates. Labour also is suspicious of moves to supranationalism. However, the leadership supported the proposed constitution, even though it was forced to cancel the referendum. Reasons for support included better democratisation, the introduction of universal rights and the establishment of a clear division of sovereignty between the EU and Britain.*
3. For what reasons are the majority of the British people opposed to the constitution and greater European integration in general? (15 marks)
   Guidance: *The passage demonstrates worries over issues such as taxation and the euro. It also implies that anti-European feeling is stirred up by the media. In addition, the Conservative Party is opposed – reasons should be cited – together with general concerns about loss of sovereignty and the possible threat of federalism in the future.*
4. What are the main arguments in favour of further European integration? (20 marks)
   Guidance: *This is not referred to in the passage, so the student's own knowledge must be used. Include such factors as the economic benefits, the benefits of pooled sovereignty, establishment of peace throughout Europe, creation of a strong trading and diplomatic bloc, and so on.*

Resources and Web Guide

Books

For a general review of the workings of the EU, look at:

E. Bomberg and A. Stubb, *The European Union: How Does it Work?*, OUP, 2003.

Also:

N. Nugent, *The Government and Politics of the European Union*, Palgrave, 2003.

For an analysis of Britain's relations with Europe, see:

Colin Pilkington, *Britain in the European Union Today*, MUP, 2001.

Alternatively, see:

J. Mather, *The European Union and British Democracy*, Palgrave, 2000.

A book that covers both the current state of the constitution and some reform issues is:

Robert Hazell, *Constitutional Futures: A History of the Next Ten Years*, OUP, 1999.

Useful websites

The best site for comprehensive information is that of the European Commission:

www.europa.eu.int (accessed 11 November 2005)

A pro-Europe site is:

www.britainineurope.org.uk (accessed 11 November 2005)

A site about the single currency is:

www.euro.gov.uk (accessed 11 November 2005)

UKIP has a Eurosceptic site:

www.independence.org.uk (accessed 11 November 2005)

In addition, party attitudes to the EU can be found in the British party websites. See guide to Useful websites at the end of Chapter 1.3.

Index

Note: page numbers in **bold** refer to Key Concept definitions.